D1084652

Chopin Through the Window: An Autobiography

Copyright © 2021 Franziska I. Stein and Amy Crews Cutts

ISBN

Paperback	978-1-68547-048-7
Hardcover	978-1-68547-049-4
eBook	978-1-68547-050-0

Printed in the United States of America

101 Foundry Dr,
West Lafayette, IN, 47906, USA

www.wordhousebp.com
+1-800-646-8124

CHOPIN
through the
WINDOW
AN AUTOBIOGRAPHY

Franziska I. Stein
Amy Crews Cutts

Praise for Chopin Through the Window

"*Chopin Through the Window* is an enthralling memoir that tells the story of a young Czech woman of German ancestry caught up in the turmoil of World War II. So effortless is the writing, so entrancing is the story, that the book is impossible to put down. Ms. Stein's memoir should be required reading for history students. Her eye for detail, her unflinching honesty and her extraordinary memory make this an unforgettable read. More important, she recounts a slice of history that is not well known. She was a member of the German minority living in the Czechoslovakia when Hitler came to power and unflinchingly recounts the hope that ethnic Germans experienced when they first heard him speak, their gradual disillusionment, and the terror and uncertainty that they suffered when they were expelled with millions of other Germans from Czechoslovakia at war's end."

—Eileen Welsome, winner of the 1994 Pulitzer Prize for national reporting and author of *The Plutonium Files* and *The General and the Jaguar*

"When I met Franziska Stein in 2016, I knew that I had come into the company of an extraordinary woman. In her remarkable autobiography, *Chopin Through the Window*, she confirms my impression as she chronicles the incredible life she has led over the past nine decades. Her story is detailed and sweeping in scope, replete with events and episodes played out against the historical backdrops of the times and places where they unfolded. Throughout, she demonstrates time and again courage, resolve, family commitment, drive, and an unending quest for justice. Her book holds lessons for all of us, but especially for those who cannot at times see the way forward. Ms. Stein shows us in so many ways how we can cut through immense difficulties and move on, and in doing that she has done us all a favor. Get the book and you'll see what I mean."

—U.S. Ambassador Johnny Young (Ret.) Sierra Leone, Togo, Bahrain and Slovenia

To the women of my family:
Barbara, my daughter;
Amy, my granddaughter; and
Karen and Brenda, my adopted granddaughters.
You have brought me much joy.

God was in a good mood. Because it was never in his nature to be sparing, he smiled and, in doing so, endowed Bohemia with thousands of attractions.

—Eighteenth-century proverb

Table of Contents

Editor's Note

Franziska weaves within her story historical essays written in the third person. These essays are offset with section headings that lead with "**Perspective:** ..." They provide a broad outline of events to help the reader understand the context of the situations in which she lived. These background notes and essays are written from her perspective, reflecting the broad historical record and her take on their meaning. Quotations that have been taken from other sources are cited.

Foreword

The author of this book, Franziska I. Stein, was born in 1922 near Karlsbad, a city in Bohemia, now a region in the Czech Republic. For many, the word *German* refers to a citizen of the country Germany. However, the same word represents an ethnic identity among many Europeans, an identity based on language. Franziska was a Czech citizen through birth, but an ethnic German through her ancestors, the Sudeten Germans of Bohemia. They were a minority within a larger Slavic-speaking Czech nation, but prior to 1919, they were citizens of the Austro-Hungarian Empire, a central European kingdom composed of a German-speaking majority.

Many ethnic Germans in Czechoslovakia chafed at their minority status, and some supported Adolf Hitler and his lust to reunite the Germans of the Sudetenland with Germany. This would have tragic consequences for all ethnic Germans in Czechoslovakia, including Franziska.

In 1939, when Franziska was seventeen years old, WWII began. From this moment onward, she lost the freedom to chart her own destiny. Expelled from her homeland in 1945, she made her way to the devastated city of Berlin with her young daughter and a knapsack on her back, not knowing if her in-laws were still alive or if her husband and father would return from the war on the eastern front.

Unfortunately, when WWII ended, the Cold War began, and Berlin was on the front lines of this ideological conflict. The unending daily struggle of living there eventually became intolerable for her and her family. They decided to immigrate to Colombia, South America. While running a hotel in Cali, Franziska blossomed as she embraced the rich culture, history and geography of her new home. Franziska also began a side job assisting countless victims of

Germany's National Socialism, helping them obtain compensation for the losses they suffered under Nazism. This temporary job would last over forty years.

Immigrating to America in the mid-1960s, Franziska and her husband settled in the small town of Lyons, Colorado, founding and operating the iconic Black Bear Inn restaurant there. She would come face-to-face with cowboys, rattlesnakes, celebrities, and the Cold War. But America was not home, and the reunification in 1990 provided the Steins with a reason to return to Germany.

Throughout her life, people and events weaved Franziska's story together across continents, and a vigilant guardian angel by her side gave her courage in the bleakest of times. A world war, a civil war and the Cold War all left their marks, but this remarkable woman prevailed.

It has been a tremendous honor to bring her story to you. She is busy planning her ninety-ninth birthday celebration, with much of her youthful energy and wit still very much apparent. To me she is "Oma," my grandmother, my hero.

Amy Crews Cutts
Reston, VA
November 2021

A Chronology of Franziska's Life

1922   Born in Pirkenhammer, a village near Karlsbad, Czechoslovakia. (Pirkenhammer is now known as Březová, Czech Republic, and Karlsbad is now known as Karlovy Vary.)

1923   Baptized Irmtraud Franziska Katharina Anna Slansky.

1928–1933   Elementary education in Karlsbad.

1933–1940   Secondary education in Karlsbad.

1940   Completed secondary education with an emphasis in French.

1941   Studied French and philosophy for a semester at the Karls University in Prague.

1941–1944   Performed civil service obligation as nursing assistant in Karlsbad.

1942   Marriage.

1944   Birth of daughter, Barbara.

1945   Expelled from Czechoslovakia. Mother died.

1945–1956   Resided in the Lichterfelde section of Allied-occupied Berlin, Germany (within the US occupation zone).

1948–1949   Soviet blockade of West Berlin; Berlin Airlift. In May

1949 Germany was divided into two countries, the Federal Republic of Germany (West Germany) and the German Democratic Republic (East Germany).

1956   Immigrated to Cali, Colombia. Name changed to Franziska Irmtraud Stein by Colombian Immigration Authority.

1956–1957   Secretary for Químicas Unidas (a subsidiary of Bayer) in Bogotá.

1957–1966   Hotel owner, Residencia Stein, in Cali, Colombia.

1957–2000   Worked for German lawyers to process claims under Germany's *Entschädigungsgesetz* (post–Second World War compensation law).

1966   Immigrated to the United States.

1966–1977   Restaurant owner, Black Bear Inn, in Lyons, Colorado.

1967   Granddaughter born.

1977   Sale of Black Bear Inn restaurant.

1977–1983   Volunteer at Denver Art Museum. Worked with pre-Columbian and colonial art. Attended art courses at the University of Colorado for two semesters.

1984–1990   Restaurant owner, Franziska's, and art gallery owner, F&B Gallery, in Longmont, Colorado.

1990   Moved back to Berlin, Germany.

1996   Widowed.

2010   Great-grandson born.

2011   Returned to the United States, living in Reston, Virginia.

CHAPTER 1

Karlsbad, Czechoslovakia, 1922-1945

Germany, Austria, Czechoslovakia and Poland shown with borders from 1945-1990.

Longmont, Colorado, 2011

I came here to visit my daughter, and after hearing that I was in town, my adopted granddaughter Karen Crews Gregg asked me to go to Lyons, a small town nearby, that I called home from 1966 to 1977. She wanted me to visit Lyons Middle-Senior High School, where she was a teacher, and meet with the students in the world history class to talk about my experiences during the Second World War. They wanted to know what it was like to be in an occupied city, living with American soldiers. What were the soldiers like? How did you get the food and things you needed? Why are we still fighting wars today?

But where to begin? At the time I spoke to the class in 2011 I was eighty-eight years old. I have had an exciting life full of diverse experiences. In one fell swoop the war erased all the hopes and dreams I carried when I was a girl, hurling me into a future I never would have imagined possible. Now I think back on when it all began, on the time and people with whom everything started.

Karlsbad, 1922

"God gave Hope a brother. His name is Remembrance." This beautiful expression can be attributed to none other than Michelangelo, the famous Italian sculptor and painter of the Renaissance.[1] He surely must have known that memories are treasures which don't require much room, just a little space in our hearts.

The first memory I carry with me is of my home in the Bohemian fatherland, in what is now the Czech Republic. I have always considered it a privilege to have grown up in one of the most beautiful areas in the heart of Europe. My hometown, Pirkenhammer, is only three miles from one of Europe's most beautiful cities—Karlsbad. Nestled in the narrow Teplá Valley and surrounded by steep tree-

---

[1]   Although widely quoted in German, the exact source in Michelangelo's writings for this quote is unknown to me. However, it was used in the April 24, 2007 speech in Berlin, Germany, by Bundestag President Dr. Norbert Lammert remembering the victims of the Armenian genocide. https://www.bundestag.de/ parlament/praesidium/reden/2007/007/246420 Accessed August 18, 2018.

covered hills, for many years Karlsbad was one of the crown jewels of the Austro-Hungarian monarchy.[2] Founded in the fifteenth century, Karlsbad has had its share of disasters over the years, such as great fires and floods. The city's founding was, in fact, tied to the discovery of a hot mineral spring. According to legend, Charles IV, the Holy Roman emperor, discovered the source while hunting for deer in the woods. In those days many believed that the hot mineral water had healing powers, a belief that continues to this day. Soon people arrived in Karlsbad not only to bathe in the water but even to drink it! Some of the more notable visitors to this spa city included the famous musicians Beethoven, Tchaikovsky, and Brahms, and Mozart's son is buried there. Johann Wolfgang Goethe, the renowned German author from the eighteenth century, visited Karlsbad twelve times. He has been quoted as saying, "There are only three places in this world where you can live—Weimar, Karlsbad and Rome."

Central Karlsbad, 2003.

2   A wonderful book about Karlsbad is Mráz, Bohumír and Miloš Heller, *Karlovy Vary & Grandhotel Pupp.* Karlovy Vary: Karlovy Vary, 1991.

Karlsbad Hotel Imperial, 1992.

In my youth Karlsbad was the beloved center of the Austro-Hungarian imperial tradition, always festive and bustling with one event or another. Today, Karlsbad has a new name—Karlovy Vary. It is once again a popular spa destination, but now its visitors are mostly Czechs and Russians. Gone is the luster of the visitors who brought culture and fame to the pearl on the Teplá River.

The Beginning in Pirkenhammer, 1922

First there was a cry of rebellion, then a shallow breath, followed by a whimper. It was a cold yet sunny afternoon, just two days after Christmas, when I saw the light of the world for the first time. The women of my family later remembered this event with astonishing detail. My mother, for example, raved about the beautiful winter sun. My great-grandmother remembered that I was born just as the postman delivered some of the Christmas mail to the house. Perhaps inside his mailbag he also carried the small part of me that hungers for travel.

Practically all the women of my family were present at my birth. This was part of our family tradition, a belief that their presence would bring the newborn good luck. Each of them brought along a gift for me, to symbolize their hope that I would have a good life.

Was I ever long overdue! When I was born, my mother was already thirty years old. In those days doctors would have told her that she was too old to start having children. Finally, after she had spent years yearning for a child, her dream came true. The importance of this event for my mother is one reason everyone remembered all the small details of my birth. I was baptized under the name Irmtraud Franziska Katharina Anna Slansky, the first child of Irma and Paul Slansky, the first great-grandchild of Aloisia and Johann Friedl on my mother's side of the family, and the first granddaughter of my paternal grandmother, Katharina Slansky.

My Maternal Great-Grandparents

My great-grandmother Aloisia may have been one of the first woman business owners in the region. At the end of the nineteenth century, Karlsbad was undisturbed by industrialization. People still went to a central market to purchase their groceries, and Aloisia had a brilliant idea to make grocery shopping more convenient for the resorts in Karlsbad. She began to raise chickens, ducks, and geese. With a horse-drawn wagon she delivered the meat and eggs to large hotels under contract. Her business thrived.

Great-Grandmother Aloisia could tell the best stories. All snuggled up in her Biedermeier-style sofa, I loved to listen to them. Sitting on a footstool, she spoke of her childhood in Engelhaus, a small village near Karlsbad with its own fortress.

I was nine months old in this photo, in Pirkenhammer, 1923.

Johann, my great-grandfather, made a living as a building contractor. He assisted in the construction of the school in Pirkenhammer. In addition to this project, he also built a house for the school's principal and a new addition for the church. My great-grandfather loved to leave his mark on whatever he constructed, so it is little wonder that when I visited my parental home in 2003, I found a relief inscribed with "J.A.F. 1899." Somehow this house managed to survive two world wars and nearly forty-five years of communism.

My great-grandparents had four children. Anna, the oldest, was my grandmother. Her brother Hans studied meteorology and lived for many years atop Bjelasnica, a mountain near Sarajevo. Marie, the second-oldest daughter, was a beauty and, to the dismay of her parents, married quite late. The fourth child, Ernst, became a bank clerk in Triest and died at an early age from tuberculosis. My great-grandmother always said that the dealings with dirty money caused his demise.

My Mother and Her Family

My maternal grandmother, Anna, met Josef Dobrowolny, my grandfather, around 1890 in Karlsbad. After their wedding, Anna and Josef moved to Vienna. They had three children. My mother, Irma, was the oldest and was born in 1892.

My grandfather made a living as a tailor and furrier between the spa seasons. Among his famous patrons in Vienna was the actress Katharina Schratt, the mistress and confidante of Franz Josef, the Austro-Hungarian emperor. His wife, Empress Elisabeth, or Sissi as she was more commonly called, tolerated the relationship. She even gave the mistress a more dignified title, "Madame Schratt." After the tragic death of her son, Crown Prince Rudolph, the empress traveled as much as possible to avoid an intimate relationship with her husband. Sadly, she was murdered in 1898 by an assassin who stabbed her with a knife.

I still own a portrait photograph of the imperial couple that Franz Josef personally gave to my grandfather, certainly representing a fleeting moment of fame in my grandfather's life. An American guest who visited me in Colorado in 1968 saw the portrait on the wall and asked if they were my grandparents.

In 1898, my grandmother Anna became pregnant with her fourth child. Desperate, with three children under three years old, no family support, and unable to find an angel-maker, a doctor who performed illegal abortions, my grandmother attempted to induce the abortion herself using a knitting needle. She died painfully at the age of twenty-six from the infection that followed. Shortly after her death, my grandfather married his cousin. This marriage produced nine children. The family continued to live in Vienna, where they experienced both the rise of the industrial age and the disaster of the First World War.

Upon completing her education, my mother moved to Pirkenhammer and lived with my great-grandparents. She wanted to complete an apprenticeship at one of the many spa resorts in Karlsbad. There she met Paul Slansky, my father, and in October 1920 they married. After the wedding my parents moved into an apartment inside one of the two apartment houses that my great-grandparents owned in Pirkenhammer.

The apartment had large rooms with inlaid flooring. The kitchen contained a magnificent oven that was used not only for baking and cooking but also for heating. In the living room and in each bedroom stood a *Kachelofen*. These stoves transmitted heat through glazed tiles, which my great-grandfather set by hand. Today I wish I could have just one of these tiles, but I was not able to keep any after the war and the exodus from my home.

My mother maintained a distant relationship with her half-siblings in Austria. Vienna was too far away for frequent visits. Moreover, the aunts and uncles seldom visited them because they could not afford the price of a train ticket. To help her impoverished family in Vienna, my mother often sent her brother, Uncle Toni, parcels stuffed with food and hand-me-down clothes.

One of these parcels contained something purportedly valuable of mine, when I was forced to part with a coat that I had detested from the moment it was given to me. It was made of good material, bottle green on the outside, gray on the inside, and crowned with a collar made of fur. I don't know exactly why, but I simply hated this piece of clothing. But because I had no other option, I had to wear the coat. Whenever I threw a fit, my mother gave me the evil eye and said, "You should be proud to wear the coat. Many girls your age would give their right arm to have it." Besides, it had "cost a million." Impressed by a number that I could not fathom, I listened to my mother and wore the coat until my arms were too long for the sleeves. Finally, we mailed that awful coat to my cousins in Vienna. As a little girl, I had no idea how worthless the Austrian schilling had become as the result of hyperinflation. A million schillings may have been just enough money to buy a loaf of bread at the time.

My mother, Irma Slansky, in 1920.

My Father and His Family

Long before the start of the First World War, my paternal grandfather, Adalbert Slansky, founded a successful sign-painting business. He was also among the first in Karlsbad to market furniture with a special *Schleiflack* treatment, a type of matte lacquering. Adalbert and his wife, Katharina, had three children. Lina, the oldest, was a great beauty who married a Czech and had two children. Lina's daughter married an American general after the war, and her son became a journalist and remained in Czechoslovakia. Anton was the second son of Adalbert, and my father, Paul, was the youngest.

Before World War I, my grandfather sent my father to Constantinople (Istanbul) in Turkey to learn a trade. He was supposed to complete an apprenticeship with one of the famous silversmiths in the city. But after the war started, my father decided to leave Constantinople and returned home. Soon the Austro-Hungarian Army conscripted him for military service, and he spent most of the First World War on the Isonzo front in the Italian Alps. Twice he was severely wounded. Given the historical record of the war battles fought on the Isonzo front, I cannot imagine how my father survived.

While my father was suffering in the trenches, his father, Adalbert, died, leaving his business to his sons. Anton ran the business alone while my father was away, and they ran it together upon his return.

With great passion, Father designed all the signs adorning the business facades in Karlsbad. This was before the advent of neon and other electric lighting. Some of the signs designed by my father are still around today. Probably for nostalgic reasons, they are still displayed by several businesses along the promenade.

Everyday life in the business was not always easy. A bitter rivalry existed between my father, the more artistically minded, and his brother, who was more business-focused and domineering. Anton would have preferred that my father pull out of the partnership. This caused a lot of friction that often erupted into terrible fights with the door slamming. My grandmother tried to intervene, but in reality, she depended on both of her sons.

After the outbreak of the Second World War, my uncle had a second chance to run the business by himself. In the fall of 1940, at the age of forty-six, my father was once again conscripted for military service. This was quite astonishing since most new recruits entered military service while in their early twenties. Father became a military policeman. His main area of responsibility was logistics. Military business took him to both Munich and Vienna. We grumbled over his conscription orders, but we did not have a choice. We had to bend just like so many other families. Anyway, Father earned a military salary and could feed his family.

Whether it was because his father had been ill or because they had a business to run or just luck, Anton was not drafted into the army during the First World War. Neither was he conscripted for the Second World War. I look back now and wonder whether he had been a member of the Nazi Party, and if maybe he made a deal to get his brother out of the way. Perhaps it was just a cruel streak of luck for my father.

Anton was happy to run the business by himself, at least for a while. Fate can have a strange way of giving and taking that which is most dear. Two years after my father was called to duty, Anton died of cancer. As if a bad curse had landed on Anton and his family, his only son, Adalbert, was severely wounded in Africa, losing one leg completely and part of the second. He was not able to work in the family business because his physical wounds were too severe. During the rest of the war, Anton's wife tried to hold the business together, until the end of war brought an end to everything.

My father was an unusual man, a passionate reader and talented painter. This artistic man could work with gold leaf, and he used this talent to gild the dome at the Anglo-Lutheran church in Karlsbad. Father was also a terrific role model. Whenever I made a fuss or said I couldn't do something, he gave me the most serious look and responded with the following words: "I-can't is at the cemetery, and I-don't-know is buried right next to him." After he was drafted back into the military, I did not see much of my father. He seldom received leave, and even then, his visits were short.

Me with my parents in the mountains near Karlsbad in 1930 or 1931.

Father almost never spoke of his day-to-day army life and his military experiences, even after the war had ended. Once he mentioned to my mother that the war had destroyed his life and the horrible memories could never be erased. I am still puzzled as to what caused him to say this, yet in my heart I know he was a good person.

My Childhood in Pirkenhammer, 1922–1929

Just like so many of the other dwellings in Pirkenhammer and the surrounding area, our apartment house was built into the mountainside and had a high garden that was connected to an upper floor of the main building by a bridge. Directly behind the bridge was a terrace with a white-painted trellis and a tree-covered hill that ascended into the unknown, a perfect place for retreating into a make-believe world. In the winter, deer often approached the bridge looking for the food we had set out for them. I spent a lot of time with a friend who lived in the same apartment building. We played in the house and garden and explored as much of the surrounding area as our parents allowed.

The traditional holidays were a welcome break from ordinary day-to-day life. Our holidays usually had a religious connotation and were celebrated with great pomp and enthusiasm. On Easter, the *Ratchenbuben* walked through the streets—boys carrying strange rattles or other noisemaking devices that were supposed to replace the church bells "flown" to Rome for the pope's blessing. In my young mind I tried to imagine how these large bells were freed from their supports in the church towers and lifted into the air. I just couldn't imagine how it could happen, yet it must have happened because the bells were silent on Easter, Pentecost, Corpus Christi, Christmas, and the church anniversary. For every holiday, the women devoted themselves to cooking whatever tradition required. The men also participated in these celebrations, which included parades, dancing, and church services.

Life was ever so peaceful and stood before us like a broad avenue disappearing somewhere on the distant horizon. Author Stefan Zweig said of this time:

Hatred between country and country, nation and nation, the occupants of one table and those of another, did not yet leap to the eye daily from the newspaper, it did not divide human beings from other human beings, nations from other nations. The herd instinct of the mob was not yet as offensively powerful in public life as it is today; freedom in what you did or did not do in private life was something taken for granted—which is hardly imaginable now—and toleration was not, as it is today, deplored as weakness and debility, but was praised as an ethical force.

—Stefan Zweig[3]

I have wonderful memories of the apartment belonging to my godmother. She had a "spy glass" in the living room, fitted into a window. The glass was highly polished and presented a distorted view of the outside world. People, horse-drawn carts, and even the occasional automobile appeared larger, closer, and even stranger than they actually were. This was great fun for a little rascal like me, a source of wild laughter and fanciful stories. Only through the greatest effort could anyone lure me away from the windowsill.

At the end of town stood a special attraction—the Epiag china factory. Founded in 1803, the factory employed many not only from Pirkenhammer but also from Karlsbad. Bohemian china is still famous. Patterns designed and produced before the Second World War have become collector's items. Moreover, porcelain from Pirkenhammer received the 1937 Gold Prize in Paris and the 1958 Gold Medal at the Brussels World Fair.

Sometimes we went to the factory to visit friends of my parents who were supervisors. Abandoned in the courtyard of the factory was a mountain of broken and second-rate china, the latter of which often had only a small design flaw in the pattern. We played hide-

---

3 Stefan Zweig, a famous Austrian writer, fled Europe in 1934 to escape Nazi persecution. He lived in exile in Great Britain, the United States, and finally Brazil, where he died in 1942. This excerpt is from his autobiography, *The World of Yesterday*, trans. Anthea Bell (Lincoln: University of Nebraska Press, 2013), 46.

and-seek around the pile and made up other games. It was great fun to dig through the pile, tossing pieces of porcelain into the air just to watch them fall and shatter on the ground. Sometimes we climbed onto the pile of broken china to sort through the shattered pieces, looking for those with an unusual shape. Then we returned home with bloody hands and knees.

The quality and unique patterns of Meissen china from Germany are world-renowned. After the First World War, the working conditions at the Meissen china factories became difficult because of the deteriorating economic situation, and many workers were laid off. Some of the artisans looked elsewhere for work and quite a few highly skilled and talented porcelain painters from Meissen came to Pirkenhammer. Epiag china became famous for its cobalt blue glazing, which was integrated into the unique designs produced at the factory. In 1994 the Epiag factory had to close its doors. The company could not withstand the international competition after the fall of the Iron Curtain.

In the troubled times that followed the First World War, I was sheltered from the war's repercussions that had been painful for many ethnic Germans in Central Europe. Karlsbad remained an island of the blessed. Our eternal hot spring offered visitors from near and far welcome relief from their aches and pains. However, the socioeconomic changes that occurred after the war meant the resort guests were no longer rich nobles, as many of them had to surrender a life of luxury to fight for survival in one of the large cites of Europe, such as Berlin or Paris. Instead, the nouveau riche, the war profiteers, walked our promenade and bathed in our hot spring. After any war, there are always some who lose and some who win.

When I was seven years old, my great-grandfather Johann Friedl died. With him a very important piece of my childhood disappeared, tucked away in my memory.

I remember the funeral like it happened yesterday. It was held in the old tradition, wherein it was customary to collect the coffin with the deceased from his residence and carry him in a funeral march through the city to his resting place. The priest of the parish came with the altar server, and for me the most impressive act was the march itself. As the march progressed, what started as just the priest, altar boys, and family soon grew to a whole parade, with friends and prominent community members joining in. People brought so many flowers, it was as if the town bloomed just for him.

At the gravesite, the priest gave a speech, followed by the mayor of Pirkenhammer, who spoke of my great-grandfather with affection and reflected on his importance in the community. After the funeral our family and a few members of the town council joined together for a typical Egerländer meal[4] at a local pub.

Following the funeral of great-grandfather Friedl, which came less than two years after the death of my great-grandmother, the large houses in Pirkenhammer were sold, and we moved to Karlsbad, so my father wouldn't have to walk so far. For years he had walked three-mile miles each way between our house in Pirkenhammer and the shop in Karlsbad where he painted the signs.

Banned from paradise! I now had to exchange the open spaces of the countryside for the narrow streets of the city.

Our new apartment in Karlsbad was on Röhrengasse and close to the spa district. Later we moved to another, bigger apartment on Pragergasse.[5] Although our new home seemed very nice, nothing could replace the natural surroundings of my early years in Pirkenhammer. I often felt trapped and missed the closeness of my great-grandmother, who told bedtime stories. I also missed the godmother with the "spy mirror," the deer next to the bridge, and the nearby hills. Like a bird with clipped wings, I felt caged in the big city.

Whereas my mother constantly scolded me, telling me to quiet down, my father recognized the awakening sense of adventure inside my little body. Whenever possible, we hiked in the woods. Starting

---

4   Egerländ is an historical region in the far northwest of Bohemia. The meal would have included Schweinebraten (roast pork), wein kraut (white cabbage cooked with white wine) and Knödel (potato dumplings).

5   "Gasse" in German generally means street, for example, we lived on Rohren Street. More specifically, gasse denotes a narrow street often limited to pedestrian traffic.

when we lived in Pirkenhammer and continuing during my life in Karlsbad, sometimes I had to cut loose and wander off alone. I was a familiar face with the local police, who often picked me up and hauled me home.

I was a highly energetic child, not able to sit still, constantly whining and peppering the grown-ups with questions. I was happy only when something grabbed my attention, a need usually satisfied by the books that I devoured. I could sit on the sofa reading for hours at a time. Afterward I filled my mother's ears with commentary about what I had just read.

Perspective: A Short History of the Sudetenland

Ethnic Germans first settled in Bohemia within the western portion of the Austro-Hungarian Empire in the thirteenth century. In the twentieth century they became known according to three groupings of Germans within the empire. The Sudeten Germans were primarily located in what would become Czechoslovakia, and the other two groups were the Alpine Germans, in what would later become Austria, and the Balkan Germans in Hungary and regions east of it.

In 1348 Emperor Karl IV (Charles the IV), who married a Bohemian princess, founded the first university in Central Europe and locat-

Our apartment on Pragergasse in Karlsbad, Photographed in the 1960s. The arrow points to our windows.

ed it in Prague. The university was structured into four parts called nations: Bohemian, Bavarian, Polish, and Saxon, denoting the regions from which students would come. In 1784 German replaced Latin as the dominant instructional language, reflecting the local influences of the region. Demographic changes in the nineteenth century caused German-speaking people to lose their majority status in Prague by 1860.

When the First World War began in 1914, the multiethnic Austro-Hungarian Empire had 53 million inhabitants and controlled the most territory in Europe apart from Russia. The western half of the empire was controlled by Austrians, whose ethnic identity was German. Hungary controlled the eastern section of the empire. In terms of ethnicity, Hungarians are often called Magyars. Magyars and Austrians shared power, and various Slavic people, including the Czechs and Slovaks, and citizens of the Balkan countries formed the minority.

The Austro-Hungarian emperor, an ethnic German, was also the king of Hungary. The emperor traces his lineage through the Habsburg Dynasty, which reigned in Europe for over 650 years. Whereas other European powers expanded their territory by acquiring overseas colonies, the Habsburg Dynasty spread its influence through carefully arranged marriages with other European nobility. In doing so, it played an influential role in the history of France and Spain.

On June 28, 1914, Franz Ferdinand, heir to the Austro-Hungarian throne, and his wife were assassinated in Sarajevo, the Bosnian capital, by a Serbian nationalist. The Austro-Hungarian Empire sent a ten-point ultimatum to Serbia, which Serbia rejected. On July 28, 1914, Austria-Hungary responded by declaring war on Serbia. The conflict in the Balkans soon spread like wildfire, thrusting the world into four years of chaos and destruction.

After the outbreak of the conflict between Austria-Hungary and Serbia, the nations of Germany, Austria-Hungary, and the Ottoman Empire formed the Central Powers and waged war together against the Entente, the armed forces of France, Great Britain, Italy, and Russia. During most of the war, Germany and Austria-Hungary fought a war on three fronts, in France, in Russia, and in Italy. In November

1917, Vladimir Lenin and his Bolshevik army seized power from the czar. Shortly after creating a communist state, Lenin signed a peace treaty with Germany. The Treaty of Brest-Litovsk ended the war on the eastern front, allowing the Central Powers to shift most of their military manpower to the war of attrition on the western front. However, this shift of resources to the western front was counterbalanced by the arrival of American troops in France. In April 1917, the United States, which was previously neutral, sided with the Entente and declared war against Germany and Austria-Hungary.

On January 8, 1918, US President Woodrow Wilson outlined the United States' war aims in a speech given to Congress. He outlined what was to become known as his "Fourteen Points," the enactment of which, he believed, would form the basis for a just and lasting peace in Europe. The tenth of these points stated, "The peoples of Austria-Hungary, whose place among the nations we wish to see safeguarded and assured, should be accorded the freest opportunity of autonomous development."

The First World War ended on November 11, 1918, when all the parties to conflict agreed to an armistice. At the end of the war, the economic and sociopolitical structures of Europe collapsed. The war touched the lives of millions of people, claiming 37 million casualties, of which more than 16 million were deaths—nearly 10 million military and 6.5 million civilian.

The Austro-Hungarian Empire was dissolved. Karl I (Charles I), the last Habsburg emperor, renounced his participation in state affairs, but did not formally abdicate his title, and went into exile on the Portuguese island of Madeira. In January 1919, peace talks began in Paris. These negotiations ended the conflict through five separate treaties. One of them, the Treaty of St. Germain, signed in September 1919, created the Republic of Austria, a country with seven million inhabitants. The same treaty also created Czechoslovakia from Bohemia, Moravia, and Slovakia, regions that were once part of the Austro-Hungarian Empire.

Before the war, Tomáš Garrigue Masaryk was a university professor in Prague. At the outbreak of war, Masaryk left Central Europe along with Edvard Beneš, a prominent lawyer. Both identified themselves as Czechs, a Slavic minority in the Austro-Hungarian Empire. They viewed the new European conflict as an opportunity to create a Czech state. During the war Masaryk and Beneš pressed the Entente to support Czech nationalism. Both delivered public lectures presenting arguments for a Czech state. The Czech independence movement received financial support, in part, from a fundraising tour Masaryk conducted in the United States. During the war thousands of Czech soldiers also fought on the side of the Entente, which generated additional support for Czech independence.

When the armistice went into effect in 1918, prior to the ratification of any peace treaties, a provisional Czech government had already been formed in the city of Turčiansky Svätý Martin.[6] Masaryk became president of the provisional government, and Beneš became his foreign minister. The multiethnic population of Czechoslovakia consisted of a Czech majority with Germans, Slovaks, Hungarians, Ruthenes, and Poles as minorities. The creation of an independent Czech state caused ethnic strife, a situation different than in Austria-Hungary, where minorities were deeply integrated into communities where they lived. Before the war, ethnic groups sometimes migrated from one region to the next in the Austro-Hungarian Empire, but they did so for economic instead of political reasons.

Masaryk undoubtedly had good intentions when he became president. Perhaps he envisioned a Czech society based on the multiethnic Swiss model, yet soon it became apparent that Czechoslovakia would implement the French model, where the nation-state would reflect only the aspirations of a single ethnic group and its language. However, the German minority continued its fight for independence from Czechoslovakia.

On March 4, 1919, ethnic Germans across Czechoslovakia marched in protest against Czech rule. On orders from the provisional government, Czech soldiers fired grenades and bullets into crowds in several cities. When the day was done, fifty-four German civilians were dead and eighty-four wounded. Among the dead were children as young as eleven years old.

---

6   The city is now Martin, Slovakia.

Wilson's suggestion with regard to the regions occupied by the ethnic Germans of Bohemia and the Sudetenland and their inclusion in Austria were ignored, and they were appropriated into the new Czechoslovakia under the Treaty of St. Germain on September 10, 1919.

In 1920 a permanent constitution went into effect in Czechoslovakia. This time of transition was marked not only by ethnic strife but also one of extreme political differences, where conservatives and liberals, nationalists and communists, all competed against each other for power in the fledgling democracy. Despite ethnic and political turmoil, living conditions in Czechoslovakia were better than those in other European countries, where the aftermath of the war brought massive political and economic upheaval.

In the early 1920s, the situation in Austria as well as in Germany was extremely tense. Many could not come to terms with the loss of imperial rule and the democratic alternative presented to them. Austria and Germany struggled to pay reparations; a huge debt imposed on them during the Paris peace talks. Germany, for example, was expected to pay the crippling sum of 266 billion gold marks over the course of sixty-six years. Even though this sum was later halved, the two billion gold marks annual payment from the reduced reparations in 1923 represented more than three percent of Germany's nominal net national product at the time. Part of the reparations were to be paid in gold, and the rest in commodities such as coal. The navy fleet of Germany was also confiscated. In 1923, when Germany defaulted repeatedly on its payment, French troops occupied the Ruhr, an industrial area in Germany.

By 1925, the postwar economic crisis stabilized, but the German economy remained weak. However, in 1929 the economic situation spiraled out of control with the start of the Great Depression. More than eight million Germans were unemployed in 1932. The workforce consisted mostly of men with families, and when they could not find work, their wives and children were also dragged into poverty. Radical groups exploited the growing bitterness and hopelessness to become more influential.

My Childhood in Karlsbad, 1929–1933

In Karlsbad I attended a new school, which was on top of a steep hill. I already had a year of elementary school behind me in Pirkenhammer, but now life started to become serious. On the first day of school in Karlsbad, I met Gerda, the girl sitting next to me. Although our personalities were completely opposite, we became the best of friends. I daydreamed constantly of the forest, the animals, and the weekend outings, anything that allowed me to escape from the dreadfully dull classroom. With her quiet, soft-spoken manner, Gerda was the only one who could pull me back to reality. Our friendship would continue until her death in 2014, and she would become my daughter's godmother, though she stayed in Karlsbad when I moved to the other side of the ocean.

Gerda's father was a Czech who abandoned his German wife after the birth of their third child. This forced the family he left behind to live among the working-class poor. Gerda was and remained a very quiet and unemotional person, so different from myself. I was the one who was charged full of energy, ready to take on the world, doing things Gerda never would have done because she was far too reserved.

With a seven-year-old's taste for adventure, I experienced my first winter in Karlsbad. The city had gone into hibernation. The promenade was empty, and the elegant shops closed. An icy wind swept down the street whenever I made the steep uphill trek to school. With lots of laughter and screaming, we raced our sleds down the same street when it was iced over and hoped we would stop in time before crashing into the wall at the end. Hand in hand, Gerda and I strolled through the sleeping city, the frosty air swirling about our faces, our voices echoing back in the stillness from the houses in the spa district.

Our favorite pastime was ice-skating on the small romantic lake outside the city limits in an area called Little Versailles. From a small booth on the bank, a constant stream of waltzes and polka music was broadcast over the ice through a loudspeaker. The ice-skaters gracefully floated over the ice, appearing to us as the dancers from the ballet *Swan Lake*. We admired the easy, graceful movements of the skating pairs who seemed to glide over the ice as if on rails, as they completely focused on no one other than themselves.

When I was seven or eight years old, we lived near the Hotel Imperial. The hotel was on Helenenstrasse (now Libušina), just around the corner from our apartment on Rohrengasse. A fun diversion for me and my friends was to go to the hotel and view the guests and activities through the tall wrought iron fence that surrounded the hotel grounds. We could hear the music from the dance club and see the couples dance. Gradually over several months, the polkas and waltzes were replaced by real American jazz. It was so exotic!

The women changed their style from long curly hair and formal gowns to short dresses and hair to match—the flappers had come to Karlsbad. I loved everything about it, but my grandmother scolded me, "Never go there again! Only loose women and dangerous men go there."

Some of the jazz musicians were African-American men, the first black men I had seen that were not dressed in the tribal clothes of African nobility or the formal gaudiness of military dictators from Africa.[7] They had a grace that was mesmerizing, and they wore formal dinner jackets with tails. I remember thinking they were beautiful with their dark skin and white teeth. I knew nothing then of the struggles for racial equality these people faced in America and elsewhere in the world.

On weekends we often traveled to a nearby mountain range, the Ore,[8] to go skiing. My father was a ski enthusiast and experienced mountain climber, skills he acquired while stationed on the Isonzo front in the Italian Alps during the First World War. His natural ability for these activities must have been genetic. Soon I became just as proficient as he. Because I was such an active and adventurous

---

7   By African American I mean that these black musicians were from the United States of America and descendants of African slaves, not simply people with dark skin from Europe or Africa.

8   Also known as the Erzgebirge.

child, I sometimes found myself in rather dangerous situations. Once, when I was nine, I got lost while cross-country skiing. After searching for several hours, my rescuers finally found me crying and with a broken ankle. I had never seen my parents more horrified. That frightened me more than the fall itself.

When we went to the mountains, we stayed in a cabin belonging to a friend of my father. The cabin was in Hirschenstand, a small village tucked away in a beautiful corner of the world, surrounded by forests, steep hills, and winding roads. Inside the cabin stood an enormous stove with a warming shelf for keeping the *Malzkaffee* warm.[9] After an exciting day on the slopes, returning dead tired and soaked to the bone from the wet snow, we could always look forward to a warm beverage. As we felt the warmth from the fire, our cheeks began to glow, and as quickly as possible, we climbed into our pajamas and set out our clothes to dry on the wooden beams over the stove.

The deaths of my great-grandparents, so close together and at such an early time in my life, affected me profoundly. Never again would I feel their warmth and kindness. After they died, we no longer had a reason to visit Pirkenhammer. I stored the memories of my life there away in my heart.

Shortly before I was ordered to leave my home after the war during the German expulsion in 1945, for what I thought would be my very last footsteps on Bohemian soil, I went to the old cemetery in Pirkenhammer to visit the graves of my great-grandparents. I took as a souvenir of my visit a few oak leaves from the tree closest to the graves. I remember how I admired the old iron fence that encircled the cemetery, protecting its inhabitants.

After many years of living in South and North America, I went back to Karlsbad to make arrangements for my fiftieth wedding celebration in March 1992. I wanted to see the place of my birth, Pirkenhammer, once again and walk in the cemetery with my ancestors. By now Pirkenhammer had been renamed Březová, but there were so many other changes. The cemetery wasn't there any

---

9   Malzkaffee is coffee made from malted barley.

I am standing second from the right in this photo with my father's friend Otto Stein (center) and other children skiing, in January 1933. We are near the village of Hirschenstand, in the Ore Mountains.

Playing in the Ore Mountains at about age ten.

longer. A large parking lot had replaced the graves of the forgotten German population. But I still have the oak leaves, now placed together with photos of generations of my family. They now belong to one of many fragments of my life.

We did not travel that often to visit our relatives in Vienna, but after my great-grandparents died, we decided it was time to see them

A school play in 1930. I am in the center of the front row, with a dark ribbon on my collar contrasting against the white dress. Gerda is in the center of the back row, the short girl with the dark-colored scarf around her head.

with which she could create meals rivaling the best that any imperial kitchen had to offer. My parents tried to show me several museums and castles, especially the famous Schönbrunn Palace, to raise some affection for the once-great monarchy with all the glamour that it still had to offer. I, however, was not so interested in these cultural pursuits. For me, the crooked walls of the old hunting lodge were the height of luxury and fantasy.

It was a shame that the visit came to an end, but our journey continued. Mother and I traveled toward Melk, where one of my aunts owned a summer house. Melk, located in the Wachau region of Lower Austria, is a city with a unique monastery built in the Austrian baroque style. We found time to tour some of the castles in the area. Many of the castles have lain in ruin for hundreds of years, a powerful reminder of past conflicts. Never shall I forget Dürnstein, a castle dating to the twelfth century, whose dungeons held Richard the Lionheart hostage as Robin Hood battled the unlawful ruler of England.

---

10   Vienna is located about 210 miles from Karlsbad.

The Wachau belongs to one of the most beautiful areas of Europe. Small picturesque villages line the banks of the Danube River. Behind these villages, numerous vineyards produce award-winning wines. My mother was born in the great city of Vienna, less than thirty miles away, and her blood pulses through my veins. I am proud to claim this scenic region as part of my heritage.

The School Years, 1933–1940

My classroom in Karlsbad. I am in the third row from the front on the far right of the photo. The photo is from the early 1930s.

In 1933, at ten years of age, I began my secondary school education at the Reform Real Gymnasium.[11] Once again, Gerda was at my side to keep my energy under control. I was a very slender girl with big

---

11   Gymnasiums in Europe are elite, academically oriented high schools, somewhat akin to community colleges in the United States. Reform Real Gymnasiums featured the liberal arts, particularly languages, and Real Gymnasiums were more oriented toward math, science, and engineering, in addition to more intensive studies of Latin and Greek than in the reform curriculum.

brown eyes displaying a bit of Gypsy spirit that caused my family to say that I had the temperament of a wild young horse. My mother would have preferred to keep me tied to the household. In her opinion I should have been prepared for my duties in the home, no matter what the price. She came from an age that viewed the lives of women as consisting of *Kinder, Kirche*, and *Küche*, meaning children, church, and kitchen. Mother was almost reluctant to send me to school, and before letting me leave, she felt compelled to give me a daily lecture. "Be on your best behavior. Listen to exactly what the teacher says. And the reverend too, you understand? And no goofing around, no gossiping, and no speaking out of turn!"

In Karlsbad I had a lot of friends. We were always meeting at one place or another, going out, playing jokes on people, and romping around the street like lost puppy dogs. I remember something that happened when I was fifteen, something that illustrates how uninformed I was about life and the world around me. I had just gone to Mass with several of my classmates. After several minutes the piety would wear off, and I was back to having fun. I went to the park for a stroll with an eighteen-year-old boy who lived next to us. After a while we sat on the park bench. He slid closer and closer to me and, with a jolt, placed his arm around my shoulders. Gently, he pressed his face against mine. Then he placed his lips against my mouth, carefully at first, and within a few seconds, he stuck his tongue between my lips.

"You idiot!" I screamed. I stormed home with tears in my eyes.

"What's wrong?" asked my mother as she wrapped her arms around me.

Sobbing, I said, "I am having a baby."

After a few seconds of terror came my tear-filled explanation and finally embarrassed laughter from my mother. Noticeably absent from her reaction was a more enlightened explanation.

Perspective: The Annexation of Austria and the Sudetenland, 1938

The Sudetenland is the historical German name for the border districts of Bohemia, Moravia, and Czech Silesia of former Czechoslovakia which were inhabited primarily by Sudeten Germans from the time of the Austrian Empire. To understand how this area fell into the hands of Nazi Germany, an event with enormous political significance, it is necessary to return to the Paris peace negotiations of 1919. The Treaty of Versailles ended the conflict between the Entente and Germany. The negotiations were held at the Versailles Palace near Paris, and importantly, Germany was not invited to participate. Germany was forced to cede one-fourth of its territory and to pay reparations. The Entente also limited the size of the German military and the type and number of weapons it could possess. However, the most controversial demand made of Germany was the so-called war-guilt clause of the treaty. The German government, the newly formed Weimar Republic, was presented with an ultimatum: either sign a statement admitting responsibility for the war, or the war would resume. Faced with these choices, the Weimar government admitted responsibility for the war. Many in Germany felt betrayed by their new government, finding the war-guilt clause humiliating.

The Weimar government and democracy never achieved widespread support among Germans. Out of the political and economic chaos emerged Adolf Hitler. He stepped into the political arena armed with excellent public speaking skills and a deep understanding of how to use mass media to build support. Both radio and newsreels delivered his message. Born in Austria, he served on the western front during World War I. Since his childhood, he had an irrational hatred of Jews, seeing signs everywhere of a Jewish conspiracy. After the war he joined the German Workers' Party in Munich and in 1921 became its chairman. The party was later renamed the National Socialist German Workers' Party – the Nazi Party. In 1923 he led a coup attempt in Munich, which failed, and he was arrested. Hitler spent several months in prison, where he wrote *Mein Kampf,* a book that detailed his anti-Semitic and fascist views.

More and more Germans turned to National Socialism, believing the radical ideology as well as the promise of more jobs and greater prosperity. During the 1932 elections in Germany, the Nazi Party received the most votes. In 1933 Hitler became the German *Führer*, meaning leader, a title he bestowed upon himself. Shortly after seizing power, the Nazi Party banned the Communist Party, along with freedom of speech and freedom of the press.

One of Hitler's goals was to reunite all the German-speaking areas of Europe under the umbrella of a "Thousand-Year Empire," the Third Reich. He also planned to incorporate other areas of Europe into the Reich for economic or military reasons, with the area in the east reserved for resettling the Jews. While emphasizing his desire to live in peace with his neighbors, Hitler secretly prepared for war. He tested the resolve of France and Great Britain to enforce the Versailles Treaty; Germany stopped paying war reparations. In further violation of the treaty, Hitler also reequipped the German armed forces with modern weapons and introduced conscription. As the military received new equipment, government contracts provided Germans with desperately needed jobs.

In 1935, while Hitler was rebuilding Germany's military strength, Edvard Beneš succeeded Tomáš Masaryk as president of Czechoslovakia. He signed pacts with France and the Soviet Union, pledging military assistance in the event of an attack against Czechoslovakia. Beneš also pursued political policies more hostile to the ethnic Germans and Hungarians than those under Masaryk.

Hitler's testing of French and British resolve to enforce the Versailles Treaty continued when, in March 1936, Germany sent soldiers into the demilitarized Rhineland. France and Great Britain refused to use military force in response to this flagrant violation of the treaty.

On March 12, 1938, German troops invaded Austria. The next day, the once-sovereign Republic of Austria became the Ostmark, a territory of the Third Reich. German soldiers encountered no resistance. The Austrian chancellor, Kurt Schuschnigg, in a very emotional radio address, gave his last order as head of state asking his countrymen not to resist because this would cause senseless bloodshed.

On Sunday, March 13, 1938, the *New York Times* featured the following headlines on the front page[12]:

HITLER ENTERS AUSTRIA IN TRIUMPHAL PARADE; VIENNA PREPARES FOR UNION, VOIDS TREATY BAN; FRANCE MANS BORDER; BRITAIN STUDIES MOVES

LINZ HAILS HITLER

He Defies World to Part Two Peoples—Will Go to Capital Today

GERMAN TROOPS POUR IN

By G.E.R. Gedye, Wireless to the *New York Times* from Vienna

...

Both the German and Austrian banks were lined with enormous crowds to witness the historic moment when the Nazi leader should enter into possession—for it is clear that after the formality of a plebiscite under Nazi control Austria will become part of a new, great Germany—of the country where he was born and raised and where he acquired the political philosophy that has brought him greater power than any German has had in history.

It is the country that ever since his accession to power had formally rejected his doctrines and where his followers until a few weeks ago had been outlawed as members of an illegal government.

Goes from Braunau to Linz

---

12   This article is remarkably similar in tone to the stories reported in the German papers. I have included this story as it would not be subject to my translation.

Amid the deafening cheers of the Nazis both in Germany and in Austria and the pealing of church bells, the Fuehrer's car slowly crossed the bridge over the Inn into Braunau, which was a mass of swastika banners. Then he proceeded to Linz, his first extended halt.

There, amid scenes of the wildest enthusiasm, he made a speech from the balcony of the City Hall in which he proclaimed the unity of Germany and Austria and warned the world that any effort to part the two peoples would be in vain.

In greeting Hitler at Linz, Dr. Arthur Seyss-Inquart, the new Austrian Chancellor, proclaimed the annulment of the peace treaty of St. Germain, which stipulated that the Austrian republic must remain independent and forbade union with Germany except with the consent of the League of Nations.

And, once again, Great Britain and France did not take any military action against Germany for this act of war.

During the summer of 1938, discontent among the Sudeten Germans came to the political forefront. The British sent Lord Runciman to Czechoslovakia to observe and report on the intensifying situation of minority peoples. He recommended that Germany take over control of the Sudetenland, areas of Bohemia and Moravia where the majority of the ethnic Germans live. The British government pressured the French government to accept this position, although France was committed under a treaty obligation to protect Czech sovereignty. Although it initially resisted this decision, the Czech government under Beneš acceded to the decision on September 21, 1938. The terms of this decision were ratified by Great Britain, France, and Germany on September 29 and 30, 1938, at the infamous Munich Conference.

Through the Munich Agreement, France, Great Britain and Italy allowed Hitler to take 11,000 square miles of Czech territory, a decision with far-reaching yet unforeseeable consequences. The decision also caused Czechoslovakia to lose much of its glass, chemical, and textile industry and much of its coal reserves.

Neville Chamberlain, the British prime minister, returned from Munich and told his countrymen "My good friends, for the second time in our history, a British Prime Minister has returned from Germany bringing peace with honour. I believe it is peace for our time."[13] Winston Churchill, at the time a Member of Parliament, was among the few in the British government who condemned the Agreement.

In the mid-1930s the fascist regime in Germany made a series of financial investments in the Sudeten German Party in Czechoslovakia led by Konrad Henlein. In return, this political party stirred up sentiment against the Czech government and paved the way for Germany to annex the Sudetenland without encountering opposition from other European powers.

On October 1, 1938, German troops occupied the Sudetenland. Nazi flags with the swastika adorned the streets. A large majority of the people welcomed annexation by the Third Reich. The *Völkischer Beobachter* reported on that date, "There is indescribable rejoicing on Bohemia's northern border. The Sudetenland spruces up, waiting to receive the German troops. Konrad Henlein to the *Führer*: Words are too weak to express the gratitude of the Sudeten Germans."[14]

Perspective: The Scapegoats

Beginning in 1933, denunciation became commonplace in Germany, and was mostly used to settle personal scores. Because of this, nobody was free to tell a joke about Hitler or to complain about the Nazi party.

---

13   Prime Minister Neville Chamberlain's statement in front of #10 Downing Street, London, after his arrival home from the Munich Conference on September 30, 1938.

14   The *Völkischer Beobachter*, meaning the "People's Observer," was the official newspaper of the Nazi Party from the early 1920s until the collapse of the regime in 1945.

Homosexuals and those not of pure Aryan descent or anyone who had unauthorized contact with forced laborers faced punishment, ranging from a physical beating to deportation to a labor camp or even the death penalty. In numerous cases the administration of justice became arbitrary and capricious.

The National Socialists found it relatively easy to stir up hatred against Jews. Despite the creation of jobs through rearmament and public works projects, the economic situation remained difficult for many. People were quick to blame the Jews for the dreadful state of affairs. In the schools, children learned a revised version of history, in which the pure German people were oppressed by external forces that colluded with the Jews to strip them of prosperity and honor. Discriminatory laws against those of the Jewish faith appeared as soon as Hitler came to power, the first steps toward a "final solution." The Nazis staged public burnings of books written by Jewish authors. They urged fellow citizens to boycott Jewish-owned businesses. Jews were not allowed to practice certain occupations or use public transportation. The Nazis devised a variety of measures to remove Jews from society, including the so-called work camps. In Czechoslovakia, discrimination against Jews began as soon as the German soldiers arrived in October 1938.

The infamous night of November 9, 1938 came to be known among Germans as the Night of Broken Glass (*Reichskristallnacht*) and as the November Pogrom among those of the Jewish faith. The *Sturmabteilung* (SA) was the paramilitary unit of the Nazi Party, providing security for members at rallies and promoting the regime's propaganda through intimidation and violence. News of the assassination of a German diplomat in Paris by a young Polish Jew provided the SA an excuse for a night of mob violence. Storm troopers of the SA, joined in some cases by young people and others stirred to violence, roved about the streets smashing in the windows of Jewish-owned businesses and dwellings. They also torched synagogues.

Since Karlsbad did not have a trained SA detachment, one was sent to the city from Saxony, a German region on Bohemia's northern border. Using cobblestones or anything else that could be thrown, these thugs smashed the front windows and then the glass cabinets, lighting fixtures, and mirrors of Jewish citizens. The police remained out of sight and did not respond to calls for help from frightened citizens. In the early morning hours, a large mob wearing civilian clothes appeared. Using steel bars, they smashed any remaining panes of glass, as well as trash containers and business signs, until the sidewalks were covered with shards of glass and other debris.

During the Night of Broken Glass, Jewish men from every age group were taken into custody and later deported to concentration camps such as Buchenwald, Dachau, and Sachsenhausen. *Kristallnacht* marked the first instance in which the Nazi regime incarcerated Jews on a massive scale simply on the basis of their ethnicity.

The civil authorities never prosecuted those who perpetrated the vandalism on November 9. Moreover, Jewish property owners did not receive any compensation for the damage to their homes and businesses. In fact, the Nazi regime required them to pay the cleanup costs.

Throughout Nazi Germany a final solution to the Jewish question gained additional momentum. The Nazi regime took additional steps to exclude Jews from participating in professional life. Jews could no longer belong to unions and trade associations. Jewish midwives, doctors, and other health care providers were prohibited from practicing their occupations. A ban on cultural activities, such as going to the theater, concerts, or even into cinemas, was also enacted. Jewish children and university students could no longer obtain a public education. The Nazi regime also curtailed housing rights and freedom of movement among the Jewish segment of the population.

The majority of people in the Third Reich gave no serious objections to these measures, and some even agreed that they were justified.

The Start of Changes, 1938

When I was fifteen, Germany annexed the Sudetenland. The German annexation of our neighbors in Austria was accepted with a shrug of the shoulders. A weekly newsreel, *Deutsche Wochenschau*, showed us that everything was in order. I was able to see the cheering crowds in Vienna. Since the early 1930s, the *Deutsche Wochenschau* had stood right next to newspapers and radio as the most important news media. Played in movie theaters, these newsreels were the equivalent of the television news broadcasts of today.

Letters from our relatives in Vienna confirmed the official news. The Austrians themselves appeared to greet annexation. Shouldn't we have the same aspirations? Hope for our situation began to sprout.

Even I felt a more nationalistic tone in Czechoslovakia among the Czechs, who became more suspicious of the German minority. Newspaper headlines announced that the German minority opposed the Czech state and common government. The public greeting of German troops in Austria was denounced. Afterward, many Czechs feared that the Sudeten Germans would be emboldened to turn to the Third Reich.

Owned by Sudeten Germans, the *Karlsbader Badeblatt* was the only German newspaper in Karlsbad. News articles often described discrimination against the German minority. Just as often, the newspaper was censored, with the offending article taken out and the print column simply left blank.

In a 1938 edition the following statement from President Masaryk was printed as a headline: "Where there is not freedom of the press, democracy does not prevail." Masaryk said this in the early 1920s when he formed his first government. Underneath this headline, a list of discriminatory measures taken against the German minority was supposed to have appeared, but instead the rest of the front page remained empty. We learned through the propaganda reaching us indirectly that many Sudeten Germans had become dissatisfied with the status quo and were becoming more confrontational toward the Czechs. In diplomatic protests they demanded support from the Czech government for their own industry and agriculture.

I did not understand the propaganda that I heard on the radio or saw in the headlines. I could not have cared less about political squabbling, yet I could not comprehend why our neighbors of Czech origin should be different or why we Sudeten Germans should be marginalized. People from both ethnic groups, not only in our own apartment house but in all of Karlsbad and even in all of Czechoslovakia, had coexisted peacefully next to each other for centuries. As can be expected, politicians from both groups took advantage of certain differences between these segments of the population. They did so to stir up tension and to advance their own political agenda in the process. Discord was then sown between neighbors, and soon they began to see each other as dangerous and suspicious.

Still, many Sudeten Germans enthusiastically followed the events within the Third Reich. They soaked up the propaganda as though they were sponges. They thought Hitler was the Napoleon of the twentieth century. They also desired the same economic revival that was occurring in Germany. Maybe we wanted someone to rescue us. We also hoped to be freed from the unpopular Czech government. Although many Sudeten Germans were not particularly enthusiastic about the Third Reich, they believed it might well represent the lesser of two evils. We wanted equal rights and to have our needs addressed and our culture respected.

In reaction to the statements made by Hitler regarding the Sudetenland, the Czech Army stationed troops around Karlsbad in the summer of 1938. This made the propaganda real for us, creating real fear but without any meaningful change in our lives.

The uncertain times in Europe did not seem to penetrate my corner of the world. My life was peaceful and sheltered. I can't describe it any other way.

Certainly, my teenage perception of life in Karlsbad distorts the true picture of events in Czechoslovakia after the First World War. The Hungarian and German minorities encountered discrimination. Those of German ancestry were removed from public office. In the rural areas, those of German heritage suffered the most economic hardship. Czechs no longer shopped in German-owned businesses, and the corresponding loss of business income affected the families of German business owners.

Although I didn't know who Runciman was, I remember there was a saying, "Dear Lord Runciman, please make us free from Czechoslovakia!" There was a lot of hope and excitement about his visit, but there were no changes in our day-to-day lives.

A dumb joke about Masaryk was enough cause to be arrested. The Czech authorities also relied on informants. Those who spoke out against the Czech government were locked up in one of the old buildings at the infamous Pankrác Prison in Prague. The Czech police paid special attention to the German minority. Sudeten Germans were placed under surveillance, their day-to-day activities carefully scrutinized. In response, many acts of rebellion, both large and small, occurred to undermine police activity. For example, a white hand towel in front of the window told the owner of a house, "Danger! Stay away!" Perhaps the Czech police were searching through the house, something they often did without cause.

Many things were discussed only in secret among very close friends. If children came into the room, discussion of current events or the government suddenly came to an end. Children have a tendency to babble about things not intended for others to hear.

Can a fifteen-year-old be expected to have political foresight? I did not pay attention to the propaganda from Prague accusing the minorities of social problems. Why? My friends were both Czechs and Sudeten Germans. Was I supposed to harbor a grudge against one or the other? In the time before the war, as well as the periods during and after the war, Karlsbad had less ethnic tension than other nearby cities. Karlsbad was a tourist destination with an international clientele. Nobody wanted to ruin the business climate with rumors and strife among the inhabitants.

I had hardly any contact with people outside the city. In my family nobody spoke about any problems between ethnic groups, nor did I have these discussions with my friends, all between fifteen and eighteen years of age. Furthermore, I did not read any of the newspapers, and even if I had, one could not find any unbiased and uncensored comprehensive news source.

Because I did not live before the First World War, I perceived things as normal. We were a minority, and this was clear among the Sudeten Germans. Although the older Sudeten Germans might have missed the old Austro-Hungarian Empire, when Germans were the majority, this was not especially significant for someone like me. For me, being a minority meant that although my family spoke German, I also had to learn Czech.

Our family sometimes discussed the events unfolding inside Nazi Germany. My mother was a staunch supporter of the monarchy that existed before the First World War. She could never warm up to the idea of a democratic state. Masaryk and Beneš shaped her prejudices. At least a hundred times a day, she could be heard saying, "Now if only the Kaiser were still around..." Hearing Hitler on the radio was enough to make her see red. She called him the "screaming throat." Over and over, my mother said he would lead only to a disaster. Father was quite naive. He always strived for harmony and felt content when his little corner of the world was in order. Father avoided politics and preferred to escape from worldly concerns by painting for hours at a time. Totally ambivalent about the new political developments, he simply adopted a wait-and-see attitude. Mostly he stayed out of the political discussions, leaving this assignment to his wife.

The promenade in central Karlsbad in March 1992.

I lived in the present just like any other teenager, never asking about the past or thinking of the future. Nevertheless, I could sense a change in our city. Usually in the late autumn, after the stress of the harvest season was over, many wealthy landowners from Hungary and Poland traveled to Karlsbad to relax. Not this year. The city remained deserted and lonely, the cold autumn wind blowing over the empty promenade, forcing most of the hotels to reduce their business operations to a bare minimum. We in Karlsbad were like the mouse sitting before the snake, waiting to be swallowed whole.

On October 4, 1938, heavily armed German soldiers reached Karlsbad around noon. Celebrations took place throughout the city, and the children were given a school holiday. Many of the Sudeten Germans, other inhabitants with mixed marriages, and a few Czechs lined the streets. With astonishment and cheering, they greeted the German soldiers as they marched past. Young women and children received them with flowers and small flags displaying the swastika. When Hitler drove by in an open-air car, the festivities boiled over. Everyday life in the city came to a standstill. On this day Hitler spoke to the "new" Germans from a balcony at the city theater. He spoke without notes yet was able to deliver a rousing speech that flowed quite well. Those in the audience, including teenagers like myself, held their breath as this charismatic man cast his spell over us. He told us how we were now delivered from years of oppression and fear. I looked at those present, at how they held their mouths wide open, how speechless they were during that stirring address. I saw a glimmer in their eyes and felt the hope that everything would improve. Although not especially prevalent in Karlsbad, the humiliation felt by many after the First World War was detailed for us in the crudely explicit words of the speech. Hitler told us that this era in our history had come to an end. We could now look to the future with pride.

Like the others around me, I was impressed by Hitler, by the eloquence of his speech, and by the enthusiasm for his plan to change the lives of Germans. Could we have seen through the facade paraded before us? The performance given by Hitler's entourage and the soldiers was scripted to the smallest detail by the propaganda ministry. They set out bait in a trap to deceive us and the entire world. We were not accustomed to such things and fell for it. Whether rich or poor, who would not have wanted the economic improvement and prosperity he promised? The events leading to the Second

World War have been analyzed by many historians, who have then accused us of failing to heed the warning signals of the impending disaster. How could we have known what kind of plans Hitler and his ministers were plotting? Almost nobody among us had followed the details of Hitler's rise to power in Germany—perhaps the upper class, but not average people. Nobody had read the book *Mein Kampf.* How were we supposed to interpret the kind of plans he made, so many years in advance, before he set everything in motion? We were the masses who believed without question what we heard and saw because he spoke to our hopes and fears. My heart throbbed with pure excitement when I thought of the changes about which Hitler spoke. I know now that he told us what we wanted deep down inside ourselves to believe. The experience in front of the city theater was so rousing that I can still sense the excitement of that day. We were promised a new start.

In the weeks that followed the arrival of the German Army, not much changed within Karlsbad. Among the people on the streets, those wearing German uniforms mixed with the common people and the now-former Czech government employees. The atmosphere was like that of a carnival, full of laughing faces, along with hand-shaking and friendly nods of the head. It was an orderly transfer of power.

The cinemas were always full whenever the *Wochenschau* newsreels ran. We saw now our new German brothers, how they worked, harvested, and celebrated and how they pushed their way into the shops to spend their money. We had no doubt that the economic crisis was over. Overnight, thousands of the unemployed found work. In the newsreels, Jews, other non-Aryans, and political opponents to the Reich were held responsible for the problems of the past. The Nazi regime began to harass and oppress the minority that did not conform to its vision of a future defined by boundaries that were black-and-white.

We saw how the new German Army celebrated its success and how it bragged about its weapons of war—the best-equipped army in years. The way the German soldiers appeared and how they carried themselves, with elements of ceremony and arrogance, made just as strong an impression on a civilian population as the military bands with their many trumpets and drums. What a difference compared to the Czech Army, whose soldiers wore the same old Austrian uniforms from the First World War along with faded leggings. The rifles and pistols the Czechs carried were half-rusted relics from the era when Bohemia manufactured weapons for the royal armory. The Czech soldiers did not bathe that often and reeked of body odor. The German soldiers, on the other hand, dressed in brand-new uniforms, looking very polished and clean, and wore leather boots so new they often creaked with every step.

Like a wounded animal, the Czech Army left the city a few days after the German Army arrived, almost crawling back to Prague. Adding insult to injury, as they were leaving the city, they ran out of gasoline. With a patronizing attitude, appearing superior and benevolent to the whole world, the German troops helped the pathetic Czech soldiers out, to send them back to a country that had just been amputated. How humiliating for Beneš, whose hatred of Germans became further inflamed.

The Sudeten Germans had had a love-hate relationship with the Czech majority under Czech rule. After the German soldiers arrived, this ethnic conflict retreated to the background. However, shaped by media reports and new laws, the marginalization of a new segment of the population began: the Jews. People always seem to have a need to make another person or group responsible for their own inadequacies.

I observed the changes around me with suspicion but had not formed my own opinion. Gerda, on the other hand, avoided anything to do with politics. She refused to participate in any discussion of current events. Perhaps these events frightened her because her father was of Czech origin.

The German soldiers in Karlsbad were housed in barracks outside the city limits. Soon we saw less of them on the streets. Sometimes we saw them alone on the promenade or on the banks of the Teplá River, casually smoking a cigarette while leaning against handrails, sizing up the inhabitants, sometimes with a girl hanging on their arm. The soldiers maintained a friendly yet distant presence. After the invasion, German uniforms replaced the Czech uniforms, but otherwise nothing else changed.

The Beginning of the End, 1938–1939

However, we still sensed something in the air. We waited and held our breath. Rumors surfaced in Karlsbad, unbelievable horror stories about the *Schutzstaffel* (SS)[15] and Gestapo and the brutal oppression of Jews and anyone who resisted the Nazi regime. We could not believe what we heard. We cautiously distanced ourselves from the men who suddenly appeared in Karlsbad. Perhaps the rumors were true. We did not want to provoke anything.

Within a month of annexation, we knew in no uncertain terms that life would never be the same as before. Under the authority of the Third Reich, "special measures" were taken throughout Bohemia. On the main shopping street in Karlsbad, the German SA thugs and others caught up in the moment broke the windows of Jewish-owned businesses during the night. Soon the business owners were taken into custody. None of us dared to leave the house. We were in a state of shock when the loud and angry mob roamed about the streets.

The victims of this attack were generally well-known and respected in our community. Otto Stein, a former classmate of my father, a friend of the family, and a Jew, owned the apartment building in which we lived. On the ground floor of the building, he also owned a grocery store. The day after the attack on Jewish-owned businesses, one of Otto Stein's apprentices went to the Gestapo and offered his help.[16] He returned with a squad of SS soldiers, who confiscated

---

15   The Schutzstaffel, commonly called the SS, was a major paramilitary organization in Germany. In 1925 Heinrich Himmler joined the unit, which had by then been reorganized from its origin as a small guard unit into one of the most powerful organizations in the Nazi Regime. Under Himmler's leadership from 1929-1945, the SS was the foremost agency of security, surveillance, and terror within Germany and German-occupied Europe.

16   It is difficult to render in English the extent to which Otto Stein was betrayed. In German-speaking countries, young people perform an apprenticeship as part of their high school education. The relationship between the master and the

and searched the business. Those who knew Otto Stein, both in the apartment building and in the surrounding area, regarded him as a fair businessman. He was also part of the fabric of our community— one of us. He was a good man, a life-long friend of my father. That he was a Jew was irrelevant.

We didn't know what to do when the SS arrived. My mother, always very courageous and bold, attempted to enter the store and show her support for Otto Stein by purchasing some groceries. A baby-faced SS man blocked the way. "My God," said my mother, angrily rolling her eyes. "You've just liberated us from the Czechs, and now comes the *Führer* to oppress once again." The man, like most of the young and zealous SS soldiers, was not very bright. He looked at my mother, terrified, and without saying a word, he let her pass. Unfortunately, our support for Otto Stein failed to help him. That same day, he was arrested and taken way.

We were horrified, not able to understand what was happening. There always seemed to be a segment of the population that followed the crowd, which would join forces with the SS or SA just to commit acts of extreme violence. On the day they broke the windows, there had been calls for a demonstration against the Jews, but the outbreak of mob violence occurring during the night took us completely by surprise.

Most of those taken into custody were transported to Dachau, a concentration camp near Munich. From the bottoms of our hearts, we sympathized with these men and women, many of whom we knew personally. Yet we remained silent and did not speak openly about this event. We feared the Gestapo for very good reasons. They regarded the Jews as public enemy number one. Those who objected could be summoned to appear before the police and made to register as subversives. The years we spent living under state-sponsored terror in Czechoslovakia have become a bizarre episode in history, something nobody would ever want to experience. The oppression embodied by the Pankrác Prison under the Czech government was

---

apprentice is often close, almost a parent–child closeness. The mother of the young man who reported Otto to the authorities came to my family some months later and said she was horrified that her son had committed such an act.

continued by the Nazi regime, but instead of prisons, they now confined people in "work camps."

Some of those deported to the work camps committed suicide to escape their desperate circumstances. Olga, a relative of the Otto Stein family, swallowed poison during the train journey to a concentration camp. She could not stand being confined inside a cattle car crammed full of people. Before Olga died from the poison, she jumped from the train. Her corpse remained alongside the railroad tracks for several days. Of all the terrible news I heard during this time, Olga's death was the most distressing, imposing itself like a ton weight upon my shoulders.

Otto Stein returned home shortly before Christmas in 1938. He hardly talked about his experiences in the camp. Because of his silence, I wanted to believe that his detention had not been that terrible for him. A small ray of sunshine occurred in this otherwise dismal time when Otto gave me a cheesecake recipe he had learned by heart from a Jewish cook at the camp. In January 1939, Otto left his family behind in Karlsbad and moved to Prague, to live with his sister-in-law, who was of Aryan ancestry. There he hoped to be outside the reach of the hatred toward Jewish people.

If only Otto Stein had immigrated to America, England, or someplace else. He could have

One of many weekends spent with Otto Stein and his family in the mountains. Otto is sitting on the far left, next to my mother, and the daughter of our hosts is looking over his left shoulder. Otto's son sits at my father's feet and I am behind my parents, draping my arms over their shoulders.

afforded to do so, but instead Otto stayed in Czechoslovakia. Once again, the fangs of the Nazi henchmen caught him, and now his fate was sealed. He was taken into custody for the last time and probably became one of the many concentration camp victims.

On my seventy-fifth birthday, I was surprised by a phone call from Frankfurt, Germany. For quite a long time, Otto Stein's daughter, Inge, had been attempting to contact me. Now she finally had succeeded. Inge told me a moving story about her father and mine. In 1940 or 1941, while my father was a German soldier stationed in Vienna, he met Otto Stein by coincidence on the train platform. Otto was among a group of prisoners awaiting transport to one of the concentration camps. My father impulsively called out to Otto upon seeing him, initially thinking that Otto had stumbled into this area of the train station by accident.

Otto stepped out from the group of prisoners and approached my father. For a few minutes the two were able to talk undisturbed. "Your family is doing well," whispered my father. Otto Stein had tears in his eyes as he looked around furtively. Father continued, "Here, you need this more than I." He then shoved some cash and cigarettes into the pocket of Otto's jacket. Pleading with my father, Otto whispered, "Can you deliver a message to Rosa?" After looking around and making sure nobody was watching, my father rummaged around in his pocket and pulled out a small piece of paper and pencil, which he handed to Otto. After scribbling down a few words, Otto pressed the note into my father's hand. Both said goodbye, knowing they would never see each other again. Otto rejoined the prisoners, and my father quickly left the platform. While home on leave, Father delivered the message to Rosa, Otto's wife, and told her of their encounter. Inge told me that during the many years that followed, the final message from Otto comforted Rosa, a message from her beloved husband, which my father delivered.

Through the personal intervention of Baron Konstantin von Neurath, the Reichs Protector of Bohemia (a sort of governor), Rosa Stein was allowed to keep the apartment building and rental income. However, Otto Stein's grocery store was "Aryanized" and taken over by a German owner.

At age seventeen in Karlsbad.

For some time after the terrible night of mob violence, we remained in a state of complete shock, shuffling around with drooping shoulders and speaking in muffled voices. The Christmas of 1938 was more than depressing. Those who perpetrated the violence remained faceless. The authorities never identified and punished those who had broken the windows. It soothed our conscience to think these people were outsiders who had come into Karlsbad and fled soon afterward.

Starting in the spring of 1939, life returned to normal. The spa resort business flourished, just like before the war, with one major exception: Jews no longer lived in Karlsbad. Czechs or Germans "confiscated" their property and assets. The hotels received a fresh coat of paint, with the balconies receiving a coat of gold; Karlsbad shone. Food supplies remained plentiful. Some came from the Third Reich, and some was imported. We had the worst part of integration behind us, and now we could enjoy the same prosperity as in other areas of the Reich. Or so we thought.

I do not recall receiving any news from other areas of Czechoslovakia or hearing anything critical of events in Germany. Everything was colored by propaganda, showing only positive aspects of life in the Third Reich, such as the "Strength through Joy" program. We all wanted to be part of that.

How wonderful it must have been to vacation on the Baltic Sea or in the Alps, I thought. The *Wochenschau* showed young, strong bodies enjoying organized trips that were not only fun but also a splendid diversion from working life. Dictators can certainly utilize slogans such as "Strength through Joy" as a weapon. They seduce, deceive, and enslave people. Their effect is addictive, like that of a drug.

Perspective: Indoctrination, 1933-1945

Literally translated as the "Strength through Joy", the "*Kraft durch Freude*", or KdF, program's purpose was to remove social-class inequity and create a national community independent of socioeconomic distinctions. Everyone had the right to rest and relaxation and KdF bridged the class divide by making middle-class leisure activities available to the masses and promote the advantages of National Socialism to the people. Another less ideological goal was to boost the German economy by stimulating the tourism industry, and KdF became the world's largest tourism operator in the 1930s.

Entertainment and travel made the propaganda more enticing. The traditions of the people were highlighted to strengthen feelings of loyalty toward the fatherland and a common citizenship. If these programs seemed useless and idealistic, they were based on a cunning underlying strategy to build the tourism trade, increase employment, and create deep national pride. Many became convinced of the plan's credibility. Until the start of the Second World War in 1939, over 43 million Germans set the plan in motion by finding the means to take a vacation. When the war started, shipping and railway capacity were set aside for military transport, and the KdF focused on evening activities closer to home.

While the KdF focused on families and workers, boys and girls received indoctrination by state organizations for youth starting at age ten. At age fourteen, the boys joined the Hitler Youth. The League of German Girls was a similar organization for girls.[17] New members were sworn in at a ceremony that incorporated military drills. At age eighteen, young men were required to perform civil service work for the Reich and were later conscripted for military service. At a Nazi Party rally of the Hitler Youth Movement in the

---

17   In German, Hitler Jugend and Bund Deutscher Mädel.

Nuremberg[18] stadium on September 14, 1935, Hitler described his ideal of a young German boy as "swift as a greyhound, as tough as leather, and as hard as Krupp's steel."[19] This phrase soon became a party slogan.

The League of German Girls had similar goals, of building strong, educated women, worthy partners for their future husbands, and also required compulsory service at age eighteen. The League used summer camps, romanticism and folklores, tradition, and sports to indoctrinate girls within the National Socialist belief system, and to train them for their roles in German society: wife, mother, and homemaker. They would give birth to the great Aryanized nation.

The National Socialists built their propaganda machine to the point of perfection, crushing any attempt to present alternative points of view. In his 1930 book *The Revolt of the Masses*, the author José Ortega y Gasset advocated the following:

> Share our existence with the enemy! Govern with the opposition! Is not such a form of tenderness beginning to seem incomprehensible? Nothing indicates more clearly the characteristics of the day than the fact that there are so few countries where an opposition exists. In almost all, a homogenous mass weighs on the public authority and crushes down, annihilates every opposing group. The mass—who would credit it as one sees its compact, multitudinous appearance? —does not wish to share life with those who are not of it. It has a deadly hatred of all that is not itself.[20]

In August 1933, at the opening of the Tenth Radio Exhibition, Dr. Joseph Göbbels said,

---

18   In German, the city of Nuremberg is known as Nürnberg.

19   For context, Krupp is the trade name for a German steel producer, now an international steel firm known as Thyssen Krupp Stahl AG.

20   José Ortega y Gasset, *The Revolt of the Masses,* 25th Anniversary Edition. (New York: W.W. Norton & Company, Inc., 1957), 76-77.

A government, whose goal it is to weld a people together so that they have a powerful voice in world politics, has not only the right but the duty to disseminate this goal to people from all walks of life or at least to make an attempt to include them in this goal. This also applies to radio. The more cognizant a people are of their place in the world, the stronger our goal becomes, and radio takes on a larger responsibility for the future of the nation.

This year's radio exhibition opens in this spirit. Its keynote is the People's Receiver. ... It will open new paths not only for Germany's political life, but for the work of radio throughout the world.

This exhibition stands in the shadow of this great task. It is a start, a beginning, an expression of German courage and German confidence.

It is our dearest wish that science, industry and the intellectual leadership of German radio from now on will follow a new path, at the end of which stands our common, great goal: One People, one Reich, one will, and a glorious German future![21]

The economic recovery was plainly evident among the Germans who now found work. For many, life seemed normal despite widespread discrimination against those of Jewish heritage and other minorities. Personal advantage overtook principle.

One must give some credit to the Nazi regime; almost everyone worked and earned money. The men either served in the military or participated in a government work program through the *Deutsche Arbeiterfront*. They worked in the armaments industry, in road construction, and in agriculture. Women who did not have any

---

21   Reported in the newspaper *Kreutzeitung*, August 19, 1933. Dr. Goebbels was the propaganda minister, and through his direction, the news media was heavily censored. See also https://research.calvin.edu/german-propaganda-archive/goeb56.htm accessed November 18, 2018.

maternal responsibilities were also pulled for service in government work programs. The *Wochenschau* showed rows of young people belonging to the Hitler Youth or League of German Girls lined up to greet the *Führer*. As they cheered, he received their greeting like a kind father whose pride was overwhelming. Crowds in Germany chanted, "*Ein Volk, ein Reich, ein Führer!*"[22]

Life in a German Town, 1939

The German soldiers treated the civilians of Karlsbad politely and assimilated themselves into our day-to-day life. After the Night of Broken Glass, acts of mob violence ceased. The terror of the National Socialist regime now seemed far away.

I joined the *Turnverein*, a gymnastics organization for German girls. At the beginning, it was not much more than a sports club. Later, the direction of the organization became more nationalistic, and besides engaging in hiking and gymnastics, we also sang.

Music, you might ask? In a sports club? Anyway, we sang songs about German independence, about freedom, and about how proud we were to be of German heritage. Children are highly impressionable. The Third Reich exploited this, knowing that through children, the government can easily influence parents.

Our lives continued much as they always had with some small differences. Instead of the daily Czech language class, we now focused on learning French and Latin. The teacher attempted to shape the learning environment by saying, "The world will one day speak about what is now happening in Germany. They will say that history was being written. Germany is here to change the world." This was said to us over and over again. It is simply amazing: what they foretold actually happened. Of course, the outcome was far from what they had expected. What they thought would be famous is now infamous.

From afar, an observer 30,000 feet in the sky would not have noticed a change. Relative calm prevailed, yet behind the scenes one

---

22   The English translation is "one people, one nation, one leader." The word *Volk* has an ethnic connotation.

noticed subtle developments. We, the local folks, saw these signs but could not interpret them.

Perspective: German Occupation of Bohemia and Building Tensions, 1939-1942

In the spring of 1939, German troops occupied the rest of Czechoslovakia. The Nazi Regime designated the region as a German protectorate and appointed Baron von Neurath to be the Reichs Protector. The term "protectorate" follows the logic, or excuse, that other European powers used to acquire colonies in Africa. After Hitler annexed the rest of Czechoslovakia, Edvar Beneš, who fled to London at the end of 1938, set up a government in exile. His postwar goal, after Czechoslovakia regained its sovereignty, was an ethnically pure Czech society in his homeland.

In the early 1930s, following a court-martial and dismissal from the German navy, Reinhard Heydrich joined the Nazi Party. A cunning and ruthless man, he soon became the deputy of Heinrich Himmler, a former poultry farmer and now the leader of the SS. Himmler placed Heydrich in charge of the security service within the SS, the *Sicherheitsdienst* or SD, whose task was to observe and combat opponents of the state. Within the SD, was an even more elite guard, called the *Einsatzgruppen*, the training of which fell under Heydrich's authority. He assembled a 3,000-man task force for assignments that the regular army rejected as undignified and contrary to military tradition. That is, the *Einsatzgruppen* were death squads.

As *Einsatzgruppen* entered towns and villages in occupied territories, they ordered the Jewish inhabitants to assemble in predetermined areas, where men, women, and children were murdered with machine guns. These mass executions proved not only inefficient but also difficult for many of those ordered to carry out the killings. Himmler sought another solution and for this reason scheduled a conference to be held at Wannsee, the name of a lake in Berlin. Heydrich helped organize the Wannsee Conference, one of the most infamous events in world history, which took place in January 1942. There, the Nazi leadership found a more efficient "final solution" to the Jewish problem, deciding to transport the Jews in occupied territories to extermination camps.

In September 1941, Baron von Neurath resigned, and Reinhard Heydrich took over as the Reichs Protector of Bohemia and Moravia. Heydrich was far more brutal than his predecessor. He soon quashed black-market and partisan activities and increased factory production, particularly of weapons for the war on the eastern front.

At the end of 1941, Jan Kubis and Joseph Gabik, two Czechs living in England, were recruited to perform a special assignment for their country: to assassinate Heydrich. They parachuted into Czechoslovakia and found an ideal location for the ambush, a curve in the road where Heydrich's driver would have to slow the vehicle. Kubis and Gabik waited for Heydrich. Soon the Heydrich car approached the curve; the top down on the convertible, leaving him unprotected. Gabik stepped forward to fire his machine gun, but the weapon jammed. Kubis then tossed a hand grenade into the car, which exploded, wounding Heydrich. He died from these injuries nine days later, on June 4, 1942.

Gabik and Kubis took refuge in a church in Prague. Eventually, the SS discovered their whereabouts, and they were killed. The Nazi regime took revenge for the assassination. In Lidiče, a small village west of Prague, 173 men were rounded up by German soldiers and executed. The soldiers then gathered the women and children of the village and sent them to concentration camps. Afterward, the village was razed to the ground.

Dancing in the Summer, 1939

I was young, wanting to enjoy my life, taking to the limit each bit of new freedom given to me. I wanted all the experiences and mistakes people at this age make. I simply wanted to be a teenager like so many before me and around me. I didn't see or want to see that we were on the verge of losing the most-valuable asset we had: our carefree youth.

Scenes from everyday life continued. I attended a dance school and floated like a feather over the dance floor with my partner. Partly because I could speak French and some Italian, in the summer of 1939, the city government asked me to represent Karlsbad at official events. As if sitting on a powder keg, during this summer I could sense the apprehension surrounding this uncertain time, a storm gathering on the horizon. Nevertheless, I also retained the typical teenage denial of the inevitable.

Together with the other young representatives of our city, I looked after visitors who came to Karlsbad from all over the world. From the first of May to the first of September, they came to relax and rest at our spa resort.

I owned two evening dresses. One was made of blue organza and decorated with small flowers. The other dress was made from a peach-colored silk. After putting one of them on, I would stand in front of the mirror and slowly turn myself around. Together with a stylish hairdo and a touch of red lipstick, I felt on top of the world. I was certain I could win any beauty contest. Elated and full of confidence, I set out to fulfill my duties as a representative of my city. A distinguished gentleman from Hungary was the first to kiss my hand, an act so flattering it nearly swept me off my feet.

The threat of war had not yet affected us—we didn't think about the burden and fear the actual fighting might bring to our city. Besides, the propaganda said that any war would be not only short but also one we would win.

The summer of 1939 was an extraordinarily busy and profitable one for Karlsbad.

To celebrate the end of the season, the city held concerts everywhere in August. The highlight of the August celebrations was a grand ball to honor an Italian delegation. It was held at the Grand Hotel Pupp, one of the most magnificent hotels in Europe. I recall giving the ladies of high society a rose to match their dresses. One of these roses survived for four years pressed into the pages of my diary. Now the rose and the diary of the girl, with all her hopes and dreams, have vanished.

Fast and with brute force, reality has a way of catching up with us. Guests at the grand ball were gliding across the dance floor as the orchestra played a waltz when abruptly the music stopped, and an SS officer swaggered onto the stage. He grabbed the microphone, and with a somber voice, he spoke words that changed our future forever. "Comrades and guests, because of the ongoing Polish aggression against the Third Reich, our *Führer* finds it necessary to meet force with force. Our soldiers are shooting back. The counterattack has begun."

Another world war engulfed Europe.

Perspective: The Invasion of Poland, 1939

During the summer of 1939, secret preparations for the attack on Poland were underway. The world was supposed to think that Poland attacked Germany and that Germany responded in self-defense. Polish-speaking SS soldiers dressed in Polish army uniforms and executed prisoners from a work camp, setting up their bodies to play the part of dead German civilians. During the night of August 31, 1939, two fake attacks by the Polish military were staged near the border towns of Groß Rauden and Kreuzburg. In the early morning hours on September 1, 1939, another Polish attack, at a radio station near Gleiwitz, was reported, which the SS also staged.

Without an official declaration of war, these staged attacks became the excuse for a massive invasion of Poland by two German Army groups. Using a new style of warfare, known as blitzkrieg or lightning war, the German Army advanced across Poland supported by modern tanks and aircraft. Warsaw, the capital, was soon surrounded.

The *Völkischer Beobachter* reported on September 2, 1939, "By order of the *Führer* and the high military command, the armed forces have taken steps to protect the Reich. To fulfill their duty to stop Polish aggression, soldiers of the German Army have crossed over the German-Polish border this morning to conduct a counterattack."

The following day, September 3, 1939, France and Great Britain declared war on Germany.

Two days after the German invasion began, outraged Poles took revenge against several thousand ethnic Germans living in Bromberg, Poland.[23] One of the first tasks of the advancing German Army was to punish the Poles for the attack on the German civilians. In the following weeks, *Einsatzgruppen* murdered tens of thousands of Poles, including doctors, civil servants, clergy, military officers, and Jews.

Prior to the invasion, the Soviet Union signed a pact with Germany and agreed not to intercede on behalf of Poland. On September 17, Soviet troops invaded eastern Poland to claim a share of the spoils. On October 4, Poland surrendered.

The War Begins and My Life Is Forever Changed, 1939

The outbreak of the Second World War, especially for those who had lived during the First World War, was deeply shocking. However, the propaganda had already brainwashed many young people, who now approvingly greeted the attack against Poland. They wanted to correct the injustices committed against Germany by the Versailles Treaty and the Polish government. Clearly, life had changed dramatically. The time of dancing and vacation was over. I stored my evening gowns in the attic, where they waited with our hopes and dreams for peace. If I remember correctly, shortly after the end of the war, my mother sold the dresses to a female Soviet Army officer in exchange for some bacon and other meat, a rather ho-hum replacement for my lost beauty and youth.

During school holidays the students in the secondary schools

---

23   Now Bydgoszcz, Poland. Poland and Germany provide differing accounts of the number killed and historians are undecided on whether German troops in the city opened fire on the Polish troops (and if so, whether they were composed of members of the Bydgoszcz German minority), or whether Polish troops (or panicking civilians) overreacted in the confusion and targeted innocent German civilians.

had to perform community service for the Reich.[24] The government sent me to Saaz, a Bohemian town, to pick hops. Nobody provided us with gloves for protection against the sharp leaves and vines of the fruit or with any lotion to soothe our swollen, beet-red hands.

During the early part of the war, the civilians in Karlsbad did not experience any serious food shortages. The farming sections of Bohemia were dominated by Czech farmers, and many of the Czechs living in Karlsbad became black marketeers after the German occupation. These families supplied us with food smuggled in from other parts of Bohemia.

At the end of the school year in 1940, the first of the slave laborers, French prisoners of war, arrived in Karlsbad. Their task was to expand our airport to convert it into a military base. Because of my foreign-language skills, the government assigned me to the airport to translate for the prisoners, part of the community service work required of me and the rest of my classmates during the school holiday.

I translated and typed into French the written orders of the German commander, certainly a difficult assignment for a seventeen-year-old girl to accomplish. Constantly, I needed to look up words in a French-German dictionary. Even then, I seriously doubted that the prisoners understood much of what I attempted to write in French. *Did I choose the right word?* I often wondered. *Was the grammar correct?* For two months I worked in the office assigned to the duty sergeant. Not even once did I see any of the prisoners up close and in person. They remained totally hidden from the civilian population, and consequently, I could never determine how they were treated.

In this depressing and frightening time, I found the first love of my life, a test pilot at the military base, a major in his early thirties who fell in love with a shy seventeen-year-old. Very tender and innocent, the love affair lasted several wonderful weeks. I was in seventh heaven. He gently stroked my hair, and we bashfully held hands and

---

24   I use the term secondary schools because in Germany this might mean a trade school or and academic high school – students in both types of schools had to do mandatory public service.

exchanged innocent kisses. He visited my family's home and brought over books for the women of the house. He read romantic poems aloud, with endless enthusiasm. Our relationship was like a flower found in the dead of winter, blooming in dark and troubled times.

Nothing lasts forever, especially during a time of war. He was a fighter pilot and was stationed in Karlsbad for just a few weeks. My major test-flew the fighter aircraft put into service for the air campaign over England. These small nimble machines accompanied the larger, heavier bombers to protect them from enemy aircraft. In the fall, when I had to return to school, he received orders to return to his unit.

On Christmas Day in 1940, I saw him for the last time, when he was able to spend a few days in Karlsbad. He seemed depressed and left me with tears in his eyes. I felt the same, bidding him goodbye with fear in my heart for his safety.

In February I received the fateful telegram: "Major Joseph H., during the performance of his duties for the German Fatherland, was shot down over the English Channel. We would like to convey to you our deepest sympathy. Central Command."

How fragile life can be. For days I walked around as though in a trance. Not even my mother could cheer me up. I maintained contact with his family. A few years later, after the birth of my daughter, his sister sent me a pair of baby shoes as well as a baby blanket. After the war the letters I sent to his family were returned to me unopened. They lived in Aachen, a city on the Belgian border. I assumed they had not survived when Allied artillery and aircraft destroyed the city.

Clothing and shoes remained in short supply because the military consumed almost all the materials needed to produce these items. In response, our motto became "from old make new." The government urged civilians to show their patriotism and solidarity with the soldiers by donating all their unwanted clothes. Furs were a different matter. They were confiscated for the war effort. The government also rationed foodstuffs, but nobody went hungry. Those who wanted to purchase something out of the ordinary often turned to the black market.

As Germany fought a war on the western and eastern fronts, we in Karlsbad had no idea that the Nazi regime was constructing extermination camps to annihilate people they called the "undesirables." There was no free press, and so, early on, none of this information filtered down to us. Much later, we started to hear rumors about special camps, but we could not have imagined what occurred there in our worst nightmares.

Two years after the outbreak of hostilities, the war continued. In the spring of 1941, I finished my secondary education. What were my options? What kind of career choices did I have in a time of war? I wanted to obtain a degree in French and philosophy at the Karls University in Prague.[25] I attended this university for four months. When the compulsory order for military service landed on my desk, I knew that not even I was outside the reach of the war. To fulfill my obligation, I had to choose between fieldwork, piecework in a munition's factory, military service, or working for the Red Cross—I chose the Red Cross. The freedom to chart my own destiny had come to an end. Instead, decisions in my life were now shaped by events outside my control or simply by the need to survive. I was just eighteen years old.

Perspective: The Second World War, 1939–1941

> For months a problem has tormented us, a problem caused by the Versailles Treaty, a degenerate and depraved dictate, which has become unbearable. Danzig was and is a German city! Danzig was taken from us! The German minority living there has suffered agonizing mistreatment. In 1919 and 1920 over a million people of German blood had to leave their homes.
>
> —Adolf Hitler, in his address to the German Reichstag on September 1, 1939 [26]

---

25   Karls University in Prague is recognized as the first German University.

26   After the First World War, the German-speaking port city of Danzig

Germany achieved easy victories in the beginning, encountering poorly equipped opponents who were dominated quickly. By July 1940, Poland, Denmark, Belgium, Norway, Holland, and France had fallen under the control of the Reich. The arrogant military high command feasted on the spoils of war and the luxuries offered in the great cities of Europe, especially in Paris.

Despite these victories, the occupation of the Baltic countries in June 1940 by the Soviet Union was interpreted by Hitler as a violation of their nonaggression pact and a personal affront. For him the response was clear: an attack against the Soviet Union, which was code-named Operation Barbarossa. Operation Barbarossa would start soon, but before attacking the Soviet Union, an invasion of Great Britain was planned, known as Operation Sea Lion.

To prepare for a ground invasion, one that would require Germany to transport soldiers across the English Channel by ship, the German air force (Luftwaffe) attacked British naval ships, ports, airfields, radar installations, and other military targets. On August 24, 1940, several German bombs fell on a residential area of London. The Royal Air Force retaliated four days later by dropping bombs on Berlin. Infuriated, since he promised that Germany would be spared from enemy attack, Hitler directed the Luftwaffe to shift from military targets to civilian targets. Although thousands of British civilians were killed by the aerial bombing that followed, the Royal Air Force and Royal Navy remained strong enough to oppose any land invasion of Great Britain. Had Hitler not redirected the focus of the aerial campaign, the air war over Britain may have had a different outcome. In September 1940, Hitler had to postpone actions under Operation Sea Lion indefinitely to focus on an invasion of the Soviet Union. The air war over Great Britain also deprived Hitler of thousands of desperately needed aircraft and pilots that could be used on the eastern front.

In the first years of the war, life for the average German remained relatively undisturbed by world events. In Karlsbad, the only sign of world conflict was that most of the men in the city were wounded

---

(now Gdańsk) was placed under the jurisdiction of the League of Nations to provide sea access to the newly formed Polish state.

soldiers or slave laborers. To raise morale, Nazi Germany distributed food to the civilian population, food often taken from the occupied countries. However, the situation was much bleaker for those who were members of any group ostracized by the Nazis, such as Jews, homosexuals, and later, the handicapped. As of 1942, about 500,000 Sinti and Roma (Gypsies) also became part of the "undesirable element," having fallen into the hands of the Nazi regime.

As other areas of Europe came under the control of the Nazis, so did millions of people of the Jewish race. After the Germans took a city, ghettos were cordoned off, where the Jewish population lived under inhumane conditions. Hunger and disease claimed thousands of lives within a short period of time.

The German armed forces encountered unexpected resistance in the Balkans yet eventually achieved military success in Yugoslavia and Greece. The fierce resistance, however, delayed the planned invasion of Russia by six weeks. On June 22, 1941, the German invasion of the Soviet Union began. Hitler planned and conducted a war of annihilation. The Nazis considered all Soviets to be subhuman, and as such, no quarter was given. The advancing German Army either exterminated or enslaved the Soviet people, while plundering the vast natural resources of the Soviet Union. Operation Barbarossa, envisioned as a *blitzkrieg*, a lightning-quick and very unrealistic defeat of the Soviet armed forces, became instead a four-year-long war of attrition that culminated in the complete destruction of Nazi Germany.

The army gathered for Operation Barbarossa was the largest invasion force ever assembled. On the Soviet border, the German force was supplemented by soldiers from Finland, Romania, Hungary, Italy, and Spain. Still, this invasion force of 3.5 million men opposed 178 Soviet divisions, around 4.7 million men. Moreover, at this stage of the war, Germany had already exhausted its military reserve, whereas the Soviet Union could still mobilize 12 million men of military age. For this reason, the German victory depended on the *blitzkrieg*, which never materialized.

The *Führer* issued crystal clear instructions: this war has no rules. His special order, the so-called Commissar Order required the summary execution of any Soviet officer or Communist Party member taken prisoner. German soldiers believed they had immunity from war crimes prosecution and unfettered discretion to commit the most heinous of atrocities. *Einsatzgruppen* interpret the Commissar Order as the legal authority for the mass execution of Soviet Jews. Not one German general raised an objection to the Commissar Order in Hitler's presence, although a few, such as General Henning von Treskow, had the courage not to carry out the order.

The War and the Patient, Part 1: 1941

At the start of my Red Cross service, I attended a training program held at the only prewar hospital in Karlsbad. It was operated by nuns. After the training program, the other trainees and I mostly cared for wounded German soldiers who needed surgical care and had been transported to hospitals recently constructed in Karlsbad. The ambulance trains that brought the wounded to Karlsbad arrived nonstop from the eastern front.

An endless stream of military convoys rolled through my town, taking thousands of soldiers to fight on the eastern front in the Soviet Union. Red Cross workers traveling with the men were usually responsible for their care until they reached the front. Sometimes the other nurses and I had to report to the train station, to give the soldiers traveling through Karlsbad coffee and something to eat. Over time we collected a great number of small cards printed with a military postal number, cards that the soldiers had slipped to us. The postal numbers directed mail to soldiers who either did not know their destination or perhaps were not allowed to give out this information. Anyway, the numbers enabled the men to remain anonymous while, hopefully, receiving some news from home. Often, we heard the soldiers say, "Write to me at the front. Send me a card and photo." Only a few found the strength to tell us how frightened they were of going into combat, yet the faces of these young men spoke volumes. Within two or three years, many of them were dead.

In late August 1941 my fellow trainees and I received news from the head nurse that we had long expected: within a few days, we would receive our first group of severely wounded soldiers. "Listen up, ladies," she said. "Shortly, the first of those wounded in the fighting in Russia will arrive. I must insist that you treat them with respect. And don't be frightened of them. They are unfortunate men." Indeed, army ambulances brought a steady stream of these men to the hospital, wounded soldiers suffering from every conceivable injury. I was supposed to remain in the maternity ward, to help bring new lives into the world instead of comforting those who were about ready to depart. But I simply could not resist the innate curiosity inside of me. I just had to see the wounded men with my own eyes. Sneaking away from my post, I went to the entrance hall and hid myself behind a support column.

In a strange, silent procession, the first-aid workers carried the wounded men on narrow stretchers through the hospital entrance to the elevator. Many were taken directly to the operating room. As my eyes grew wide, I saw men with pale faces, some of them very close to death, barely alive. That day the stretcher-bearers transported almost all the wounded soldiers to the operating room. Only one man, pale-white and wearing a giant cast covering most of his torso, waited for the orderly to arrive. This man wore a dark brown pullover with a khaki army shirt underneath. There, in the entrance hall of that hospital in Karlsbad, lay my future husband, Georg Stein.[27]

How could I have known that he would become a part of my destiny? As I leaned against the railing, half-hidden behind the support column, he saw me. Ever so charming, a lifelong trait, he tried to smile. With a deep, hoarse voice he said, "Hello up there." Shocked and horrified at having been discovered, in the blink of an eye I darted behind the large glass door leading to my work area in the maternity ward. Flushed with embarrassment, I returned to work.

About two months later, I finished my basic training to become certified as a nursing assistant. I waited for a permanent post, which did not take long. Soon I was working in a new and hastily converted military hospital, at the former Hotel Hopfenstock.

---

27   Georg is pronounced "Gay-org" in German.

The army requisitioned most of the hotels in Karlsbad for use as military hospitals, plainly evident by the Red Cross flags displayed over the entrances. Soldiers in wheelchairs or on crutches, along with those who loitered about waiting for their next assignment, shaped the street scene in Karlsbad. The dwindling number of resort guests arrived to a city full of army hospitals and mingled with soldiers out on the promenade.

The military lacked trained nurses and doctors, so in a pinch we chipped in, whether we wanted to or not. The nursing assistants, including myself, had to make medical decisions that only the head nurse, or even the doctor, was qualified to make. None of us received the necessary training, and the medical decisions we had to make demanded too much from us. I was about to turn nineteen, not mature by any means, and many of the other nurses were even younger. Right from the start, I cared for patients afflicted with typhus and wound infections. Every day I confronted my deepest fear: contracting an infectious disease. It seems as though my guardian angel stood over me and protected me from all those germs floating around in the hospital.

The odor of perfume that had wafted through the air during the last ball now had been replaced by the horrible stench of wounds that had been disinfected with Lysoform. Hygiene counted for very little. We lacked the necessary cleaning products. The hospitals held far too many wounded men while not employing enough staff to give each soldier the attention he deserved. These unfortunate men often received care from inexperienced and uncertain nursing assistants who had no one they could turn for help with tough decisions. In each military hospital there was usually only one doctor and a head nurse to care for 100 to 120 wounded men. The doctor delegated triage to the nursing assistants and dealt personally only with the most critically wounded.

At the end of November, we received this hospital's first group of German soldiers who had been fighting on the Russian front and who were suffering from frostbite so severe that their hands and feet had turned black. Due to the lack of adequate hygiene and proper medical care, many arrived with open wounds that were infested with maggots crawling around under their bandages. The sight of these men upset me terribly but knowing that horror and disgust do not bring healing, I would take a deep breath, straighten my shoulders, and return to work, trying to give these men the best medical care I could provide.

I still remember very clearly my first medical crisis. It was a Saturday. Neither the doctor nor the head nurse was on duty. An officer with a gunshot wound to the stomach called out to me in a terrified voice. Pulling aside his blanket, he showed me his wound, which had just ruptured, spilling out his intestines. My first impulse was to flee from this situation. *My God, no!* I said to myself. As the thought of him dying right before me raced through my mind, the expression on my face must have been just dreadful. His hand started shaking violently, and he turned pale.

I silently told myself, *Calm down, Irmtraud, just stay calm. Don't lose your nerve. You can do it; you can save him.* This and other similar thoughts raced through my head as my heart pounded with anxiety and fear. Then, somehow, I calmed down. My training took over, and I remembered that before I could push the intestines back into the abdominal cavity, I had to flush the wound with saline solution. This I did. Then I applied a sterile bandage to the wound and prayed everything would hold until the doctor came on duty. Afterward I sat in a quiet corner of the hospital and cried.

It appears I made the right decision in this case. The officer survived, and after his recovery, he returned to the front. He wrote me several long thank-you letters.

In no way whatsoever was I prepared for these types of emergencies. Each day brought a new challenge. For those working in the hospitals, death became an everyday occurrence. Responding to questions about how caregivers could prepare for the trauma they might witness at terrorist attacks or other catastrophes, a psychologist recently said that one can become accustomed to the dead bodies, but there should be a long period of counseling to prevent future psychological problems. During those days in Karlsbad, nobody gave any of us psychological counseling.

The news we received from the weekly *Wochenschau* newsreels, as well as the occasional eyewitness reports from soldiers, really frightened us. I had already seen such horrible things from the soldiers who came under my care. The Russian winter had set in, and conditions were deteriorating fast for soldiers on the eastern front. Now we were hearing from the news reports that things were worse than expected and that we, citizens of the Third Reich, would have to toughen up and make greater sacrifices. I wondered what could be worse than what I was already living.

> Every national-socialist has no doubt whatsoever that this war, which the British-Jewish world order has instigated against us, must be waged with extreme hardship and uncompromising determination. Therefore, as we reflect upon this moment in time and the German Eastern Front spread from … [the Barents Sea] to the Black Sea, it becomes apparent that we have undertaken this offensive out of absolute necessity.
>
> —*Völkischer Beobachter*, June 23, 1941

It had now been two months or so since I saw Georg for the first time, as he lay in the entrance hall of that military hospital. Like most of the new nursing assistants, I had to work the universally unpopular night shift. I had just started my nightly rounds and entered a hospital room, which, as far I knew, held three patients. In the dimly lit room someone called out, "Finally, there you are!"

Standing there bashful, with my head lowered and shoulders raised, I whispered timidly, "Um, did you ring the bell? Sorry, I didn't hear it."

"No, no, it's just that I've been looking all over for *you*," the man replied. Since our first brief encounter, he had not forgotten me. Determined to find me, Georg had asked every nurse or nursing assistant about me, without success, as he wandered from one military hospital to the next to obtain medical treatment for his injuries. Recently he had been transferred to my post. The way he lay before me did not exactly make a good impression. A plaster cast covered most of his body. A severe injury had sent him back from the front with a broken pelvis and three broken vertebrae.

Like the other soldiers in the heavy artillery, Georg often rode a horse. Near Gomel in Belarus, his horse had stepped on a landmine, reared up, and fallen to the ground. Georg was not thrown from the saddle—he had fastened his blanket and gas mask to the back of his saddle, and he couldn't get his leg over in time. The horse landed right on top of him. When the horse made a desperate attempt to stand up, Georg was crushed underneath, his pelvis and lower vertebrae shattered. The injury confined Georg to a body cast for several months. The injury also crippled Georg for the rest of his life, causing pain that never left him, not even for a single day.

Perspective: The War on the Eastern Front, 1941

At the beginning of the military campaign against the Soviet Union, the condition of the Soviet Army was wretched. During the bloody purges of 1937 and 1938, Stalin ordered the execution of 30,000 of his high-ranking military officers. He disbanded the huge tank division and downgraded the Red Army to a citizen militia. As a result, Soviet ground targets were completely defenseless against air attack by German bombers. Within a short period of time, the Germans eliminated the Soviet air force. Regardless of these advantages, Germany could not stop the fighting potential of the Red Army. The Soviets had an almost inexhaustible supply of military manpower to throw out onto the battlefield. In the first weeks of the campaign, German panzer units encircled and drove back the Red Army. After heavy fighting near Kiev, 665,000 Soviet soldiers surrendered to German troops. Almost none of them survived in the improvised prisoner-of-war camps. Just a few days after Kiev fell into German hands, around 30,000 Jews were murdered near Babij Jar, outside Kiev, one of the many atrocities committed against Russian civilians by the advancing German Army.

This victory concealed the heavy losses sustained by the German armed forces. By September 1941, about a half million German soldiers had been killed, wounded, or listed as missing in action on the eastern front, 15 percent of the original invasion force.

In late summer of 1941, the German Army confiscated the entire grain harvest in occupied regions for its own troops, leaving the civilian populations to starve. Behind the front lines, *Einsatzgruppen* carried out the worst of atrocities. Hitler's policy—to treat the subjugated peoples as subhuman and to eradicate them in order to create *"Lebensraum"* (living area) for the Aryan race—would have fatal consequences in the end. Had the Germans treated the civilians better, perhaps Hitler would have been seen as a liberator who offered a better alternative to Stalin's reign of terror.

By the beginning of September, the Germans and Finns encircled Leningrad (now St. Petersburg). The Siege of Leningrad lasted for almost nine hundred days. Almost a million people died of famine. The winter of 1941–1942 was especially difficult for the citizens of Leningrad, when the Germans cut off almost the entire supply of food and heating fuel to the city. Out of desperation, the Soviets trucked supplies over Lake Ladoga, whose surface freezes during the winter months.

On October 2, 1941, orders were issued to take Moscow. In the middle of this same month, constant rain set in, and soon the roads turned to mud. Nevertheless, on October 25, Hitler prematurely announced that the Soviets had been beaten. By December 4, the German Army had the Kremlin in sight but could not advance any further because its tanks remained stuck in snowdrifts and mud. The German soldiers lacked proper clothing for a winter battle, and many perished from exposure to the bitter cold. At the beginning of December, the Soviets launched a full-scale counterattack, and the Germans had no choice but to dig in and wait for spring.

On December 7, 1941, Japanese aircraft attacked the American military base at Pearl Harbor in Hawaii. The United States and Great Britain responded by declaring war on Japan, a German ally. A few days later, Italy and Germany respond by declaring war against the United States. The war in Europe had expanded to a global conflict.

By the spring of 1942, the Germans had already lost a million soldiers on the eastern front. Although the Soviet casualties were much greater, with about 5 million dead and 4.5 million taken prisoner, Germany had already lost the war. Like a child who picks a fight with someone twice his size, Germany was no match for the superpowers.

As the German Army advanced from one victory to the next in the Soviet Union, *Einsatzgruppen* remained behind the front lines. They carried out a systematic annihilation of groups of people marginalized by the Nazi regime. These units forcibly assembled the Jewish population living in the occupied regions of the east and immediately executed them, often with a bullet to the head. German-speaking populations in occupied areas often participated in these atrocities.

In the beginning, these extermination operations were somewhat chaotic, but at the end of 1941, the annihilation apparatus was running according to plan. By the beginning of 1942, more than 500,000 people had fallen victim to the extermination campaign. However, a more efficient means of carrying out the exterminations was sought. After the Wannsee Conference in January 1942, existing labor concentration camps, such as Auschwitz and Lublin-Majdanek, were refitted with gas chambers and crematories. The Nazi regime also constructed new camps, such as Treblinka, Belzec, and Sobibor, to carry out industrialized mass murder.

Georg the Patient, 1941

When Georg was injured, he was assigned to the Second Army, Central Military Command, advancing from the area around Gomel in Belarus and south to the Ukrainian border. They had orders to establish a bridgehead over the Desna River, near the city of Novgorod-Siversky. The injury he suffered in August 1941 took him out of the encirclement and siege of Kiev that began in September.

Even while recovering from his severe and painful injuries, Georg still retained his charm. Today I would say he was a cross between Frank Sinatra and the German actor Harald Juhnke. Even though he was concealed inside a large plaster body cast, I found him handsome. Today, sixty years later, when I think about what it all meant, it seems that somehow things got way out of hand. I honestly did not think of him as good husband material. Of course, Georg was bound and determined to marry me. He kept sending me notes, which he got the other nurses to deliver.

By the beginning of December 1941, Georg had made enough of a recovery that he could now hobble around on crutches through the hallways. He often visited me at the nurses' station, and I had to endure the disapproving gaze of the head nurse. One day, Georg came through the door and struggled to extend his arm. In his hand were roses, which he gave me. God only knows where he got them! Roses in November? And on top of that, during a war and from a soldier who could barely get around! I was impressed, and for the first time I could feel my heart jump.

By Christmas Day, Georg was able to walk short distances without the crutches. Together we strolled back and forth in front of the hospital. Instead of giving Georg the cold shoulder, I found myself warming up to him. Young, inexperienced, and raised according to old-fashioned ideals, I wanted to be courted and won over. Georg was as daring and romantic as the man I had always imagined in my dreams.

Many years later, when we lived in Berlin, I asked Georg, "Why were you so determined to marry me? Was I really good enough? Surely you could have found a woman in Berlin who was more self-confident and more elegant than me."

He looked me straight in the eye and said, "In that awful time, you allowed me to still trust in human kindness during that disgusting war, when the world had gone to hell. Never before had I realized that home is where the heart is." I knew he meant every word.

Over the next several weeks the relationship became even more intense. When it came to a point where I knew that Georg would be my lifelong companion, I introduced him to my mother. Several months later, when we were already married, and when Georg had been called back to duty on the eastern front, my mother told me that at first, she had not exactly been pleased with him. You see, Georg was a Prussian. She was an Austrian after all, and the animosity between the Austrians and Prussians went back hundreds of years. Now her only child wanted to marry one of those detestable Prussians from Berlin! However, Georg, with his natural charm and always the great flatterer, managed to clear this hurdle with plenty of room to spare.

The Stein Family

Georg's father, Max Alexander Stein, was born in Thorn, an old town in West Prussia.[28] The famous astronomer Copernicus also came from this town. Max was the oldest of three sons. Long before the start of the First World War, Max's father had abandoned the family under the cover of darkness. He wanted to try his luck in America. Max's mother must have been a strong woman—deeply religious and superstitious, she took charge of her own life and that of her sons, instilling in them a tremendous work ethic and devotion to the church.

After attending military school, Max obtained a position with the Prussian government. Before and during the First World War, he collected taxes from the wealthy landowners in Prussia. Sometimes I asked myself how he must have felt, a man of middle-class origins, as he feasted at the great manor houses on the estates of wealthy landowners who, in turn, wanted to offer the tax man nothing but the best. In the rural areas of Prussia, the journey from one estate to the next could be rather difficult. During wintertime the streets iced over under a deep layer of snow; even trains remained stuck in the deep snowdrifts. The spring that followed brought mud that no wagon or horse could overcome.

My mother-in-law, Margarethe Sophie, came from the same area of Prussia as Max, her husband. Her father, a devout and practicing Catholic, made a living as a teacher and organist. As was common among large Catholic families at the time, Margarethe's oldest sister, Maria, entered a convent, taking the name Sister Heriberta, and later became an abbess. Margarethe's mother died while giving birth to her eleventh child. As the oldest girl still living at home, Margarethe

---

28   Now called Toruń, the city is in the north-central part of Poland.

now had to take on the responsibilities of a large household. After receiving some home economics training at a convent, she began to look for a suitable husband, one who would free her from a life filled with obligations to her younger siblings.

Through her relatives she became acquainted with Max Stein, then known as Max Katharszinsky. From the way they got along with each other, I would not say they married for love. Although I never asked, I think it was likely an arranged marriage. Before the wedding could be held, Margarethe had to pass a rigorous test. When she arrived to visit Max's family, the future mother-in-law dumped a variety of chores on her future daughter-in-law. During the entire visit of maybe three or four days she didn't have a day of rest. One night the future mother-in-law inspected Margarethe's underwear, trying them on to determine whether the buttons were securely sewn and whether the lace was of top quality. Margarethe passed the test, and she received what she wanted—the status of a married woman, the children who followed, and a sheltered life. Was it worth the price? Max, for his part, received a pretty wife and a competent homemaker, one who had already proven that she could manage a large household.

Georg was born in 1915 in Thorn. His sister, Ursula, followed about a year later. Max continued to work for the finance ministry during the First World War. His work took him to remote areas of Prussia. Often Max could return home only for a short visit. During one of these short visits, young Georg became so frightened of the tall leather boots and the sharp uniform worn by the fearsome-looking stranger who had just entered the house that he hid from his own father.

After the First World War, the Versailles Peace Conference created an independent Polish state from territory formerly controlled by Russia and Germany. Thorn now belonged to Poland, and Max did not want to live under this new government. He decided to resettle in Berlin, where his family was not exactly greeted with open arms. This large city, now struggling under the hardships caused by the reparation obligations imposed by the Versailles Treaty, became further burdened by the postwar flood of refugees from the east.

At the end of the First World War, as a result of social upheaval, the once-prosperous landowners and nobility of Poland and Russia needed to find a new identity. The great cities of Europe, such as Berlin and Paris, were perfect for them.

Upon moving to Berlin, Max understood that his family name would be an impediment to his success. There was clear hostility toward the people coming from the east, but he was German, not Slavic or another ethnicity. So, he formally changed the family name from Katharszinsky to Stein, a good German name, though unfortunately, also a good Jewish name, and his family blended right in.

The 1920s, despite the economic problems, or maybe because of them, ushered in an exciting era of decadence, hedonism, and liberalization from social norms, especially among women. It was like dancing on top of a volcano. In Paris, Gertrude Stein (no relation to Georg's family) opened her famous salon, where prominent painters such as Picasso, Magritte, Chagall and other well-known artists gathered. In this era of changing social norms, women now wore pants and other risqué clothing and smoked in public, and love between members of the same sex suddenly became socially acceptable.

The Stein family, on the other hand, led a life far removed from these excesses. Fortunately, when Max lost his position in the finance ministry, he received a severance payment and was still able to support his family. Max also had a second source of income and had managed to save some money for his family's security. In the years he had worked as a tax collector, many of the field hands working the large estates also owned a small plot of farmland that they cultivated for themselves. However, they often did not have a chance to set aside seed for winter vegetables such as rutabagas and potatoes. Max Stein purchased several large sacks of seed, repackaged them in smaller packets of one or two ounces, and then sold them to the farmers for a tidy profit. In doing so he laid the cornerstone of his prosperity. This income, together with the severance payment, enabled him to purchase a large lot, a piece of fallow land in Lichterfelde, one of the city districts in Berlin.

Through hard work with his own hands and the hard work of his family, Max had built two large houses on this lot by 1925, both of which are still standing.[29] Margarethe was very committed to making her new home comfortable and worked hard to achieve this. Both houses were surrounded by a large garden that she tended with devotion. Around the house or in the garden, Georg spent much of his time performing a variety of chores.

Georg received a secondary education at the Lilienthal (Real) Gymnasium in Lichterfelde, where his academic area of emphasis was languages. At home he did not have a warm relationship with his parents. Georg's parents had received a typical, almost military-like Prussian upbringing where feelings were taboo. Never was a kind word spoken between father and children, nor any hug or praise given. Georg's mother always controlled her emotions, playing a minimal role in the upbringing of her children, letting her husband impose discipline. It was a cold household environment that was made even less nurturing through the arduous work in the house and garden.

After finishing his secondary education, Georg had to complete six months of compulsory community service, which was followed by four years of occupational training as a hotel businessman. Just as he was about to complete this training, the long arm of the German military reached out to grab him. After Hitler came to power, the young men of Germany were subject to conscription, and Georg had to perform two years of mandatory military service. Men of military age such as Georg were trapped. The German government did not allow them to leave the country and, in fact, stopped issuing them passports. Imprisoned in an uncertain future, many would die in the tragic war that followed. When Georg's two years of service expired, the Second World War began, and Georg's military obligation continued indefinitely.

We Are Married! 1942

Georg asked for my hand in marriage, and I accepted. My parents also gave their blessing. About six months after we met, Georg and

---

29   In Germany, a "house" can also be part of a duplex structure, connected but independently accessed homes. Max's houses were of this style.

I were married at the Church of St. Mary Magdalene in Karlsbad, a beautiful church in the baroque style. My father, now stationed in Munich, could not obtain a pass to attend our wedding nor come to visit, not even for a few days. In the church my mother was well-known and popular. She always sang at Mass and was valued as a soloist for the Christmas oratorio. For the wedding Mother obtained special treatment for us. The priest gave her free rein of the church, to decorate the interior and altar as she wanted. We even had a horse-drawn coach decked out in flowers for the wedding, an absolute luxury in a time of war. I wore a silk dress. The bridal arrangement I carried consisted of orchids, a gift from a florist who was also a friend of my mother.

Georg looked much different than when I had first met him. After being released from the hospital for rehabilitation, he wore his uniform almost every day, along with the regulation riding boots. In a spotlessly clean and perfectly ironed uniform, Georg looked very sharp. On our wedding day Georg decided to wear his dress uniform, and to match its more civilian-like appearance, he wanted to wear (heaven forbid because soldiers are born with boots) ordinary dress shoes! He asked his mother to bring a pair from his closet in Berlin.

After the ceremony my mother ran up to me, sobbing. "For heaven's sake, what will our friends think of the man you just married?"

I looked at her astonished; after all, she had agreed to the marriage.

My mother continued. "The soles of his shoes have holes. Everyone could see them when you both knelt in front of the altar."

Oh well, I thought. This was the only normal pair of shoes Georg owned before the war. He hadn't had time to take them in for repair. On top of that, the cobbler probably would not have had any leather available to put new soles on the shoes, and we surely didn't have time to find the materials for the repair.

I could not have cared less. "Just so long as it doesn't rain and get his wet feet," I said to my mother. I shrugged my shoulders and made my way over to the coach with my brand-new husband. We climbed inside and drove away with the procession. How we felt like royalty!

The meager reception afterward brought us back to reality. We could only invite a small group of friends and relatives for lunch at the Hotel Loib, now called the Hotel Central. There everyone raised a toast to the newlyweds and, hopefully, a happy future. As a gesture of generosity toward her new daughter-in-law, Georg's mother also brought with her a diamond ring, a family heirloom, which he gave me on our wedding day. Like many of the nice things we had, this ring helped us survive after the war and was later exchanged on the black market for some food.

Church of Saint Mary Magdalene, Karlsbad, Czech Republic, in 1992.

It was painful for me that my father could not attend the wedding. I was pleased that Georg's parents made the journey and I could accept the fact that his sister could not attend, but my father? In order to celebrate with him, Georg and I traveled to Munich, where we stayed for a couple of days. Then we traveled to Küstrin, a small town on the now Polish–German border, where Georg's artillery unit was stationed.

Our wedding on March 15, 1942.

In the center of Küstrin stands a famous fortress, where in 1730 Lieutenant Hans Herman von Katte was beheaded in the interior courtyard. He was a close confidant of the crown prince, Frederick II, who later became Frederick the Great. Von Katte conspired with the crown prince to help him flee his violent father, and the two planned to go to Great Britain. When the king, Frederick William I, learned of the planned escape, he had von Katte tried before a military court. Rejecting the life sentence imposed by the court, the king ordered von Katte to be put to death and forced his son to witness the execution.

The horse-drawn carriage that my mother arranged for our wedding day. It was a very cold day.

Anyway, we were there, in a town divided by the Oder River and surrounded by swamplands, a town completely lacking any social life. To me the town seemed to consist primarily of unattractive red stone buildings, dating from around the time of Frederick the Great, and some randomly added barracks and horse stables. Was this the best place for a honeymoon? We rented an old house on the banks of the river. At least we could experience the onset of spring, watching the first flowers as they appeared on the shoreline and hearing the trills of chirping birds as they accompanied our every step. In the early morning hours, the fishermen returned with their catch from the river, bringing in fresh delicious fish and crab. If you took away the barracks, the area around Küstrin had a certain appeal. Very rural, very quiet, and a bird paradise, this area evoked feelings that were both peaceful and sentimental. Once Georg reported for duty I was alone and spent my time taking long walks.

The German Army depended on horses to haul supplies and artillery. At the military base in Küstrin, Georg's assignment in the remount service was not only to break the young horses gathered from this area but also to train the other soldiers in how to ride them. For the first time since his injury, he sat in the saddle. It seemed rather strange that the military had assigned him once again to a mounted unit. Georg could hardly bend over or stand for long periods of time. It would take several more months to obtain a transfer and reassignment to the officer school in Dresden, which would eventually lead to a new assignment. Georg attempted to spend as little time as possible in the saddle, but even then, he often returned home sore and exhausted. Sitting on a horse for even a short time caused him more problems than he wanted to admit.

I had brought along a large stash of ration cards for food, yet they did not help that much because the choice of food available to us was rather sparse. With the limited cooking knowledge I had and the few ingredients I could obtain, I tried to feed us but really did not succeed in this endeavor. I often thought about what Georg's mother would have served him and afterward felt insecure because of my lack of culinary skills. Despite all this, we were happy. The war was far way, somewhere behind the haze in the east that turned the morning sun golden yellow. Subconsciously, we knew the reality of the situation—that this was only temporary and that our luck would not hold out forever. We knew that everything would drop out from under us. But we didn't know how far we would fall.

In all I spent four weeks with Georg in Küstrin. That time together had to sustain us until one of us could get leave again. We felt blessed to have such a long time with one another to start our married life together. I left Küstrin with images in my mind of the young man who was now my husband, and I prayed that we would both survive this terrible war.

Sixty years later, in 2002, I visited the area around Küstrin with Barbara, my daughter. I wanted to remember once again how it felt to be in love, to refresh the memories of my time there. My husband had already passed away in 1996. I recalled how we strolled through the fields. Forgetting for a moment the terrible battle that had occurred here, I felt happy to return to this area.

My daughter saw things differently. On her face I could read the disappointment, after hearing me talk about this place over and over again. "You know, Barbara, you can take your credit card and fly almost anywhere. Everyone goes to the Bahamas or Venice, or even to some town above the Arctic Circle for that matter. But we've traveled to Küstrin! Now that's something to brag about, right?" At least she laughed about it. Today Küstrin has become a modern Polish city. I made this visit to experience the past once again, and the more I thought about what had happened here, the more it certainly seemed as though Georg and I were lucky.

A couple of years after I went with Georg to Küstrin, this region attained a tragic notoriety after a terrible tank battle occurred here in 1944–1945 between the Soviets and the Germans. When Barbara and I wandered through the same area many years later, we saw a peaceful countryside that concealed this horrible event. Horses and cattle grazed on the banks of the river, and wildflowers blanketed the meadows. Perhaps this was nature's way of paying homage to the heartbreaking loss of so many lives, to the souls of thousands of unknown soldiers who perished in what was then a decisive battle. We will never know their names or where they lie, for not even a simple cross marks their graves. Barbara, who now views herself as an American, seemed to feel uncomfortable. Quite often she had heard of this place, where her father had been stationed, where her parents had spent their honeymoon, and where her father had become a prisoner of war. During our visit she was very quiet, and only during the return trip to Berlin did she admit how glad she was to have seen this place.

Farewell and the Promotion, 1942

The war was in its third year. In the *Wochenschau* newsreels we saw goal-driven soldiers advancing to "imminent German victory," as well as joyful citizens in the cities and countryside. Almost nothing was written about any defeats or setbacks. Even in the military circles, to which Georg belonged, the news was rather scant. All we knew was that the military was fighting a war on two fronts for our security and for more territory, what they called *Lebensraum*. This war hardly seemed to affect those of us on the home front. After the Germans bombed London, the Allies retaliated by dropping bombs on German cities. Although this caused the supply situation to become a bit tighter than in peacetime, we could not really complain of our situation in Karlsbad.

The situation was different for the Jewish population. We knew about the work camps for the Jews and prisoners of war and were given a plausible justification for their existence, but we knew nothing about the extermination camps and the inhumane treatment that occurred there. None of these camps were located near Karlsbad. I cannot really say whether the civilians near the larger camps knew about these events. The only news updates we received were deliberately falsified reports of an imminent victory.

We all lived under the threat of government surveillance and denunciation by someone close. Any discussion of the progress of the war was strictly taboo. A rash comment made in the heat of the moment could bring the worst of consequences. The thousands of soldiers maimed and mortally wounded in Russia affected us greatly. The thought of losing a husband or father occupied our thoughts more than events in the next town or even those on the eastern front.

In Karlsbad, not a single word was mentioned about the planned "final solution to the Jewish problem." The organized extermination of the Jews lay beyond anything we could have conceptualized, beyond anything we could possibly have imagined. What happened at the Wannsee Conference was so secret that the participants were urged to personally destroy the minutes of the meeting after having read them. How were we supposed to know about something that happened so far away? I was young and probably too naive to take a serious look at the events around me.

From the beginning, Georg opposed National Socialism, a political ideology that in no way was a part of his values. Did he know of the war crimes committed against the civilian population behind the front lines? He never spoke about it if he did.

Georg was still assigned to Küstrin with countless other soldiers. Since his assignment included taking care of the horses, occasionally he had to stand the night watch. Horses played a role almost as important as the soldiers in the heavy artillery unit at that time. The military spared no expense for their safekeeping, and that included assigning soldiers to watch them throughout the night. Of course, Georg was not particularly suited for this task, which was far too boring, far too quiet, and far too uneventful for a charming man such as himself, whose passion was music and other entertainment. One night he and some of the other soldiers felt ready for fun and mischief. They helped themselves to several glasses of homemade liquor they had procured from the local farmers. After telling jokes for a while, this became boring for them, and they looked for something more exciting to do.

"Over there are some bicycles," giggled one of the soldiers, pointing with his thumb to an adjoining shed. No sooner said than done. Soon the boys were bicycling through the stalls. Georg, who always liked a good tune, started singing a very loud rendition of "Sur Le Pont D'Avignon," a traditional French song and certainly not a marching hymn sanctioned by the German military.

Well, that didn't last long. An officer stormed into the stable, having been startled by the noise. "All right knock it off and come to attention." The singing ended abruptly, and the bicycles were quickly abandoned, landing in the straw, as the men stood up straight, hands pressed tight against their pants, fearful of the punishment awaiting them. For the rest of the night, the men resumed the boring task of watching the horses. The next morning, they reported to the master sergeant. Luckily, they received a relatively mild punishment: three days in confinement. The master sergeant punished them not so much for depriving the horses of a restful night's sleep as for singing a French folk song, somewhat unfair since Georg had studied foreign languages and since the rest of the men were just a bunch of farm boys who had never even heard a word of French and weren't part of the singing. The soldiers accepted their sentence without any grumbling, grinning at Georg as they were led to their cells.

Shortly after this incident, Georg began the three-month officer training program in Dresden. Finally, he could transfer to the infantry. I was overjoyed that Georg would be stationed in Dresden, a city much closer to Karlsbad. I visited him on weekends. After all, I wanted to spend as much time as possible with my husband.

On one weekend in July we went to Berlin to visit his family. We used the nice weather as an excuse to relax in the garden and enjoy our time together. Berlin was only one-and-a-half hours by train from Dresden.

A summer day in Berlin in July 1942. This photo was taken a few months after we were married and during our brief visit with Georg's family. Sitting in the chair was Georg's mother, Margarethe. I am sitting on the stoop between Georg and his sister Ulla.

The decision to attend officer school in Dresden would become a problem years later when we attempted to emigrate to America. But we did not know that until 1965. I will tell you more about this later in my story.

In Dresden the military assigned Georg to a room that he shared with three other men. One of the four men in each barrack room was always a spy who determined the political orientation and convictions of the other three. He immediately reported anyone who criticized or opposed the Nazi regime. The result was always the same. Any officer candidate who ran his mouth eventually received an order to carry out a suicide mission. Apparently, Georg opened his big mouth. As he had mentioned to me at one time or another, Georg believed Germany would lose the war. Such sentiments were considered undermining of the war effort and were dangerous for whoever said them. Whatever he might have said, Georg received a suicide mission.

After completing officer training, Georg began making his way back to Küstrin. During the journey he received word that his earlier request for leave had been approved. Immediately, he turned around and traveled to Karlsbad. We enjoyed the astonishingly peaceful atmosphere of the city, not allowing the great number of wounded soldiers to ruin the mood or our love.

Our precious time together was suddenly interrupted by a telegram from military headquarters. Georg had to leave immediately for Meseritz, another remote place in the flatlands of Prussia. There he would receive further orders.

We did not want to leave each other. When would we see each other again? "Come along for a few days," my husband suggested, and I agreed. The journey would take us close to where Georg's step grandmother had been living alone since the death of her husband, Georg's grandfather. There we planned to pay the old woman a visit and then part company, with Georg traveling to his area of deployment while I returned to Karlsbad.

Once we arrived in Meseritz, we discovered that she wasn't there. She had gone to Berlin to stay with relatives. This gave us all the time together for ourselves. Then the day we were to go our separate ways, we were thrilled to learn that transport problems on a stretch of railway would give us two more days together. In times like this you certainly count days and even hours. Every little moment, every word, and even the smallest gesture becomes important; anything could become a memory, for the next goodbye could be the final one.

One day we made our way over to Kalzig, a small village near Meseritz. We strolled over the flat terrain. Next to the road we saw fields of sunflowers interrupted every so often by dense forest. At an intersection I noticed mushrooms at the edge of the road, wonderful, edible mushrooms. For us they were a special luxury, almost like finding gold. We tossed as many of them as possible in my scarf and in Georg's army hat. Then we walked the remaining stretch into the small village. Paul Handke, Georg's grandfather, had played the organ here on Sundays and taught in the school. The neighbors around the schoolhouse still remembered Georg from when he visited his grandfather many years earlier during a school holiday. One family invited us in, and the farmer's wife prepared the mushrooms with lots of butter and bacon, a meal we would not forget for a long time. Late in the evening, we decided to leave these friendly people and make our way back to Meseritz. Arm in arm, we strolled along the empty roads, the starlit sky guiding our way back. Georg's train departed the next morning, packed with soldiers on their way to fight on the eastern front. We'd had two wonderful extra days granted to us. This would have to sustain us for a long time.

We said goodbye to each other on the train platform. Then I stood there all alone in the cool morning haze. I felt empty and hollow inside, as though someone had stolen my heart. I didn't want to think about what the future would bring or how that final embrace could be the last.

From Meseritz I traveled to Berlin, where I spent several days with my in-laws. Afterward I made my way back to Karlsbad and resumed my duties as a nurse. I was reassigned to a large military hospital. There I had to learn how to use the new medical equipment that had recently become available. A young doctor led me through the operation of an x-ray machine, but he didn't seem to have any more experience than I did. We lacked all kinds of trained specialists, and I was forced to become a jack-of-all-trades. I didn't have a way to describe my feelings then, but many years later, I read a book by Marilyn Ferguson in which she wrote, "Denial is a way of life. More accurately, it is a way of diminishing life, of making it seem more manageable. Denial is the alternative to transformation."[30] This described my situation perfectly.

The November sky turned gray and dreary, only adding to the depressing thoughts shaped by longing and fear. To distract myself, I often worked a double shift at the hospital. In the meantime, Georg was experiencing even worse things. When he reached his deployment area, somewhere near Lake Ilmen in Russia, a fellow soldier asked him, "What the hell are you doing here among us poor dumb grunts?" Suddenly, it became very clear to Georg: someone had squealed on him, and now Georg was past the point of no return.

Perspective: The Turning Point of the War, Stalingrad, 1942

On August 19, 1942, the Allies staged a raid near Dieppe, a coastal town in northern France. For the Allies, this raid was a total disaster, with three-fourths of the soldiers, mostly Canadians, killed, wounded, or taken prisoner. Yet the Allies delivered a preview of the Normandy invasion that would follow in June 1944.

In November 1942, German soldiers under the command of General Friedrich Paulus had pushed the Soviet defenders into narrow zones along the west bank of the Volga River in the Battle of Stalingrad. Led by General Vasily Ivanovich Chuikov, the Soviets then launched a two-pronged attack targeting the weaker Romanian and Hungarian armies protecting the German 6th Army's flanks. Easily overrun, the Axis forces on the flanks were defeated and the 6th Army was cut off and surrounded in the Stalingrad area. Hitler ordered his troops to keep fighting, and sent in supplies by air, but the

---

30   Marilyn Ferguson, *The Aquarian Conspiracy: Personal and Social Transformation in Our Time.* New York: Jeremy P. Tarcher/Putnam, 1980. p 74.

winter, and the superior numbers of the Soviets eventually brought an end to the 6th Army. The Battle of Stalingrad lasted five months, one week, and three days

Here, Nazi Germany reached the zenith of its territorial conquest. From that moment onward, one defeat followed another, and Germany fought a defensive war instead of an offensive war.

Hunger and a policy of deliberate maltreatment exacted a heavy toll on Soviets confined in the German prisoner-of-war camps. Of the roughly six million Soviet prisoners of war, 57 percent died. German forces also engaged in indiscriminate killing of civilians and showed little mercy to Soviet deserters. In German-occupied territory, mass murder continued in the concentration camps. Upon prisoners' arrival, the guards screened them to determine which prisoners were capable of work. Those not able to work—mostly women, children, and the elderly—were ordered to report to a showering facility, which was actually a gas chamber where they were murdered. Prisoners capable of work were assigned to simple barracks and confined under the worst and most inhumane conditions. Often, they labored in gigantic factory complexes that supplied the German war effort. The most dreadful of the extermination camps was Auschwitz in Poland, where two million people perished.

This mass murder of people overburdened the war effort. The thousands of freight trains bringing Jews from Western Europe to the extermination camps in the east were not available to haul supplies needed by the soldiers on the eastern front.

Nazi Germany planned to resettle the Ukraine with Aryans, a policy of racial eradication, even though at this time, the winter of 1942–1943, the military defeat of Germany was already foreseeable. Starting in February 1942, the Allied bombing of Germany became more widespread. Air Marshal Arthur Harris of the British Royal Air Force decided to subject German cities to constant aerial attack. This decision affected mostly civilians instead of soldiers, with the aerial bombardment killing about 600,000 civilians in German cities, compared to 62,000 who perished in Great Britain. At the end of the war, almost every large city in Germany and Austria had been reduced to rubble and ash.

The slow turn of events also brought changes inside Germany. The arbitrary and brutal abuse of political authority replaced the rule of law. The Enabling Act of 1933, valid for four years and twice renewed, was a constitutional amendment that gave virtually unlimited authority to Hitler's government to pass legislation without the approval of the parliament. The act, as read out by Hermann Göring on April 26, 1942, states that:

> The *Führer*, in his capacity as leader of the nation …, must therefore be able at any time—without being bound by existing legal provisions—to prevail, if necessary, upon all Germans …, by every means he deems appropriate, to fulfil their obligations.

This opened the floodgates to totalitarianism.

By this time the heavy loss of life on the eastern front had touched almost every family in Germany. People on the home front concentrated on surviving as they contended with hunger, the Allied air campaign, and a deteriorating political situation, one of tyranny and persecution. In January 1943, during the Casablanca Conference, the Western Allies decided to demand the unconditional surrender of Germany. This was angrily rejected by the Nazi regime.

The resistance against terror also grew inside Germany. Several groups planned the assassination of leading figures within the Nazi regime, and some officers had already fallen victim.

The War and the Patient, Part 2: 1942

December came around, and I had not received any news from my husband. I did not know where he was but knew only that he was somewhere out there on the eastern front. Whenever I saw the newsreels covering the heavy fighting in Russia, I became absolutely horrified. Shortly before Christmas, a telegram arrived. My heart sank as I sat there shaking. What was in the message? Was this the end of my marriage? Once again, I thought of my major. I had learned of his death over the English Channel from a similar telegram.

Georg had been severely wounded while fighting somewhere near Lake Ilmen, near St. Petersburg (then called Leningrad). Now he was in a military hospital in Lötzen (in East Prussia on the border between Poland and Russia). His injuries were life-threatening, and I had to prepare myself for the worst. I was supposed to make my way to the hospital as soon as possible. *Thank God he is not dead*, I thought.

A message like this was nothing out of the ordinary. Often, when a soldier was gravely wounded, the hospital would summon his wife, in part to help the dying man and in part so they could say goodbye to each other. In most cases the visit with the soldier lasted less than a week. Sometimes the patient's condition improved, but too frequently, the patient died.

Many things leave an indelible impression in our minds, especially when we are thrown into a hopelessly desperate situation. The telegram was signed by the doctor in charge of the military hospital, a Dr. Hühnerbein, whose last name, literally translated, means "chicken leg" in English. This laughable detail stuck with me from that moment on.

As far as I was concerned, I had no other alternative than to travel to the military hospital in Lötzen as soon as possible. On top of that, I had no intention of staying just a few days. I wanted to care for my husband as long as I could. That meant I had to figure out how to quit my job in Karlsbad and then find a way of traveling to East Prussia. The only way to do so was to become a nurse at the military hospital in Lötzen, which should not have been too much of a problem. The hospitals at the front desperately needed help, and I was determined to go there. This would allow me to take care of Georg, even though it meant taking care of several other patients too.

My mother was beside herself when I told her about my travel plans. "For heaven's sake, child! On the front? Don't you know how dangerous it is?" she yelled, wringing her hands.

My journey would take me to a military hospital about sixty miles (one hundred kilometers) from the fighting. My mother's attempt to convince me to stay was in vain. She gave me the evil eye, and I gave a mean look back. What could she hope to achieve? I was already an adult and perhaps even too grown-up. She certainly knew how stubborn I could be. When I make up my mind to do something, I carry it through.

I took an indefinite leave of absence from work. The train journey first took me to Berlin, then to Königsberg (now Kaliningrad), and finally to Lötzen (now Giżycko in Poland). I have forgotten the number of unheated and uncomfortable train cars in which I traveled over those three days, with nothing to eat and filthy toilets. What I remember about this long and tortuous journey are the soldiers who casually smoked and told themselves dirty jokes, while all I could care about was the cold and hunger. After the first two days of travel, I finally reached Königsberg. There a train engineer took pity on me and let me board a train whose final destination was the Wolfsschanze near Rastenburg (now Ketrzyn), Hitler's secret headquarters in East Prussia. Somewhere en route, when I was not in the best of shape, the train stopped in the middle of nowhere. In an almost incomprehensible East Prussian dialect, the attendant at the train station told me that I could not go any further on this train and that the engineer had disobeyed his orders by taking me this far. On top of that, there would be severe consequences for everyone involved.

I looked at the end of the train and its red taillights as it departed without me. The situation seemed totally hopeless as I stood there on that windy, makeshift train platform. I felt terribly alone and dejected, and at the same time I just wanted to sleep a little. Whatever would come tomorrow could wait, for at this moment I simply needed to rest and get out of the cold. The station attendant showed a bit of human kindness and allowed me to wait inside his small house. Grumbling, he offered me some warm tea, but otherwise not another word was spoken between us. At least I had found shelter from the bitter cold. Later that morning, a connecting train arrived, and I reached my destination around noon.

I had been traveling for three straight days. I was so tired that I almost forgot the purpose of my journey. With my last bit of strength, I dragged myself over to the military hospital to obtain information about my accommodations. I rented a room at the home of a general who was fighting somewhere on the eastern front. His wife still lived in the house, and the occasional tenant kept her company. The bed inside my room, with its cool white sheets, was calling my name, but I could not rest. I tossed my small suitcase in the corner, washed my face, and returned to the hospital to visit my private patient.

Georg had a high fever and was suffering from delirium. "What happened?" I asked an orderly. With a gentle voice the orderly explained how Georg had come to the field hospital. A bullet had passed through his foot. Despite the severe swelling, the doctors did not consider the injury itself to be life-threatening. Nobody could make sense of Georg's condition, why he was so terribly sick. None of the doctors wanted to amputate his foot, something to be avoided if at all possible, for a soldier with a missing limb became useless, and the army badly needed soldiers. The general rule was that doctors were to patch the wounded soldiers up and send them back to the front as quickly as possible.

Much later, Georg told me what had happened. His unit, the Northern Army Group, Sixteenth Army, had found themselves fighting on swampy terrain near Lake Ilmen. They fought desperately to save themselves from imminent death in the Battle of the Demyansk Pocket. He was supposed to take out the Soviet tanks that were closing in on them from all directions, blocking their retreat. With an antitank weapon, he attempted frontal shots to set the tanks on fire, destroying them in the process. It was a last-ditch attempt. Georg had a clear line of fire and managed to destroy eight or nine tanks. Finally, a Soviet sharpshooter found Georg's position and took him out of action with an aimed shot. Months later, he would receive the Iron Cross First Class, a prestigious German military decoration for bravery. Of course, at this very moment, as he struggled to live, the possibility of a medal meant very little.

After Georg was wounded, the Soviets took him prisoner. They let him lie around for three days in a camp without providing any medical attention. Of course, they were not able to do so, partly because no nurses were available and because they were also fighting for their own lives. In Georg's situation a soldier was lucky to receive some bread and water. He was rescued by German soldiers, and the evacuation to a military hospital took two additional days.

Georg now had received treatment for typhus, Wolhynia fever, and a number of other diseases that he could have contracted while in captivity, yet his condition had not improved.[31]

Somehow, I caught a second wind and no longer felt tired. I spent the entire night next to Georg's bed, cooling his face and head and holding his hand, wanting to do anything to comfort him. Throughout the night, I administered fluids, just a drop or two at a time. By morning the fever had fallen a bit. Still, he remained unconscious. The next day the doctors decided to transfer Georg to another military hospital, to the fortress at Boyen, outside of Lötzen,[32] where more specialized care was available for the severely wounded. This fortress, a true citadel, had withstood attacks from the east for hundreds of years. Three tunnels led to an interior section where the wounded were hospitalized. The main house contained numerous small rooms with unbelievably thick walls and windows protected by heavy iron bars.

In order to take care of Georg, each day I had to walk a three-mile path in freezing weather. I clearly remember the first of these many daily treks. When I returned to the house where I rented a room, the landlady opened the door for me. I must have been a strange sight, shivering from the cold, my nose, ears, and hands red from the frost. "Young lady," she said sternly, "you can't take care of your husband going out like that." Then she placed a thick wool pullover in my hands. I looked at her gratefully and was dumbstruck when she then presented me with a long scarf, one that I could wrap around my face and head to protect myself from the bitter cold.

When I returned the next day, the condition of my patient had not improved; rather, it had deteriorated. He was suffering even more from delirium and was sleepwalking, if it could be called that. One time he tried to stand up and go on a rampage through the hospital room he shared with many other injured soldiers. Due to

31   Wolhynia fever is a bacterial infection that is now treated with antibiotics.

32   Lötzen is now called Giżycko in Poland and is near the northern part of the Polish–Russian border.

the carelessness of one of the orderlies, his pistol had been left with his belongings, which had been placed next to the bed. During one of these attacks of delirium, he grabbed the sidearm and began looking around the room with rage in his eyes. With the weapon in his shaking hand, he bounced around the room and suddenly aimed the pistol at a child who was visiting one of the soldiers. While pointing the pistol at the child, either he thought clearly for a moment and became aware of what he was doing, or he simply lost his strength. He let the weapon drop and collapsed. Then the nursing staff was all over him and took the pistol away.

After this incident the hospital assigned Georg to a smaller room with two beds, to prevent his having so many visitors around him. He continued to run a fever and still tried to leave the bed. "Take the bandages off! The doctors are coming!" he yelled out to the other patients, wanting to rip the dressing from his leg.

In the few days I had been at the hospital, Georg's condition had deteriorated to the point where he now required constant medical attention, something the nursing staff could not provide because there were far too many patients with pressing medical needs. "Do you think you could ...?" asked the doctor, as he motioned with his head in Georg's direction. I had already prepared myself for this request, and I nodded my head without saying a word. If the need arose, I would care for my husband around the clock. All that bothered me was that nobody knew what was wrong with him. I spent most of my time with Georg, giving him plenty of fluids and paying attention to the slightest change in his condition, giving him the care he needed.

According to the calendar, Christmas was just a few days away. During the day I always had some time to myself, when the nursing staff provided Georg with his treatments. One day the landlady invited me to tea at a nearby palace. She was of noble birth and maintained contact with the other nobility in the area. Masuria, a region in former East Prussia where Georg was hospitalized, possessed many large estates and castles, remnants of a bygone era when the Teutonic Knights from this region were renowned throughout Europe. On this cold afternoon the landlady and I journeyed to one of these estates in the village of Nikolaiken, the residence of a rather old count who also appeared to be a relic from another era.

A horse-drawn wagon, very ornate with wood carvings and tiny bells, took us to the estate. Inside the coach, fur blankets kept us warm. I remember the bright winter sun, how sunshine radiated everywhere, and how our breath appeared like miniature clouds. The beautiful scenery and the quiet panting of the horses gave me a strange, peaceful feeling that lasted for but a brief moment, during which I was a princess enjoying the luxury of a coach ride instead of the wife and nurse of a critically wounded soldier.

When we reached the estate, an elderly servant opened a large door at the entrance of the mansion, silently stepping to the side to let us into the large room with a huge fireplace. Above the elaborately cut stone fireplace hung a colossal moose head that stared back at us. We were led to another room for tea, elegantly furnished with valuable tapestry, exquisite furniture, an elegant silver set, and fine porcelain. After I introduced myself, one of the servants began to pour tea into cups for us.

The count's facial features looked like they had been chiseled from marble. He had pale skin and elegant prominent cheekbones; features shared by many of the nobles. For two hours the count and the landlady talked about the most unbelievable things, not just about the war. I could not add a whole lot to the conversation that took place. I was not accustomed to the elevated style of speech used by them, nor was I accustomed to people who talked without really saying anything.

"How is it going for your husband?" the count asked my landlady.

"Well, as you may already know, one does not hear from the front too often. But I believe he is making progress."

"Of course, that is to be expected."

"How is the winter crop?"

"I have already instructed my tenant farmers to begin sowing the seed. We are already prepared for next year and hope to sell much of the harvest to the new settlers in the east."

"That is splendid. By the way, how did you come across this

exquisite tea? It has been quite a long time since I drank something so wonderful."

I must have sat there gaping with my mouth open, staring at them. Every once in a while, they glanced over in my direction and then quickly redirected their gaze toward each other, occasionally showing approval with a slight nod of the head.

When we departed, I received a picnic basket and a bottle of French cognac to strengthen my dear patient. The coachman took us back to Lötzen and reality. As we traveled in the light of the setting sun, once again I felt as though I was playing a part in some fairy tale, perhaps the role of the little Clara in *The Nutcracker*.

Christmas, 1942

Shortly before Christmas, an experienced surgeon from a hospital in Dresden, now assigned to the military hospital in Lötzen, conducted a thorough examination of my patient and decided he needed another operation. The doctor felt that the swelling and inflammation had obscured the cause of Georg's illness. Early in the morning on Christmas Eve, he began to operate on Georg. During the operation I paced back and forth in front of the operating room. Finally, after several hours, the exhausted physician approached me and briefly stated that the operation had gone well. The fever had been caused by blood poisoning, which in turn had been caused by bone fragments still in the foot. The gunshot wound had, in fact, left permanent damage behind. Both the heel bone and the metatarsal were shattered. For the rest of his life, Georg would require special orthopedic shoes and boots with arch supports to get around, and occasionally a remaining bone fragment would cause infections and painful swelling. Though I was relieved, the whole ordeal left me drained and tired. My patient, still under the effects of the anesthesia, would not need me for at least several hours. I decided to return to my room for some badly needed rest.

I felt very alone on this Christmas Eve night. As I walked home, the snow crunched under my feet, and the winter scenery before me was illuminated by the light of a full moon. Suddenly, I heard voices stirring in the wind. Several days prior, during a return trip, I had noticed a huge cross not far from the road. The cross had been erected to commemorate the life of Bruno von Querfurt, a German missionary martyred in 1009. On this night, several Soviet prisoners were gathered around the cross with their German guards. Their faces reflected the glow of numerous candles, and together they sang a melancholic Russian folk melody: "Not the wind blows, nor the branches move, nor the old oak tree rustles, for it is only my poor heart that moans and shakes like a leaf in the fall."

I shall never forget this unique experience. In the dark, wrapped in my wool scarf, I looked at these men now bound together by the spirit of Christmas. I thought of my parents, of Georg, of the virgin birth in Bethlehem, of the irrationality of this situation in some godforsaken place, in this war-torn land. A shiver ran down my spine as I looked upon these emaciated Soviet prisoners in East Prussia.

When I returned to my room, the landlady surprised me with roasted goose. The smell of baked apple wafted through the house like sweet perfume. For Christmas she gave me a book about Mozart, a book that later accompanied me on my transatlantic crossings.

On December 27, 1942, I celebrated my twentieth birthday. The nursing staff at the hospital gave me a pine branch decorated with pieces of chocolate, a small token of appreciation for my helping them.

Going West, 1943

The New Year brought unusually cold weather accompanied by snowstorms. Apart from some squawking crows, a numbing silence covered the landscape.

In the still of the night, as I was walking back to my room from the hospital, and as wind blew from the east, out in the distance I could hear something like thunder. I wondered if the noise had come from the fighting on the eastern front, but this seemed rather strange since the front was a good distance away. At the hospital some of the soldiers insisted that I had heard Katyusha rocket launchers, the so-called choir of many voices, often called "Stalin's organ," a terrible, deadly weapon of war rolling out of the Soviet factories for deployment on the eastern front. My heart went out to the men who were somewhere on the front, huddled in their icy foxholes, fighting for their lives.

Things improved for my patient after the operation, a weight off my shoulders. The chief surgeon who had operated on Georg started to look for patients who could be transferred to the west, to free up hospital beds for the fast-growing number of wounded arriving from the front. Georg was among those selected. He would be taken on the next hospital train to another military hospital further west, in Pleschen.[33]

Before they loaded him on the train, I looked after Georg until the very last moment. I then stood there at the station as the westward-moving locomotive grew smaller and smaller in the distance. Taking my time, with slow steps, I made my way back to my room. My work here was finished. After a final adieu to the landlady, which included a short embrace, I took the next train west and traveled to Berlin.

With me I had the rations every wounded man received: butter, cheese, salami, bacon, chocolate, and coffee. Of course, these items were in short supply among the very deprived civilian population and consequently were much sought after. These rationed goods came from a package given to the wounded soldiers, a noble gift from Hitler, and for this reason they were called the *Führer* Package.

I wanted to visit Max, my father-in-law in Berlin, to give him a personal account of his son's condition. I knew from his last letter that he had been left alone in the house, his wife and daughter having fled to safety in the countryside, to escape the air raids. He was not really in a position to take care of himself, and his situation was gradually deteriorating due to loneliness and hunger.

On a cold and gray January night I arrived at the Görlitzer train station in the eastern part of Berlin, where countless soldiers waited on the platform, often for the entire day, for the next train to the front or the one heading home. Among them were soldiers

---

33   Now Pleszew in Poland, a small town about seventy kilometers from Posen (now Poznan). Posen was then and still is the largest city in the western half of Poland.

wounded in combat, who should have been anywhere else but there. Now and then refugees pushed their way through, people wanting to escape from the bombed-out city, attempting to find safety out in the countryside.

The trains no longer ran according to schedule. Allied bombing raids had already damaged many stretches of track, making connections difficult. In addition to this great inconvenience, people faced the fear of a nighttime bombing raid while waiting for the train and the fear that the train would be attacked en route to the next destination.

I could hardly endure the stench underneath the train station, where I had gone to catch the *S-Bahn*.[34] The misery of war left behind an unmistakable stench, a mixture of sweat, rotting garbage, cigarette smoke, train soot, and sewage overlaid with disinfectant cleaner, a smell that still haunts me. Holding the *Führer* Package close to my body and with a firm grasp on my suitcase, I climbed aboard the *S-Bahn* train shortly before midnight and traveled in the direction of Lichterfelde, one of the districts in Berlin. As I peered out the train window, it seemed as though someone had thrown a shroud over the city. Because of the air raids, blackout conditions remained in effect. Not even the train cars were illuminated.

Looking out the train window upon the deserted streets, I felt as though I were traveling through a ghost town. In the darkness I could hardly make out the houses covered with soot and dust; the air raids had damaged or destroyed many of them. The train station at Lichterfelde seemed like a haunted house. I was the only passenger who stepped off the train. Alone, I still faced a twenty-minute walk through the dark streets. I have to admit, my heart ached at the sight of what had happened here. To get the distance behind me, I walked at a brisk pace. On the deserted streets, not even a prowling tomcat crossed my path.

I rang the bell at my in-laws' house. My father-in-law opened the door, perhaps expecting a neighbor because he was responsible for the air-raid shelters in the neighborhood. He was speechless when

---

34   "*S-Bahn*" refers to an interurban railway or a city train that is above ground.

he saw me, and I had to gently push him back into the house and set him in a chair. Without saying a word, I opened the *Führer* Package from underneath my coat, the gift from his son. In all the time I had known him, not once had he ever given me a kiss or a hug, but on this night, he wrapped his arms helplessly around me and stammered, "I am so happy to have you here."

Donning one of my mother-in-law's aprons, I prepared him a real, proper cup of coffee and bratwurst. I couldn't eat a thing. Dead tired, I wanted only to sleep, to forget the fear and the sadness for just a short while. Tomorrow I would be traveling again, back to Karlsbad. Still quite young, only twenty years old, I had just endured a long and difficult month. In this short period of time, I had grown up considerably. I had become a new person, stronger and more self-disciplined. Shakespeare wrote the following in *Cymbeline*, one of his plays: "Let's withdraw; and meet the time as it seeks us." I thought of this line at that moment.

Now it was the beginning of January, just over two months since that fateful day when Georg had received his injury. I learned that Georg had arrived at the new hospital, a comforting sign, meaning that he still lived. Then came the bad news. He was suffering from a nerve inflammation and was paralyzed from the waist down. Nobody knew how long this would last. I could not bear to be so far from home again, so I worked on getting Georg moved closer to me. Somehow, I managed to organize a hospital transfer to Karlsbad for him.

It is ironic that whenever I wanted to do something good for my husband, I not only had to sell my soul but also had to risk life and limb. The approval for a transfer came with a prerequisite: I had to accompany Georg during the journey. That meant another journey for me eastward, now to Pleschen. Though only maybe 250 to 300 miles as the crow flies from Karlsbad, the reality of travel so late in the war meant I would have to take many different trains on an uncertain schedule and spend perhaps days of travel without sleep, with only the food I could carry with me.

During the journey to Pleschen, I would have to spend the night in Posen. On the train I met a German woman traveling with her daughter. Both were returning home from a spa visit in Karlsbad.

After hearing my story, the woman took pity on me and offered me a bed in her home, which happened to be in Posen. I gladly accepted the offer, but almost immediately afterward, I began to suspect that this seemingly nice woman and her family sympathized with the Nazis. Her political views surfaced during our conversation, propaganda slogans that praised the Nazi Party as a shining example of law and order. Later I realized that the woman's husband owned a wood products business. I suspected that he had been able to secure some type of a lucrative contract with the regime.

At her house, my traveling companion treated me like a long-lost daughter. On the table she set out a huge spread of freshly prepared food. Perhaps she viewed my deathly ill husband as a great German hero, something that stirred a sense of patriotism and compassion in her, and maybe for this reason she took pity on me.

Two Polish maids lived in the house, very young, helpless, and afraid. It seemed as though they were tied to the house like serfs in the Middle Ages. The next morning, when I was preparing to leave, one of the girls pulled me aside. She whispered in my ear, "Tell my father everything is okay." Then she pressed a crumpled piece of scrap paper in my hand. After sitting down in the train, I unfolded the paper and saw a Posen address written on it. I simply did not have enough time to deliver the message, and on top of that, I was not familiar with the city. It could have been very dangerous. I didn't know whether her father lived in a bad section of town. The whole thing could have been a trap.

In the early 1970s, some thirty years later, I found out it was not a trap. While living in Colorado, I worked on compensation claims submitted by those persecuted during the Nazi era. A lady who had lived in German-occupied Poland contacted me to offer her support. We arranged a meeting, and right from the start of the conversation, something about me apparently caught her eye. She stared back at me as the conversation continued, and suddenly, she stopped and took a deep breath. Then she said, "I know you from the war. Did you once live in Poland?"

Showing regret, I shook my head. Nothing about her, the name or the face, seemed familiar. The conversation continued and then stopped again, and after a longer pause, she exclaimed, "You were that woman who spent a night with the W. family in Posen! I gave you my father's address."

Suddenly, everything came back to me. I remembered how I could not fulfill her request. Red with embarrassment, I tried to find the words for an apology.

"That's okay. I understand completely. There just wasn't enough time." With that she abruptly changed the conversation, and I sat there wondering how we could have crossed paths again.

Back to the moment in 1943, after another train journey I finally reached Pleschen. In Lötzen in December, I had said to myself that there could not be any place more terrible. I was wrong. Pleschen was even worse. The military hospital consisted of a couple of shacks thrown together, a makeshift setup for wounded soldiers. And there were many of them.

Georg shared a room with several soldiers who had been wounded in the Battle of Stalingrad, among the last who had been airlifted before the German Army surrendered. They had received what the soldiers called a *Heimschuss*, a ticket home. A *Heimschuß* was a severe-enough war injury that a soldier could go home.

Were they really lucky? Severely traumatized, malnourished, and suffering from exposure to the cold, they lay in their beds, indifferent to what was going on around them. Looking into their eyes, I had to ask myself how the human body could survive the abuse that these men had endured. I wondered what kept them going. Was it the thought of family members, perhaps a wife and children, or perhaps a sweetheart back home? On the nightstand of a dying soldier, I found this short poem:

> The *white wax drops*
> *Like quiet tears*
> *The red wax flows like young blood*
> *I think of you*, my love.

I kept this poem for many years, pressed inside a book, and often thought of this unfortunate man, who in that drafty hospital had thought one last time of his loved ones before dying alone.

At the beginning of February, while still in Pleschen, we received the news about Stalingrad. The German Sixth Army had surrendered. Among the men in the hospital, the news was devastating. We women did not understand the depth of what it meant, but we knew it was bad. Completely shocked, with pale faces, we went into the hallway and just looked at one another without saying a word. In the recovery room some of the men started to cry uncontrollably. How senseless the sacrifice was—how senseless that so many on both sides had to die in a war waged by two dictators lacking a conscience.

Perspective: Stalingrad, 1942-1943

In July 1942, Hitler gave the order to take Stalingrad, and eventually, the German Sixth Army seized two-thirds of the city. The city had symbolic value because it bore the name of the Soviet leader. It also had strategic value because of the Volga River, an important supply route, flowing through it. By the end of November, the Soviets managed to encircle Stalingrad, and the German Sixth Army was cut off from its chain of supply. Hitler personally forbade a retreat after Reichs Marshal Göring guaranteed that the German troops in Stalingrad could be resupplied by aircraft. Although aircraft managed to bring supplies into the city, the air force delivered only a third of the amount needed. Conditions deteriorated inside the besieged city, which the Germans called the "cauldron." The German soldiers were exhausted by months of street fighting. Moreover, their food rations were continually reduced, and they faced starvation.

As the German troops in Stalingrad faced imminent defeat, German soldiers in the Caucasus and other areas of Russia began a fighting retreat westward, pursued by a relentless Red Army now on the offensive with brand-new equipment rolling off the assembly lines not only in the Soviet Union but also in the United States.

By the middle of January, the supply situation in Stalingrad had completely collapsed. The noose around the cauldron became even tighter, and finally on February 2, 1943, the German troops surrendered. Of the roughly 285,000 German soldiers trapped when Stalingrad was encircled by the Red Army on November 22,

1942, 150,000 died fighting, and about 91,000 soldiers were taken as prisoners. Of this latter number, only 6,000 returned to Germany. The rest perished in captivity. The surrender of the German Sixth Army represents the turning point of the war on the eastern front, an important step toward the defeat of Nazi Germany.

The *Völkischer Beobachter* reported on February 4, 1943:

> They die so that Germany lives. For years to come their example will serve to defy the false Bolshevik propaganda. The divisions of the Sixth Army have already become a legend. As Germans reflect upon this moment in time, they are not weakened in their resolve, but rather find collective strength. The sacrifice of the Sixth Army shall embolden the will of the German people, a will that shall never be broken.

More than seventy years later, people from Russia, Germany, and other countries still attempt to collect the remains that these fighting men left behind. Remains such as bone fragments, buttons, and identification cards are often found. Organizations such as the German War Graves Commission maintain the graveyards of the two world wars to preserve the history of these events, work for peace among all nations, and guarantee the dignity of the men who died in these fields.

In the aftermath of the surrender, General Paulus, the German military commander at Stalingrad, became a prisoner of war along with several other generals. Shortly before the surrender, Hitler promoted Paulus to field marshal. Never had a German field marshal surrendered, and Hitler expected Paulus to take his life instead of disgracing this tradition. While a prisoner of war, Paulus joined the National Committee to Free Germany, an organization consisting mostly of German prisoners of war, who called for Germany's surrender. During the Nuremberg war crimes trials, he appeared as a witness for the prosecution. In 1953 Paulus returned home from captivity, and three years later, he died in Dresden.

Leaving Pleschen, 1943

Georg was paralyzed from the waist down. Because of severe neuritis, he could not move or stand. Constant pain made his life miserable. In order for Georg to move about, someone had to push him in a wheelchair, and wheelchairs in a war were as rare as Fabergé eggs in times of peace. On top of that, because of a severe shortage of medical staff, soldiers well enough to leave Pleschen often had to wheel themselves to the depot for the next available train departing to the west.

I felt sorry for all those who had to stay in that hospital in Pleschen. The conditions there were simply indescribable. Hospital staff failed to maintain even the most basic standards of hygiene. Furthermore, lice and other vermin infested the hospital. During an attempt to delouse the facility, nobody shielded the patients from the pesticide, not even the severely wounded.

I shall never forget the few days I spent there. I so wanted to help the poor unfortunate men in the hospital, to do anything to make them more comfortable or ease their suffering as they died. I wanted to take them in my arms, to give them a bit of warmth, to let them feel human goodness, to offer them encouragement. But there were just way too many bodies, and consequently, they became objects instead of people.

The family in Pleschen from whom I obtained accommodations reminded me of the family that I had stayed with in Posen; both were dyed-in-the-wool Nazis. They used every conceivable opportunity to express their loyalty to the Nazi cause. At the breakfast table, to mark the start of a new day, they stretched out their right hands to give the Hitler salute: "Heil Hitler!" Constantly, they talked of a victorious German military, one that still controlled Europe despite suffering a devastating defeat at Stalingrad. They talked of the *Führer* and how he would lead the German people to glory.

One thing I knew from the very beginning was that I had to watch what I said and what I did. Once again, my husband had survived a very severe injury, and the last thing I needed now was to disappear in some camp. No, thank you!

As I waited until Georg could leave with me, time seemed to drag on forever. By luck, an orderly was assigned to escort Georg first to Berlin and then eventually on to Karlsbad. In Pleschen they were always grateful whenever a patient could leave, and I was grateful to have help on our journey.

Once I knew our travel plans, I called ahead to Berlin to Max to let him know we were coming and to ask him to arrange a place for the orderly to stay. He seemed happy to hear my voice and assured me all would be ready when we got there, since Margarethe had returned from the countryside.

During the journey I kept hearing a particular song on a *Volksempfänger*, a small inexpensive "people's radio" that the Nazis had mass-produced for the public. They usually played this song, which had become quite popular throughout Europe during the war, at the same time each day. "Before the barracks by the large gate stood a lantern, a lantern that still stands, like before. There we will see each other again. There will stand Lili Marleen once more."

Sung by Lale Anderson, *Lili Marleen* describes a girl waiting for her sweetheart, a soldier. The song, recorded in German and English, became popular with soldiers on both sides of the conflict. The melancholic melody reminded the men of their girls back home and made the women long to hold their men once more in their arms. This song became one of the greatest hits of the war, and like Glen Miller's *In the Mood*, became a hit among the postwar generation. After the war, *Lili Marleen* records became collector's items among the American soldiers in the occupation army, who offered up to one hundred dollars to have one, a fortune in those days. This sentimental song still portrays the senselessness of war, no matter where it occurs. It evokes feelings of yearning and fear caused by the separation from loved ones, the desire to return home, and the fear one may die too soon.

The journey from Pleschen to Berlin was tortuous. We rode in train cars filled to bursting. Whenever we had to catch a connecting train, we sat in a waiting room for hours on end, without food or anything to drink. The Red Cross, hopelessly overburdened by the mass migration of people, could do little to help us.

In the train cars we saw young mothers and their children, fleeing to the countryside to escape the constant aerial bombing of German cities. They often sought refuge in the rural areas of Bavaria and the Sudetenland. Traveling westward with them were soldiers on leave as well as the wounded. When we arrived in Berlin, I asked God to help us avoid another air raid. We could see the aftermath of the Allied bombing—entire rows of homes reduced to rubble and ash. Like ants around a giant hill, the inhabitants of the city scurried about the ruins, attempting to dig out those trapped inside or to salvage some of their belongings.

Once we reached the home of Georg's parents, and with the help of the orderly traveling with us and my mother-in-law, I was able to give Georg a bath, the first one he'd had in a long time. We lifted his emaciated body, which felt limp in my arms, into the warm water. He could not have weighed more than a hundred pounds.

Following a few short days in Berlin, the final stretch of our journey took us home to Karlsbad, and the closer we found ourselves to our ultimate destination, the easier the journey became. Bohemia remained almost undamaged by the war, even though the war had turned Karlsbad into a giant army hospital, a city whose streets now teemed with doctors and nurses, the wounded, and their visitors.

It was the beginning of spring. The daffodils bloomed, having just pushed their way through the soil, and needles from fir trees covered the ground. As I inhaled the cool fresh air, a feeling of hope flowed through me, hope and desire for a new beginning, hope for peace and harmony. *Everything will improve*, I thought. The war is almost over, Georg is with me, and nothing more can happen to us. It was almost like culture shock. We slowly got used to the quiet and relative luxury found in Karlsbad.

Georg's recovery dragged on. Over several weeks the neuritis began to diminish and eventually disappeared. Now he could move around on crutches, but he was very weak after being off his legs so long.

My mother was beside herself with joy to have both of us back, safe and almost sound. She pulled whatever strings she could to obtain groceries to fatten up Georg and me. It was an unbelievable time, being with her, enjoying the great cooking, and feeling her warmth and endless help.

Some seventy years later as I write these lines, I notice how challenging it is to describe how I felt during this time. I find it quite difficult to overcome inhibition and even think about this troubling time, to think once again about what burdened us during those difficult weeks and months, and to finally speak about this time in my life.

Now that I was home and Georg was in much better condition, I returned to my official nursing duties. I was assigned to work at the former Hotel Imperial, which had been converted into a military hospital. As Georg recovered, I spent as much time as I could with him. As a result, at work I was meticulous about leaving on time. Georg began a long course of physical therapy in order to walk again. He slowly started to gain more weight, and with the improvement in his condition, we wanted to get to know each other again, to share our experiences, to rekindle the passion that somehow had been lost. The entire time we had been married, a little more than a year, sickness, grief, and desperation had overshadowed our relationship, leaving little room inside us for romantic feelings. Not exactly a good start for a marriage.

Whenever possible, we strolled along the promenade or wandered through the park, areas still undisturbed by war. Sometimes we rented a horse-drawn wagon and enjoyed the peacefulness of the surroundings.

Our life together almost returned to a kind of normal. Once again, I stood on cloud nine. Despite the disturbing news from the eastern front, I wanted to enjoy the present. The future seemed too distant to be of concern, obscuring the inevitable like a dense fog.

Perspective: Propaganda

Reichs Minister Dr. Göbbels spoke Thursday evening at the Berlin Sports Arena, which was filled to capacity. His speech detailed the state of Germany's struggle for freedom with unvarnished clarity. He posed a question to the German Nation, whether it still had the will to do whatever it takes to achieve an ultimate victory. He questioned whether the German People were prepared to make the sacrifices that the *Führer* requires of us. The audience, who often interrupted Dr. Göbbels during his speech with several minutes of applause, echoed the agreement of the masses, reflecting the resolve of the German people, expressing their never-ending faith in the war effort, and their rock-solid conviction that Germany will emerge victorious.

—*Völkischer Beobachter*, February 19, 1943

The *Führer* has ordered us to follow him. This moment in our history is a test of our devotion and steadfastness. He stretches out his hand to save us and we must only take hold. We must resolve to subordinate all aspects of our lives to his will. That is what is required of us in this hour of need. And like the slogan reminds us: Now arise people and let the storm loose.

—Joseph Göbbels, speaking in the Berlin Sportpalast, February 18, 1943

As Joseph Göbbels called for total war in his speeches, the Allies advanced on all fronts. The newspapers, newsreels, and radio broadcasts all spoke of great German victories and weak opponents, grand battles, and brave men. The reality that touched the civilian populations throughout Europe and the young men in the trenches could not have been further away.

Karlsbad and the POWs, 1943

The war brought a prisoner-of-war camp to Karlsbad. During our excursions into the countryside, we sometimes came across work details consisting of Soviet prisoners. Whenever the guards were SS soldiers, whom we could recognize by their uniforms, we immediately avoided eye contact and left the area as quickly as possible. Trouble with them could be fatal, for us or the prisoners.

However, sometimes only civilians guarded the prisoners. Without saying a word, we knew exactly what to do. Georg would let one of his crutches fall to the ground, pretending it was an accident, and when he bent over to pick it up, he would leave several cigarettes on the pathway, hoping a prisoner would find them. When the prisoners took a break, Georg would strike up a conversation with the guard, distracting him while I secretly left behind some of the food we had brought along for the picnic.

We were perfectly aware that what we were doing could land us in a lot of hot water, yet somehow the sight of the prisoners moved us to show some compassion and to provide a bit of help. According to secondhand information we often received, some of the other women around Karlsbad also supplied the prisoners with food. The Red Cross prescribed a minimum food ration for prisoners of war, one that was not sufficient for the longer-term survival of these men, who often performed heavy labor. For many on the home front, making the lives of these prisoners more comfortable represented an act of desperation. They hoped for reciprocity by someone on the other side of the war; perhaps someone else would show compassion for a German prisoner of war floating around somewhere in the Soviet territory or imprisoned in a Siberian gulag.

Georg made a slow but steady recovery. Finally, he could leave the hospital and begin the next phase of his rehabilitation. Then came a bit of news that seemed sent from heaven itself. We were going to Austria for two weeks, to Lake Wörther in the southern province of Carinthia, for rest and recovery. We simply could not believe it. During the train journey we sat there stunned, hardly believing our good fortune. From the balcony of the hotel room, we could see a few boats sailing on the lake. And the "hospital food" there was something else. Our host set out on the table an enormous spread of scrumptious food. For the first time in a long while, we were able to stuff ourselves with as much food as we wanted. On top of that, we could eat as often as we wanted. This was truly the land of milk and honey.

The war seemed far away, but then again not so far away. Our hotel was located near the Mittagskogel, a mountain on the border with Yugoslavia covered by heavy forest. The Yugoslav Partisans, a Communist-led resistance to the Axis powers in occupied Yugoslavia used this same forest to hide and plan their activities. The Partisans, led by General Tito, became Europe's most effective anti-Axis resistance movement during the war. During the night we often heard strange noises, perhaps partisans creeping past the houses, looking for a chicken, a lamb, or just anything edible. If the partisans ran into one of the locals, they did not hesitate to gun the person down. Even if someone promised us all the money in the world, we would not dare take one step outside our hotel after dark.

Despite the nighttime danger we found ways of making the most of our time. We swam in the warm lake, went boating, and sunbathed. Sometimes we felt a little down. We imagined how much more pleasant and tranquil our marriage could have been if only we had lived during a time of peace. The two weeks flew by way too quickly, especially because we dreaded the inevitable end to our vacation and the journey home. All too soon, we waved goodbye to the innkeeper and headed back to Karlsbad.

Perspective: The Yugoslavs and the Italians

Josip Broz Tito was the general secretary of the Yugoslavian Communist Party. After the Germans invaded Russia in 1941, he waged a partisan war against Germany, one shaped by his tactical skill and unscrupulousness. The Germans put a concerted effort into capturing Tito, but he successfully evaded them. In December 1943 the Allied countries recognized the provisional democratic Yugoslav government in exile. Tito's partisan army fought their own war with Germany but were never officially granted equal status with the allied powers of the United States, England, France and the Soviet Union.

Like the Germans, many Italians also turned to fascism during the political and economic instability that followed the First World War. By 1922 the fascist movement in Italy had seized control of the government. Its leader, Benito Mussolini, became the dictator. Known as "Il Duce," Mussolini's regime was not as brutal as its counterpart in Germany. Moreover, Mussolini served at the pleasure of the Italian king, far different from the *Führer* in Germany, who remained accountable to no one.

Mussolini dreamed of expanding Italy's influence in Africa and the Mediterranean. In 1935 Italy invaded and conquered Ethiopia. In an effort to create a new Roman Empire, in 1939 Mussolini signed the Pact of Steel with Germany, an agreement that pledged both countries to provide military assistance to the other. However, rather than advance the interests of Hitler and Mussolini, the Italian armed forces performed miserably on the battlefields of Africa and Europe. This forced Hitler to divert military resources from the eastern front to aid Mussolini.

On July 23, 1943, Benito Mussolini received a summons to appear before the Italian king, Victor Emmanuel III. In that meeting, the king removed the dictator from office. King Victor Emanuel and others in the Italian government took this step as part of a secret plan to surrender to the Allies. The Italians had no desire to resist the planned Anglo-American invasion of their country. After the meeting with the king, Mussolini was arrested. Marshal Bodoglio then undertook the task of forming a new government.

After shuffling Mussolini from one secret location to the next, Italian police eventually brought the former dictator to the Hotel Imperatore, a ski resort near the Gran Sasso, a 9,554-foot mountain in central Italy. An aerial tramcar traveling a distance of nearly 10,000 feet provided the only means of access to the resort.[35]

Shortly after the coup in Italy, Hitler placed Captain Otto Skorzeny, a fellow Austrian, in charge of a rescue mission to free Mussolini. The Italian dictator was one of the few people whom Hitler regarded as a friend. On September 12, the Germans landed twelve gliders and 120 soldiers on a meadow next to the hotel where Mussolini was held. The daring rescue mission succeeded, and Skorzeny took Mussolini to Germany for a meeting with Hitler. The Italian dictator spent the rest of the war in northern Italy.

---

35   The mountains of Italy feature sheer cliff walls and other difficult features. The tramcar thus had to both climb vertically and travel horizontally as well as make other allowances for terrain.

Following Mussolini's rescue, Skorzeny became an overnight hero. The rescue fueled German propaganda, as an attempt to control the fallout stemming from the Italian surrender to the Allied Forces. Nothing could undermine the war effort in Germany. Skorzeny spent the rest of the war planning covert missions against the advancing Allied armies. After the German surrender, he was arrested and placed in a prisoner-of-war camp. Three years later Skorzeny managed to escape and spent the rest of his life in Spain.

Just days before the German surrender, partisans captured Mussolini near Lake Como as he attempted to flee from the approaching Allied armies. He was executed, and his body was hung upside down in a public square.

Back to Karlsbad, 1943

Our return trip brought us close to the Italian border, where we could witness the chaos and confusion occurring inside of Italy. Some in the Italian armed forces supported the new government, whereas others opposed the change. The new government had ordered a change in military uniforms. To put it mildly, the Italian soldiers looked like something out of a circus act. Each soldier wore what looked like a pointy cowboy hat with a green feather. We saw these men standing on the train platforms as we rode past. They had been detained by German soldiers who formerly had been their allies. This political development delayed our journey home. We would be underway for two days before we reached our destination.

As we sat in our train compartment, we hoped and prayed the war would not break out in front of our window. Then my stomach started to rumble and grumble, followed by a burning sensation in my throat. Suddenly, I started to vomit. The nausea stopped when I fainted and landed on the floor.

"A doctor! Is a doctor aboard?" my husband, still wobbly on his injured legs, yelled as he ran through the train like his hair was on fire.

The fainting spell and the examination that followed lasted but a few minutes. Afterward, the army doctor looked at Georg and said nonchalantly, "She's just pregnant." From his tone of voice, he could have been reading the cooking instructions on a soup-can label.

Perspective: Scorched Earth

As the German military retreated on the eastern front, it pursued a scorched-earth policy: the destruction of the regions it left behind. One desperate battle after another took place, such as the great tank battle at Kursk, which ended in a German defeat. By the beginning of 1943, the Red Army had won back most of the Ukraine.

The scorched-earth policy would come back to haunt civilians and German soldiers at the wars' end, as it made the war personal for citizens of countries conquered by Germany. Getting caught in the war's crossfire is one thing, casualties of one army fighting another, but deliberately burning homes and destroying farms and businesses, and deliberately taking civilian lives is unforgivable.

In stark contrast to the Red Army, the German armed forces had exhausted almost their entire reserve of soldiers. The German ground war was now being fought on two fronts, one in the Ukraine and the other in Italy. Battle fatigue and inadequate supplies exacted a heavy toll on the German military machine. Yet, the official story was unchanged.

> Several of our tank units counterattacked, driving back the enemy who penetrated German lines just the day before, depriving them of an opportunity to launch a larger offensive. In the last ten days in this sector alone, 12,000 enemy soldiers have been killed, and 1,000 have been taken prisoner. On top of that, 30 tanks, 380 machine guns, 140 mortars, and countless other weapons have been destroyed. Fighting with the enemy is particularly heavy north of Orel. In this area of the Eastern Front, a defensive tank battle keeps the enemy in place as he makes a futile attempt to advance. Southeast of Lake Ilmen, our armed forces have repelled five waves of enemy attack and destroyed thirteen tanks.

> —*Völkischer Beobachter*, February 19, 1943

Our Little Bundle of Joy, 1943–1944

The war continued, and just as Georg was halfway put together again, he received orders to report to Berlin in two months' time. There he would receive his assignment in the struggle for a "final victory." In Karlsbad the number of soldiers crammed into the hospital rooms grew steadily, not a good sign for a nation that was supposed to be winning the war, according to the message broadcast to us through propaganda.

For several months my mother had not been feeling well. She suffered from persistent pain and always felt exhausted. Her doctor sent her to a professor in Prague, Dr. Knaus, one of the foremost gynecologists at the university hospital. He was known for having developed a technique for birth control that utilized a woman's body temperature to prevent conception, a means of birth control that received recognition by the pope. Of course, no means of birth control received approval from the Nazis, who viewed women as birth machines providing a future supply of soldiers to fight wars.

After two weeks in Prague, she returned with my father in tow. Mother had devastating news. She had been diagnosed with an inoperable form of abdominal cancer. To ease the considerable pain, Mother depended on very potent pain pills.

The day-to-day stress became almost unbearable. I was pregnant. My work was physically and emotionally exhausting. The front was closing in on us, and once again the army had separated me from my husband, who obeyed orders and left for Berlin. Then, on top of all that, my mother, the closest friend I had at this time in my life, was dying. Now when I think back upon this time, everything appears murky, like I am looking through a glass of milk, but the problems I faced were very real.

I look back now and know that I was ridiculously unprepared for marriage and motherhood. I think that perhaps when my mother gave her blessing on Georg's marriage proposal that she already knew she would not live much longer, and she wanted me to have some security in having a husband. I don't think that anyone can be prepared for living in a country at war, with death and destruction a daily event.

Every day I fired off a quick prayer to heaven. "Dear God, let this child be born before the war reaches us, and let him or her be healthy enough to survive the war." I took care of my mother the best I could. My godmother came over three times a week to help around the home and to obtain our food rations. On my days off I marched several kilometers to a farm outside of Karlsbad, owned by some people we knew. There I traded some of our household goods for butter, cheese, and vegetables.

At Christmas Georg received some leave from the military. After he returned to his unit, I applied to work in an office. Until the birth of my child, I still had my civil service obligation, and I did not want to spend the rest of my pregnancy working in a hospital.

As best as I could, I tried to prepare for the birth of the baby. Almost none of what the baby needed was available in the stores. Diapers, romper suits, shoes, blouses—we had to knit or sew these things on our old sewing machine. Our relatives and friends scoured their attics, looking inside suitcases or boxes they had packed away, attempting to find the sewing material that we needed to equip the baby for the journey ahead.

From an army hospital my father cadged some old flannel sheets and sent them to us, which we immediately sewed into diapers. We carried on a bustling exchange trade with those we knew, bartering for enough wool to make the baby's jacket and socks. It certainly became a lot of work, but we threw ourselves into this endeavor because it distracted us from the war and the dark future we faced.

Georg was able to obtain leave for an Easter visit. The day before he arrived, I cut some willow branches and wildflowers, which I arranged into a welcoming gift for my husband as well as for the baby, who was supposed to be born on Easter Sunday.

On Good Saturday, Georg returned from Berlin. I could not believe they had granted him leave. Proudly, I walked into the church with him to attend Easter Mass. I felt we had finally become a real family. As the two and one-half of us sat down in a pew, we were under the gaze of the rest of the congregation in a full church. The war and the loss of loved ones, which touched families even in

Karlsbad, drove people to Mass. People prayed for themselves, for others, and for peace. Just like before the war, the nave was decorated with candles that glowed with a heavenly brilliance. In his beautiful sermon the priest attempted to show compassion to those who mourned and at the same time tried to present hope for a better future. He concluded the sermon by saying, "After the chaos, all that is eternal shall remain."

Right on time, during the early morning hours of Easter Sunday, our little bundle of joy decided to come into the world. The birth caused me quite a bit of concern. Around Karlsbad the hospitals were reserved for either wounded soldiers or emergency surgeries. Located up high and on the other side of the valley, a single maternity clinic served as a hospital for women going into labor.[36] Like the rest of the civilian population, we did not have a car. Hardly any taxis were around, certainly none at four o'clock in the morning, nor did we have the option of calling for an ambulance because none were available.

With me clinging to Georg's arm for support and becoming more and more breathless as the contractions overwhelmed me, together we set off on foot, down one steep hill and up the other. The distance was about one kilometer in total, but it was a marathon in my condition. I must have been huffing and puffing like one of those old steam locomotives.

The look of terror on Georg's face was something else. "Is it coming out?" he asked. "Please, just hold on for a few more seconds. The clinic is just right up there, not too far now," he whispered.

Finally, a midwife ran toward us. Pushing and pulling, she and Georg managed somehow to drag me inside the building. Despite all the commotion, the birth was not coming anytime soon. The labor dragged on. After two hours everyone had had enough of Georg, his nervousness, and his constant questions. He was sent home.

During my entire life nothing ever went according to plan, including the birth of my child. The baby's umbilical cord was wrapped

---

36   For reference, Karlsbad is in a steep, narrow valley with hillsides rising so sharply that many roads feature switchbacks, and many sidewalks are made into stairs.

around her neck, posing a life-threatening risk of suffocation. I can no longer remember all that the midwives did for me, but finally at three o'clock in the afternoon, the torture was over with, and our little girl saw the light of the world for the first time. With trembling hands, my arms weakened by the prolonged labor, I held the baby up next to me. I saw her silky black hair, ruffled in the back, and some redness on the back of her neck, chafing caused by the umbilical cord. At first, I was shocked, but the doctor calmed me down.

Patting my arm and giving a laugh, he said, "The young lady will certainly develop a taste for necklaces."

Since it was not customary for fathers to be present at the birth of a child and Georg had been sent home, word had to be sent to him that we were finally parents. He came immediately to be with me and our little girl. The three of us spent our first hours together, a time I shall never forget.

But once again, my talent for attracting trouble appeared. Whether from the stress of the last week and concern about the child or just from random bad luck, I suffered an episode of eclampsia. My kidneys started to fail, and I could not see or speak. Now the staff scurried about the hospital because of me and not my daughter.

In all that commotion, and, despite the fact that he was exhausted, Georg had to take care of a legal matter; he was required to appear at the Civil Registry Office and report the birth of our child within 24 hours. Before the birth we had not discussed any possible names, and now I had lost my opportunity to contribute to this decision because I could not speak. It was now up to Georg, and he had to make this decision on short notice. He was losing his mind under the stress of making this decision on his own, and the only name that came to him was Barbara, the patron saint of artillerymen, among whom, as the saying goes, "the Holy Barbara is never far." He spoke briefly with my mother about a possible name, and she insisted on the name Brigitte. That is how Barbara Brigitte came to be named.

Georg didn't have much time to celebrate with his new family. A few days after the birth, he had to return to his unit. *Dear God, I prayed, let things stay the same, even just for a month. Then my precious baby will be a bit older, and I can deal with whatever comes.* I prayed like this every day.

At the top of this Photo is the building that housed the maternity clinic in 1944 where Barbara was born. The steepness of the terrain in and around Karlsbad meant that I had to walk a very long way to get up that hill to the clinic. The retaining wall below it is all that remains of the synagogue that existed in Karlsbad prior to the war. This Photo was taken in 2001.

Three months after Barbara's birth, Georg received a few days of leave. At this time Karlsbad met the same fate as many other cities and experienced an air raid. It was not a planned raid but rather, in all honesty, an accident. A British bomber encountered mechanical problems and had to drop its bomb load to avoid crashing. The pilot, on his way to bomb a target in Germany, had plenty of reason to fear not only a potentially fatal crash landing but also the possibility of being captured alive and tortured. Unfortunately, the pilot dumped his bomb load as he flew directly over the spa district. The explosion destroyed several houses, killing the occupants inside. That day the British Broadcasting Corporation, or BBC, announced an official apology for the incident.

The short reunion was over, and Georg had to return to his unit. The next time he saw Barbara, she was almost two years old, the war was over, and our world had changed from the ground up.

Barbara's christening took place without Georg in the Church of St. Mary Magdalene. My best friend, Gerda, was the godmother in a rather plain and small ceremony that initiated my daughter into the Catholic faith.

On a hot July day, I encountered a woman on the staircase outside our apartment. She lived with some neighbors, a married couple, who had offered this woman a place to stay after she lost her apartment in Berlin, destroyed by a direct hit during a bombing raid. As we met each other on the stairs, she sobbed uncontrollably and had to lean on me for support. I finally found out what had happened.

"Did you hear the news? Someone tried to assassinate the *Führer*. My God, haven't you heard?" The woman could barely speak. "But the Almighty was looking out for him. He is only slightly injured." Then she climbed down the rest of the stairs, continuing to sob quietly.

I could not have cared less. My daughter, now three months old, required every bit of my attention. The political events playing out in Berlin and at the Wolfsschanze in Prussia did not interest me in the slightest. Was this a postnatal mood? I don't know. In any case I had my child in my arms, now the most important thing in the world. At this time in my life, I was so completely disinterested in politics that the world could have been coming to end, and I would not have noticed. Indeed, this was about to happen. Somewhere out there in the west, the Allies had already landed on the shores of continental Europe, the significance of which I did not really grasp.

This photo of Gerda was taken in 1943 or 1944.

Perspective: The Arrival of the Allies and Assassination Attempts

On June 6, 1944, British, American, and Canadian soldiers landed on the beaches of Normandy in France, the beginning of a relentless drive toward Germany. The *Völkischer Beobachter* reported on June 7, 1944,

> Acting on orders from Moscow, the British and Americans have now decided to take the incalculable risk of an invasion they had postponed for a long time. The German leadership is prepared for this engagement, which is about the defense of Europe, its freedom and eternal greatness.

> In this hour they [the people] grow to meet the challenge this general offensive imposes on them. They rely on their historical duty to overcome any hardship handed to them. The German people gather together in this momentous hour, convinced that their righteous cause will triumph, which embodies a belief in the *Führer*, a belief in ultimate victory, and a belief in a future that our nation deserves, one that fulfills our historic destiny.

Between 1939 and 1944 about ten assassination attempts against Hitler had failed. On July 20, 1944, Klaus Schenk, Count von Stauffenberg, planted a bomb inside the Wolfsschanze, the secret Nazi hideout in East Prussia. He was a severely disabled war veteran, a colonel, and a staunch opponent of the Nazi regime. Even with a careful plan this attempt failed. Hitler escaped, almost miraculously, with only slight injuries.

Believing that Hitler was killed in the explosion, Count von Stauffenberg and his accomplices returned to Berlin and set in motion the planned coup, Operation Valkyrie. When the failed assassination attempt was finally reported, and everyone learned that Hitler survived, support for the coup crumbled.

Soon, von Stauffenberg and other coconspirators were arrested and executed. The Nazi regime then held a series of show trials to publicly disgrace others involved in the assassination attempt. The witch hunt that followed eventually resulted in the arrest and execution of thousands of leading military officials, which ultimately hastened the defeat of Nazi Germany.

> I swear to God this sacred oath that to the Leader of the German empire and people, Adolf Hitler, supreme commander of the armed forces, I shall render unconditional obedience and that as a brave soldier I shall at all times be prepared to give my life for this oath.[37]

This oath that the soldiers had sworn brought fatal consequences for the military resistance movement. In heated discussions prior to von Stauffenberg's attempt, it was decided that the situation in Germany required them to violate this oath and betray the military code of honor. Following their conscience, these men decided to carry out the assassination attempt even though the chance of success was questionable, and they faced certain death.

General Major Henning von Tresckow, one of the leaders of the resistance movement, said in reference to the Valkyrie plan to kill Hitler,

> The assassination must be attempted at all costs. Even if it should not succeed, an attempt to seize power in Berlin must be made. What matters now is no longer the practical purpose of the coup, but to prove to the world and for the records of history that the men of the resistance dared to take the decisive step. Compared to this objective, nothing else is of consequence.[38]

---

37   In German, "Ich schwöre bei Gott diesen heiligen Eid, daß ich dem Führer des Deutschen Reiches und Volkes Adolf Hitler, dem Obersten Befehlshaber der Wehrmacht, unbedingten Gehorsam leisten und als tapferer Soldat bereit sein will, jederzeit für diesen Eid mein Leben einzusetzen."

38   Joachim Fest, *Plotting Hitler's Death: the Story of German Resistance* (New York: Metropolitan Books, 1996), 236.

After the coup on July 20 failed, von Tresckow committed suicide in the early hours of July 21, 1944.

The *Völkischer Beobachter* published the following remarks on July 21, 1944:

> Through the personality of the *Führer* we approach a new era in the history of Germany and Europe, one which belongs among the most awe inspiring ever seen. Never before has a struggle been so hard-fought upon on our continent.
>
> Under the eyes of the world-hungry Roosevelt, countless newspaper articles, and even brochures, have appeared in the USA, which through words and pictures have either suggested assassination attempts against our *Führer* or have provided a full description of the completed act, a depiction shaped by pure Jewish fantasy. The fact this filthy trash was allowed to appear in "God's own land," even before America's entry into the war, would be enough to stand Roosevelt before a world court and pronounce him guilty of murder.

At the beginning of August 1944, Churchill spoke of a war of attrition among the elite of the Third Reich. Even Roosevelt says that the assassination attempt reminds him more of a dark criminal underworld than of something one would expect from an officer corps in a civilized country.

Long before the assassination attempt, the conspirators attempted to secure the support of the Allies but were not successful. The Allies had no interest in an internal German resistance movement because this would jeopardize their demand for an unconditional surrender.

As the reign of terror intensified in German political circles following the attempt, it became apparent that this purge would have fatal consequences for the Nazi regime. The thousands of officers who were arrested and murdered could not be replaced.

In 1944 the remaining Jews in the Warsaw ghetto formed resistance groups. On August 1, 1944, they undertook an armed revolt against the German occupation force. They hoped the advancing Soviet Army would rescue them, but it never came. The uprising lasted until the beginning of October, ending when the Germans started setting fire to sections of the ghetto. During the revolt around 16,000 resistance fighters perished, and afterward the remaining survivors faced summary execution or death inside a gas chamber at one of the concentration camps. Throughout Warsaw civilian deaths exceeded 150,000.

The propaganda called for total resistance against the Anglo-American "terror-bombing" and the Red Army's "raging lust for revenge." In September 1944 the so-called Volkssturm ("People's Storm") was put into effect, declaring all men between sixteen and sixty fit for military service. At this point the Allies stood at the edge of the Reich's borders. In the east began the mass exodus of refugees, ethnic Germans fleeing from the advancing Red Army. The mass flight of refugees from Prussia, Pomerania, and Silesia was triggered by "propaganda" that accused the Soviets of committing atrocities against civilians.

In this case, the propaganda turned out to be fiction only in its failure to adequately prepare the civilians for the horrors to come.[39]

This mass migration of people became heart-wrenching, as they marched during the winter months on foot or made the journey on horse carts, left unprotected from the bitter wind and storms of the coldest winter in Europe during the twentieth century. They fled amid the fighting armies and indescribably cruel mistreatment of civilians.

Historians later concluded that the delusions of victory among those who once were strong changed them into the weakest. The Germans paid a heavy price for the injustices launched from their own soil.

First Christmas, 1944

We celebrated Barbara's first Christmas and the last one in our hometown. Despite all that worried us, we baked Mother's famous

---

39   An excellent book on the plight of civilians in the last days of the war and the early days of the peace is *After the Reich: the Brutal History of the Allied Occupation*, by Giles MacDonogh (New York: Basic Books, 2007).

Christmas cookies. My mother stood there in the kitchen and said, "Child, I don't know if I'll experience another Christmas. So, let's go ahead and use up all the food that we have." Barbara was mesmerized by the lights on the Christmas tree, reaching out with her tiny hands to grasp the glowing candles, the warmth of which reflected constantly on her face, bringing peace to all for just a short while.

Somehow my mother managed to get a carp for our Christmas dinner, something close to a miracle.[40] We prepared two additional place settings for the table. According to our tradition, there should always be an extra place setting for the "missing guest." This time two guests failed to attend, Georg and my father, from whom we had not received any news for a long time. Almost every day the postman brought Christmas cards. As we sat there reading the Christmas greetings, we could not help but say, "My God, they are still alive."

Dresden, 1945

It was February 1945. Sirens sounded throughout the night, summoning us to the bomb shelters. For this contingency we always had a small suitcase ready that contained various belongings, including important papers and some clothing. Although we had planned for this, it still took a bit of time to reach shelter. Barbara, not even one year old, had to be carried. On top of that, someone had to help my mother. The struggle with cancer had made her very weak. Neighbors finally helped

Bath time for Barbara, around Christmastime 1944.

---

40   The common carp, or European carp (*Cyprinus carpio*), is a widespread freshwater fish in Europe. It is often served during the Christmas meal in Germany.

us find cover. Just as we climbed into the cold and dark cellar, an intimidating squadron of heavy bombers flew directly overhead, bringing a sense of anxiety and approaching danger.

Although countless aircraft flew over us, we did not hear any explosions. Still, our cellar shook and rattled, vibrations caused by the drone of the aircraft engines making their way to some target in the northeast. After two hours it was over, and the last of the machines disappeared in the distance. Still unnerved, we returned home and attempted to get some sleep. We had been spared, yet nobody felt triumphant or even gave a sigh of relief for that matter. We knew that the bombs had fallen or would fall on somebody else. May God help them.

I could not calm Barbara. She was terrified, sitting there on my lap, looking at me with her huge dark eyes that just ripped my heart out. We adults had an idea of what was playing out in our country, even though it was difficult to comprehend the destructive frenzy and hatred. But how was a small child supposed to deal with this situation? We gave her some extra attention, attempting to provide a feeling of peace and security, yet we ourselves certainly did not feel this way. The situation was simply wretched.

The Red Cross summoned me for extraordinary service, something I shall never forget for the rest of my life. I reported, as ordered, to the train station. There they arrived, survivors of one of the largest and most devastating air raids of the war. Dresden had been almost obliterated, reduced to ash and rubble. Thousands of people had lost their lives. Thousands more had lost everything they owned. Now some of them had come to Karlsbad, the elderly, mothers with infants, desperate women covered in gray ash, exhausted and frightened, climbing out of the trains slowly, with hesitation.

They sent us into the train cars to check on those who might need some extra assistance. After opening the door to one compartment, I reared back in horror at what I saw. On the floor, in a pool of frozen blood, lay a woman and the body of a recently born child. The woman still breathed, but the child had clearly died. Although the child might have been born a bit premature, under different circumstances he or she probably would have survived, but nobody had been able to help the mother and child. In the chaos and confusion, in the rush to flee from the burning city, nobody had lifted the child from the floor and provided the baby with warmth. While I fought back tears and sadness, the mother regained consciousness. "My child, my child!" She cried, her entire body shaking with deep sobs. All I could do was offer the woman some comfort and wrap the baby in a sheet. I sat next to her, resting her head on my lap. "Everything is going to be all right. Don't be sad. Soon the war will be over," I whispered in her ear, while stroking her hair.

It took a while for the first-aid workers to arrive. One of them discreetly placed the small bundle in the ambulance as I continued to comfort the woman. A short while later, I was sent to assist with other injured people. I don't know whether anyone registered the birth or took down the name of the mother. They were among those thousands of nameless faces in this inhumane war.

In each train car we saw something horrific, memories that today have disappeared for me behind the merciful curtain of forgetfulness. Only the mother with the frozen baby comes back to haunt my memories. These survivors of the bombing raid received totally inadequate care. Karlsbad was simply unprepared for their arrival, not even able to offer something as basic as a piece of bread or a hot cup of coffee or tea.

During the day, more air-raid sirens sounded. A hundred planes must have flown overhead in a northeasterly direction. The next day everyone was talking about it. Dresden had been bombed to smithereens; the Florence of the Elbe obliterated. The famous baroque buildings, with their flamboyant architecture, had disappeared. Famous buildings, such as the Semper Opera House and the Frauenkirche Church, had been reduced to rubble. Bombs had killed or maimed thousands of already-wounded soldiers as well as refugees from the east, those who had sought refuge in this city from the advancing Red Army.

Perspective: The Bombing of Dresden

The bombing of Dresden represents one of the most tragic examples of the escalation of the Allied air campaign in Germany. By 1942 the Allies achieved air superiority over the Third Reich. Starting in 1943, the Allied air campaign increasingly targeted residential areas, city centers, palaces, and estates in the countryside, starting with those in the west and moving later in the war to targets in the eastern sections of the Third Reich. Under the leadership of Air Marshal Arthur Harris, in 1942 the British Bomber Command pursued a strategy of wiping out the industrial cities of the Ruhr as well as Berlin, the capital of Nazi Germany. For the most part they were successful. They intended to demoralize the civilian population, who are supposed to pressure the regime to surrender.

Dresden, known for its cultural heritage, was renowned for its historic buildings, whose beauty bore tribute to the past rulers of Germany. During the war the city had already been attacked, but the damage was limited. In February 1945, Dresden lacked any defense against air attack except for some antiaircraft cannons that protected a hydrogen plant. Fighter aircraft were not available to defend the city because they had already been sent to the eastern front.

During the night of February 13, a total of about 725 heavy British bombers took part in the attack on Dresden. They came in two waves, the second following the first three hours later. This second wave was supposed to interfere with fire-suppression efforts and prevent the survivors of the first attack from fleeing. Then, on February 14 and 15, 1945, more than 525 American bombers participated in the third and fourth waves of the attack on Dresden, with many of the bombs falling on residential areas in the city center. Of the nearly four thousand tons of bombs dropped on the city, half of those were incendiary bombs, which generated a firestorm.

In one of the most devastating air raids in history, in just fourteen hours about eleven square miles, mostly the downtown area, was destroyed. Phosphorus bombs ignited an inferno that reached 2,700° F. The flames created a vacuum effect that sucked some people into the fires. Many of those seeking refuge in bunkers and cellars died from a lack of oxygen or from carbon monoxide poisoning. The firestorm knocked over train cars and caused the asphalt to burn. Institutions of city life ceased to exist.

Dresden burned for several days. Although many of those who perished had burned to ash, thousands of corpses littered the streets and underground shelters. The damaged city lacked the resources to place the bodies in a mass grave. In the downtown area, sandstone blocks taken from the girders of a destroyed department store formed a surface upon which the bodies were cremated.

Historical accounts differ as to how many people died during the bombing raid. An exact number will probably never be available because the city didn't keep an exact record of the thousands of refugees who had recently arrived there, and the bombs destroyed what records might have been kept. Before the war, Dresden had 630,000 inhabitants, but the population may have swollen to as many as 1.2 million at the time of the attack. Many estimates place the number of deaths at 35,000 to 50,000.

Early estimates from the German Propaganda Ministry put the number of deaths from the Dresden raids at over 100,000 and then a week later used an estimate of 202,040, a value taken from a police report with an extra zero tacked onto the end. This propaganda was quite effective, as it not only influenced attitudes in neutral countries at the time but even reached the British House of Commons when Richard Stokes quoted information from the German Press Agency (controlled by the Propaganda Ministry). Historian Frederick Taylor suggests that, although the destruction of Dresden would have affected people's perception of the Allies' claim to absolute moral superiority in any event, part of the outrage involves Göbbels's master stroke of propaganda.[41] Starting within days of the raids and lasting to today, many questioned the justification for the air raid on Dresden, which Churchill personally ordered.

After the public outcry, stoked by the German reports, Churchill distanced himself from the highly decorated Arthur Harris, air

---

41   Taylor, Frederick (2004). *Dresden: Tuesday, 13 February 1945*. New York: HarperCollins.

marshal and commander in chief of the British Bomber Command. His unit was excluded from some of the honors bestowed on other branches of the British military, and it is not until the 1990s that Harris finally received a bronze statue in Hyde Park in London.

According to some historians, the bombing of civilians in urban areas constituted a flagrant violation of the Hague Convention. They view the destruction of German cities, including Dresden, as a war crime.

Until the political reunification of Germany, the ruins of the Frauenkirche stood as a monument to the thousands who died on this night. The communist East German government haphazardly reconstructed some of the historic buildings, such as the Zwinger and Schloss. After the fall of the Iron Curtain, the Germans finally undertook a comprehensive renovation and reconstruction program to preserve these cultural landmarks.

Private contributions financed most of the reconstruction costs for the Frauenkirche. Noteworthy among the donors was the Dresden Trust (Great Britain), which financed the pinnacle cross and orb that adorns the church dome and, in addition, supports reconciliation through educational and cultural initiatives, memorials and visits. The trust counts among its patrons HRH the Duke of Kent, cousin to Queen Elizabeth II. In November 2004, the queen and her husband, Prince Phillip, travelled to Berlin for a state visit and hosted a charity event featuring the Berlin Philharmonic, the proceeds from which were donated to help cover the costs of the reconstruction effort. The televised event featured a heartfelt speech by Prince Phillip, in German, recognizing the horrors and costs of war on civilians.

In 1994 I bought my granddaughter, who lives in the United States, a wristwatch, inside of which small stones from the old Frauenkirche were inlaid. Proceeds generated from the sale of this watch and others like it helped finance the reconstruction of this church. At the time, my granddaughter did not fully understand the historical significance behind rebuilding this landmark—and why should she? How could a young person born 22 years after the event and thousands of miles from Dresden understand the meaning and history that these small stones conveyed? For many

Germans, however, the rebuilding of the Frauenkirche represents coming to terms with a painful and tragic episode in their history. For many Europeans, the rebuilding of the Frauenkirche has become a powerful symbol of reconciliation.

Perspective: The Killing of Refugees and Civilians in the Final Months of the War, 1945

The defeat of Nazi Germany was now a foregone conclusion. In February 1945 the Allies held a conference at Yalta, once a popular retreat on the Black Sea for Russian nobility. On the agenda was the division of Europe into various zones of occupation. Indeed, the German armed forces faced imminent defeat on all fronts. In many combat zones, the Allies had separated the German Army from its chain of supply. Especially in the east, a savage bloodbath ensued, taking thousands of lives on both sides up until the last moments of the war.

In many areas, civilians attempted to flee the fighting but were often encircled and perished alongside the soldiers. The mass exodus of refugees clogged the roads, preventing the escape of others down the line of evacuation. Everyone was vulnerable.

As the war came to its end, both sides tossed any remaining standards of decency to the wind, a familiar feature of twentieth-century warfare. Among the worst atrocities was the sinking of ships refitted for evacuating civilians and wounded soldiers from East Prussia. Sailing from the harbors in Danzig (now Gdańsk) and Gotenhafen (now Gydinia), these vessels became easy targets for torpedoes and other weapons of war as they sailed across the Baltic Sea. Ironically, many of the refugee vessels were once luxury liners that traveled through the Baltic, North, and Adriatic Seas under the auspices of the Strength through Joy program. Although these vessels now evacuated mostly civilians and wounded soldiers, fleeing with them were also high-ranking military officers, civil servants, and their relatives.

The most tragic sinking occurred on January 30, 1945, not far from the harbor in the Gulf of Danzig, when torpedoes from the

Soviet submarine *S-13* struck the *MV Wilhelm Gustloff*. Within an hour this once-proud passenger liner sank, becoming one of the largest shipping disasters in history. Built to carry 1,880 passengers and crew, the ship's complement and passenger lists cited 6,050 people on board, but this did not include many civilians who boarded the ship without being recorded in the ship's official embarkation records. Historians now estimate that the ship held over 10,000 passengers and crew, of which there were 9,000 civilians, some 4,000 of whom were children. Fewer than 1,230 survived, rescued by other naval vessels in the area that were at risk of being torpedoed themselves.

Although the sinking of refugee ships claimed thousands of lives, the evacuation effort at sea still succeeded in bringing more than 1.5 million civilians and 500,000 soldiers from East Prussia, Pomerania, and the Baltic States to safety in Denmark and northern Germany.

Did the Red Army deliberately seek civilian targets? The acts may well have been revenge, intended to inflict as much damage as possible on the enemy and those who had destroyed much of the Soviet Union.

In March 1945, Hitler issued the "Nero Order," which required the complete destruction of any infrastructure remaining in areas from which the German armed forces retreated. This decree included factories, transportation networks, and supply depots. Not all the military commanders carried out this order, but in many combat zones this order resulted in a fight to the last man standing. The fact that the Germans refused to surrender, attempting to hold out for so long, was considered by many to be senseless. However, they forget that up until the very end of the war, the Nazi regime summarily executed defeatists and deserters, those who did not believe in the final victory of the Reich.

The Down Comforter and the Prophesy

The agony of peace. The sun goes down on Rome. Our day is gone. Clouds, darkness and danger have come, our deeds are done.

—Shakespeare, *Julius Caesar*

Several years before the outbreak of the war, when I was still a little girl, I heard the prophesy of a clairvoyant. Years later, this prophesy would come true, having foretold with phenomenal accuracy all the horror and terrible things to come. This is how the prophesy came about:

It was the second of February, in 1932 or 1933, which was not only the birthday of my great-aunt Marie but also the beginning of our annual feather party. According to an old tradition, each woman who had a daughter had to prepare feathers twice a year for the down comforter that eventually would be given as a dowry. Lots of women participated while their husbands fended for themselves until the evening. It took several days not only to pluck the feathers from the skins of ducks and geese we had consumed throughout the winter, but also to remove the quills so that the down was soft and pliable.

The feather party was always great fun, an event accompanied by laughter (restrained, though, lest we stir up the feathers), interesting stories, and tall tales. It was a chance for everyone to catch up with the local gossip and spread a few good jokes. Everyone there had to move around gently, to avoid scattering the mountain of feathers we had accumulated. The ladies allowed only one person at a time to speak. Even the air we exhaled was enough to send feathers flying around the room. During the gathering, feathers clung to our hair and stuck to our lips. In the evening, delicious food was set out on the table, to satisfy hungry appetites after a long day of laughter and gossiping. Every year, we kids begged to be allowed to remain with the ladies as they plucked all those feathers. We wanted to be part of the excitement and hear the funny stories and maybe even some of the sad ones. "Stay under the table, stop fidgeting, stop whining," my great-aunt always said with a raised index finger and a funny look on her face. "Or else," she said, pointing to doors and the way out with her thumb, as though she meant it.

Among the women this year at the feather party was a friend of my mother, a fortune-teller. According to rumors, she had contact with the supernatural world. She told us the following prophesy:

> In the not-too distant future there will come a time when
> two friends will meet at some place in Karlsbad. They
> will be amazed that both still live in this area. They will

say to each other, 'Where did you hide so you could go on living? Nobody is still here. All of our friends have gone.' They will tell each other what fate brought them, explaining what happened to the others, how they are the only ones who remain. They will talk about how the people in their town now speak another language and why every farm has a new owner.

We shook our heads and tried to imagine what kind of catastrophe could occur that would explain what the fortuneteller had just told us. Yet nothing came to mind that was as bad and horrible as the reality of the war that would come several years later.

Perspective: The Battle of Seelow Heights and the Battle for Berlin, 1945

One of the largest battles of the modern age took place over four days in April 1945 near Küstrin. The defensive line on the Seelow Heights was the last major defensive line outside Berlin. From April 19 on, when the slaughter on the fields of Küstrin ended, the road to Berlin—about 55 miles to the west—lay unchallenged. By April 23, Berlin was fully encircled, and the Battle in Berlin entered its last stage. Within two weeks, Adolf Hitler was dead and the war in Europe was effectively over.

Like most of the battles on the eastern front, this battle was characterized by its brutality and ghastly loss of human life. Once again, German soldiers confronted a superior opponent and fought to the last man standing in a futile attempt to prevent the enemy from taking more of the Fatherland. Although this fight delayed the advance of the Red Army, it proved senseless. Thousands of soldiers in the prime of their lives were slaughtered. Nobody bothered to bury their bodies, which rotted on the battlefield over several miles of countryside, emitting a sickening odor. Even more than seventy years later, as farmers plow their land, the remains of those who perished here will occasionally surface.

This senseless war, one that was supposed to build the Thousand-Year Reich, ended after almost six years with more than 60 million people killed—over three percent of the world's population at the time. Seventy years later, it still burdens the descendants of the war generation.

The drama of humanity is that it has no memory. Four decades after the end of the war, on May 8, 1985, Richard von Weizsäcker, the president of the Federal Republic of Germany, said in a speech to the Bundestag,

> The young and old generations must and can help each other to understand why it is vital to keep alive the memories. It is not a case of coming to terms with the past. That is not possible. It cannot be subsequently modified or made not to have happened. However, anyone who closes his eyes to the past is blind to the present. Whoever refuses to remember the inhumanity is prone to new risks of infection.

Despite the defeats on the eastern and western fronts, the extermination machinery at the concentration camps continued to run. In 1944, as the Allies approached the concentration camps for the first time, Nazi officials attempted to prevent the prisoners from falling into the hands of the "enemy." To conceal the atrocities, concentration camp guards shot some of the surviving prisoners. Other prisoners were burned in barns or driven to the gas chambers. Still other prisoners had to endure a death march in the opposite direction of the advancing front. Nevertheless, German efforts to kill the eyewitnesses to their inhumanity failed. In many camps, Russian, British, or American troops found survivors. Often the prisoners' health had deteriorated so far that despite intensive medical care, they succumbed to the effects of malnourishment and mistreatment days later. Former prisoners who managed to survive had to eventually fend for themselves and join the postwar flood of refugees that overwhelmed Europe.

During the Holocaust, the Nazi regime and its collaborators murdered about six million people of the Jewish faith, roughly one-third of the worldwide Jewish population. Millions of other civilians were also murdered by the regime—those considered inferior, undesirable, or dangerous. These included homosexuals, Gypsies

(Romani), Poles, the mentally ill and disabled, political opponents, and religious dissidents.

After the war many of those responsible for committing the atrocities attempted to justify what they had done by claiming they were but small cogs inside a giant machine, and that they had to follow orders. Yet the lack of moral courage on the part of thousands of government officials, including police officers and guards, fueled and enabled the extermination machine.

On April 25, 1945, American and Soviet soldiers meet for the first time at Torgau on the Elbe, a symbolic gathering at a river crossing, signaling the closure of an offensive on two fronts. The bitter, hard-fought battle for Berlin was underway, and the Soviet Red Army undertook it alone. General Dwight D. Eisenhower, the commander of American and British forces, decided not to participate in the battle for Berlin, a very controversial decision that questioned whether a city that the Soviets desperately wanted was worth the sacrifice of the lives of thousands of American soldiers.

Hitler's insanity became more and more obvious as the war progressed. In the last year of the war, he isolated himself from the outside world, rejecting any information that did not conform to his picture of how the war was supposed to progress. Supported by his team of loyal advisors, he lived in a Germany that drove victoriously toward world domination. Only in the last weeks of the war did he come to terms with reality and the inevitable defeat of the Reich. Meanwhile, his physical health deteriorated rapidly. He placed his last hopes on a miracle, trusting in wonder weapons that did not yet exist, such as the V-1 and V-2 rockets and jet fighters. He waited for Berlin's liberation by an invisible German Army. Hitler finally accepted defeat when Soviet troops were seen fighting just blocks away from his bunker underneath the Reich Chancellery, his headquarters in Berlin.

On April 30, 1945, Hitler committed suicide inside the *Führer* bunker in Berlin. Almost at the same time, Josef Göbbels, the Reich propaganda minister, took his own life, along with the lives of his six children and wife. Other high-ranking Nazi officials also escaped the clutches of the Allies by committing suicide. Just hours before Hitler shot himself in the underground bunker, he ordered the execution of his closest advisors, claiming they had gone behind his back and betrayed him.

On May 2, 1945, Berlin surrendered unconditionally to the Soviet Army. This was followed by the unconditional surrender of Germany to the Allied Forces on May 7, 1945, effective at midnight, May 8, 1945. The war in Europe finally came to an end and with it the so-called Thousand-Year Reich ended after just twelve years.

After the Red Army had taken the German parliament building (Reichstag) in Berlin, in a staged photoshoot, a Soviet soldier hoisted his country's flag on top of the roof of this nearly completely destroyed structure. Although similar photos were taken by several photographers at the time, a retouched photo by Yevgeny Khaldei was the one circulated worldwide, becoming an iconic image of the fall of Berlin. The original photo shows another soldier holding his foot to provide support. Present on both exposed arms of the second soldier were wristwatches that he "confiscated." The photo was edited to show the second soldier with only one wristwatch and added a different flag billowing dramatically in the wind.[42]

The deployment of large numbers of troops utilizing modern weaponry determined the outcome of the Second World War. Battles on a massive scale decided Germany's fate on the eastern front, where millions of soldiers and civilians were killed. Extensive aerial bombardment by the Allies also took the lives of hundreds of thousands of civilians in German cities. This war, including the effects of famine, disease, and crimes against humanity, depopulated large sections of Central and Eastern Europe. Worldwide, the war claimed the lives of more than 70 million soldiers and civilians. For individual countries, the numbers read as follows: in the Third Reich, 5.3 million soldiers and up to 3 million civilians perished;[43]

---

42   Sontheimer, Michael (May 7, 2008). "The Art of Soviet Propaganda: Iconic Red Army Reichstag Photo Faked". *Der Spiegel Online*. http://www. spiegel.de/international/europe/the-art-of-soviet-propaganda-iconic-red-army-reichstag-photo-faked-a-551972.html (accessed September 7, 2018).

43   *Statistisches Jahrbuch für die Bundesrepublik Deutschland 1960*, (Bonn: Statistisches Bundesamt (Destatis), 1961), 78-79.

in the Soviet Union, 9-11 million soldiers and more than 16 million civilians were killed;[44] in Poland the war claimed the lives of nearly 6 million people, about a sixth of the prewar population.[45] Those displaced throughout Europe, those who were eventually scattered to every corner of the world to rebuild their lives in poverty, should not be forgotten. In Germany an estimated 2 million refugees were listed as missing while attempting to flee the approaching Red Army.[46]

The End of the War, 1945

The long, hard winter with its cold temperatures and huge snowfall finally came to an end. Karlsbad, in the southeastern part of the Third Reich, became sandwiched between two fronts that were closing in on us. Rumors about the horrible fighting on the eastern front circulated, yet we did not receive any of these reports from official sources. On the contrary, the propaganda told us that the Third Reich continued to struggle against the threat of Bolshevism and world Jewry, that the setbacks were only temporary, and that we would emerge victorious.

The gap of contradiction between the slogans of a regime that expected us to fight to the last man and the information from other sources that told us of impending defeat could not have been any wider.

People we knew from East Prussia, former spa guests, sent us desperate letters, which arrived after much delay, describing their situation, their fears, and their plans to leave their homes to escape the advancing Red Army. They spoke of the thousands of refugees fleeing the horde that approached from the east, bringing murder,

---

44   Michael Ellman and S. Maksudov, 1994. "Soviet Deaths in the Great Patriotic War: A Note," *Europe-Asia Studies*, 46(4): 671-680.

45   Materski, Wojciech and Tomasz Szarota, *Poland 1939-1945: Personal Losses and Victims of Repression Under Two Occupations (Polska 1939–1945: Straty osobowe i ofiary represji pod dwiema okupacjami)* (Warsaw: Institute of National Remembrance (IPN), 2009), 9.

46   Christoph Bergner, Secretary of State in Germany's Bureau for Inner Affairs, outlined the stance of the respective governmental institutions in an interview with Deutschlandfunk (German Public Radio) on November 29, 2006.

plunder, and rape. Everything in the east was set afire, and the people had lost all that they had. They wrote to us and asked us for a place to hide. But how? We did not need these letters to remind us how desperate our own situation was, for even in Karlsbad, where we were comparatively sheltered from the fighting, the refugees had begun to arrive. These refugees hoped for safety, always a false and deceptive hope. After the train brought them to Karlsbad, they set up camp in any site available. Now the refugees lived among us, emaciated, wearing torn and tattered clothing—women, children, and the old, people who had lost everything, even their belief in their country and a *Führer* who had promised them heaven on earth and then so shamefully abandoned them.

We hoped with all our hearts that we ourselves would not have to flee. When logic told us that this was wishful thinking, we turned to superstition and the spirits. Mother owned an old chest that was locked with an unusual key. We imagined that this key could predict the future for us. After tying the key to a piece of string, we swung it like a pendulum to ease our fear of the unknown. Of course, the key predicted exactly what we wanted. When the first attempt was not successful, we simply tried again, until the pendulum had a positive swing. The perception that one can control future events is indeed the purest form of wishful thinking.

Now we were cut off from any outside news. We had no idea what had happened to our men. We had no idea what was going on in Berlin—no news whatsoever from my in-laws. Mail delivery stopped. Perhaps nothing new was occurring, or perhaps the postal system had collapsed. We simply did not know.

As though Mother Nature wanted to brag, we had a beautiful spring. The trees turned green, and the flowers bloomed. With refreshing air and sunshine that radiated everywhere, it was a spring we would remember for a long time. On Barbara's first birthday we decided to enjoy the warm weather and sunbathe for a while somewhere outside of Karlsbad. We sat in a small quiet clearing and listened as the birds in the green branches overhead sang, while rebuilding their nests from the previous year. It felt so warm as we looked up at a blue sky with a few clouds, such a stark contrast to the storm brewing inside my soul. I thought about the great battlefields upon which thousands of dead lay and the civilians who suffered the fear of arbitrary punishment from their government.

As beautiful as this spring was, we knew we were doomed. The war was approaching its final stages, which we knew based on the rumors that circulated as well as our own interpretation of the propaganda from the Reich. Now we wanted to know our fate. Would we survive?

Rumors surfaced that the Americans were approaching the city, the lesser of two evils, civilized troops from the West who would respect our homes. Of course, we had no idea of the postwar plans formulated at the international level among the leading political figures of that era, decisions made by those who won the war, decisions that would affect us. We essentially interpreted our own situation based on very little information, which was then enhanced by our hopes and desires and greased with hunches and rumors that we picked up from the refugees. Although it was illegal and very dangerous, some of our neighbors listened to the BBC with a *Volksempfänger* radio.[47] The consequences for this could be quite severe if an eavesdropper heard the broadcast and reported the owner of the radio to the police. Listening to a foreign news broadcast was punishable by deportation to a concentration camp or even summary execution, which became more and more frequent as the end of the war approached.

Some German soldiers, often young men and even boys, attempted to flee rather than endure the madness of fighting to the last man in a senseless final battle. The regime punished these men for desertion and hanged them from trees or street lanterns in Karlsbad without any great fuss. We could not escape the terrible, cruel reality. Karlsbad, a friendly and artistic city, once mercifully spared from the brutality of war, now had to pay its tribute. The

---

47   *Volksempfänger*, or "people's receiver," radios were inexpensive radios, mass-produced for the public. The radio was a relatively new technology in the 1930s, and the regime realized its potential for widespread distribution of propaganda. The radios were manufactured to receive only German stations, but foreign stations could be heard with the use of an external antenna.

wretched bodies, which hung for days on end, testified to the defeat of the Nazi regime. I wanted to shield Barbara from the bodies of these men, a sight that instilled fear and terror inside of me. We kept her inside the house, taking her out only into the garden for fresh air.

It must have been the beginning of May. Throughout the day air-raid sirens sounded the alarm. A wave of fighter bombers flew overhead as we hid in the cellar. We could feel the concussion of bombs that seemed to be exploding nearby. The ceiling over the cellar shook and vibrated as we endured these fearful hours. Karlsbad sustained several direct hits, and many buildings were destroyed. The air raid reduced our central train station to ash and rubble. When the attack began, a train had just pulled into the station to transfer wounded soldiers to one of the military hospitals. During the attack, the wounded men on board the train could do nothing but hope the bombing would be over quickly, especially since many could not move themselves to safety and avoid the explosions. Fortunately, none of the bombs hit the train. Once we were able to get to the soldiers, the other nurses and I caught a glimpse of the horror of war as we provided care to them. We saw how bomb fragments, sharp as a scalpel, had cut a path right through anything that stood in their way.

During the last weeks of the war, we noticed the collapse of military and civil authority within Karlsbad. High-ranking officers and leading political figures made themselves scarce. The soldiers who remained behind, mostly the wounded in hospitals, lacked leadership and direction. Those once in charge now feared falling into the hands of the approaching Allied armies. One day somebody knocked on the door of our apartment. I opened the door just a few inches, just to peer out and see who it could be. Standing there was a German soldier wearing a dust-covered uniform. "Would you happen to have any of your husband's suits that you could lend me?" he whispered. "You see, I've got to get back to Bavaria. There I can hide out. But with this uniform I'm not going to make it too far. They'll just gun me down." We didn't have a whole lot to offer him, but his request was sincere, and we did what we could. So off he went as a civilian, and to this day I just hope that he somehow survived.

While foraging around near Karlsbad for food, I was accompanied by a lady we knew, a Mrs. L. Suddenly, we heard the drone of low-flying aircraft approaching us, which meant only one thing: we were being targeted, in the hunt for anything that moved on the ground. We barely had a chance to jump into the ditch alongside the road before the aircraft flew directly over us. To my right and left, pieces of earth and gravel sprang up as bullets flew past my ears. The attack lasted maybe a few seconds, which seemed like an eternity in this situation. Only when the airplanes disappeared into the distance did I dare raise my head. Mrs. L., who was next to me in the ditch, had been hit by one of the bullets and was dead.

Desperately, frantically, in utter panic, I screamed. "Help! My God, she's dead! Help!" I ran toward the last of the houses that we had passed.

"For heaven's sake, woman, what happened to you?" called out one of the residents as I ran toward her.

Deeply shocked, shaking uncontrollably, and sobbing, I told her about what had happened to poor Mrs. L., how she had lost her life in such a horrible way, so close to the end of the war.

But then, like a light being switched off, I got myself together. I had to regain my composure and continue with the task at hand. I was alive. And others at home depended on me to place food on the table.

By now it had become quite difficult to scrounge up something edible. Food deliveries to Karlsbad had ceased. Agriculture was in dire straits. One could only hope that the farm animals, the ones that gave us meat, milk, and eggs, would have enough to eat so that they could continue to sustain us. During the last several months of the war, my mother had hoarded as many canned goods as she could lay her hands on, exactly for the situation we found ourselves in when Germany surrendered. As we ate the canned goods, we ignored the expiration dates. If the food wasn't moldy or rancid, it was considered edible. Even then, if you could just scrape away the mold or remove the spoiled part, the rest was good to go. The taste of freshly prepared vegetables now became a luxury, but in our situation, we had to take what we could get, and anything halfway edible was gladly consumed. We also found ourselves participating in the black market. From a Yugoslavian prisoner of war, my mother once bought some dry milk for Barbara.

There are so many details that keep coming back to me as I think about this time in my life. We did whatever it took to survive, to obtain the most basic necessities of life. But I don't seem to remember exactly what we talked about then. I remember just that we sat around the kitchen table and tried to distract each other from how desperate our situation had become.

My mother was in the last stages of her struggle with cancer. Now she could barely get around. Despite this, she didn't feel sorry for herself one bit or make a fuss about her ailing body. Her entire focus was on me and what little Barbara needed. We didn't know what had happened to my father or to Georg. We had no idea whether they were still alive. On the other hand, our day-to-day struggle to survive preoccupied us so much that we frankly had little time to worry about them. The adrenaline flowed constantly. This was the source of energy that mobilized our bodies into action, the power that kept us going, the drive behind our will to survive. Survival meant doing whatever it took to get the job done. In survival mode, life centered on eating, drinking, going to bed, sleeping, and waking up the next morning to continue the struggle. Life was plain and simple. Suddenly, one appreciated that which once had been taken for granted—the soft glow of white wine; the boldness of red wine; the music that spread throughout the room and lifted the heart; the book that you couldn't set down; the brilliant sunset out on the horizon that stirred the soul; the dog who thrust his cold, wet, slobber-covered nose into your face; the warm, quiet Sunday interrupted only by the soliloquy of singing birds; the aroma of freshly cut hay and poppy flowers alongside the road. For us, survival was the only thing that remained. Of course, that was difficult to face. More often than not, it left behind a feeling that made me sick to my stomach.

One morning at the beginning of May, we heard a commotion in the streets. Over the main highway leading into town, heavy equipment rolled in from Eger, a nearby town. We saw American troops forcing their way into the city. Although we still had not heard of Hitler's suicide, the Americans had obviously won the war.

They seemed indifferent and acted superior to everyone else, which is perhaps the right of victors. At least they treated us comparatively well, not like a herd of cattle, but rather like people.

After several days the American troops left, replaced by Soviet troops, many of whom entered Karlsbad in horse-drawn wagons. They were fresh, unused troops specially chosen for this assignment. Crude and uncivilized, many came from the eastern part of the Soviet Union. They knew but three words of German, words they had mastered quite well: *Frau* (woman), *komm* (come), and *Uri* (wristwatch).

What a paradox. Some Soviet soldiers were dangerous, and others had a heart of gold. One day at the end of May, I set out to buy some milk with Barbara in my arms. As I exited the apartment building, I placed Barbara down on the ground outside the door so that I could turn around and pull the baby stroller through the doorway. Suddenly, a rough-looking Soviet soldier appeared, a huge man whose face had distinct Asian features. He looked at Barbara and me. Then he snatched my daughter and ran around the corner. My heart pounded. I was struck with terror. I didn't know what to do. Before I could think of what to do, he came back with Barbara and a large can of milk. He attempted to explain something to me with words and hand gestures, but my knowledge of Russian was very limited. I could not completely understand what he said, but I caught the gist—that he would return tomorrow with another can of milk. For five days in a row, while he stayed in a neighboring house, he brought us a can of milk. He wanted nothing from me. For us the milk was a gift from heaven. I learned how to make cheese from the extra milk, which I exchanged for other groceries.

Not all our encounters with the Soviet soldiers were as pleasant. One day, while I was standing in line in front of a store with some other women, a Soviet soldier strolled alongside us and noticed the watch on my arm. With a grin, he said, "*Uri!*" I wasn't in a position to refuse, so I handed over the wristwatch. He seemed fascinated by it, staring at the watch face, twisting the armband back and forth. Suddenly, he grabbed my hand, bent over slightly, and kissed it. This was the strangest hand kiss I ever received.

We left the house only to obtain groceries, mostly bread and milk. It was almost impossible to obtain anything else. We planned our shopping and errands so that several women left together, at the same time—safety in numbers. Other than that, we barricaded ourselves inside our homes. We repeatedly heard stories of how the Soviet soldiers attacked and raped women, yet somehow in Karlsbad the occupation soldiers behaved differently. Maybe the picturesque surroundings quelled any desire to seek revenge. Who knows? I am just glad we were spared from this violence. Today I am frequently asked to talk about my experiences during this period of history. I know from my discussions with other women about the brutality that occurred. Back then I did not appreciate the fact that the women of Karlsbad received better treatment. I thought only that another day had occurred without violence, and this seemed good enough.

Perspective: A New Government and the Return of Beneš

As soon as the war ended Beneš returned to Czechoslovakia to reassume the role of president. But one year earlier, Beneš corresponded with Stalin and obtained his support for the reestablishment of Czechoslovakia and its former government. In exchange, Beneš pledged his support for Stalin's plans for Soviet influence, including making the new Czechoslovakia a communist state. In February 1945, Beneš gave himself legislative power over the yet-to-be-formed Czechoslovakia in anticipation of the Soviet capture of the territory. Soon thereafter, he traveled to Moscow and followed the Red Army's progress westward with eager anticipation.

Beneš' hatred for Germans and other non-Czech minorities and his thirst for power grew exponentially while in exile. While in London he formed a diabolical plan for freeing Czechoslovakia of all ethnic minorities that was just short of extermination. In 1944 he gave a speech in London in which he stated, "We have to get rid of all the Germans who plunged a dagger in the back of the Czechoslovak State in 1938."[48]

---

48   Beneš in broadcast, quoted by Louise W. Holborn (ed). *War and Peace*

On April 5, 1945, in the northeastern city of Kaschau (Košice), Beneš proclaimed the program of the self-appointed Czech government, which included elements of barbarous oppression, inhumane persecution, and immediate expulsion of the non-Czech, non-Slovak, and non-Allied population of the restored Czechoslovak Republic.

Starting with the Kaschau Proclamation, Edvard Beneš issued a total of 143 decrees, known as the "Beneš Decrees," including 15 in 1945 that deprived ethnic Germans and Hungarians of their civil liberties and property rights:

> On May 19, 1945, invalidated real property acquisitions made by Germans, Hungarians (Magyars), traitors and collaborators (GHTC) that occurred during the wartime occupation; these assets were placed under national control.
>
> On June 21, 1945, GHTC agricultural holdings were confiscated.
>
> On July 20, 1945, GHTC agricultural holdings were transferred to Czech, Slovak, and other Slavic farmers.
>
> On August 2, 1945, German and Hungarian peoples were stripped of their citizenship and were given refugee identity cards along with white armbands that they were to wear on the outside of their coats to identify them as German. By agreement with the Allies at the Potsdam Conference on this same date, ethnic Germans and Hungarians will be expelled from Czechoslovakia.
>
> On August 23, 1945, social benefit eligibility for GHTC people was revoked affecting the disabled, elderly and poor.
>
> On September 19, 1945, anyone who had lost citizenship under previous Decrees was subject to forced labor.

Aims of the United Nations, Vol. 2: From Casablanca to Tokyo Bay, January 1, 1943 – September 1, 1945. (Boston, MA: World Peace Foundation, 1948) p. 1036.

On October 19, 1945, all bank deposits belonging to GHTC people were confiscated.

On October 25, 1945, all real property belonging to GHTC people was confiscated.

On October 27, 1945, persons deemed untrustworthy were subject to indefinite incarceration.

Between July 17 and August 2, 1945, heads of state from the United States, the Soviet Union, and Great Britain met at the Cecilienhof, a palace in Potsdam, Germany, near Berlin. The Soviets made special arrangements to have an imposing table flown in from Moscow for the conference. President Harry S. Truman represented the United States. Joseph Stalin represented the Soviet Union. Winston Churchill represented Great Britain until July 28, when he had to relinquish this task to Clement Atlee, the newly elected prime minister. Together they finalized plans for the division of postwar Europe, including territorial boundaries and zones of occupation. They also set in motion a plan that ultimately expelled and resettled three million ethnic Germans from Czechoslovakia and millions of German citizens residing in territory that Poland had just acquired through the redrawing of its borders. The Polish border with Germany was shifted about 150 miles to the west, with the countries now separated by the Oder and Neisse Rivers.

At Potsdam the Allies decided to resettle millions of ethnic Germans without considering the logistics such an undertaking would require and the human misery it would entail, nor did they consider that the expulsion would occur starting in late summer on into the early winter. It proved nearly impossible to properly feed, clothe, house, and provide medical care for those who were suddenly uprooted and sent to the nearest border crossing. The Allies made this decision without considering that many of those expelled from Czechoslovakia and Poland were deeply rooted in the communities where they lived, having ancestors who moved into these regions several hundred years prior. Furthermore, most of those expelled did not participate in the atrocities committed by Nazi Germany.

When the war in Europe came to an end, chaos reigned throughout the continent as a result of the destroyed infrastructure, ineffective government, and the flood of refugees. In many areas, the war had reduced roads to rubble and disrupted rail service between cities. In many European countries, hyperinflation occurred as currencies became worthless. Poor sanitation sparked waves of epidemics. As territorial boundaries were redrawn, and expulsion orders issued, millions of Germans, who fled mostly on foot or on carts, became the targets of revenge by those once oppressed by the Nazi regime.

First at Yalta and now at Potsdam, Stalin received approval for using German prisoners to rebuild the Soviet Union. This was viewed as an additional "reparations payment" in addition to the $20 billion reparation imposed on Germany.[49]

What they did not discuss was how Stalin would obtain the manpower, that is, the prisoners, needed for rebuilding the Soviet Union. Not only were German prisoners of war utilized for this task, but also an estimated 874,000 German civilians were taken from sections of the former Reich.[50] At the end of the war, the Soviet Union transported many of these civilians to remote and distant areas behind the Ural Mountains, where they undertook the rebuilding of the Soviet Union under the worst and most inhumane conditions.

In the middle of August 1945, the Czech government began the systematic expulsion of ethnic Germans from Czechoslovakia. Street by street, homes belonging to ethnic Germans were cleared out. Some of the younger adult Germans were separated from their families and sent to work on Czech farms for the harvest. The rest had to find new shelter elsewhere, with friends or relatives if they were lucky, or maybe a room rented with several others in ever smaller zones. With the transportation network in disarray, it would be several months before the mass expulsion could be enforced, but already real property and businesses of ethnic Germans were being taken by the state and given to ethnic Czechs and their financial assets in banks were seized by the government.

---

49   More than $280 billion in 2018 dollars.

50   Böhme, Kurt W. *Gesucht Wird—Die Dramatische Gesichte des Suchdienstes* (München: Suddeutsche Verlag, 1965), 275.

Reprisals against ethnic Germans started to increase, carried out by those not constrained by the rule of law. The tables had been turned. Now the Germans had to surrender their homes and businesses. From Prague, the capital of the resurrected Czechoslovakia, came hate-filled tirades accusing the Germans of acts that only a small minority had committed. Czech militias were quickly formed, free to do anything they pleased against ethnic Germans without fear of punishment.

Today, the Beneš Decrees remain in effect, never having been repealed by the communist Czech government or the new, free government that emerged in 1989. Although intense debates still occur on the international level as to whether the decrees violated human rights standards, very few within the Czech government will discuss the matter. Surprisingly, the Czech Republic was allowed to enter the European Union with these laws still on the books, although respect for human rights is normally a prerequisite for admission.[51] The United States and international human rights organizations continually bring to public attention human rights abuses in other countries, but the discrimination against ethnic Germans and Hungarians in the Czech Republic has been largely ignored. In the years since the end of the war, the Federal Republic of Germany has awarded compensation to many of the Sudeten Germans, but none has come from either the former communist Czechoslovakia or the current Czech Republic. Hungary and organizations such as Sudeten German Homeland Association (Sudetendeutsche Landsmannschaft) continue to apply pressure on the Czech government but no action has yet resulted.

Indeed, President Miloš Zeman of the Czech Republic (elected in 2013) has stated repeatedly that the expulsion of the Sudeten Germans was just. In an interview on April 23, 2013, to the Austrian

---

51   The Treaty of Lisbon (initially known as the Reform Treaty) is a treaty that was signed by the European Union member states on December 13, 2007 and entered into force on December 1, 2009. It amends the Treaty on European Union (TEU; Maastricht, 1992) and the Treaty Establishing the European Community (TEC; Rome, 1957). The Czech Republic was the last country to ratify the Lisbon Treaty on November 13, 2009. To ensure ratification by the Czech government, the Czech Republic was allowed to opt out of certain provisions of the treaty. This included being allowed to deny claims from Second World War expellees.

Press he said, "When a citizen of some country collaborates with a country that has occupied his state, expulsion is a subtler [form of] punishment than, for example, a death penalty." The Czech president also argued that the expulsion was not an act of collective punishment because an "estimated ten percent" of the Sudeten Germans who were opponents of the Nazis were allowed to stay.[52] Scholars and political commentators have argued that it was collective punishment because the burden of proof lay with the individual rather than the group, and the brutality of the expulsion would be considered a war crime today.

The Expulsion Order and Exodus, 1945

The Beneš Decrees could not have come at a worse time for us; the situation for us Sudeten Germans became even more desperate. The government had further reduced our food ration. We now stood in the same shoes as the Jews who had been confined in the ghettos by the Nazi regime. Nobody could survive on the meager food ration allocated to us. The black market represented our only hope. For Barbara, her ration of milk amounted to one glass every two days. How could we possibly feed her? Our dear friends, farmers we had known for a long time, helped us survive. With them we could trade the unimportant things in life, such as jewelry, for the essentials.

As though the attempt to starve us was not enough, we faced discrimination in each of the smallest areas of everyday life. The new Czech government banned us from using any public transportation or gathering in public. The government closed all the German schools. Payments to Germans ceased, and their property was confiscated. To identify us as ethnic Germans in public, the new government required us to wear an armband indicating we belonged to this segment of the population. Increasingly, we faced verbal abuse, and some people spat on us. Some of us were physically assaulted or chased.

---

52   K. S., "The Expulsion of the Sudeten Germans Is Still Raw," *The Economist*, May 7, 2013.

I remember the supply missions that took me outside of Karlsbad to forage for food, a trek of six or seven miles on foot just to obtain something to eat. We had to avoid the main roads. Instead, we detoured along the back roads and through the forest to maintain a low profile and remain out of sight.

One day I left the protection of the woods to take a shortcut on a narrow back road. My feet ached, and I felt totally exhausted. I just wanted to get home. This was careless. Suddenly, as I stepped onto the road, I recoiled back in terror. Directly in front of me, like a bronze statue, was a huge Cossack riding a giant horse. He stared at me, and I froze. I first thought about the cheese, bread, and butter I carried with me. I had just exchanged jewelry for these things, and now everything would be lost. Then I fired off a quick prayer to heaven. *Dear God, just let him take the food and leave me alone. Don't let him hurt me.* On this lonely road I was completely at the man's mercy.

What happened next was totally different from what I feared. Motionless, he continued to look at me. After tapping two fingers on the brim of his hat and quickly nodding his head, he kicked his horse and galloped away. I just stood there as he disappeared around the next curve in the road. Although very relieved, I could not help but cry for I was so terrified. I still sobbed even after I had returned home.

The cancer was progressing, limiting my mother's strength. But she would rally each day to ease the burden on me. Meanwhile, rumors from the peace talks at Potsdam filtered down to us, international diplomacy that would decide our future and seal our fate. With horror we heard that the Allies approved the Beneš Decrees.

We didn't dare to leave our houses, but the dwindling food supply started to worry me. I knew, as we all did, that only the smallest excuse was necessary to trigger mob violence against the new enemy, the ethnic Germans. In Karlsbad, for reasons that I cannot explain, ethnic Germans faced comparatively little hostility. However, in many towns and rural areas of Czechoslovakia, the picture was quite different. In Aussig Fischern, Komotau, and Tetschen-Bodenbach, Czech militia groups roamed freely to wreak havoc. Of course, we should not forget Prague. Once again, the infamous Pankrác Prison became the focal point of the arbitrary abuse of ethnic Germans.

Nobody bothered to help us. Even the Western Allies looked the other way. Only after two months or so, when eyewitness reports finally surfaced in the British press, did the Western Allies finally insist that the Czech government follow the conditions imposed for the expulsions, which were supposed to be "orderly and humane."

Sometime during this period, as the expulsion was underway, someone rang our doorbell. Startled, knowing it could not be a relative or one of our friends, I opened the door. Five men from the Czech militia stood at the entrance to our apartment. I asked politely in Czech what they wanted, and without much hesitation they forced their way into our home. As I held Barbara in my arms, they began to ransack our home, looking for anything of value. My heart pounded, and my hands shook violently. Suddenly, the leader of the squad reached behind the heating stove and retrieved Georg's military pistol, a Walther PP. According to the new laws, which subjected Germans to arbitrary and discriminatory treatment, he could have shot me and the rest of my family on the spot. Fortunately, not everybody behaved like an animal. Looking at me sternly and without saying a word, he discreetly hid the pistol inside his jacket. None of the other men saw this.

My face must have been as white as a sheet. Shaking like a leaf, I almost fainted. This was my second terrifyingly close call with death. How many more times would he allow me to defeat him? The men finished looting, and as the others departed with their spoils, the leader of the squad remained behind. He whispered to me in a soft voice, "I didn't see a thing, and neither did you. Auf Wiedersehen." My guardian angel must have been working overtime on that day.

Despite all the displays of government hatred toward ethnic Germans, on a personal level many of the Czechs did not view us as the enemy. Of course, they intended to move into the apartments and houses we had to forfeit, but still they remained civil toward us, and some were even sympathetic. Yet during this time I had almost no contact with Gerda, the friend from my childhood who had a Czech father and German mother.

One of the Czechs I knew gave me a bit of insider information: our neighborhood was next on the list for "cleanup actions." One certainly could not ignore such a warning. Hurriedly, we packed our things in a rucksack. That same evening, we made our way over to Aunt Marie's apartment on the edge of the city. Mother was so weak that she could barely move, yet with a little bit of cunning, I was able to obtain an ambulance, something remarkable because as ethnic Germans we really couldn't expect such help.

We could not stay with Aunt Marie for any length of time. We knew that this was just a short-term solution, that the Czech authorities would eventually force us to leave. Most of our possessions remained in the apartment, which we needed to retrieve if possible. Compounding the hopelessness of the situation was my mother's deteriorating condition. I can still remember that evening as I sat with Aunt Marie in her kitchen. I felt so lonesome, like a nomad in a bare and desolate land. We had already brought Mother to bed, and Barbara was fast asleep. From time to time Aunt Marie shook her head in frustration. She kept asking, with increasing urgency, "My God, what's going to happen to us?"

Then she asked me where I planned to go, and I responded, "Where am I supposed to go? We can't stay in Czechoslovakia. One thing is for sure—we will not survive here. But for heaven's sake, where do we go? We don't have anybody."

Then suddenly an idea came to me. Georg! I belonged to him. That I knew, even though he wasn't around. But it seemed hard to believe he could still be alive. We had heard how the Red Army had overrun all the German positions. We had heard about horrific battles, where afterward thousands of dead bodies littered the ground. We knew that some of the Soviet soldiers thought it was great fun to collect souvenirs from bodies of dead Germans, such as identity cards. A feeling of impending doom set in, and I felt alone in the universe. Finally, I fell asleep.

Since I was a little girl, I have always found a way to overcome any obstacle thrown in my way. After the shock of the cleanup action wore off, I began to consider a possible solution to our dilemma. For a while I sat there just tossing ideas back and forth in my head. Then I made a decision: to pay our new chief of police a visit.

I went to the police station and waited patiently to talk to the chief of police. To be on the safe side, I brought along a note from my mother's doctor, explaining that she had a terminal illness and not much time to live. Finally, the guard let me through the door. Once I entered his office, I handed the doctor's note to the chief. I then told him the reason that we needed to return to our home. This was the only place where I could properly take care of my mother. After quietly listening to my request, nodding his head from time to time, the chief scribbled something on a piece of paper. "All right, you can stay there, but only until the final order comes for you to leave the country. After that nothing can be done for you. If you have any problems before then, please feel free to come and see me." This was unexpected, that he would take pity on us and understand our situation. Sometimes human decency allows us to bend the rules. This was an important learning experience for me: judge the person, not the group.

I felt so happy after having gained a little more time for us. We returned to our apartment. And who cared about tomorrow? Today was important, the here and now.

Now it was fall. Like a squirrel preparing for the approaching winter, I attempted to hoard as much food as possible. I had no idea when we would have to leave Karlsbad. From the forest I collected wood and mushrooms. I begged potatoes from the farmers. I also managed to cook up a huge pot of rosehip marmalade. During the war my mother had managed to stash fifty pounds of sugar—thank goodness! I used most of it, keeping just a little for the trip to Berlin. I also made cheese and collected acorns, which I roasted. It's simply amazing what you can achieve with a little imagination.

In the middle of October 1945, the letter that I had dreaded finally arrived. Within ten days I had to leave Karlsbad and Czechoslovakia. Because of her Austrian origins and failing health, Mother could remain in her home. I gladly would have taken her with me, but in her condition such a journey was simply out of the question.

I now had the citizenship of my husband. What a joke! Nobody had the faintest clue where he might be or even whether he still lived. On top of that, I had no idea whether my in-laws in Berlin had survived or whether their house still stood. For all I knew, Lichterfelde, the area in Berlin where they lived, could have been destroyed. Perhaps only a sea of rubble waited for me, and my in-laws were among the thousands of missing Germans. I had no means of assessing the situation in Berlin. We still depended on rumors to keep us informed of events outside of Karlsbad. Mail service, working telephones and newspapers had become a thing of the past.

This time in my life seemed so surreal. Sometimes it was as though I stood next to myself, staring at someone who was being dragged through the currents of social collapse, helpless to shape whatever outcome was ahead. It was just one problem after another, and Mother's failing health compounded everything else that was happening. The reality of the situation was that I had to leave. Fortunately, my godmother offered to take care of my mother until I could return. I didn't know how I was going to do it, but for me it was abundantly clear: I would return to Karlsbad to be with my mother during the last days of her life. But for now, priority number one was taking my daughter to safety.

On October 25, 1945, I left Karlsbad to comply with the order issued by the Czechoslovakian Ministry for the Expulsion of Former Citizens of German Descent.

We were allowed to bring only twenty kilos (forty-four pounds) of personal effects with us, which was comparatively generous considering what had happened to many of the early-expulsion Germans. This small allowance was due to the intervention of the Allies who enforced international laws on humane expulsion. The first groups to be thrown out had not been allowed to take anything with them. Still, it seemed such a pittance relative to my family's possessions.

Early in the morning, I said goodbye to my ailing mother and gave my relatives a final wave. Wearing a rucksack and holding a suitcase with one hand and my daughter with the other, I dragged myself to the train station under the supervision of heavily armed policemen.

Nobody would ever describe the train that transported us out of Czechoslovakia as luxurious. We sat inside unheated cars, many of which had broken windows.

The Move to Berlin and the Trip Back, 1945

I did my best to keep Barbara warm. She was wrapped inside a small sleeping bag lined with rabbit fur, the same material used for the mittens protecting her tiny hands from the cold. I was terrified as I looked out the train window onto the countryside that sped past. Barbara's eyes were wide with worry, and I am sure she felt the same as the adults around her. Occasionally, the train let out a whistle, a sound that carried my despair straight to heaven. That is how I left the town of my birth, the place I called home, and the end of my life in Bohemia.

Heading toward the German border, the train made numerous stops along the way so that additional refugees could board. The train cars were not furnished with toilets, and consequently, we had to take care of our business at the train depots during the few minutes that the trains waited there to load additional passengers. On the train we were given nothing to eat or drink, and perhaps this decision was made to prevent the need to use the toilet in the first place. The further north the train traveled, the more the train cars filled with refugees. Former German soldiers on crutches also joined us while the Czech police stood guard, preventing those on board from leaving except to use the toilet facilities or find the nearest bush.

Around twilight we reached Johanngeorgenstadt, a small German town near the border with Czechoslovakia, in the Ore Mountains. The first day's journey had taken us a little over 20 miles from Karlsbad, and this was the end of the line. From here our next train was uncertain, but it would not come until tomorrow at the earliest.

In Johanngeorgenstadt, the Red Cross had set up a camp for the expelled Germans, which was like a harbor providing refuge from the rough and stormy sea. Small groups of young women congregated together. Many desperately attempted to search for their husbands or other loved ones, hoping that someone out there still waited for them.

The Red Cross provided temporary housing for us inside a small room that Barbara and I shared with three other women and their children. We must have had the greatest luck on earth. This room was furnished with a small stove, something totally unexpected. We could prepare a warm meal and heat milk for our children. Barbara emptied her bottle in record speed. Afterward, I could not pry her tiny fingers from it. Once someone has tasted something delicious, like the milk she had just inhaled, it is difficult to quell the expectation for more of the same.

To make all of us a little more comfortable, one of the ladies managed to get a hold of a metal bathtub, and we were able to wash the children. Soon they were fast asleep, dead tired after a long and stressful day. We slept on makeshift beds, and little Barbara held my finger tightly, not wanting to let go. After the children were settled in and sound asleep, we women talked into the early morning hours. Each of us felt uncertain about the future, yet we also felt there was still hope. The war was now over, and things could only get better, even if we had just lost our homes.

About 200 miles more to go and an even more stressful day awaited Barbara and me. We were expected to figure out for ourselves the connecting trains to our final destination. We got to the station very early, before sunrise, and then sat around for hours, waiting for a train that would take us farther north. Eventually we boarded and were on our way, but we had to endure numerous detours because bombs had rendered many sections of track impassable. We would get off the train, carry our things without assistance, and then board another train some distance away. Sometimes it was a few hundred feet further on and sometimes quite a long way. Worse, the new train might be going east or west, not north.

A little before one o'clock in the afternoon we reached a major tributary of the Elbe River (after so many train changes, I don't remember where it might have been). Now we faced another obstacle. The station where we needed to catch another train was on the other side of the river, and the bridge over the river had been blown apart. A temporary suspension bridge had been erected to permit foot traffic from one bank to the next. This arrangement seemed precarious. As people crossed over, the wobbly bridge swayed side to side. I fired off another quick prayer to heaven. After putting on the rucksack, I grabbed my suitcase with one hand and Barbara with the other. There I was, making that death-defying crossing over deep and treacherous water, when suddenly I heard someone screaming at me. I am almost certain that I would have fallen into the water if not for a Soviet soldier who ran toward me from the other side of the river, causing the rickety bridge to sway even more violently. "Halt! Halt!" he kept saying, until he met me somewhere in the middle. This was so frightening that I considered jumping into the water below rather than postponing the inevitable plunge to my demise. When the soldier caught up to me, he took the suitcase from my hand. If he wanted to steal it, he could have it! At this very moment I had other priorities, like getting off that bridge. Even today I have nightmares about that bridge and falling into the water below. But, the soldier did not steal my bag. When we reached the other side, he set the suitcase down, nodded his head, and disappeared.

The remaining part of my journey was just as traumatic. Now the train cars were packed beyond full with other refugees carrying everything they owned. On top of that, we could not put any distance behind us because the locomotives often had only enough fuel to reach the next station. As the day wore on, I became even more discouraged. I can't quite remember all the train stations I got to know, going so slowly on my journey that it seemed I was making no progress at all. Berlin was still a long distance away. Now at the end of my rope, and while waiting for yet another train, I just wanted to cry. Then a Soviet supply train rolled into the station, idling on the tracks for several minutes and providing me an opportunity to come up with a new strategy. I pleaded with the supply train's conductor, "Please, please! Can you help me get to Berlin?" At first, I didn't think he would believe my story—or care, for that matter—and then suddenly he stepped aside and let me climb aboard. This is how I completed the final part of my journey, one that would bring me to my in-laws in Berlin.

When I think back on what happened, I realize how fortunate I was; I could have been one of the thousands of women who were taken in the direction of Russia, killed, and then thrown from the train, their bodies left to rot alongside the track. You really couldn't trust the word of a man, especially if he was a recent enemy. But by luck, the conductor treated me well. He offered me something to drink and found a small corner of the train where Barbara could sleep undisturbed for a while. At one of the stops, he managed to steal a box from the luggage compartment, which he handed over to me with instructions that it was for the little one. After reaching Berlin, I would discover the treasure inside: potatoes, carrots, and a thick piece of bacon.

In midafternoon we finally arrived at the Anhalter train station in Berlin, now mostly a pile of rubble, one of many such piles in postwar Berlin. The train conductor, a Soviet officer, the one who had already helped me so much, arranged for a horse-drawn wagon to take me the several miles to Lichterfelde, where my in-laws lived. A grumpy Soviet drove the wagon.

I had hoped that when we got to the station in Berlin that I could get some water for Barbara and myself. I had milk powder but nothing to mix it with. She alternated between whining and crying, not understanding why I didn't have something for her to drink. I had not expected the station to be a mound of rubble, but there was nothing I could do about the water situation on the train either. The grumpy Soviet was likely made even grumpier by the upset child, but alas, he had no water to offer either.

Underway we endured a bumpy ride that jolted us side to side. Even though I was dead tired, I could not help but notice the devastation that surrounded us. Berlin, the capital of the former Third Reich, lay in ruins. It seemed that not a single house had survived the war. I remember seeing people living among these ruins, cooking something to eat over a fire between piles of rubble. They were mostly women, children, and the elderly, without any means of bathing, insufficiently clothed, without shoes in many cases, and emaciated from the lack of food. As we made our way, it seemed that a pile of rubble stood along every yard of this stretch. Shortly before arriving in Lichterfelde, I noticed a change in scenery. Somehow this part of the city had been spared from the devastation caused by the carpet bombing. The buildings remained mostly intact, barely damaged except for broken windows.

During the conference that took place in Potsdam in the summer of 1945, the Allies divided Europe into Soviet and Western spheres of influence. After redrawing the German borders, the Allies divided Germany into four occupation zones under the control of Great Britain, the United States, France, and the Soviet Union. Berlin, which lay in the middle of the Soviet occupation zone, was also divided among the four occupation powers. Similarly, Austria was divided into four occupation zones, and Vienna also became a divided city within the Soviet zone.[53]

The American occupation force in Berlin had established its headquarters in Lichterfelde. Having just won the war, the American army was certainly not going to house its soldiers among the ruins. What a difference compared to the other city districts in Berlin! American soldiers leaned against their jeeps, which were parked alongside the streets. Glen Miller and his swing music blared from the radio. They wore immaculate uniforms and looked very sharp—clean-shaven, hair combed. They smelled like aftershave or cologne. Some casually smoked a cigarette, others told jokes, and some just whistled a happy tune to themselves. Their demeanor spoke volumes—we won the war!

Since many of the homes in Lichterfelde had survived the war, they were confiscated by the American army for office space and housing. Unbeknownst to me, the Americans also had moved into the large house belonging to my in-laws.

The grumpy Soviet stopped the wagon in front of the house. He became even more disgruntled when I asked him to help me unload my bags from the wagon. Immediately after he dropped my bags on the stoop, he headed back to the Soviet zone. Some GIs who were standing around stared at us. I must have been a strange sight, especially after that awful journey from Karlsbad. As I approached the doorway to the house belonging to my in-laws, someone wearing a uniform blocked my way. I stuttered a bit, pointing to the door, and he just shook his head emphatically back and forth. After directing me to leave my bag outside, he led us into the house, to my father-in-law's study, where I saw an American staff officer lounging in an armchair, his feet on the desk. On

---

53   Whereas Germany was divided into East and West Germany in 1949, Austria remained under joint occupation of the Western Allies and of the Soviet Union until May 15, 1955. Austria agreed to perpetual neutrality to gain its independence.

this desk there was a large regal replica statuette of Michelangelo's *David*, upon which the officer conveniently placed his army cap.

In broken English I asked for the owner of the house.

The American officer, moving the wad of chewing gum from one cheek to the next, looked at me rather coldly and uttered, "Oh, you mean the communist?"

I was stunned. I thought I must not have heard him correctly. My father-in-law may have been a lot of things, but he was no communist. Then the officer said, "Ya know, he's always dressing in red, so he's got to be a communist."

I learned later that when the Americans took the house, my father-in-law had been allowed to gather only a few things before he and my mother-in-law were assigned other housing. The only piece of warm clothing that he could grab was a red pullover, which he wore whenever he went out in public, and the red made him look suspicious.

I found the officer intimidating, and for this reason I made the mistake of responding to him in Czech. Suddenly, all hell broke loose. He jumped to his feet, screaming, "The Soviets have infiltrated the building!"

"But … but …" I said frantically, trying to find a way out of this mess with the few English words that I knew, trying to explain that I was the owner's daughter-in-law from Czechoslovakia. After a while the officer finally calmed down and realized I wasn't some secret Soviet agent. Another GI, much calmer and probably somewhat brighter than his commanding officer, led me over to the apartment where my in-laws were housed. Barely able to keep myself standing on two feet, I knocked on the door several times. My mother-in-law finally opened the door. She didn't say a word but just stood there and looked at me. Several seconds later, I staggered into the room. Timidly and with hesitation she took Barbara from my arms, her first and only grandchild, whom she had never seen before.

We only wanted to sleep. After a few bites of bread, my daughter bedded down in a large chair and fell fast asleep before her head even hit the upholstery.

During that first night in Berlin, I slept on the floor. The Americans had assigned my in-laws to a small apartment belonging to an old woman. There certainly wasn't room for two more, but I didn't care. Somehow, I had made it to Berlin and had found my family. I was now safe. Things could only get better. Of course, all these changes were traumatic for little Barbara, and she required several days to become accustomed to the new environment. We all tried to give her a bit of extra attention to ease the transition, including Mrs. Stiller, the apartment owner.

The first days of my new life in Berlin seemed like the last days of my life in Karlsbad, with the desperate search for food and the hunt for the rations cards to which I was entitled. Once again, the need to acquire food consumed my thoughts, as well as the need to find a roof over my head before the snowflakes started to land on my face. This extinguished all other concerns, and I didn't have any room left inside me to worry about Georg or my father. During this time the only things I felt were an empty stomach, cold hands, and sore feet, my constant companions.

I had left Karlsbad with about 10,000 Reichsmarks in my pocket. Upon arriving in Berlin and looking out the train window, seeing the devastation that the war had left behind, I had thought to myself that with this huge sum of money, I could buy half the city. How wrong I was! Reality had set in when I had to pay 1,000 marks for the ride from the Anhalter train station to Lichterfelde.

After several days of eating and sleeping better, I became restless. My mother was dying. I had to return to Karlsbad—there wasn't any other choice—even though I had no idea whether she was still alive.

One morning I said to my mother-in-law, "You have to do something for me, Margarethe."

She gave me a puzzled look.

Then I dropped the bombshell. "You'll have to look after Barbara for a few days."

Margarethe was stunned. "Now what are you up to? You are here in our home waiting for your husband. What else could you want?"

Somehow, I managed to keep my composure. "I am going back to Karlsbad."

The look on Margarethe's face was one of shock and disapproval. Then Max, my father-in-law, had something to say. "Well, you're going to have to take Barbara with you. We don't even have enough food for ourselves, and certainly not enough to feed her."

Now it was time to talk business. "First of all, she's *your* granddaughter. Second, if I don't make the trip, you'll never see the family silver again. I can only carry it back with two free hands."

During the war Max had imagined that a bomb might fall through the ceiling of his house and destroy everything he owned, including a set of precious Russian silver flatware that he treasured. While visiting my in-laws early during our marriage, Georg and I brought the silver set to Karlsbad, where it was well hidden in our apartment along with Margarethe's fur coat.

After the First World War, Max had smuggled the silver set out of Poland. I knew that he was very fond of it and that it was an asset. He sat there for a while, pondering the matter inside his head, and then finally relented. Even today as an old woman, I remember how worried I was to leave the little child in war-torn Berlin with people who had no love for her, and yet I pushed the thoughts away so that I could see my mother before she died.

Times have changed, and the fashion of fine silver cutlery and porcelain china has been replaced by less formal tableware. Today, my granddaughter owns the silver set, which lies unceremoniously in a cabinet of her house. It's funny—something for which one person is willing to risk his life, the next will allow to remain hidden and disregarded, accumulating dust.

The Journey Back to Karlsbad, 1945

Two days later, on November 12, 1945, I began the train journey back to Karlsbad. Right before leaving, I purchased a bottle of whiskey and several packs of cigarettes from an American soldier. I didn't realize how useful these two items would become.

The train would take me via Dresden, where I was to change to a Soviet military train to Tečin and then, with some luck, to Karlsbad. To my surprise, the train had windows—a rare luxury!

We crossed the southern suburbs of Berlin quickly. The landscape lay still in the darkness of the evening. In a way, this was a good thing because I was unable to see the miles upon miles of devastation from the war.

As we got closer to Dresden, the first snowflakes of the season began to fall. They were tentative in the way they fell, as though they were shy about covering the burned soil with so many dead lying there.

We pulled into the Dresden Neustadt railroad station. It was then that I learned that I had a nearly two-mile walk[54] ahead of me to reach the Dresden Hauptbahnhof station, the main rail station, from where my next train would depart.

In February 1945, the firebombing of Dresden had taken place over two nights. When you hear the description of what occurred there, you cannot really imagine the extent of it, and no picture could possibly capture the vastness of it. Some ten months later, I would find myself walking through the old market square. I saw the remains of one of the funeral pyres used to dispose of the bodies of those killed in raids. At the time, I was not aware that the city officials had burned the corpses rather than burying them—some 25,000 bodies had to be removed, and given the already burning buildings around them, this likely was the best way to do that. Nevertheless, a cold shiver ran down my spine.

At the Red Cross station, I obtained a train schedule providing a rough timetable for trains traveling south. I wanted the train going to Tečin-Prague-Vienna-Budapest. After firing off a quick prayer to heaven, I used some of the cigarettes that I had brought along to bribe a Soviet guard into letting me claim a seat in the first-class section of that train.

Now that I was on board, I had to find a "traveling companion." I introduced myself to a civilized and nice-looking Soviet officer who

---

54   Approximately 3.1 kilometers.

seemed to be trustworthy. At least I hoped so. After I explained my plan to him in Czech—I wanted to travel across the border to Tečin—and bribed him with the bottle of whiskey, he laughed. Then the officer placed his army jacket around my shoulders and said nonchalantly to anyone who wanted to know, "She's my girlfriend."

Several police patrols passed through the train cars, and each time, they received the same "she's my girlfriend" story from the officer. Once, to keep up appearances, he leaned over to kiss me, but instead of placing his lips on my mouth, he kissed my ear. At the German-Czech border, my Soviet companion sent the border police on their way with a quick flick of the wrist.

I had a ten-dollar bill with me that I had stolen from the American staff officer on the day I arrived in Berlin. I asked my companion to buy me a train ticket to Karlsbad. He gladly accepted the money, and I am certain it went a long way. Although the Soviet soldiers had managed to win the war, most of them received only a small fraction of the pay owed to them. Part of the reason is that the war probably drained the Soviet treasury dry, but I also suspect that after the war Stalin cared little about his soldiers and their sacrifice.

After I said a quick farewell to the Soviet officer, I departed on the next train to Karlsbad. I joined up with a woman and her young child, and with this arrangement I somehow managed to escape four police patrols that made their rounds through the train cars. Several prayers and a few hours later, I arrived at the train station in Karlovy Vary, the Czech name for Karlsbad.

Climbing out of the train, I felt a bit of nostalgia, but then I realized there wasn't any time for that. *Irmtraud*, I said to myself, *remain sensible and take one step at a time.*

Through hidden pathways and backyards, I made my way over to my former apartment. After I softly knocked, the door slowly opened, and there was the loving face of my mother. We embraced each other tightly, the tears choking the words we attempted to utter. Mother had lost a lot of weight, and now her cheeks were sunken and her face very pale.

She could barely contain herself. "You came back," she stammered again and again.

I was overjoyed to be with her. The dangerous journey and the even more dangerous return trip that awaited me didn't seem to matter. Our friends helped us out, and with some donated food I managed to prepare a halfway decent meal, something that neither my mother nor I had eaten in a long time. But we could not really enjoy it. I had barely finished the last bite when my eyes closed shut. Mother now spent most of the day in bed, and I lay next to her until the next overcast November day appeared.

Mother was clearly in the final stages of her illness, even if I didn't want to accept it. Instead of dwelling on what was inevitable, I attempted to experience every remaining hour with her as though it might be our last hour together. To distract myself, I ran the household, organizing our possessions into items I wanted to take with me and items that we could sell. I sold these items mostly to the Czechs who had just moved into the apartments formerly occupied by Sudeten Germans. Most of them were quite nice to us, even though I had to be careful and distance myself from them.

One day a young doctor visited us, a Jew who recently had been released from a concentration camp. He had returned immediately to Karlsbad to set up a medical practice. His diagnosis was the most devastating moment of my life. "She will not survive another week," he said in a quiet voice, looking sad.

In effect I was waiting for my mother to pass away. Each day that she lived was a gift. On the other hand, I had a young daughter in Berlin who depended on me. I could not abandon her. This was morally unacceptable. Each day spent in Karlsbad meant a greater risk of arrest and possible deportation to Siberia or worse. Staying in Karlsbad became more and more dangerous for me.

On December 1, 1945, my mother died. It might well have been the most dignified death considering the circumstances. My godmother and I remained with her until the very end, when she closed her eyes forever.

I find it difficult to remember what occurred after she died. At one point I went outside to the garden. Then I returned to Mother's room to lie down next to her for a while, to feel her presence one last time. I needed another day to think straight again. However, several important tasks required my attention. I had to notify the authorities of her death and pay for the burial.

The longer I stayed, the more dangerous the situation became for me. Paranoia set in, and I started to imagine that a policeman lurked around every corner. My nerves were shot.

Through contacts I still had at the army hospital, I was able to track down a Soviet chauffeur named Arcadi. He made weekly trips between the Imperial Hotel (then converted to a Soviet Army hospital) in Karlsbad and the Soviet headquarters in Berlin. After the end of the war, any German soldiers remaining in the hospitals in Karlsbad were transported to the west, and wounded Soviet soldiers filled their beds. After recovering, the Soviet soldiers traveled to Berlin to receive their discharge papers. Arcadi came from Gomel, a city in Belarus, where my husband had received his first war injury. Fate had then brought him to the army hospital and to me.

During the evening of the day my mother died, Arcadi came over to the house for a short visit. Two days later, he would be making one of his runs to Berlin, and he could take me along. That's how I was rescued in the nick of time. The undertaker announced that he would remove the body the following day, which in turn would bring the police to the apartment.

I clearly remember this evening. "Arcadi, take anything you want for yourself," I said. What use did I have for these things? I couldn't take them with me.

Arcadi selected an elegant dark blue dress, my father's patent leather shoes, and a grandfather clock. Then he took a pair of opera glasses that were inlaid with mother of pearl. In the next few days he became my rescuer and guardian angel. I think I did the right thing by letting him have these things; I hope they made him happy.

I spent my last two days in Karlsbad with Frau Rosa Stein, the wife of Otto Stein, the former owner of the apartment building who had died in the concentration camp.

I also paid a final visit to Katharina, my paternal grandmother.

She was still awaiting her expulsion order and by luck was still living in her apartment. She died shortly after I returned to Berlin, a blessing perhaps as the journey surely would have killed her. She had been a wonderful grandmother who gave me a tremendous amount of love.

During the night before our departure, Arcadi and I met once again. Together we went back into Mother's apartment. A curfew remained in effect, and I didn't dare to even cross the street unless escorted by someone wearing a Soviet uniform. Arcadi was young and very handsome, and the way he carried himself conveyed confidence and assertiveness. I suspected that he carried a pistol in his coat pocket, ready to pull it out on a moment's notice to set things right if someone said a cross word to him.

Together we loaded my belongings into his car, everything I wanted to take with me. Among the belongings was the precious silver set belonging to my father-in-law. I made one last tour through the apartment, taking my mother's handwritten cookbook as a memento. Later, this book would travel with me to North and South America, and I still possess several recipes from the book.

Near daybreak I stood in front of my old apartment building, waiting for Arcadi. Suddenly, three men with the secret Czech police service approached me. Thank God it was still dark out, and they could not see how ashen-white my face had become from the terror I felt.

"Do you know a Pani Steinova?" they asked. "She is in the country illegally, and we need to arrest her."[55]

I swallowed hard and then realized the opportunity just handed to me. "Yes, Pani Steinova lives in that apartment building over there. I think she is still at home."

The three men tapped their fingers on the brim of their hats and made their way over to the building. They would soon be knocking on Frau Stein's door. I knew this might cause her a little inconvenience, but it would buy me some time. Since the Nazis had persecuted her husband, the new government gave her special protection, and the police would not harm her. Then I fired off another quick prayer.

---

55   Pani is Czech for Mrs.

Please, God, get Arcadi over here before the police find out that they are talking to the wrong woman.

Just as the three police officers entered Frau Stein's apartment building, Arcadi pulled around the corner. I jumped into the car as fast as my shaking legs permitted. After a short while, I noticed that my fellow passengers were high-ranking Soviet officers, mostly older men, also traveling to Berlin. Arcadi had told them about my situation.

In the hazy morning sun, I took a final look at the Church of St. Mary Magdalene, which we passed on our way out of town. We also drove past the cloud of steam rising from the *Sprudel*, a natural geyser of hot mineral water in the center of Karlsbad—the breath of benevolent gods. Although I would someday return to Karlsbad, it would be just as a visitor.

It was early December, and I noticed with a heavy heart that as we passed houses and shops on our way out of Karlsbad, not one sign of the beginning of Advent or approaching Christmas was visible. There was just the gray and hostile landscape.

Sadly, I could not attend the funeral for my mother. It was simply too dangerous to stay any longer. My heart was heavy. This was something I could not reconcile. When I look back, missing this final farewell seems like a shadow that covers my soul. Yet the shadow is an offspring of the light. Light and darkness, war and peace, rise and fall—these are polarities one must accept.

Together Again, 1945

Our journey took us over the Czech border to Dresden. To avoid problems at the border crossing, Arcadi handed me a Soviet officer uniform, which I wore. I also had to memorize several words of Russian so that I could play the part. But everything ran smoothly at the border, and I didn't have to pretend that I was a member of the Red Army. One of the officers in the car was especially kind to me, carefully placing a coat around my shoulders and offering some vodka to calm my nerves. He reminded me of a picture I had seen of Frederick the Great with sideburns.

We spent the night at a hotel in Dresden called the White Stag. Located on the outskirts of the city on a hill, this building had managed to survive the bombing, although the surrounding area had not fared as well. Soviet military personnel now filled the rooms and were scurrying about the hallways when we arrived. As bad as I felt, I could have spent the night in the car. I just needed to get some sleep, to take a short break from all that troubled me. Arcadi found a room for me, and I fell into a deep sleep as soon as my head hit the pillow. The next morning, I couldn't eat anything, which was probably my body reacting to the stress and tension of the last few days. I developed acute stomach pain and ran a fever. A Soviet army doctor gave me a strong sedative, and I slept until we reached Berlin.

Before we drove into the city, two of the officers had parted from our company, and only the KGB officer remained.[56] The KGB officer, who sat in the rear seat, planned to visit Potsdam the next day to obtain his discharge papers, but for now he stayed with us in the car. Around noon we drove through Steglitz, a city district in Berlin. For the first time in several months, streetcars could be seen rolling along and picking up passengers. In front of the city hall, Arcadi stopped the car for a traffic signal. Tired, I looked out the window upon the destroyed city, and my heart just froze. On the other side of the street, next to the streetcar station, stood Georg.

His head was shaved, and he appeared to have lost a tremendous amount of weight, but without a doubt it was Georg, my husband, from whom I had not received a sign of life for over a year. I called out his name, but he turned around, attempting to ignore the voice coming from a Soviet car.

"Georg!" I called out. "Over here, Georg."

Finally, he couldn't ignore me any longer. Hesitating for a second, he crossed over the street, and only when he stood right next to the car did he recognize me. Georg stood there looking at me as though I were a creature from another planet coming after him with slimy

---

56   The NKGB, or People's Commissariat for State Security, was the Soviet secret police, intelligence and counterintelligence force that existed between 1943 and 1946. The service became known as the KGB in 1954 after going through several more name changes. Here I use the more familiar KGB for simplicity.

tentacles. After hesitating, he finally climbed into the car, but even then, he distanced himself from me and kept silent.

Sometime later, he told me that when we picked him up, he had been in Berlin for only a few days, and was in Steglitz to see if any rations were available. He had written me a letter as soon as he crossed the border into Germany, but I hadn't received it. He told me he had just made his way back to the city from a prisoner-of-war camp. After fighting the Soviets for several months, he had been taken prisoner by them.

There are not sufficient words to describe the suffering endured by prisoners of war in Russian camps—suffice it to say, they broke his soul. At the official end of the war, Georg was lucky, and they released him. But then Georg had to make a perilous march to Berlin—no one provided the former prisoners any transportation back to Germany. Understandably, he became paranoid when he heard someone in a Soviet car yelling at him. *Now they want to bring me back*, he thought. Last, and what was even more strange, he saw his wife wearing a Soviet uniform. He was terrified they would take him again.

With Georg in the car, we drove to Lichterfelde, to the apartment where his parents lived. As we passed through an American checkpoint, the GIs appeared edgy, and of course, they got the same response from us. For the American and British troops, the Soviets seemed stranger than ever. Their culture and the way they acted made them seem almost like visitors from another world. We almost got the same edgy reaction from Georg's parents when we pulled up in front of their apartment in a Soviet car. Ulla, my sister-in-law, immediately began to remove anything of value from her fingers and wrists as we climbed out of the vehicle.

Georg, still in a state of shock, tried to provide an explanation for the Soviets in the car and me wearing a Soviet uniform, but he wasn't making any sense. In the meantime, Arcadi and I began to unload the car and carry my belongings inside the house: a can of cooking oil, a bit rancid but still usable; a small package of sugar; and a large bag of wool that, unfortunately, consisted exclusively of darker colors. Nevertheless, wool was still wool, and our Barbara needed winter clothing. Today I can still see my daughter wearing the dark blue pants we knitted for her. Of course, the wool scratched her skin, and we had to soften it up before she would wear it, but without this material she would not have had any winter clothing. Finally, we brought the silver set into the house, as well as Margarethe's fur coat.

Arcadi needed to make his way over to the Soviet zone, which meant it was time to haggle over the price of my adventurous journey from Karlsbad to Berlin. "How much is she worth to you?" Arcadi asked Georg mischievously.

I slipped Georg a wad of Reichsmarks, and he forked over a thousand of them, which made a rustling sound as he counted. The payment wasn't that much, perhaps enough to buy a kilo of butter on the black market.

Arcadi continued, "Isn't your wife worth more than a few banknotes? If someone were to ask me, I'd say she's worth a lot more."

Georg thought for a second, looking rather puzzled, and then noticed a bottle of whiskey on the dresser, which he grabbed and handed to Arcadi. Anyone who knew the Soviets knew that they appreciated their spirits.

For Arcadi, the bottle was something special. But after tucking it away, he continued to haggle over how much I was worth and raised the stakes. "She's got to be worth more. After all, she's the mother of your daughter."

So, Georg forked over another 1,000 Reichsmarks.

The haggling continued. "Isn't she worth—"

Georg finally interrupted Arcadi, raising his hands, signaling enough was enough. "She's really not worth any more," he said.

Arcadi happily conceded, kissed my hand and that of my mother-in-law, and then drove away. Notably, he did not ask the KGB officer to join him as he left.

The KGB officer still sat in our living room. Tomorrow he was supposed to obtain his discharge papers in Potsdam, but what were we to do with him now? While he sat upright in the chair, looking in the opposite corner of the room out of decency, we huddled together in the other corner and discussed our strategy. We really didn't have any other choice but to offer the bedroom my in-laws slept in, leaving the living room for us, where we would have to squeeze together for an uncomfortable night of rest.

That night, just as we had made ourselves halfway comfortable in the living room, I saw a look of complete shock on Margarethe's face. "My jewelry," she whispered. "I left all my jewelry underneath the pillow in the bedroom."

Now the rest of us became worried. This jewelry represented the only liquid wealth the family had, our only hope for rebuilding our lives in postwar Berlin, or at least some guarantee we would survive a few more months.

Enraged, Georg whispered, "Tomorrow, when he goes into the bathroom, I'll check underneath the pillow, and if anything is missing, I'll just kill him."

After a night in which we could not sleep a wink, morning light flooded the living room. Singing a happy tune to himself, the officer entered the bathroom, and as promised, Georg slipped into the bedroom to see whether the officer had stolen the jewelry. Georg found all the jewelry underneath the pillow, exactly where my mother-in-law had left it.

After the KGB officer took a bath, we ate breakfast together. The officer did not notice how nervous we had been. When we finished eating, he offered us a can of excellent tea, a jar of caviar, several cigars for Grandpa Max, and an exquisite fruitcake for the ladies. Then the officer asked Georg to take him to Potsdam. Georg explained that the car was almost out of gasoline.

"Not a problem," said the officer. "We'll just get some from the Americans." That they did indeed.

Georg drove a friend's old DKW (Dampf-Kraft-Wagen, the predecessor to Audi), which had been hidden in a secret garage during the war. Through some miracle the car had managed to survive the war intact. After breakfast Georg drove into the heart of the Soviet command in Potsdam, a city south of Berlin. The whole day, I feared that he would not return, that once again the Soviets would take him prisoner. That evening he came back.

Over the next couple of days, we spent a lot of time searching for a place to live. The temporary arrangement with his parents was not a long-term solution, sleeping crammed together in the small apartment. Plus, we desperately wanted to build a life together, one without the threat of another final farewell, one with intimacy and even the occasional squabble. After all, Georg and I were married, we had a daughter, and it was about time we lived together as a family.

We finally found an apartment not far from where his parents were staying. Our new home was just a single room on the fourth floor of a building, with the bathroom below us on the first floor. Perhaps this arrangement was a little complicated, but under the circumstances, who cared? Georg and I had been separated for quite a long time, and I had forgotten what it was like to be in his arms. It took a while before I could let down my guard, to feel comfortable with him. Physically, I wasn't much more than skin and bones. Emotionally, I felt close to having a nervous breakdown. I can't say that Georg fared any better. Then there was Barbara. Every day we strove to give her some peace and reassurance, something we lacked for ourselves.

We really had to get to know each other all over again, which meant finding out what the other had experienced during these many months apart. Georg told me about his experiences during the final months of the war. In December 1944, the army ordered him to train new recruits. He couldn't believe his eyes when he first saw them. Boys, only fifteen to seventeen years old, stood before him at attention, most wearing a uniform several sizes too large and a steel helmet that covered most of their face. A few seemed mature for their age, eager, waiting to stomp the enemy into the ground, but most of the boys were simply terrified. For many, the obligatory "yes, sir!" was whispered back with trembling lips, a tear rolling down their cheeks. "Sir," many of them pleaded, "I don't want to go into battle."

Even Georg had a lump in his throat. Yet his hands were tied. Georg delayed sending them to the front lines as long as possible, hoping the war would end in time to spare their lives, but this did not help most of them.

In February 1945 Georg and the rest of his unit were taken prisoner at Küstrin. The Soviets transported them to Landsberg, inside recently occupied territory. Later, they were taken to the Black Sea to unload ships. Georg remembered the first days of captivity and the mistreatment that occurred. Many of the German soldiers lost some teeth during that first week, including Georg. A guard hit him in the face with a rifle butt. Someone also stole Georg's special orthopedic riding boots, which he needed after the most recent war injury. As a prisoner of war, he performed hard physical labor. The crippled foot, combined with the traditional Russian felt boots that he now wore, known as Valenkis, made this work even more agonizing.

In the prisoner-of-war camp he witnessed the arrival of an elite squad of officers from the German air force (the Luftwaffe), who had been most recently stationed in Berlin. They entered captivity still wearing their elegant uniforms, including silk socks and handkerchiefs. They didn't receive much respect from the fighting men, who now wore tattered clothing. The men showed their disdain for the elite squad by spitting on the ground in front of them.

The first chance he got, Georg asked for a transfer. Through some incredible stroke of luck, the Soviets transferred Georg to a prisoner-of-war camp in Poland. It became increasingly difficult for him to move around, as constant pain tormented him day and night. They assigned him to the kitchen, representing at least a bit of success for him. There, he could stop the rapid loss of body weight by eating some of the leftover food. Still, even this new assignment was too much for Georg. As he approached the point of total physical exhaustion, Georg needed to find a way to get out of performing the daily physical work. Out of desperation, he pressed his hand against the red-hot heating element on the kitchen stove. Within seconds a huge burn blister appeared. His legs buckled because of the excruciating pain, but he had accomplished what he had set out to do: he had become unfit for work. He spent several days in the camp hospital.

When they reassigned him back to the barracks, Georg had not made much of a recovery, and he was very close to the point of physical and psychological collapse. Several weeks later, he came down with erysipelas, a dangerous skin infection that caused his face to swell to twice its normal size. As Georg lay in the hospital, the swelling was so severe he could not open his eyes. It took a while for Georg to recover, partly because the Soviets could only treat his illness with aspirin. Today the same condition is easily treated with antibiotics.

Georg's recollection of his time in captivity often seemed fuzzy and incoherent, time and space distorted by mental and physical anguish. Shortly before the onset of winter, he found a notice on the camp bulletin board, an announcement that streetcar drivers were badly needed in Berlin to rebuild the city's infrastructure. That the Soviets had some interest in rebuilding the city seemed too good to be true. Anyway, many of the prisoners ignored the advertisement, thinking it was a trick or lie, a one-way train ticket to Siberia. Georg, desperate to escape his present circumstances, took a risk and arranged a meeting with the camp commandant.

"All right, comrade," the commandant said. "You say you once drove a streetcar in Berlin. Prove it! Tell me where the streetcar stops."

I can only imagine the grin Georg must have had on his face. Georg had lived in Berlin since he was three years old, and he was ten when the family moved to Lichterfelde. He had ridden the streetcars perhaps a thousand times. He rattled off one stop after another: "Unter den Eichen, Drakestraße, Holbeinstraße, Karwendelstraße, Görtzallee, Ostpreußendamm…"

The commandant finally had had enough of Georg's enthusiasm. He signed the release papers, and Georg was a free man standing outside the gate.

Now Georg had another problem: he had to walk most of the way to Berlin with a long line of refugees headed in the same direction. His crippled foot made the journey even more agonizing as he joined up with the millions of Germans who had just been expelled from Silesia, Pomerania, and Prussia, former German territory now incorporated into Poland. This mass migration of displaced people moved as an endless human stream from east to west, not knowing where to go but knowing they had to keep moving. The destination seemed not important for they encountered more immediate problems: hunger, cold, and the loss of their homes, their wealth, and an entire way of life, having suddenly been expelled from communities where their ancestors had lived since the Middle Ages.

This forced ethnic migration consisted mostly of the elderly, women, and children. For the children, the march to the west was especially strenuous, and many perished along the way. In many cases their small corpses were wrapped in a towel or sheet and left alongside the road, their rigid forms becoming food for wild animals and former house pets. The line had to keep moving, and nobody could afford the time to give the dead a decent burial.

After several weeks Georg finally reached Berlin, emaciated and with a shaved head, having just been subjected to delousing. He bore both physical and psychological wounds, having suffered greatly during the war, and he yearned to be with his family once again, to feel the affection of loved ones and solace in what had comforted him in the past.

Perhaps Georg should not have had such great expectations, but his family did not welcome his return home.

"We didn't expect you to come back. We thought you were dead," his mother and sister said to him, looking a bit surprised when they saw him. "We don't have room for you."

Moreover, after having taken the long way home, Georg now found his former house occupied, forcing him to find more humble accommodations. Gone was everything that Georg had left behind before going off to war. His suits, for example, had been sewn into women's clothing. Other belongings had been sold. In fact, when he arrived in Berlin, Georg had no choice but to wear the same pair of tattered pants issued to him while he was a prisoner of war. A friend finally loaned him something better to wear.

I think this blow after the war hurt Georg deeply, and he could never forgive his family. I couldn't offer him much support either, after my experiences with the loss of my mother, the two journeys from Karlsbad, and the daily struggle for food. I was exhausted and emotionally drained. With every type of home remedy, I attempted to calm my nerves, but I could not find any peace of mind during that cold, wet winter.

Georg looked for work and found a job cooking for the American soldiers stationed near our house. Because of his war injury, and because he could not get the orthopedic shoes he required, this work was hard on Georg. However, the job had one benefit: he was able to bring home some of the leftovers.

The depression I experienced was crushing. Sometimes I sat in front of the window and thought back on my time in Pirkenhammer. I recalled my mother's living room in summer and how the sun cast small circles on the walls. I thought about sledding in the Ore Mountains and how I had clung to my father's back. I thought about those happy times when I turned myself around in front of the mirror, wondering what life would bring me. Memories are life's safety net. They often cushion the fall.

That is how I began my life in war-torn Berlin, the start of a new chapter in my life, which the hand of history wrote for me.

Perspective: The Suffering

Dante once wrote that one is supposed to find paradise after suffering greatly. Enormous human suffering occurred during the two world wars of the twentieth century, and there is still no peace on earth, and certainly no paradise. For many years historians and writers have analyzed in excruciating detail what happened in twentieth-century Europe, to determine how things went so awry. Nobody has come up with a satisfactory explanation. One unresolved question lingering from events immediately following the Second World War is the treatment of almost 14 million ethnic Germans or German citizens in Czechoslovakia, Poland, Romania, Yugoslavia, and the Baltic States of Lithuania, Latvia, and Estonia. Their treatment could be seen as an attempt to collectively punish an entire people for the misconduct of a few. Unfortunately, Amnesty International did not exist then, nor was "human rights" a recognized slogan. In those dark days, the term "orderly and humane transfers" was seen as the minimum standard for expelling millions of ethnic Germans or German citizens from their homelands, uprooting them from areas settled by their ancestors several hundred years prior. Mostly children, the elderly, and women were forced across Eastern Europe into Germany, where they joined millions of others suffering from cold and hunger. Many died of disease, hypothermia, or exhaustion before reaching Germany, and conditions were little better there. Only after several months could the Allies provide the cities, which had to accept this human migration, a regular supply of food.[57]

The United States remained the only country in the world with the means, technical know-how, and desire to provide war-torn Europe with a comprehensive aid program. Initially, the United States distributed this aid through the UNRRA (United Nations Relief and Rehabilitation Administration), the predecessor of the more familiar Marshall Plan. The United States sent billions of dollars' worth of food, clothing, medicine, and agricultural and industrial equipment to European countries in need, without distinguishing friend from foe, courtesy of the American taxpayer.

Scientists have calculated how much food energy a person needs to survive, about 1,200 calories per day for women and 1,800 per day for men. For a healthy, active person, the typical calorie intake required to maintain weight is about 1,800 to 2,500 per day. Of course, the harder a person works, the more calories she or he needs. Today this bit of trivia may seem a little strange to Americans or Europeans who battle daily to avoid excess body weight, but in postwar Germany millions of people struggled to obtain enough of calories to survive. Along with the struggle to find sufficient calories came malnutrition, which occurs when the body does not receive enough of the required vitamins and minerals.

In addition to the vast amount of food required to feed the hungry, the logistics of transporting the aid were also challenging. Nearly all communications systems were rendered useless by either the allied bombs or the scorched earth policies of the German military.

---

57   Three excellent sources on the expulsion of ethnic Germans from Eastern Europe are R. M. Douglas, *Orderly and Humane: The Expulsion of the Germans after the Second World War* (New Haven: Yale University Press, 2013), Alfred-Maurice de Zayes, *A Terrible Revenge: The Ethnic Cleansing of the East European Germans*, 2nd ed. (New York: St. Martin's Griffin, 2006), and Giles MacDonogh, *After the Reich: the Brutal History of the Allied Occupation* (New York: Basic Books, 2007).

How was Germany supposed to have regular postal delivery in the chaos that followed the Second World War? How could anyone find an address if whole sections of the city no longer existed? How could you find people whom the war had displaced and scattered to different areas of the country?

Damaged walls and barricaded entrances to uninhabitable buildings were used to post messages and pass along news or missing-person information, such as "Everyone survived, now staying at Steinitz residence" or "Today at noon: potato delivery at the corner of Augustaplatz and Manteuffelstraße." This means of disseminating information was perhaps only effective within a radius of two hundred yards, but it was the only means after the city had essentially died.

Chapter 2

Berlin, Germany, 1945-1956

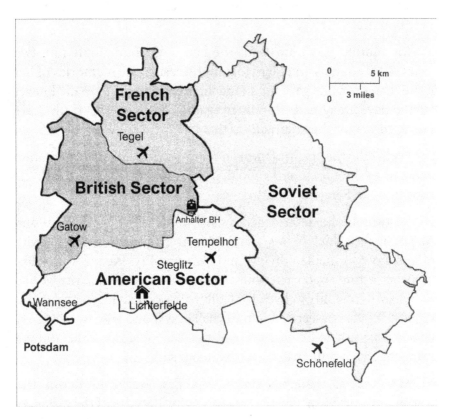

Berlin Germany with Allied Occupation Sectors marked. House icon shows location of Max Stein's house in Lichterfelde.

The Stein Family and Winter in Berlin, 1945–1946

During those first months in Berlin, when that city became my new home, I felt as though I had been pulled from the soil in which my roots had grown deep over many generations. My former life lay in ruins like the cityscape around me. It had been an eternity since I last received word from my father. Was he still alive? How could he ever find me?

My mother was now dead. She had died young, only fifty-two years old. Today, as an older woman, I treasure the memories of her more than ever. She gave me so much, preparing me for a life I never would have imagined. But then again, could anyone really have prepared me for the aftermath of that terrible war?

We lived at the height of the Iron Years—stripped of ornamentation and shine. The epoch of the Golden Years had disappeared with the shots fired in Sarajevo in 1914.

Postwar Berlin represented a time of tremendous political and social change, which in turn changed us in terms of relationships with others, how we made a living, and our morality. We were now like pioneers setting out on a new voyage to rediscover the security we had once had, to rebuild our lives, to create a life worth living, to regain our dignity. We had descended into the hell of war and witnessed its fiery conclusion, only to be disappointed by a so-called peace that did not bring the much-anticipated end to human suffering.

My greatest challenge during my first weeks in Berlin was learning the art of survival in this great city. Because of the distances involved, I could no longer walk from farm to farm, foraging for food, as I had done in Karlsbad. I had to become accustomed to what countless other women in Berlin did every day: standing in a long line for several hours at a time in front of a store. Today when I walk into a well-stocked modern supermarket, I am overwhelmed at what I see. In Berlin, the market nearest our house had been set up in an old garage. An incredibly long line always stood before this store, and more than once, after spending several hours in line, I found that everything was sold out when it was my turn to enter the business. Ration cards were worthless when there were no rations to be had. That said, the more cards the better because we could trade them on the black market.

I sometimes worked as a maid in the house that the Americans soldiers had confiscated from my in-laws. It was hard work, but the job also had its fringe benefits—extra ration cards for food. Although the basic need to survive dominated everyday life at home, at work my prewar ideals of everyday life surfaced. The need to maintain decorum replaced fear and hunger.

During the war my mother-in-law had stored her valuable KPM china set in the basement for safekeeping. These initials stand for *Königliche Porzellan-Manufaktur*, or "Royal Porcelain Factory" in English. After the Americans took over the house, they found the china set and used it for serving food. However, instead of washing the china afterward, the Americans simply discarded it, throwing it into the trash, where it broke into hundreds of tiny pieces. To me it was sacrilege that someone would be so thoughtless as to discard such a valuable and treasured home furnishing, a symbol of status and gracious living, as though it were the wrapper from some fast-food hamburger. Of course, some GI from Alabama or a small farm in Idaho probably found this difficult to comprehend, or maybe they thought we deserved it.

Well, I wasn't going to tolerate this, no way! I managed to save the rest of the china set by pounding into the head of the sergeant how much this china was worth. I fished some pieces out of the trash and tossed them on the table. Then I yelled, "That is KPM, you understand! Frederick the Great founded the factory. He's for the Germans what George Washington is for you Americans."

The young man shrugged his shoulders and gave me a dumb look. What did he care about the German George Washington and his china factory? Whether he understood completely was hard to say, but he and the other men got the hint and learned to come to me for advice. Sheepishly, they would present a glass or something else to me and wait nervously for a response. When I shook my head left and right, that meant "toss it." When I nodded my head up and down, that meant "wash it in hot water and put it back in the cabinet." For me it was like saving a part of our heritage, another lifestyle, maybe a better way of life, that now had disappeared.

My ability to speak English was quite limited. I knew French, German, and Czech, but English had never been a part of my school curriculum. But you can adapt, especially when you must. After several weeks I could imitate the lingo of the GIs. Hundreds of times every day, I muttered, "Okay." On top of that, I became an expert at extending my thumb and holding it upright.

The two houses from Max Stein, Spindelmühler Weg 10 and 12, Lichterfelde West, Berlin, 1950.

The large house belonging to my in-laws became office space for the American occupation army. When I first arrived in Berlin, I had found the staff sergeant, a red-haired giant with hands the size of plates and the man who accused me of being a Soviet spy, intimidating. Now things were different. The mere sight of him made me laugh, the way he slouched carefree in the renaissance chair with delicate thin legs and lion's claw feet, which cracked and creaked under the strain of his weight. As he issued orders to his men, he rested his giant feet on top of the desk while a lit cigarette hung from the corner of his mouth. The elegant bookshelves behind him, carved from oak, were now adorned with pinup girls, competition for space that the heavyweights of German literature, such as Goethe and Schiller, never would have expected. Perhaps it was inevitable. The victors almost never appreciate the culture and traditions of a people they have just conquered.

Perhaps it was providence, or perhaps just luck, that we lived in the American sector. Most of these soldiers were very friendly to us, slipping us chocolate for the "baby" or occasionally a can of coffee. Once a soldier asked me, "Ma'am, how's the little girl? Is there anything I can get you?" It reaffirmed my belief in human kindness.

Whenever I arrived home from work, Barbara ran up to me crying, "Candy, candy!" That was the first word of English she learned. Knowing full well what she could expect, she extended both hands, demanding with a look of anticipation something sweet and delicious. One day we got a completely new treat: peanut butter! An American soldier gave us a couple of cans of this delicious and sticky concoction, and Barbara was in ecstasy. It was so filling and creamy and sweet that for the first time in a very long while, her tummy was full.

Now that the cannons had fallen silent, we turned to the task of rebuilding our lives. As conditions improved a little, we began to confront the daunting task of overcoming the postwar devastation.

We set up our one-room home with our meager possessions and furnished it with a hot plate for preparing meals. This early attempt to return to a normal life had unforeseen consequences. An oil painting hung on the wall in our room, in a niche next to the heating stove, directly over the hot plate we used to heat Barbara's milk and our dinner. It was a portrait of some seventeenth- or eighteenth-century noble that we had received from Georg's parents. Every morning when we heated the bottle of milk for Barbara, steam would rise, swirling about the painting. One day we noticed that the facial features of the noble seemed to be elongated and that the fingers of his crossed hands extended out into the frame. One could say that he mutated right before our very eyes. After a close inspection we noticed that the paint felt wet and that gravity was forcing it to run to the bottom of the frame. Perhaps the portrait was a forgery because it's hard to imagine that simple water vapor could bring about this type of damage.

Barbara at age three, in Berlin.

We stood there in front of the painting, and Georg, looking at me from the corner of his eye, remarked, "Now that's one long finger!" At first, I tried to choke back a chuckle, and Georg tried to hide a smile, but the pressure kept building and building, and both of us busted out laughing, laughing so hard our ribs hurt, amusing ourselves with how odd our ancestor now appeared. Like nothing had ever happened, we removed the picture from the wall and set it upside down in a corner of the room, hoping the paint would flow in the opposite direction, correcting the damage that had been done. After a few weeks we returned the painting to the in-laws without explanation, hoping the elongated face and fingers were not too conspicuous.

Barbara became accustomed to the postwar "menu circa 1945," potatoes fried in usually nearly rancid oil that we bartered for, along with applesauce and homemade syrup. Like a hawk, I made sure she got all her milk ration, but like so many of the other children, she also suffered from vitamin and mineral deficiencies. We spent many of our evenings in the apartment belonging to my in-laws. The wallpaper pattern was enough to make you scream, extremely ugly, having not been replaced in decades. Every so often, we caught Barbara licking the wallpaper and were puzzled as to why she would do such thing. Did the paper or paste have some mineral that she lacked, inducing an instinctive response from her? We will never know.

On top of all the problems confronting all families in postwar Berlin, I still encountered a special little personal problem. I could not find my place in the Stein clan. The rivalry between Prussians and Austrians, which had lasted for hundreds of years and passed from one generation to the next, did not exactly help my debut in the family. Added to this, and for some reasons I will never understand, Max Stein hated his children, especially Georg. This hatred destroyed his life and that of his family. Order and precision military drills governed everyday life. Everything involved a plan; nothing was left to chance. Every waking moment had to be filled with doing something productive. I, on the other hand, had been raised differently. I had nothing against hard work, but I also didn't have any problem with taking a good book to the corner of the room and reading for a while.

My parents, like Georg's, provided a Catholic upbringing, but my God was different from that of his family. For me, God is kind, gentle, and understanding. For the in-laws, God stood ready to punish any small transgression with a bolt of lightning. Any display of emotion in this family was strictly taboo. All members of the family barricaded themselves in their own individual mental caves, incapable of sharing feelings with the others. My parents raised me differently, with joy and love and empathy.

I found it difficult to get along with Grandpa Max. Nevertheless, I succeeded over the course of several years in breaking that hard, impenetrable outer shell, just a little. Of course, he never would have admitted to it. In my heart I believe we developed a certain kind of friendship with each other. I still have a few items that we inherited from him that I keep to honor his memory.

Christmas, 1945

I can remember how my mother baked her famous cookies for Christmas in 1944. I had a photo of her in front of our rather humble Christmas tree with Barbara sitting in her lap, the two of them very happy, full of the holiday spirit, but it was lost in one of my intercontinental moves. The image remains indelible in my memory however, and I often think of it during the holiday season.

Our first postwar Christmas was completely different. The events of the past year and the still uncertain future had deeply wounded both body and soul. Somehow, I had to bury deep inside all those terrible experiences, to carry out the business of everyday life in postwar Berlin.

It was difficult to find any Christmas spirit during Advent in 1945. The challenge to collect enough food for a traditional meal, as well as some decorations, seemed almost insurmountable. What gifts could we give each other in this time of need? Frau Stiller, the lady who owned the apartment where my in-laws lived, gave us a broomstick. Georg cut the stick into various lengths, which we covered with leftover fabric to make dolls. The head, arms, and legs were formed from an old sheet, and we made a face using colored pencils. An old shoe box served as a doll bed, and before long we had made the perfect Christmas surprise.

Georg still worked for the American army and was able to bring home some ham and other treats. Grandpa Max raised rabbits to sell or to provide meat for his family, so on this occasion, one was sacrificed for our Christmas dinner. On the black market I exchanged my mother's wedding ring for eggs and butter. Some flour, sugar, and cocoa remained from the freight I had brought from Karlsbad. That was how we celebrated Christmas; it was somewhat meager, but still we kept the tradition going, a symbol of our hope for peace and a better future.

I can't quite figure out how we warmed the room and roasted the rabbit with the small supply of cooking gas allotted to us. Perhaps we had become accustomed to the cold, and maybe in the dim light we didn't notice that the rabbit was only partially cooked. But I remember it as a warm and comforting celebration, nonetheless.

During the midnight Mass every seat was taken. For an all-too-brief moment we forgot the fear and sadness and joined together in worship. We thanked God for peace and asked His blessing for those who had died. During this one hour we attempted to set aside all that had happened to us in the past year, turning with confidence toward the future.

We sat reverently under the scaffolding supporting the damaged pulpit, listening to the sermon. We felt revitalized by a new sense of purpose that crept into our hearts. We, the children of the Third Reich, those who had matured too fast in the recent years of immense suffering, now wanted to be young again, to re-experience the joy of living. I think you know what it means to really pray only when you wish with all your heart that God will bring light to a dark and uncertain future.

We celebrated New Year's Eve 1945 with a bit of wine that had been either home-brewed or stolen. January brought greetings from Siberia and icy cold air. As best as I remember, until the early 1950s all the winters in Berlin were bitter cold and long. Heating fuel always remained in short supply. Mostly we heated just one room in the house and routed the stovepipe out the window. Many valuable pieces of antique furniture made their way into a makeshift stove, and when the gas supply ran low, we cooked our meals over this smoking monster. The bitter cold winter weather made our situation even worse, and many of the older people, especially those living alone, froze to death in their unheated rooms.

"People Who Light the Morning Fire Together Still Spend the Entire Day Apart" A Kyrgyz Saying, 1946

After two months of working as a maid, I had to give up my job for health reasons. There was simply too much to be done at home, especially given how hard it was to obtain the daily necessities of food and fuel for our family. Moreover, whenever I went somewhere, I walked.

Berlin still lay in ruins, and it seemed as if no progress had been made in clearing the rubble and rebuilding the infrastructure, though I am sure that some improvements had occurred. During those gray winter days, the silhouette of the city reminded me of a mouth with rotting teeth. Over several miles in every direction, entire city blocks stood pulverized. Not a single upright and undamaged wall remained to testify to Berlin's former greatness. On windy days the dust coming off the piles of rubble blanketed the city.

If you visited Berlin now, say in the summer of 2018, you would not be able to imagine what the city looked like in 1945. Billy Wilder, the Austrian-born American filmmaker, described it as a "desert of rubble." As far as one could see, Berlin lay in ashes. The Western Allies had dropped 65,000 tons of explosives over the city, and the

Red Army had dropped another 40,000 tons. Statisticians calculated that for each inhabitant of Berlin, there were nearly 30 cubic meters (39 cubic yards) of rubble.[1]

What remains when a world power vanishes? Ruins, chaos, piles of stone, and immense suffering among the inhabitants. Even today you can still see evidence of the desperate street battles that took place in Berlin. For example, on Museum Island the exterior wall to the State Museum still bears the scars of battle, bullets holes and grenade fragments.

For the most part, women performed the task of cleaning up the German cities after the war. The Allies assigned this task to any woman who had been a member of the Nazi Party or whose husband had held a position within the party. This was seen as a way of atoning for misguided beliefs, both on a personal level and for the society as a whole. The so-called Rubble Women cleared away the debris from damaged houses to make them habitable once again. Many people in postwar Germany lived on the first floor of bombed-out structures or even in the basements of these buildings.

Many of the homes, however, lacked glass windows. Most of the windows in Berlin had been blown out within a few months after the carpet bombing began. And all of the factories that manufactured window glass or putty had been destroyed during the war. In many apartments people sealed off the window openings with pieces of cardboard taped together. The cardboard mostly came from the USA Care boxes that we received. I remember a time when Georg obtained a pane of glass that he wanted to set in the window, to provide a tighter seal against the air coming into the house. He didn't have any putty, so he scavenged some tape from the American barracks. Finally, we had a glass window!

Each day was the same, filled with the never-ending search for food and heating fuel. The days seemed to roll along with the same monotony as beads on a rosary. But then again, my lack of patience certainly didn't help.

---

1   Joachim Fest, *Inside Hitler's Bunker: The Last Days of the Third Reich*, trans. Margot Bettauer Dembo (New York: Picador, 2004), 86.

My health deteriorated. The emotional stress, combined with the physical work at home and the long daily trek to obtain food, became too much to bear. Georg finally decided to take me to a hospital. The news there was devastating, even though it should have been a joyful occasion. I was pregnant. According to the doctor, I also was suffering from malnutrition, not receiving enough of the minerals and vitamins my body needed. Like many young people, I had ignored the signals my body had given me, attempting to hide the need for medical attention. I lost the baby in the fourth month of pregnancy, something that is still painful for me, even though it was for the best of all of us, including the unborn child.

In the weeks that followed the miscarriage, I often cried. I imagined how the unborn child might have looked and how precious he or she would have been. I once heard that lost unborn children are the angels without bodies who surround the saints in many religious pictures. Even today, when I think of this loss, I find this image comforting.

We lived in the one-room apartment for an entire year before finding a new place. Now we had the entire ground floor of a house. It belonged to a professor who, according to rumor, had joined the Nazi Party and later had gone underground to escape from the Allies. In our new house we had two large rooms and the luxury of our very own bathroom. Although we shared the kitchen with the other tenants, this was only a minor inconvenience. What a joy it was to be able to plant a garden. We cultivated vegetables, harvested fruit, and raised some rabbits, all of which became part of the daily menu.

Barbara named all the rabbits Mumbles and became very attached to them. Every time we wanted to slaughter one of those precious long-eared rabbits, we tried to hide this reality from her, concealing the fact that one of them was now missing. "Mumbles went to the country to visit his cousins," we would say. Or maybe "Mumbles has gone to work on the other side of town and has a nice apartment now."

Fortunately, they reproduced constantly, allowing us to sell one or two to a neighbor in exchange for any leftover food that we could feed to the remaining rabbits, such as potato and apple peels. And the endless supply of bunnies helped us cover up the fact that one or two were now missing.

Just after we moved into the new apartment, we noticed that our new home came with a hidden treasure. The gas meter malfunctioned. Only when we used large quantities of hot water and ran all the stove burners at once did the meter slowly register any gas usage. About a month after we moved in, a man from the utility company arrived to read the meter. Puzzled, he just stood there in front of the distribution box, scratching his head. "Excuse me," he said. "Do you use any gas? I mean, how do you cook?"

I looked at him, astonished, and then exploited the opportunity handed to me. "Well, most days we cook together with my in-laws, so we don't use very much here," I said indifferently, trying to look innocent.

Of course, it was wrong not to report a damaged meter, but on the other hand, it sure was a lifesaver. Times were extreme, and everyone had to look out for themselves. We gladly embraced any opportunity to improve our lives.

For the second peacetime Christmas, we made our own decorations for the tree. We sold another piece of jewelry and scraped together enough money to buy something special for the holiday meal, something different from the everyday fare. I don't now remember what we ate that Christmas, but it was the first holiday in what felt like a real home of our own.

From time to time, Georg talked one of the GIs into giving us some ham, powdered milk, or other household goods that were normally unattainable for us. Life can certainly be ironic at times. Fifty years later, I was a US citizen living again in Germany. Every year I returned to the United States for Christmas and brought along an entire suitcase of "unattainable" German chocolate.

One of our more frequent visitors was my mother-in-law's sister, previously known as Martha and now known as Sister Senorina. She was a Benedictine nun, a member of a convent in Gleiwitz, a town on the Polish border near where the Second World War had started. One of her responsibilities was to procure equipment for the hospitals that the order ran. This duty took her to various hospitals throughout Germany, including some in Berlin, where she often tried to obtain some badly needed equipment.

Grandpa Max, a very religious man, often supported the church and its lay institutions. He owned a large silver goblet with inlaid gold, one of the pieces I had brought back from Karlsbad. In an unexpected and unusual gesture of generosity, he gave the goblet to Senorina, telling her to give it to the mother superior, to melt down for silver crosses for the nuns. He thought this would bring him a blessing from the mother superior. Then Grandpa Max went off to work.

It only made sense that many of the silver crosses at the convent disappeared, exchanged on the black market for food. Who needed a fancy cross anyway to prove their piety? Well, Margarethe and Senorina looked at each other in silence for a while, hearing the occasional grumble of a stomach that had been hungry for quite some time. Then they thought of Max and how he might want to eat from a full plate that evening. Soon Senorina took off her habit and put on one of Margarethe's dresses. Together they went to the black market. Now I don't remember whether they received much money for the goblet, but mysteriously an unexpected and large cut of pork appeared on Max's plate that evening.

Max continued to believe that he had bought his way into heaven with the silver goblet he donated to the convent. Whenever Senorina returned to Berlin on one of her visits, Max would ask her about this heirloom, the masterwork of a Russian silversmith that was now supposedly melted down into crucifixes. Senorina could not bear to tell her brother-in-law what had really happened and always came up with some story to placate him. She told a lie, and afterward she headed back to the convent to confess her sin.

Berlin, 1946–1947

Perhaps love is like the ocean, filled with conflict, filled with pain.

—John Denver, "Perhaps Love"

Now we had been married for five years. The love we first felt for each other had changed. Buried were many of the dreams we had once shared, dominated by the daily requirements of just living. The passion we had once felt had taken a quieter path.

Couples often believe that when they can't maintain the same feeling that they had for each other when they first met, the relationship will come to a tragic end. Yet each of us must grow as a person to confront those events that eventually change our lives. In the winter of 1946–1947, I was pregnant once again. The child was supposed to come at the end of May.

Not until the middle of spring did the icy cold winter finally come to an end. The leaves began to sprout on the branches, almost bashful to make their first appearance. I spent most of my time preparing for the arrival in our family. It was almost impossible to buy the things that the baby would need, such as diapers, shirts, and shoes. I had to sew these things myself from whatever fabric I came across. Sometime at the beginning of May, I was reaching for a glass on the shelf in the kitchen when suddenly I felt liquid running down my legs—I was bleeding badly. Barbara had just left to go shopping with the neighbors, and Georg wasn't home. Like most households, we did not have a telephone. The damage to the telephone system had been so extensive by the end of the war that it would be years before the connection for residential service got established. But this time an angel must have been looking out for me. Our neighbor, a young American doctor who had just returned home, heard my cries for help. Within a few minutes I was on my way to the hospital.

When I arrived, the hospital refused to admit me because I had not made an appointment. The hospital admitted only those with a reservation, refusing to admit anyone else, even if the patient's condition was life-threatening. Berlin simply lacked enough hospitals to care for everyone who had a serious medical need. The young doctor was dismayed, but he was not in a position to order the director of the hospital to admit me. He then took me to a military hospital that also admitted Germans to make sure that I would not be turned away for a second time. They were able to stop the bleeding, but in the early morning hours the hemorrhaging resumed. It was one of the more serious complications that could occur during pregnancy. The surgeon on duty diagnosed my condition as placenta previa, which is when the placenta becomes detached from the uterus and settles on top of the cervix and birth canal. Today doctors generally perform a cesarean section to save the baby and mother. But the obstetrically inexperienced military doctors did not utilize this procedure for whatever reason. The duty surgeon gave up on me and the baby, but a young German doctor, who had just been freed from a Soviet prisoner-of-war camp, refused to accept this diagnosis. He administered several blood transfusions and saved my life. However, our boy did not survive the ordeal. After taking several breaths, he passed away.

A long time passed before I became myself again. I hit rock bottom. I was simply devastated when I heard that our son had died. Inside me I had no room left to care for Barbara or Georg. The child was born fully developed, and the birth might have turned out okay under different circumstances. Since he lived for several minutes, his birth and death had to be reported to the Civil Registry Office.

Things became very complicated when we tried to arrange a burial. Nobody in postwar Berlin had the authority to issue burial plots at the cemetery. A representative from the hospital recommended that we donate the body to medical science. Although it was a very difficult and painful decision, we accepted the advice. We received a small box for the body. On the box someone wrote the name and address of the institution where remains were to be taken. Georg managed to make his way over to the facility, staring at the small cardboard casket, very distraught and crying. The box contained a small part of his heart and mine. Only after several months could I finally come to terms with this loss. Even today I think about our son and what he might have become in life.

Several months later a policeman came to our door. "Did a Mrs. Stein once live here?" he asked.

I swallowed hard and then answered, "I am Mrs. Stein. What can I do for you?"

The man turned pale and stared at me for a few seconds. Then he opened a folder and gave me a document. He quickly scribbled something on a piece of paper, looking up at me several times, and then left. When he disappeared around the corner, I finally read what he had handed to me. I probably turned just as pale as he had. In my hands I held my own death certificate. According to the document, I had died on May 15, 1947. A clerk at the Civil Registry Office had made a mistake, reporting that I had died and that the child had survived.

The summer was almost over, and life went on. What a blessing for our entire family that Barbara was a normal healthy child. Under the watchful eye of every member of the family, she became an exceptionally bright and gifted little girl. At the end of the summer, we finally got some news from my father. He recently had been freed from an American prisoner-of-war camp and was on his way to Berlin to join us.

In 1947, shortly after I gave birth to our son. Barbara is on the right.

Father Comes Home, 1947

My father was coming from Nuremberg, where he had visited with relatives after he returned to Germany after the war's end. I nervously waited for him at the Wannsee train station in Berlin. For three years we had had no contact with him, and my father still had not seen his granddaughter. I had so much to share with him, but where to begin?

Over the last five years many things had happened. We both had endured experiences that had changed us. Our lives had become different. Now I realize that I lacked the maturity then to find the right words to comfort him, something he desperately needed. Our lives now centered on survival—the need to find food and heating fuel, as well as the need to provide a roof over our heads before the next winter arrived. We had no desire to come to terms with the past. We thought of those who had survived instead of grieving for those who were buried. This was the spirit of the times. But it didn't make the grief go away; it just ate at us from the inside.

By nature, I have a proactive approach to life, preparing ahead of time for the next event to come. In the morning I am usually planning for the evening. This personal characteristic had tragic consequences for my relationship with my father. The era to which he belonged was something that I had had to put behind me. Father had not been a part of my life for five years, and he no longer belonged in my future. The problems of everyday life did not permit me to help him escape from a painful past. In retrospect I think it was my duty to help him, and now, when I think about it, my heart is troubled.

Father shared with us the tight quarters we were renting in Berlin, where he was able to set up a bed in the attic. I sensed that my father was not happy here, yet he had no other choice than to stay. The Beneš Decrees that had expelled me from Czechoslovakia also applied to him. Although he never spoke about the conditions in the American prisoner-of-war camp, I could tell that this experience and all that he had witnessed as a soldier in two wars burdened him. Father simply felt unwelcome in Berlin, and he missed Karlsbad, a situation made worse by the lack of work.

To our complete astonishment, after living in Berlin for about a year, Father met a woman who soon would become an important part of his life. Her name was Erna Eschenbach, and everyone called her Oma (Grandma) Esche. They married in 1948. A short time later, the American army no longer needed the house belonging to my in-laws. My father and his new wife were able to move into a small apartment that my in-laws partitioned off in the basement for him and Oma Esche. Then my father finally found a job. It seemed he was on his way to having a normal life again.

But after months of feeling poorly, my father visited a doctor. During the exam the doctor discovered a cancerous growth on my father's spinal column. One year later, in 1951 at the age of fifty-six, my father passed away.

I am certain Father died of a broken heart. The war had destroyed his family and had taken away his home. My father could not come to terms with all that had happened. At least Oma Esche could provide him some comfort during those last years. That is how it ended for this dear and much-loved man. Today only a few photos remain to remind me of him.

Georg and His Brilliant Idea, 1948

Once the necessities in life are taken care of, such as security and food, there is no stopping the creative impulse of a people. Soldiers of the Allied occupation became a part of everyday life in Berlin. Although the top military commanders forbade the soldiers from fraternizing with the German civilians, the German women were too enticing for many of the GIs. Far from home, they could not bury the need for female companionship. For the German women, what often started out as a casual encounter became a wedding and a subsequent move to the other side of the Atlantic.

In many of the houses not taken for use by the occupation army, rooms were rented out to the girlfriends of American GIs, a welcome source of income for the landlords and an opportunity for a soldier to spend several uninterrupted hours together with his girl. Barbara, an exceptionally bright kid, fully exploited these rendezvous to obtain the chocolate bars she craved. She learned to wait on the steps of the apartment building, knowing that any GI making his way out the building would gladly slip one of these treats to her.

Through my daughter we met a noncommissioned officer who lived next door to us. One morning as he was dressing himself, he noticed that the buttons on his uniform jacket were tarnished and dull. As he left the house, he rubbed the buttons feverishly in an unsuccessful attempt to attain a luster on them. It was the duty of every American soldier to polish the buttons on his uniform jackets until they shined. These buttons, worn on the lapel, indicated both rank and the unit to which the soldier was assigned. However, the sticky paste they used to polish the buttons became embedded in the nooks and crannies in the buttons' engraving and over time caused the unsightly discoloring.

I could read Georg's face as though it were a newspaper. Georg watched as the officer tried in vain to shine his buttons as he walked down the sidewalk. Then Georg came up with a "brilliant" idea.

During the war countless firms in Berlin had manufactured military decorations and other insignia. Now that the war was over, they were out of business. Nobody needed these products in peacetime, especially since the former customer had lost the war. Georg knew an owner of one of these firms. He showed the owner a button the American soldiers wore. Georg asked if it could be produced in two sections so that the button could be affixed to the uniform with a piece that was screwed on from the back side. If the button could be removed, then the soldier could rinse the paste off with warm water, avoiding the discoloration.

"No problem," the factory owner said enthusiastically, also sensing an opportunity to make a killing from the hundreds of GIs who clearly needed this product. "I'll get to work on it right away, and tomorrow I will have a sample ready for you."

The officer next door obtained the first batch of the experimental buttons. When he reported for inspection, he stood out from the rest of his fellow soldiers, standing proudly when the commanding officer noticed how sharp his uniform looked. Interest in this invention spread quickly by word of mouth. The neighbor officer negotiated a deal for his fellow soldiers, who paid for the new buttons with the universal currency—cigarettes. Even if you didn't smoke, cigarettes were a much-sought-after commodity. They were easily exchanged on the black market for food, building supplies, and other necessities of life.

For quite a long time this new enterprise ran smoothly. Then the head of the CIC (Counter Intelligence Corps) moved into the house across the street. From his window he could see the constant stream of visitors that entered and exited our little house. One day the military police came to the door—wearing, of course, *our* buttons—and took me to see him.

"So, can you tell me what's going on at your house?" he asked. "Why are so many of our soldiers coming and going? And what about all those civilians that we see coming and going? What's going on?"

I turned my big brown eyes on him. "Is there any rule that tells us how many visitors we can have?"

He shook his head and let me go. A short time later, Georg was arrested. Now Georg knew he could not easily get out of this mess. Somewhat proud of his ingenuity, he showed the high-ranking officer his invention, buttons that maintained their luster.

"Damn it! What gives a German civilian the right to manufacture buttons for our soldiers?" the officer growled. He also knew he could not do anything about it. On top of that, he knew Georg had a brilliant idea. Continuing to rant, the officer said, "Then anyone can come along and invent something. I see a day when you damn Germans will clothe our entire army. Well, that's coming to an end right now!"

All those who were involved in the manufacture and distribution of these buttons were summoned to appear before a military court. Most of those present were former German officers, who looked rather pathetic compared to their American counterparts. These men sat in the room wearing their worn, shabby-looking officer's coats, and accused of violating a law that wasn't on the books. Nobody had forbidden the trade in buttons; however, it was illegal to trade cigarettes. Around the Germans stood a squad of military police, wearing, of course, *our* buttons. The man who manufactured the buttons also attended the hearing, not because he had to, since he lived in the Soviet zone and did not fall under the jurisdiction of the Americans, but rather because he wanted to witness this spectacle, something he would not have missed for the world.

"Who supplied the buttons?" the judge asked of those present.

"Georg Stein," they answered in unison.

"Mr. Stein, you have been accused. How do you plead?"

"Not guilty, your honor," Georg said, shaking his head.

After all the former German officers had been questioned, the judge asked the owner of the company, "Why did you start manufacturing the buttons?"

"You know, your honor, there is simply no longer a demand for the Iron Cross or other similar decorations. Somehow, I had to feed my family. I didn't see anything wrong in it. Besides, the buttons look really sharp—German workmanship at its best."

Not even the judge could hide a smile. After a short recess he returned and announced his decision. "Gentlemen, the manufacturing of buttons must cease immediately. The court sentences you to a fine of 2,000 Reichsmarks each, payable to the clerk of the court." That was the black-market price for a carton of cigarettes, an acceptable sentence. The US occupation army liked Georg's two-part button idea and took over the production of these buttons.

They say invention is born out of necessity, and we certainly needed it to survive in postwar Berlin. After the judge imposed his sentence, we lost an important source of income. It's tempting to imagine what would have happened if Georg had produced his invention under different circumstances, if he'd had an opportunity to patent his idea. Every soldier in the world would have been a potential customer. We would have become rich. But the patent office wasn't open then, and it didn't happen.

Perspective: The Second Battle for Berlin, 1948–1949

The war had been over for four years, and four foreign powers governed Germany. Noticeably absent was the peace desperately needed to rebuild lives beyond mere subsistence. During the Nazi era the German people had been pawns in Hitler's plan for world domination. Now they were pawns in a struggle of political ideologies, communism versus democracy, and a command economy versus capitalism. During the Cold War, Berlin once again returned to the political forefront. This 700-year-old pearl of the Spree, the former capital of Prussia, imperial Germany, and the Third Reich, paid a terrible price for the status it had attained.

The Germans, especially Berliners, wanted nothing more than a democratic constitution and an alliance with the Western democracies. Why did they have such a negative view of the Soviet Union? After all, the Soviets had liberated Berlin and had been present when its starving citizens emerged from their bunkers to see the light of day. The civilians probably believed the stories spread through the Nazi propaganda machine—that for the destruction of the Soviets' country, the Germans would be repaid an eye for an eye and a tooth for a tooth.

Food and medicine became essential. Everything else was icing on the cake. Nobody had yet made the rebuilding of German industry a priority. The Soviets, in fact, dismantled many of the industrial facilities to rebuild the factories that had been destroyed in their own country during the war. For example, the Soviets carted off giant electrical generators from Berlin and Spandau, leaving behind empty buildings. Often, the Soviets loaded equipment onto railcars and then left everything to rust on the railroad tracks.

In many areas of Germany, the Western powers did not stand in the way of economic recovery. Yet those left to carry out the rebuilding consisted mostly of women, children, and the elderly.

After the war, Germany was divided into four occupation zones, governed by the United States, the Soviet Union, Great Britain, and France. Berlin, in middle of the Soviet zone, was also occupied by the same powers, who divided the city into four sectors. The Allies established an executive authority, the *Kommandatura*, which in theory would decide issues requiring attention and governance, formulate a response, and issue formal orders to the Lord Mayor and the Berlin Magistrate. The structure of the Kommandatura was based on the Allied Control Council, also headquartered in Berlin in the former *Reichskammergericht*, (an historic court building). The Allied Control Council served the same purpose as the Kommandatura for the whole of Germany and superseded the Kommandatura on issues affecting both. New laws required the unanimous approval of all four nations.

Through the Allied Control Council, the Allies began the rebuilding of Germany and attempted to cleanse the nation of its former Nazi ideology. For example, on February 25, 1947, the Allied Control Council dissolved Prussia, a political entity that existed for hundreds of years, one that played a major role in shaping European political history.

The Soviets became dissatisfied with the four-nation status of Berlin. They saw themselves as the rightful conquerors of Berlin and were looking for a means of forcing the other three powers—the Western Allies of France, Great Britain, and the United States—to abandon the city.

Ideological differences caused the gap between East and West to expand. The Soviets feared a strong Germany, a country that invaded their homeland twice in the twentieth century. However, the Western Allies felt it would be in their best interests to create an economically self-sufficient Germany. The moral and legal obligation to feed the German people were a tremendous burden on the treasuries of both the United States and Great Britain. These ideological differences come to a head in March 1948, when the Soviet representative walked out of a meeting of the Allied Control Council, ending any further cooperation with the organization.

The gap between East and West widened even further when the Western Allies proposed currency reform. To stabilize the economy, they intended to replace the old Reichsmark (Imperial Mark) with the Deutsche Mark, commonly known as the D-Mark. The United States Air Force was responsible for handling currency exchanges in Berlin, where they would offer a "door prize" for the first forty Reichsmarks, which were exchanged 1:1 for the D-Mark. The exchange rate fell to 10:1 for any remaining Reichsmarks. This was a defining moment in German history, the demise of the Reichsmark, a final relic of imperial Germany.

On Monday, June 21, 1948, Germans stood in line to exchange one currency for another. The Soviet response was swift. In Berlin, the Western Allies were dependent on rail and road transport for supplies, which they shipped from their occupation zones in the west, through the Soviet zone, and finally into West Berlin. Without this lifeline, the supply of food, heating fuel and other necessities would be exhausted within thirty days. Knowing this, on June 24 the Soviets sealed off this lifeline to the west, hoping that a starving civilian population would force the Western Allies to withdraw from the city. Transport over waterways leading into the city was also interrupted. The Soviets then cut the electrical supply to West Berlin.

In propaganda messages the Soviets spread the false rumor that the Allies were abandoning the city. Coincidentally, many Western officials had, in fact, already left the city, taking their dependents with them. Berliners began to panic. They could not foresee any possibility of the city holding out under these circumstances. For them, it seemed it was only a matter of time before the Soviets would occupy West Berlin.

Berlin became the forum for the first test of will between the Soviet Union and the Western Allies, who still insisted on a four-power occupation of Berlin. Yet as time would show, the Soviet Union did not have enough leverage to influence the changes it desired. Like so many other events in history, the struggle for power was carried on the shoulders of civilians.

In these difficult times two men would write history: General Lucius D. Clay, the commander of the American occupation troops in Berlin, and Ernst Reuter, the governing mayor of West Berlin. General Clay refused to surrender "his" city. He initially proposed sending a tank column down the Autobahn linking western Allied–occupied Germany with Berlin to test Soviet resolve, but this suggestion was quickly vetoed by President Truman. Instead, the Western Allies devised a plan to airlift supplies into Berlin, a risky and untested proposal. They took advantage of a 1945 treaty with the Soviet Union that granted them three air corridors from Allied-occupied western Germany into Berlin. Road and rail access, on the other hand, had never been part of any formal agreement. Through this technicality, the aerial resupply of Berlin, known as Operation Vittles, began. Historical accounts in English refer to this event as the Berlin Airlift, whereas the German accounts use the term *Luftbrücke*, meaning "air bridge."

This undertaking was not easy. The single runway at Tempelhof, the airport in the American sector, had to be reinforced to withstand the weight of the heavy transport aircraft. Furthermore, buildings stood at both ends of the 6,000-foot runway, making both landing and takeoff very treacherous. Frantically, and with the help of German civilian employees, the necessary improvements were made at Tempelhof, and during the operation work crews constructed two additional runways. The Americans enlisted transport aircraft from all corners of the world for this undertaking. Cargo planes arrived from Alaska, Hawaii, Tokyo, and other bases. Initially, the United States used the C-47 Skytrain (and its passenger equivalent the Douglas DC-3) with a 3.5-ton capacity to haul supplies into Berlin. Later, once the airport improvements were complete, 10-ton load C-54 Skymasters and Douglas DC-4s joined the supply effort. In the United States, pilots trained in Montana to become accustomed to the flying conditions they would encounter in Berlin.

British transport aircraft landed at the Gatow airfield in Berlin, located in their sector. The British also allowed the Americans to utilize this airfield for the airlift. The French were not able to contribute any transport aircraft because they were being used in a new war in Indochina (Vietnam). However, France agreed to build a complete, new and larger airport in its sector on the shores of Lake Tegel, an engineering feat that they accomplish in three months. The airport was mostly built by hand, by thousands of mostly female laborers who worked day and night.

Unfortunately, the French engineers had to overcome a major obstacle during the construction at Tegel. A Soviet communication tower stood in the way. After giving the Soviets ample warning to move the tower, which the Soviets ignored, French and American forces blew up the tower. Problem solved!

The next day the Soviet commander paid his French colleague a visit. Known for being very hot-tempered, the Soviet commander ranted for several minutes, swearing up a storm, arms waving, his face flushed in anger. "How could you do such a thing?" he yelled.

The French general, keeping his composure, looked at his Soviet colleague and said nonchalantly, "Avec de la dynamite, mon general."[2]

The Soviet general continued his tirade, but he could not undo what had been done. He did not want to concede that he was losing this tug-of-war for Berlin. The Soviets had seriously underestimated the resolve of the Berliners and the Western Allies.

Cargo planes landed around the clock at Tempelhof, Gatow, and Tegel. They had a nickname among the Berliners: raisin bombers. At times the Soviets sent fighter planes to harass an incoming transporter, but for the most part the resupply missions ran smoothly, and more serious obstructions to air traffic, such as aerial balloons, were never employed.

On September 9, 1948, 300,000 people gathered in front of what remained of the *Reichstag* (parliament building) in Berlin, standing at the border of the Soviet sector. They went there to hear a speech delivered by Ernst Reuter, the governing mayor of Berlin, who made a fervent appeal to the entire world, that they shall not forget Berlin. "People of this world... look upon this city and see that you should not, cannot abandon this city and this people."

The crowd saw a great and valiant man. During the First World War he fought on the eastern front and was taken prisoner. After he returned to Germany, Reuter became a member of the Communist Party. In 1922, his affiliation with the party ended when he was expelled after a disagreement with its leadership. Reuter later joined the German Social Democrat party. After rejecting the Nazi ideology, he spent the Second World War exiled in Turkey. After the war Reuter returned to Germany to help his people rebuild. His appeal to the world in 1948 did not fall on deaf ears. However, West Berlin endured a blockade that lasted almost an entire year.

West Berlin and its two and one-half million people needed an estimated 4,000 to 5,000 tons of supplies each day to survive in

---

2   "With dynamite, my dear colleague."

the summer months, especially food, medicine, and coal. When it became apparent that the blockade would last indefinitely, another 6,000 tons of coal per day was needed to heat the homes of Berliners through the winter. A total of 280 aircraft were assembled for this mission, landing around the clock every ninety seconds. Despite the blockade, life and work in the city continued. The few functioning industries still produced their goods, which were flown out in an attempt to bolster the local economy.[3]

In 1949 the Federal Republic of Germany was formed from the American, French, and British zones, and became known as West Germany. That same year the German Democratic Republic, known as East Germany, was founded in the Soviet occupation zone. However, neither East nor West Germany ratified a peace treaty with the victorious powers. In fact, the Allies did not approve a peace treaty with Germany until September 12, 1990, during the Two-Plus- Four negotiations, which also resulted in a reunified Germany.

Life under the Blockade, 1948-49

Even before the proposed currency reform, fear and uncertainty had become part of our daily lives. We never knew how the Soviets would react to local and world events, but in Berlin we certainly felt that we were at their mercy. We could feel the tension mounting but didn't know how things would develop.

We now had to give up our tiny home, to make it available to the landlord's relatives who had fled from Eastern Europe. Luckily, the American army had just vacated the home belonging to my in-laws, and we were able to move into an apartment in their house. I was just thankful that we had a roof over our heads.

We, the citizens of Berlin, were trapped in the impenetrable darkness, not knowing whether the outside world cared for us.

---

3   For additional information about the Berlin Airlift, see Gail S. Halvorsen, *The Berlin Candy Bomber* (Bountiful, UT: Horizon, 1990), and Robert Miller, *To Save a City: The Berlin Airlift, 1948–1949*, (College Station, TX: Texas A&M University Press, 2015).

Occasionally, we could pick up some news from a radio broadcast during the few hours each day when the electricity flowed. Limited one-way passenger rail service took some Berliners to the west. Georg wanted a way out of Berlin because his worst fear was that the city would fall into the hands of the Soviets. He contacted some relatives in Nuremberg and arranged to visit them while looking for work and an apartment for us. He went through a lot of trouble to obtain a ticket for the inter-zonal train without knowing whether he would be able to return after making the journey to the west.

Just before he departed, he hugged me one last time and said, "Mother, soon I'll have everything taken care of. I'll find a job and an apartment, and before long we'll be living in the west. Don't worry about a thing."

I didn't worry about the journey. I worried about the coming winter and having a roof over our heads. We needed to prepare for the cold weather and stock up on food. About four weeks later, he landed at Tempelhof. How he came back was one of those mysteries that no longer surprised me. Quite simply, Georg had come across someone who had given him an airline ticket for free. I think if Georg had been born a cat and thrown from a window, he'd land on his feet no matter how far he fell.

As Georg had learned the hard way, the economic situation in other parts of Germany was just as dismal as in Berlin. Industry lay in ruins, and the cities overflowed with refugees and displaced people.

Jobs and apartments were scarce at best. It wasn't better elsewhere. Who needed another family of refugees from Berlin? Georg stood before me discouraged. He had found neither a job nor a place to live. Despite the disappointment, Georg was happy to be reunited with his family.

When Georg came home, fall-like weather rolled in with him. Now winter approached, and my worst fears were about to come true. It was a long, bitter cold winter with extreme demands that it placed on us. We clung to each other, for in each other we found our only hope to keep going.

Household gas and electricity became rationed commodities, which were turned on for only about two hours each day. It would have been nice to have the option of consuming our two-hour supply during the evening hours, to bring perhaps a little comfort to our difficult situation. But not a chance! The gas and electricity flowed mostly late at night or in the wee hours of morning. It became quite a circus to wake up suddenly in the middle of the night and, within that short period of time, use the gas and electricity allotted to us to cook, iron, wash, listen to the news, sew, and heat the house. Of course, after our frantic attempts to accomplish all these household chores, the cold and darkness returned once again.

For the rest of the night, we depended on petroleum lamps, which became useless without the required fuel, another rationed commodity. We were terrified of lighting any candles. They became so valuable, set aside only for a worst-case scenario, when no other source of illumination could be found. Of course, we could not heat the house with a two-hour supply of gas. Compounding the heating problem was the fact that many homes in Berlin, including ours, still lacked glass windows, and many homes had a section of the wall or ceiling missing. We still had not recovered from the damage left behind by the first battle for Berlin.

Our situation in Lichterfelde was comparatively better than the situation in other parts of the city. However, the closer you came to the city center in Berlin, the more devastation you encountered. I often wondered how many citizens of Berlin went to bed wearing everything they owned, lying there as the snow filtered through an opening in the roof or as chilled air flooded the room through a damaged wall.

In West Berlin heating fuel became just as scarce as food. Before long we had exhausted our yearly household ration of coal, just fifty pounds. Because an empty cellar couldn't heat the house, a trip to the Soviet sector represented our only chance of staying warm. Many of us found the very thought of traveling to the Soviet sector repugnant, but you have to do what you have to do. In fact, traveling there was relatively easy with the city train. While hunting for a lump of coal, we sometimes came across some potatoes. Mostly, it was the women who went through the trouble of obtaining coal in East

Berlin, enduring the watchful if not offended stare of Soviet soldiers. Of course, the men could have reached the Soviet sector just as easily as the women. The question was whether they would ever return. Even then the Soviets might have selected any halfway nourished and reasonably strong male for an all-expense-paid one-way trip to the east. Several thousand German men still performed forced labor in the Siberian gulags or in other areas of the Soviet Union. The Soviets desperately needed more able-bodied men to repair the damage left behind by war. On top of that, the Soviets needed to replace the laborers who had already died in captivity.

Our husbands had already survived the hell of war, life-threatening injuries, and prisoner-of-war camps. We now hoped that the most frightening moments of their lives were behind them. That meant the women of Berlin had no choice but to drag the fifty-pound bags of coal onto the train cars and eventually to the empty coal cellars at home.

In the Soviet zone we had to pay cash for our coal. Now how were we supposed to obtain cash? Certainly not from the government. Most of our business dealings involved bartering one item for another. Some, like me, could sell something of value that had been acquired before the war, such as jewelry or a coat. Others managed to provide a service, such as sewing or baking.

Eventually, the coal trips to the Soviet sector, which were tests of physical strength and endurance, caused back problems for me, a lifelong reminder of this ordeal. While I attempted to buy coal for our stove, Georg looked after Barbara. She was four years old and found herself drawn into our desperate attempt to stay warm too. Among her chores was the collection of every branch or piece of wood or coal found on the street.

The American households always managed to remain warm. They also provided an unexpected source of free coal. Barbara had found an American friend who lived on the same street as us. Together they stood on the street corner, and as the coal truck made the turn, they would let out a yell and wave to the driver, who gave the steering wheel a slight jerk, sending some of the load onto the street. Armed with small pails, the girls picked the coal off the street and returned home triumphantly with full buckets and jet-black hands and faces. After they had spent several weeks standing on the corner in bitter cold weather, this game became old. Barbara's American friend, who was also four years old, came up with another idea. Instead of waiting outside for the coal to fall from the truck, why not wait until it had been loaded into the cellar? So, they walked down into the cellar inside the American house, loaded their buckets with coal, and brought some of it to our stove. This hungry coal-eating monster had to be fed constantly. And if we could not feed it, we received the most effective punishment ever devised: bitter cold that penetrated through the many layers of clothing we wore, tormenting us as we slept. To conserve fuel, we heated only one room inside the house with a small stove. We all slept in this room to harness the body heat of everyone present.

During the long cold winter, the Berliners burned anything that closely resembled fuel. Every park, especially the "green lungs" of Berlin, Grunewald and Tiergarten, became a deforested wasteland. In the gardens, wood fencing ceased to exist. I am also sure that many sacrificed their wooden doors, tables, and chairs to combat the cold. When I think back upon this time, I wonder how we survived. My in-laws were generous and didn't ask us to pay any rent. We prepared meals together, but because of gas rationing, warm meals were not a regular feature of everyday life. In the garden we collected every single apple that was remotely edible. Like those final days in Karlsbad, once again I became a forager.

The winter of 1948–1949 was long and difficult like so many of the previous winters of this decade. Despite the pilots' skill, weather conditions continually tested the ability of those flying the cargo planes into and out of Berlin. Those of us who shivered on the ground continually prayed for decent flying conditions, both for their safety and for our survival.

Perspective: Relationships between Nations

The squabble between East and West continued, a test of political ideologies rather than street warfare. Nevertheless, tension between the two foes sometimes brought fear and terror to the citizens of Berlin. One such incident involved a Soviet general and his convoy traveling through Zehlendorf in the American sector at excessive speed. The Soviets had headquarters both in Karlshorst, in East Berlin, and in Potsdam, south of Berlin. Zehlendorf was the most convenient route between the two. When an American patrol stopped the convoy, the general's adjutant attempted to persuade a sergeant to let them travel further. After negotiations between the sergeant and the adjutant broke down, the general decided to intervene.

"Soldier, I order you to let my adjutant pass. Stand down. We are on our way to headquarters."

The sergeant drew his pistol, shoved the barrel into the belly of the highly decorated general, and said, "I don't take orders from any Soviet."

The three men stared at each other coldly for a few seconds.

Finally, the general said, "Okay," and climbed back inside the car.

A short time later the sergeant said, "Have a pleasant journey," and the convoy departed, continuing the journey at the posted speed limit. That same day General Clay heard about the incident, and behind closed doors he let his anger be known. Of course, in public General Clay had to appear as a diplomat, which meant an obligatory journey to Soviet headquarters and a personal apology. He hoped this journey to see his Soviet counterpart would result in some sort of friendly dialogue between both sides. Instead, Clay was treated like a schoolboy on his way to see the principal. The Soviets received him coldly and did not even offer him a chair or a glass of water. Clay's Soviet counterpart entered the room, bluntly accepted the apology, and quickly left.

One day, Colonel Gail Halvorsen, an American pilot who sympathized with the plight of Berlin's children, dropped three small packages from his cargo plane while approaching Tempelhof Airport for a landing. These packages contained something sweet for the children standing near the runway below. To break the fall of these packages, he attached a handkerchief to each one, to act as a miniature parachute. Soon the children of Berlin were gathering near the runway, waiting for the "candy pilot" to drop them some more candy bars. Halvorsen used his own service ration of chocolate and some donated by his fellow airmen for this gesture of goodwill. When he ran out of handkerchiefs, he resorted to cutting up old shirts to make the parachutes. The US Air Force and public soon learned of Halvorsen's desire to help the children of Berlin. The air force relieved him from delivering freight and instead assigned him to "Operation Little Vittles." A corporate sponsor in America donated the chocolate, and American schoolchildren assembled the parachutes, while Halvorsen continued to fly over Berlin, dropping candy to the boys and girls waiting below.

To demonstrate their resolve not to abandon Berlin, on Easter Day 1949 the Western Allies staged the "Easter Parade." In a twenty-four-hour period, at a record-setting pace, American and British aircraft landed every sixty-two seconds, delivering almost thirteen thousand tons of coal for the besieged city, a phenomenal feat of unequaled logistics.

Following the Easter Parade, serious negotiations between the Western Allies and the Soviets began. Although the Soviets still had serious objections to currency reform, they had to concede that the blockade would never achieve their policy objectives in Germany. On May 4, 1949, the Allies announced an agreement to end the blockade in eight days' time.

At one minute after midnight on May 12, 1949, the Soviets once again allowed rail and road traffic into West Berlin. The Allies, not trusting the Soviets to keep the traffic flowing, continued the airlift until September 30, 1949, allowing the Allies to stockpile additional supplies in case of another blockade. During the Berlin Airlift, 278,228 transport flights delivered over 2.3 million tons of supplies at an estimated cost of $350 million to United States taxpayers, £17 million to the British, and 150 million Deutschmarks to those in Western Germany.[4] In the meantime, the citizens of Berlin earned the respect and admiration of people throughout the world.

---

4   Equivalent values in the early 2020s would be more than ten times higher.

The End of the Blockade and Finally a Little Light in Our Lives, 1949

In 2004, I had the pleasure of meeting and getting to know Colonel Halvorsen. He was in Berlin to celebrate the publication of his biography in German, and I was at the publisher's event. Like me, he was now old but hadn't lost his vitality. I hope he appreciates the very large impact he had not only on the children of Berlin but also on their parents—he brought a big ray of hope and love in every candy parachute he dropped.

By the end of February, the days had become noticeably longer. We prayed for a quick end to this nightmare. For us the war continued. Although bombs no longer dropped from the sky, and soldiers no longer battled in the streets, the years of deprivation had become increasingly difficult to endure. Under such conditions, when survival constantly hangs in the balance, freedom tends to lose its value.

The months of deprivation had been an enormous strain on all of us. Almost everyone, especially the children, suffered from malnutrition. Suddenly, the electricity flowed, and the stores restocked their shelves. A flood of help rolled into Berlin that summer, something that even touched our family. Barbara, along with many of the other children in Berlin, attended a summer camp at St. Peter-Ording on the North Sea, a program not tainted by political propaganda. Finally, she could be a kid and have fun. Through good nutrition and fresh air, she recovered from the deprivation that had plagued the first years of her life. She had a joyous and wonderful summer, full of love and laughter among Berlin's smaller citizens. When she returned home, I saw a different person. Her cheeks were rosy, and she had gained weight. Now began a new chapter in our lives, with hope for things to return to a new and better normal.

Perspective: The Race for the Scientists

After 1949, the Soviets accepted a divided Berlin, and communism was contained on their side of the Iron Curtain. Sometime later, rumors surfaced that the Americans considered using the atomic bomb to protect Berlin, which may have influenced Stalin's decision to lift the blockade.

During the Second World War, German scientists attempted to develop nuclear weapons. Thankfully, they were not successful in this endeavor. However, during the war, German engineering produced the technology to build jet aircraft and ballistic missiles, the means by which nuclear warheads could be delivered to a target.

During the final days of the Second World War, British and American intelligence officers searched for German scientists among the prisoners of war. Especially useful were those with special knowledge of atomic science, rocketry, aeronautics, and the manufacture of synthetic materials. They were offered employment in the West, and later some received citizenship.

Over 1,500 of these experts eventually came to the United States as part of Operation Paperclip. One of the foremost German scientists was Wernher von Braun. During the war he worked on the construction of the V-1 and V-2 rockets that killed countless civilians in Great Britain. Thousands of slave laborers perished while producing these weapons. In the United States, von Braun played a pivotal role in the manned space program, developing the Saturn V rocket that made the Apollo 11 mission to the moon possible. President Ford awarded him the National Medal of Science in 1975.

Hubertus Strughold, another comrade in arms and German scientist, received recognition as the father of American space medicine. In 1949 he became director of the School of Aviation Medicine at Randolph Air Force Base in Texas. His work after the war led to the development of the pressurized suits worn by astronauts. Numerous awards were bestowed on him for his work in space science, and in 1977 the Aeromedical Library at Brooks Air Force Base was named after him. However, following his death in 1986, Strughold's alleged connection to experiments conducted at the Dachau concentration camp became more widely known following the release of US Army Intelligence documents from 1945. According to these documents, Strughold played a role in conducting inhuman experiments on concentration camp prisoners, testing the effects of low-pressure conditions at high altitude. These revelations significantly damaged his reputation and most of the honors previously given were revoked, including removing his name from the science library at Brooks Air Force Base.

After the war the Soviets also managed to "recruit" hundreds of specialists who had not already immigrated to Western countries. The Soviets kidnapped some scientists from Berlin and even some from West Germany. The scientists were taken to the Soviet Union and forced to work on a variety of secret projects to build the Soviet space and atomic programs. Many lived under the worst of conditions and returned home only after several years in exile.

Our Attempt to Return to a Normal Life and Find a Bit of Happiness, 1949–1951

Money was still tight, but finally our lives made a turn for the better and started to resemble something like normal after the tragic events of the last ten years. During the blockade nobody in our family had held a steady job, though Georg did some occasional work for the Americans. Real, full-time jobs were just hard to find.

Thanks to my mother-in-law and her connections with the Christian Social Democrats, one of Germany's political parties, Georg found employment with the regional tax authority as the blockade came to an end.

It is funny how the gradual improvement in the economy lifted our spirits. With a little extra money in our pockets, I could spruce things up at home. In a secondhand store I came across some furniture that seemed to match the decor of our apartment. The curtains I sewed also made our home a bit cozier. During the few hours of free time that I allowed myself, I reminisced about the life we had once had. How I missed the nice things from my childhood. I thought about Mother's old collection of glass with ruby-red ornamentation and a bit of powdered shell for color. I remembered some of the beautiful pieces of china manufactured at the factory in Pirkenhammer. I remembered my father's paintings and my great-grandmother's antique furniture. The few pieces of Mother's jewelry that I had managed to bring from Karlsbad had been sold piece by piece on the black market during the blockade.

While serving in the armed forces of the Third Reich, Georg had attended some educational courses that helped him obtain the civil service job. After taking another intensive course, overnight Georg became a customs inspector. I wouldn't say he was born to do this kind of work, being a customs inspector and a bureaucrat on top of that, but for the moment it would suffice. His family needed a steady paycheck, and along with his new job, our lives slowly acquired a day-to-day routine. Many things were still difficult to obtain, but now the economy was starting to make a slow yet steady recovery.

I spent most of my time sewing and working in the garden. Since I took care of the yard work, the in-laws continued to not charge us any rent for the apartment. I also earned a bit of pocket money performing some office work for a young attorney who lived in our building.

Back then housework had a certain charm. We washed laundry by hand. I first boiled the dirty laundry in a large copper tub and then hand-rinsed the clothes. Finally, I wrung everything dry by hand. For a large item, such as a bedsheet, four hands were required, with   someone holding the sheet at each end, twisting in opposite directions, to squeeze out the excess water. In the summer I hung the wash in the garden to dry, and in the winter, I had to haul everything three stories up to the attic.

In the spring of 1950, Barbara's life became more serious. She started school, although it would be a stretch to call it an education. There simply weren't enough teachers, and the school buildings were random structures with some sort of makeshift repair, rather than true schools. To make the most of each classroom, student instruction lasted for half a day.

My in-laws made renovations to their properties and rented every apartment they could carve out. To me, in those early days after the airlift ended, the apartment house we lived in seemed like a beehive, the pitter-patter of tiny feet constantly audible. The blockade had triggered a baby boom.

Perspective: Prisoners of War and Homecoming

At the end of the Second World War, more than 11 million German soldiers were taken into custody by the Allies. Many of the German soldiers held by the Soviets were sent to labor camps, the so-called gulags in Siberia. Of the more than 1.5 million German soldiers listed as missing during the Second World War, a significant number of them may have perished from inhumane treatment in these camps rather than on the battlefield.

Following long-standing international military custom, most of the 11 million German prisoners of war had been repatriated by 1949. However, ten years after the end of the war, the Soviets still held an estimated 85,000 German prisoners of war, asserting that they have been convicted of war crimes.

The repatriation of German prisoners of war in Soviet custody became a foreign policy objective for Konrad Adenauer, West Germany's first chancellor. On September 8, 1955, he traveled to Moscow for the first official state visit by a West German chancellor. He personally intervened on behalf of the German prisoners of war. The Soviets informed Adenauer that the prisoners would be released if West Germany established full diplomatic relations with the Soviet Union. This proposal was problematic because neither the West German government nor the Western Allies were willing to accept a divided Germany, which the Soviet proposal entailed. Eventually, a compromise solution surfaced wherein West Germany recognized the special status of the Soviet Union as one of the victors of the Second World War while recognizing the expectations of the Western Allies, who linked an eventual peace treaty with German reunification. The compromise paved the way for the release of the remaining German prisoners of war, all of whom are repatriated by January 1956.

Those returning from captivity found a Germany far different from the one they left behind. In many cases their wives, if they had survived the war and its aftermath, had given them up for dead and found a new partner. On the other hand, when the Soviet Union finally repatriated the German prisoners of war, many German women had to give up all hope that their husband or son would return home.

My Work as a Storyteller, 1951

The Germans were rebuilding their lives, brick by brick, from the ruins that the war had left behind. Everyone lent a hand, the young and old, men and women. Many children had lost a father, and now their mothers toiled outside the home to put food on the table. Often, I babysat their children while they worked. I enjoyed watching over this lively bunch as they roamed around in the garden. There was only one problem: feeding these hungry mouths. They always seemed to have an insatiable appetite, but they gladly accepted whatever I could give, which sometimes was just a small piece of fruit.

Playing was a way for them to forget their fears and concentrate on just being kids, forgetting a home environment where the stress of everyday life in Berlin made the adults short-tempered or depressed. When they couldn't play outdoors because of the weather, we sat together in the living room, and I told many of the wonderful fairy tales that my mother and great-grandmother had taught me as a little girl. Also, in the evenings, when the housework was finished, I fetched my knitting needles and clicked one against the other while Barbara and her little friends waited to hear the stories.

How I loved telling them these fairy tales from my childhood. The children often wanted to hear the ghost stories, the ones about old spinsters and stuffy noblemen who haunted the castles and mansions because of a troubled past. The children also seemed to long for tales that told of people who perhaps had a better past than they did. Did they find in these stories hope for a better future? Fairy tales are a universal cure that always enchants children no matter where they live. Many years later, when my granddaughter lived with us in Lyons, Colorado, I just had to tell her the same stories. "Oma," she said one day (calling me by a German word for "Grandma"), "tell me about when the kids ran out of food." At first, I misunderstood what she meant, but soon I realized that she wanted to hear about Hansel and Gretel and not about the horror of postwar Germany.

When Georg worked the night shift, Barbara and I snuggled together in bed, nibbling on bits of chocolate and listing to music that played on a small radio. That's how we would spend many hours together, until we were dead tired and fell asleep. There we found refuge from the outside world and were both content and happy.

Photo taken during the blockade, the heavy coat hides how thin I was. The doll never left Barbara's arms.

Everything Is Subject to Constant Change, 1951

It was an unusually hot day for Berlin, with the thermometer pushing 105 degrees Fahrenheit. My mother-in-law and I picked berries in the garden. Around five o'clock in the evening, we finally had enough. We took the berries inside the house as Berlin continued suffocating under the oppressive heat wave. Barbara and I started to wash the berries while my mother-in-law left to buy some sugar for canning. Soon, Georg returned home, and we decided to ride off on his motorcycle and visit some friends. During the visit, which had not lasted long, Georg received a phone call. The news was horrible; his mother had just suffered a massive heart attack. We rushed home immediately. The phone call had left no doubt whatsoever that Margarethe's condition was grave, and when we arrived home, she had already passed away. She had just turned sixty and now was dead, her never-ending work—the arduous tasks of taking care of her family, her elegant home, and the garden—left unfinished.

I wouldn't say she had a happy marriage, and this plagued the union from the onset. Her husband, a tyrant, never gave his wife any affection, a form of oppression he inflicted on her every moment of every day. Margarethe, on the other hand, felt no love for her children. When Georg lay in the military hospital in East Prussia, she did not express any concern or care whatsoever. Margarethe never defended her children from their tyrannical father. Either she feared her husband, or she wanted to hide her emotional side from others. The only person in the world to whom Margarethe showed the slightest measure of affection was her granddaughter. No matter how tired she felt, Margarethe found time to make something for Barbara or perform some act of kindness, such as cut something out from a piece of paper. Through this bond between the two of them, I also felt some attachment to my mother-in-law. She and Max behaved so differently from my own parents, and perhaps for this reason I found it difficult to understand my in-laws. Over time I began to view Margarethe as someone with a troubled soul. I saw the inner conflict within her, a part of her that wanted to rebel against the life handed to her and the reality that she could not.

Margarethe's brothers and sisters attended the funeral service along with their children. I could not believe how many people were able to squeeze into that small church. The heat wave still had not broken, and I remember preparing a mountain of food in that murderously hot kitchen. The feast included cakes, salads, and grilled meats for the funeral guests. After the funeral, reality came back with a vengeance. The daily routine continued, and we sorely missed the contribution Margarethe had made to this endeavor. How could we possibly fill the hole she had left behind? Who would take care of the household, the fruit trees, the berry bushes, the roses, and other flowers? Who would cook and can what we had just harvested?

Is There Really Such a Thing as "Normal?" 1952

It seemed too overwhelming—the death of my mother, a miscarriage, a stillborn child, the death of my father, and now the loss of Margarethe. We desperately needed a break from all these tragic events. For a while I helped Grandpa Max with the household chores, but soon I was freed from this obligation. My father-in-law obviously had plans, including a second marriage. About a year after Margarethe died, Max met a nice childless widow named Erna. Although his first wife had completely spoiled him, the second wife was not about to follow in the footsteps of her predecessor, something she made abundantly clear right from the start.

Georg and I devoted a lot of effort to our marriage, and now we celebrated our tenth wedding anniversary. Yet for many years our marriage lacked the emotion and closeness that it should have had. Young love is wonderful, like the freshness of spring. The unavoidable summer then takes over, and soon obligations replace feelings. Hopefully, a more ideal relationship subsequently emerges. For both of us, political and social events, as well as personal tragedy, steered the direction of our married life. The intense feelings that couples initially experience were, in our case, set aside way too early.

After finishing high school, I had attended the university for a semester in 1940. Then I'd had to abandon my dream of a university education to fulfill my compulsory civil service obligation during the war. The dream of higher education never left me, but my family obligations and the devastation left behind by the war made it impossible to pursue this goal. Most of the universities in Germany were not fully functioning. In Berlin, the famous Humboldt University now stood in the Soviet sector, which did not accept students from West Berlin. To provide students in West Berlin with an education, the Free University of Berlin was founded in the American sector.

Whenever Georg worked the day shift, we could expect him home around five o'clock in the evening, close to the time when Barbara finished her school day. Together, Georg and I picked Barbara up from school, and we returned home together, showing everybody a nice young family. Many said Georg and I were a dream couple, something we found flattering but not always accurate.

Using every trick in the book, I tried to build a modest yet comfortable life for us, which started in our apartment and the clothes we wore. Thankfully, the days of sewing clothes from leftover wool were now behind us. Life became more natural. I would say that we were content, but not that we were happy. Despite promotions Georg did not find his work fulfilling. Perhaps part of the problem was the many years spent in the armed forces and his time in the prisoner-of-war camp. These experiences had left Georg defiant of any kind of authority.

We had a nice apartment and many friends, some of whom Georg had first met while attending high school. Dinners at restaurants, evening parties, and the occasional ball added some color to our lives. I shall never forget this homemade dress I wore to a ball in 1952. In an old suitcase in the attic, I had found several pieces of clothing from the time before the war. One of the dresses consisted of black georgette and had spaghetti straps. I tailored the dress to my size and added a few rows of frill to the skirt. I looked fabulous! I wore a borrowed pearl necklace to complete the most striking of all accessories, my youth, and we danced throughout the night to the rhythm of beautiful music, tossing aside all that had happened in the last ten years. After so many years of wandering in the darkness, we now stood in the limelight under the gaze of admiring onlookers. How they envied our youthful appearance.

I also remember how, in 1950, we put on all the finest things that we could find in our closets and attics or that we could borrow, to celebrate the wedding of Georg's best friend from his earliest years in school. It was like playing dress-up as children, only now it cleansed our souls.

During the war Georg lost many friends; some died, and others are still listed as missing. Those who survived formed a club, *Virgilia*, and met together regularly.[5] Sometimes the club invited the wives

---

5   The Virgilia Club was still active until at least the early 2000s, when I would occasionally get letters from some of Georg's friends in the club.

to attend an event they sponsored. I found it interesting to see how life treated these men, many of whom Georg had met when he was a teenager. During the early 1950s some became successful businessmen, and others attained political appointments, often through the influence of their parents. Many lawyers from Georg's youth now held important posts within the new German government.

I was surprised to learn that several American military officers belonged to the club. These men had left Germany as children or young adults to go to America, before the war. They had been deployed back to Germany after the war and joined the club to contact old friends.

The wedding of Georg's best friend from his early childhood, Berlin, 1950. I am in the front pair, and Georg is walking in the second pair. With borrowed clothes we managed to look elegant for the occasion.

But something seemed awkward. During events hosted by the club, former soldiers of a defeated nation mixed with military officers and civil servants from the side that had won. When they now spoke to each other, they did so carefully and with restraint, sounding the other out, attempting to avoid any topic deemed too sensitive. Actually, the friendships had ceased long ago. The images they had of each other had been shaped by years of propaganda and conflicting ideologies that eventually had sent the world into chaos.

Barbara was a flower girl at the wedding. She is on the right.

The Divided City, 1952–1956

After the blockade it was possible to visit with friends and relatives in East Berlin. For us in West Berlin, things had improved considerably since the Soviet blockade ended. During the airlift we had needed the East Berliners for some of the necessities of life, and now they needed the same from us West Berliners. In our section of town, the display windows showcased anything you could ever want, yet our neighbors in the Soviet sector had to resort to the black market and depended on gifts from friends and relatives because of rationing. Nobody would dare visit someone in East Berlin without bringing at least a small can of coffee, which was still a luxury for us but also a symbol of the economic recovery in West Berlin. The hope of future prosperity had something in common with this beverage; both acted like a drug that revived body and soul.

Though our day-to-day life was greatly improved by the availability of food, clothing and other necessities and niceties, we could not forget for even a moment that we were in a militarized and divided city. To meet with our friends in East Berlin, we had to go to specific border crossings and present our identification cards to the border police.

Among the more popular border crossings, the Glienicke Bridge spanned the Havel River from West Berlin into communist-controlled Potsdam. From 1948 on, it was not advisable to take a stroll along the banks of this river because it was patrolled by East German and Soviet police. The Glienicke Bridge served as a major border crossing until 1952 when it was closed to general traffic. From then until 1989 it was open only for access by the Western Allied Military Liaison Missions. The bridge became notorious during the Cold War, clouded by cloak-and-dagger intrigue, as it was used by the Americans and Soviets for the exchange of captured spies. Checkpoint Charlie in the city center was perhaps the most famous of the Cold War border crossings in Berlin. The American army was somewhat particular about the GIs assigned to this high-profile post, attempting to find men capable of exercising restraint and good judgment, at a place where Soviet and American tanks sometimes squared off just yards from each other, and where many East Germans risked their lives in attempts to flee to West Berlin.

Many books have told both factual and fictional tales of espionage using Cold War Berlin as the setting. The same events have been portrayed in numerous films. These films seem so real that I sometimes ask myself if I could have been a bystander.

Perspective: Games Spies Play

One incident that led to bad feelings on both sides of the Cold War conflict occurred underneath the Schönefeld Highway, a busy road forming the border between Neukölln in the American sector of Berlin and Teptow in the Soviet sector.

In the early 1950s the Americans discovered a point where several telephone cables converged in the Soviet sector, phone lines that they could tap with the most modern surveillance equipment of the era to intercept Soviet telephone conversations and their secret dealings. Under the direction of the American Central Intelligence Agency (CIA) and the British Secret Intelligence Service (SIS), over a six-month period, starting in September 1954, a 300-yard tunnel was constructed twenty feet underground, from a communications tower in the American sector to the telephone lines on the other side of the highway in the Soviet sector. For fourteen months, the Americans and British operated surveillance equipment inside the tunnel and eavesdropped on tens of thousands of conversations.

The intelligence agencies of these nations had no idea that this operation, code-named "Stopwatch" by the British and "Gold" by the Americans, was leaked to the Soviets during the planning stages by George Blake, an SIS agent who offered his services to the KGB. The Soviets let the operation continue for almost a year for reasons not entirely clear, perhaps to protect their informant, perhaps to spread disinformation, or perhaps even to demonstrate that they are not as aggressive as the West believed. The Soviets decided to end the whole affair in April 1956. Under the pretense of checking for possible gas leaks, the Soviets "accidentally" discovered the tunnel and shut down the surveillance activities. The Soviet Union and East Germany protested, accusing the "gangsters" in the West of breaking international law. In 1961 the British finally had enough evidence to bring espionage charges against George Blake. He received a hefty forty-two-year prison sentence, and the Western intelligence agencies learned that Operation Gold/Stopwatch was not an information gold mine after all. Adding further insult, Blake escaped from prison in October 1966 and fled to the USSR.

A Birthday to Remember, 1952–1953

The Christmas season of 1952 brought another life-changing event, especially for a woman. I turned thirty! There are significant milestones in life when you finally notice that you are, in fact, mortal. Time no longer stretches endlessly over the horizon. Before, the detours and wrong paths you took in life could merely be dismissed with a shrug of the shoulders and an "oh well." You start to seriously consider the possibility of a superficial life, an internal crisis that becomes the momentum for a new beginning. For me, my thirtieth birthday was indeed a memorable event, leaving behind a feeling that my life would now chart a new direction.

The winter came and went for our small family just like so many in years past. A thick blanket of snow covered the city, a stroke of luck for the children. Together, we sledded and skated. Barbara loved the new duffel coat I made for her out of fabric I had won at a ball event. I was so proud when people at the ice-skating rink started asking where I had purchased such a terrific coat.

Despite my tireless energy, I needed a break from the business of running a household. The idea of taking a vacation seemed more and more appealing. I felt the need to travel somewhere, to another country perhaps, something I had not been able to do since I was a young girl, when I had spent fourteen days in Italy. In February 1953 we received an invitation to attend Aunt Marie's eightieth birthday celebration in Nuremberg. Aunt Marie lived in a house she had dwelled in before the war, one that had miraculously survived the air raids and shelling during the conflict. Like me, Aunt Marie had been expelled from Czechoslovakia and had moved into the house in Nuremberg with the rest of her family, hopefully finding living conditions better than those on the divided political island of Berlin.

Together with Grandpa Max, we had invested our money in a Volkswagen, an expense I could not really seem to justify based on how little Georg and I actually drove the car. For Grandpa Max, the VW gave him the freedom to go to Mass as often as he wanted at a church located well beyond walking distance from his home. I suspect these frequent church visits stemmed from a guilty conscience over the death of his wife. Maybe he wanted to find solace and forgiveness. Perhaps he also wanted to buy his way into heaven, the motive behind all that he did on behalf of the church. It seems to me that after so many journeys to church and after numerous hours parked next to the church, the Volkswagen should have been blessed many times over. Yet during the journey to Nuremberg, it appears our guardian angel also had gone on vacation.

Nuremberg is in West Germany. To reach this destination, we had to travel on the Autobahn through communist East Germany. We departed Berlin through Checkpoint Bravo, also known as the Drewitz-Dreilinden crossing. After several hours of driving, we were about to cross the border into West Germany through Checkpoint Alpha (Helmstadt-Marienbon). At the first stop the checkpoint was manned by East German soldiers, and as requested, we handed over our travel documents and passports. The guards seemed pleasant enough, and the one who took our documents marched into the barracks next to the checkpoint and returned a couple of minutes later. He looked at me, pressed his fingers against the visor of his uniform cap, and said, "Please come with me."

I couldn't believe it. Why me? What was going on this time? The guard led me to some stuffy room while Georg and Barbara waited outside. The guards asked me a series of strange questions— if I had relatives in the Soviet Union, what my political beliefs were, and other such things—that I somehow managed to answer despite being utterly confused, not having a clue why they were questioning me of all people. All of this lasted for several hours, while Georg and Barbara waited anxiously in the next room and while our relatives in Nuremberg were presumably celebrating without us.

Finally, they decided to release us, and eventually I was able to solve this mystery. Stalin had recently ordered a purge, cleansing once again the military and political bureaucracy of anyone not loyal to him. On the most-wanted list was Rudolf Slansky, a distant cousin of my father whom we had not seen or had contact with for many years. Slansky had been the leader of the Communist Party in Czechoslovakia but after the war had been convicted of conspiracy and a variety of other charges. Stalin had ordered him executed. My passport also contained my maiden name of Slansky. The guards had called Berlin, and it had taken several hours for them to clear everything with headquarters and determine that I was not among Rudolf Slansky's renegade relatives.

My heart pounded wildly as the lights of the barracks grew dimmer in the distance and as we finally crossed over the West German border. Of course, we arrived late, and the birthday celebration had begun without us. Nevertheless, we received a warm welcome, which calmed my frayed nerves.

The birthday celebration was terrific. Despite her advanced age, Aunt Marie appeared as beautiful as ever, a living reminder of my childhood in Karlsbad and my lost family. Everyone greeted us with open arms and spoiled us rotten.

Perspective: The 17th of June Uprising

In 1949 Soviet-occupied Germany became the German Democratic Republic, commonly known as East Germany. This satellite state of the Soviet Union had no option other than to adopt a communist form of government carried out by an East German puppet regime. By 1952 many in East Germany were dissatisfied with the political situation and policies adopted by their government, especially the decision to devote the nation's economic resources to heavy industry while neglecting everything else. Stalin died on March 2, 1953, which allowed the East German government to enact a series of liberal reforms. However, these reforms came at a price, and the productivity standard for factory workers was raised 10 percent without a corresponding increase in wages. On June 15 and June 16, 1953, construction workers rebuilding the Stalinallee, a road in East Berlin, stop working and organized a protest march to the Minister House near Potsdamer Platz, the seat of government at the time. By June 17, 1953, over 40,000 people were marching in the streets of East Berlin. West German radio stations broadcasted news reports of these events, and these were also received by those living in East Germany.

Political protests spread to other large East German cities and industrial centers, such as Leipzig, Magdeburg, Halle, Bitterfeld, and Jena. Soon, political protests engulfed East Germany. Demonstrators demanded that the new work quota be rescinded and that the cost of living be lowered. They also demanded that government leaders step down and allow free elections. The protesters stormed Communist Party offices, freed political prisoners, and disarmed police officers. Some party officials were also attacked.

Soviet forces struck quickly and without warning. Troops, supported by tanks and other armored vehicles, crashed through the crowd of protesters in East Berlin, killing an estimated twenty unarmed civilians. Major-General Dibrova, the Soviet Army Commandant in East Berlin, declared martial law, and by the evening of June 17, the protests had been shattered and relative calm was restored. Later, 106 participants were executed under martial law, more than 5,100 were arrested and some 1,200 of those received lengthy sentences in Soviet labor camps. Furthermore, soldiers of the Red Army and East German police officers who refused to fire on unarmed civilians were executed before a firing squad.

To avoid an escalation of the Cold War, none of the Western democracies intervened. But in West Berlin, the commemoration of the event happened quickly. On the 21st of June, the West Berlin continuation of the East Berlin street *Unter Den Linden,* known as *Charlottenburger Chaussee,* was renamed *Strasse des 17. Juni* (The 17th of June Street), to remember those who sacrificed their lives for freedom during the 1953 uprising.

On August 7, 1953, a proclamation was printed in the West German *Federal Law Gazette* (section 1, no. 45), which read as follows:

> On June 17, 1953, the German People in the Soviet occupation zone and East Berlin rose up against tyranny and paid a heavy price for their demand for freedom. The 17th of June has thus become a symbol of German unity and their desire for freedom. The 17th of June shall be commemorated as the Day of German Unity and shall be observed as a federal holiday.

After German reunification in 1990, the Day of German Unity was changed to the third of October.

A View of the 17th of June Uprising from West Berlin, 1953

In June 1953 we witnessed an uprising occurring in East Berlin, an attempt to overthrow the communist government. Over the course of several days, we had noticed something was brewing. From the West German press we received fragments of information, telling us about large gatherings of people in the streets. Clearly, something was going on—exactly what, we didn't know, but you could feel the tension building, like turning up the heat underneath a pressure cooker until it was ready to explode.

Throughout the day on June 17, 1953, sirens in Berlin wailed almost nonstop. Special news bulletins were announced on the radio, and rumors surfaced about street fighting and dead people: "Revolt in East Germany! Shots fired!" The news reports continued. We heard about more deaths, and as the day progressed, the extent of the uprising became even clearer. The city district where we lived, Lichterfelde, stood some distance away from the middle of East Berlin, where the civil unrest occurred. We were in fact quite isolated from the uprising, and exactly for this reason, I felt rather strange and uncomfortable, like perhaps this was not entirely right.

That evening Georg failed to come home as expected, and while I continued to monitor the news reports, I began to imagine the worst. Had he gotten caught up in the fighting? After all, his office was relatively close to the border. In West Berlin the authorities had blocked off many of the streets to prevent traffic from entering the eastern part of the city. Considering the state of upheaval, I wondered why anybody would want to travel there in the first place. In this era before cell phones, I simply had to wait for Georg to come home, as the worst-case scenarios raced through my mind. Finally, Georg came home. He had witnessed some of the uprising. His office was located near the main train station, the Hauptbahnhof, a stone's throw from the border crossing into East Berlin. He had seen people running frantically around the Friedrichstraße train station. Georg also heard shots fired and the ominous sound of tanks going into action. All his coworkers stood at the window, watching the events unfold. In such conditions nobody could work. During the night we lay in bed wondering what the next few days would bring. We had struggled so hard to rebuild our lives after the end of the blockade, and we could not help but ask ourselves whether we would lose everything once again.

Diplomatic maneuvering had brought some stability to everyday life in West Berlin, while turmoil and social unrest continued on the other side of the city. In hindsight, social unrest and revolution, such as the 1953 Uprising in East Germany, have a dynamic of their own, whose aftereffects are not always foreseeable among politicians.

Although relatively isolated from the uprising in the east, we still noticed the extra military patrols throughout West Berlin. The

Western Allies did not want to actively intervene in what was largely considered a domestic issue for the DDR. However, they issued condemnations and spoke of peace. This weak response to the atrocities committed that day avoided escalating the conflict with the Soviets, and once again everyone could breathe a sigh of relief. But these events reminded those of us in West Berlin that we still lived on a dangerous political island. After the soldiers returned to their barracks, the daily routine resumed, yet I did not feel at home in this city. In fact, I felt no attachment whatsoever. My true home lay buried, tucked away in some recess of my heart, someplace that would remain forever lost. I had to ask myself, "What is keeping me here?" Nothing, actually.

Georg and I frequently discussed whether we should move to West Germany. Yet the economic situation had changed relatively little since Georg's ill-fated journey to Nuremberg during the blockade. Available apartments remained more than scarce and work impossible to find. Although Germany had already begun the monumental task of postwar rebuilding, much of its infrastructure still lay in ruin, which in turn hindered economic investment and growth. Furthermore, these problems were compounded by the flood of hundreds of thousands of displaced persons who sought refuge in West Germany after the war, representing even more people to house and more mouths to feed.

A Vacation Abroad, 1953

One of our neighbors was a young lawyer with a family, for whom I occasionally performed some office work. Now and then, I also babysat his kids. The lawyer and his wife now wanted to find a way to thank us. They invited Georg and me along on a trip to Austria and Italy. This was about as exciting as taking a world tour. For us northerners, Italy represented the ideal travel destination and certainly was a paradise for me. Our mouths watered at the thought of Italian cuisine, and how we longed for the elegant Italian clothes prominently displayed in our shop windows. Italia—sun, ocean, romance, everything that made life worth living!

This was also the first time we had together alone as a couple since Barbara was born. She stayed in Berlin with the two children from the lawyer, watched by his parents.

Full of excitement, we were on our way. The journey took us over the Brenner Pass in Tyrol. At the time, drivers on this stretch of road encountered very little traffic, which gave us a chance to take in the beautiful scenery. Nowadays the same stretch of road is among the most congested trucking routes in Europe.

We finally reached Italy. Our journey continued into South Tyrol, and we passed a town called Sterzing in northern Italy on the Austrian border. Sterzing was founded in 14 BC, and my father had been stationed here during the First World War. As we traveled further into Italy, the terrain changed, with the steep mountains giving way to vineyard-covered hills. I shall never forget all those vineyards and the vines that twisted around wooden trellises. Of course, we could not resist sampling some of the grapes, larger and sweeter than any grape I had ever tasted. We stopped in Merano, another beautiful city founded during the Roman era. Like astonished children opening their Christmas presents, we wandered through its streets, taking in the local flavor. Merano had recovered from the destruction of the previous war through the dedication and hard work of its citizens, recovering once again that joyful Italian lifestyle. There, in one of the city's many cafés, I sampled cappuccino for the first time, and I let the pleasing sound of this word roll off my tongue repeatedly. Cappuccino, a word I had never heard before, tasted as pleasant as it sounded, and the drink was served to us with almonds, chocolate, and whipped cream. Even today, when I close my eyes, I can still recall the wonderful sensation of this taste reaching my lips and tongue for the first time. Then came another new taste sensation— Campari and soda, which I also sampled for the first time in this wonderful town. These two drinks today still bring me back to that time and place.

During the vacation our friends spoiled us, taking us to fantastic restaurants serving delicious Italian cuisine, and we had such a good time together. The lawyer's wife and I bought something special just for ourselves—silk scarves. Silk, what a soothing word! Somehow, I could not keep my scarf wrapped around my neck. Time and time again, I pulled the soft, cool fabric through my fingers, another unforgettable Italian sensation. We visited Verona, the setting for Shakespeare's *Romeo and Juliet*. Around every corner, scenes from this tragic tale of two young lovers filled my imagination. At the end of our vacation, we spent a week in Seefeld in Austria, a small romantic village. After our return to Berlin, we remained indebted to this couple, full of gratitude for so many wonderful new experiences.

Rendezvous with Destiny, 1954–1955

During the winter of 1954, Barbara found a new friend—Ruta. Her mother, Anni, had attended school with Georg. Ruta and her mother had just arrived in Berlin to spend time with family. Since Ruta was almost as old as Barbara, after a few cautious encounters the ice broke, and they became the best of friends. Anni talked constantly about her life in Colombia and South America. These conversations enthralled Georg, leaving him stunned and astonished.

Eventually, we met Anni's husband, Enricas. During a casual conversation, he mentioned that Georg and I should join them in South America. "Why not?" he asked. "What is keeping you here? In Colombia you can live better. Trust me."

At first, I did not take the invitation seriously. What we really wanted was to live in West Germany, or so I thought. Colombia seemed like another planet. Georg, on the other hand, really liked the idea. Soon he was determined to go. Of course, he had to convince me. Many heated discussions followed, and finally I warmed up to the idea. We needed a new start in life, and perhaps our destiny lay in Colombia.

Even the name sounded exotic. We had to take out Georg's old *World Atlas*, the one he had used in high school, and figure out the exact location of our new home. I asked myself whether either one of us had even heard the name "Colombia" before. Who knew? During the excitement of the last ten years, it seemed that we had forgotten many things. In November 1955 we finally obtained the necessary immigration papers. Now we had to plan this new endeavor, something we had managed to delay up until this point. It would take several months to give up our life in Europe.

As unpleasant as life was in Berlin, we had gotten used to the city and learned how to cope with everyday life in this divided metropolis. In comparison, South America seemed almost alien. We had no idea what we would do there, nor did we have enough money saved up to furnish a home. On top of that, there was the language barrier.

But Georg had made up his mind and was standing firm on his plan, which was very unusual for him. He wanted to take on this challenge, and thus we began our preparations. The end of the Second World War had hurt the South American economy. Eager for a recovery, many countries in South America wanted to build better business relationships with nations in Europe. They welcomed European immigrants with open arms, hoping to exploit the infusion of money and talent they brought with them.

As the day of our departure approached, we attended numerous farewell parties, receiving lots of good wishes and perhaps even a bit of pity. The show of support made us proud of our decision but also sad and uncomfortable. Regardless of these mixed feelings, we had already passed the point of no return. One of my personal qualities is my determination. Once I decide to do something, it's best to step out the way, for I intend to charge full steam ahead, casting aside any misgivings I may have as excess baggage. In other words, when I make up my mind, I carry out the undertaking to the best of my ability without worrying about the consequences. Georg and I knew it would not be easy, but we took the plunge.

Our adventure began—we were starting a new life carrying about $500 in our pockets and knowing maybe two words of Spanish.[6]

On Our Way to an Uncertain Future, 1956

We departed Germany from the northern port city of Hamburg. It was the middle of March, and the biting cold air from the north

---

6   For perspective, in inflation adjusted terms, this would put our total financial assets at less than $5000 today.

chilled us to the bone. With the wind blowing in our faces, we took a stroll alongside the Elbe River. Every so often, I stopped, turned around, and took in my surroundings, taking one last look at the continent I was about to leave behind. How can I describe the uneasiness I felt in these last moments before the departure? We sat in St. Michael's Church for a while and listened to the *St. Mathew Passion*. I asked myself whether I would ever experience again the cultural refinement embodied by this wonderful composition by Bach. Then I pulled Barbara a little closer to me.

One of Georg's friends from high school invited us to dinner for what would be our final meal in Germany. Having mixed feelings about leaving, I sat at her table and saw a sympathetic face.

With a gentle voice, she asked Georg, "So after you arrive, how will you make a living?"

Georg shrugged his shoulders and said, "I don't know exactly, but I am sure something will come along."

Shocked at his reply, she then looked at me and said, "So, Irmtraud, it must be absolutely terrible for you, this uncertainty. I could never imagine giving up all that I own and going into the unknown, not knowing what tomorrow will bring."

Georg gave her a scornful look, and she quickly looked the other way. "I'm sorry. That's not what I meant," she said apologetically.

To be honest, I felt envious. I almost wanted to hate this woman who sat with us at the table in her beautiful home, surrounded by a nice family who made life all so predictable for her, so that life on this day would be the same as life in a year's time—a life full of all the comfort and security one could ever need. I can only imagine the look I must have had on my face, amid my doubt and fear about what the future would bring, not having a clue about what would happen next year, next month, or even tomorrow. But I had been in this place once before under worse circumstances, and I had survived it. That thought and the presence of Georg and Barbara next to me made it bearable.

Erna, Max's second wife, accompanied us to the port on the day of our departure. In her good-natured way, she attempted to ease the tension surrounding our final farewell. Handing a small package to Barbara, she said, "For you, so you will always know the hour of the day and never forget the friends you make." Only after we had boarded the ship could we open the gift. Inside were a small wristwatch and an address book.

March 15, 1956 was our fourteenth wedding anniversary and the day we boarded the *Odenwald*, a cargo ship destined ultimately for Chile. None of us had expected a luxury cruiser. Still, the appearance of the ship, an old rust bucket, did not inspire much confidence. Built during the 1930s, the ship had been interned by the Japanese at a port in Indonesia during the Second World War. It had been released back to its German owners after the war, and the many years of neglect had given the vessel unsightly discoloration. The Odenwald transported freight from Europe to South America. It was old and slow, built for its utility rather than aesthetics. Ten small cabins crammed into the ship during its construction provided accommodations to the few passengers who ventured that the ship would stay afloat during the transatlantic crossing. Even if we had been wildly rich, we wouldn't have had the option of flying to South America, and a luxury cruise remained well beyond our means. So, this sad-looking ship would be our new home for several weeks.

Looking rather solemn as we left the harbor, we stood on the deck, capturing one final glimpse of Germany as the banks of the Elbe rolled past us. I am not exactly sure what Georg was thinking at this very moment, but I am sure he had a heavy heart. As the ship made its way northward on the river, a naval station hoisted the German flag and played the national anthem. The Odenwald then sailed out into the North Sea and open water, while the German coastline slowly faded into the distance. Farewell, Germany!

Now we started to notice our fellow passengers who stood on the deck with us and who also were taking a final look at Germany. Each person seemed lost in his or her own thoughts as we left Europe behind us. Little by little we became accustomed to each other and the new surroundings. We were a colorful group.

All the passenger cabins were taken. Barbara and I shared a cabin, where we barely had enough room for the two of us and a few suitcases that we had to stow under the bed before going to sleep. The rest of our belongings remained buried somewhere deep inside the ship's hull. Other than the three of us, no one else on the ship was from Berlin. In the cabin next to us slept a young attaché to the German embassy in Lima. He shared his cabin with a man from northern Chile (but formerly from Aachen, Germany) who was also the captain of a whaling ship. The cabin next to theirs accommodated a young lady traveling to Peru to see her husband. She shared her cabin with an old woman traveling to South America to see her children for the first time in twenty years. During the war this family had become separated like so many others. The old woman had only recently been able to determine where the rest of her family now lived. Further down the line, another cabin was occupied by a young man from Bavaria. He wanted to purchase wood in southern Chile for manufacturing toothpicks and matches. Georg shared a cabin with a man from Antwerp who was bringing nine Dutch breeding cows to Chile. What cows they were! Our four-legged fellow passengers graced our dinner table with fresh milk and cream.

Like us, most of the other passengers had never crossed an ocean before. Often, we met each other at the railing, where we stood looking at the endless horizon, surrounded by rolling waves of water and pondering what would happen next.

I suspected that our skipper, an experienced seaman, was married to the ship. They had grown old together. While the Japanese interned his vessel in Indonesia, he had refused to abandon ship. Without a doubt both he and the ship had suffered from neglect, brought about by a lack of maintenance over the course of many years. The Odenwald now belonged to Hapag-Lloyd, the shipping conglomerate that had acquired the ship after the Japanese returned it to Germany. We learned from his stories that when the war started, the British had been the first to intern the Odenwald, and later it had fallen into the hands of the Japanese. After the war ended, the captain and his ship had gone right back to work and settled back into their transatlantic itinerary. He looked every bit like the stereotypical seaman, an old salt with a dark brown weathered face and deep wrinkles. And how he could tell tall tales.

And did we need to hear a good story now and then! The evenings were long and offered little to keep us distracted. What exactly can you do aboard a heavily loaded cargo ship somewhere out in the middle of the Atlantic? Play Monopoly for hours on end? Milk the cows? Go to the ball in your finest evening gown? Our only libation on board the ship was a rum toddy, a hot grog that livened things up, taking the edge off our confinement. At dinnertime we ate heavily seasoned Indonesian food, prepared according to the captain's heat tolerance, far different from the milder German fare to which we were accustomed. All the passengers had to endure this change in diet regimen except for one. The crew became especially fond of Barbara, taking her underneath their wing. For her alone the cook prepared German dishes, which he served with a glass of fresh milk.

As we headed south, the weather took a turn for the better. By the time the ship passed the northern coast of Spain and the Bay of Biscay, many passengers had spread themselves out on the deck in lounge chairs, enjoying the spring weather that we soon would learn was deceptive. Shortly after we passed the south of Spain, a violent storm ambushed us, forcing us to seek shelter underneath the deck. Plowing through the tall waves of the Atlantic, the Odenwald creaked and moaned. As the vessel encountered each wave, it rode the wave to its crest and then came crashing down, slamming hard against the water. Whenever the cycle began anew, we looked at each other terrified, wondering how much more punishment this old lady could take before breaking in two and boring a hole in the ocean floor. All of us passengers had a green face, and the toilet became the most frequented place on board. It should surprise nobody that the dining room remained empty. After all, who wanted to eat in such a storm?

While the ship pitched and rolled, and while we passengers still felt queasy and nauseous, the captain ordered us topside. "All right, up and out you go!" roared the skipper. "Take a whiff of fresh air, you land lovers!" As he stood squarely before us, a sorry-looking bunch, nothing seemed to affect his balance. Then with a clap of his hands, he drove us to the deck, where we lumbered about, grasping the railing while what seemed like a gale-force wind blew in our faces.

After three days the storm subsided. The waves grew smaller and smaller, and once again the ship floated on calm water. For a brief period, we felt safe again, and then came the bad news. Some of the crew had been lowered down in a lifeboat to inspect the hull for damage, and they had found a major crack. The constant slamming had taken its toll on the Odenwald.

Every night Barbara said her bedtime prayers. "Dear God, please don't let another storm come," she prayed out loud, echoing the plea for divine intervention that all the other passengers silently repressed. Fortunately, during the remainder of our journey, the weather cooperated. As we approached our third week on the high seas, many of us once again spent the evenings on the top deck.

During the Second World War many of us on board the Odenwald had been isolated from the outside world. Any news we received had come from newspapers or radio broadcasts, both of which were heavily censored and biased. The only foreign news that I might have received came from a couple of BBC radio broadcasts. After the war we had lived on a political island—Berlin. There, we were so consumed with survival that we had little time for following world events. Now the spell seemed to have been broken. Our long sea voyage presented an opportunity to hear about what was going on in the world, and we found much of what we heard quite astonishing.

The captain of the whaling ship told some of the more interesting tales. When he introduced himself, a shiver ran down my side. His last name was the same as that of my first innocent love, the major in Karlsbad. Like my lost boyfriend, the whaling captain also came from Aachen. However, I could not bring myself to ask this tall athletic man if he was related to my major. My life had changed over the course of several years, and now I did not want to know.

I listened to his story very attentively. Years ago, he had worked for Aristotle Onassis, a Greek shipping tycoon (and future husband of Jacqueline Kennedy). Even then Onassis owned a lot of oil tankers. These vessels transported oil from Arabia to other parts of the world. Our fellow traveler navigated some of these tankers through the Strait of Hormuz in the Persian Gulf. At the time, the Suez Canal was too narrow to accommodate these tankers, so he had to sail the longer route around the Cape of Good Hope in South Africa. The whaling captain spoke about the emerging cities in the Arab world. Until the end of the Second World War, most of those living in Kuwait, Bahrain, and the United Arab Emirates had been nomads. They had slept in tents and roamed the desert on camels. Now the tremendous amount of oil they sat on was about to change their way of life forever. The industrial world had an insatiable thirst for this raw material. Where once camels had determined a man's wealth, the standard now had become the price of crude oil. Onassis was taking advantage of this development.

We were still somewhere in the middle of the Atlantic Ocean, heading for the Caribbean. During the night we could see the Southern Cross in the sky. Often, we sat out on the deck, gazing up at the stars that glittered in the heavens. The brilliant display of light was breathtaking. The passengers also gathered on the decks to watch the moon as it followed its arch-shaped path through the heavens. The ocean now appeared as flat as a mirror. Staring down at the water, sometimes I saw dolphins directly below the surface, swimming alongside the ship. As we traveled southward, time took on another dimension and then ceased altogether. We became one with the Odenwald. For us, the world ended at the horizon.

As the journey entered its fourth week, most of the passengers had become friends. Life aboard our ship also was becoming monotonous, but soon an excursion would bring some much-needed relief from the dull and boring daily routine. We were approaching Curaçao, a small Dutch colony in the middle of the Caribbean. There, the Odenwald planned to anchor for two days. After sailing into the harbor, we had permission to visit the island just as long as we returned in time for the evening meal. Barbara had a full program. The young wood trader from Bavaria took my daughter underneath his wing, and they set out to explore the island. In the evening when they returned, Barbara was aglow, bursting with enthusiasm from all the new experiences she had acquired throughout the day on the colorful island. In her hands she carried numerous small gifts that her chaperone had given her.

Georg and I decided to go to church along with some of the other passengers. With some trepidation I set foot on non-European soil for the first time in my life. However, what I had imagined was far different from the reality. Most of the inhabitants were of African descent, yet the better restaurants and stores belonged to the Chinese. The buildings looked like gingerbread houses with icing. Then we encountered something that absolutely stunned us pilgrims from Europe. Whomever could have imagined that on this island in the tropics we would find an organ playing *Waves of the Danube,* a waltz by Ion Ivanovici, a Romanian composer? It was a breathtaking moment. My heart pounded wildly, so fast that I thought it would drown out the melody floating in our direction. A shiver ran down my spine as I thought of my long-lost relatives in Central Europe.

Although many passengers found excitement on the island, something exciting also happened on board the ship. Two calves were born. According to rumor, the man who owned the cows, an older man from Antwerp, had given the bovines medication so that they would not give birth on the open sea, but rather would give birth on Dutch territory. For the owner, this was necessary to protect the pedigree. If the calves had been born on the high seas on a German ship, then they would have been, God forbid, German and not Dutch cows.

The two days in port went by quickly, and then we returned to the drudgery of everyday life aboard the Odenwald. However, soon we stood at the entrance of the Panama Canal, through which we passed from the Atlantic Ocean to the Pacific.

Despite efforts to control mosquito populations, malaria is still an ever-present concern for anybody who spends time in the tropics. During our passage through the Panama Canal, many of us held makeshift flyswatters, attempting to fend off any rogue mosquito determined to bite one of us. It would have been nice if someone had furnished the cabins with mosquito netting, but nobody had done so, and during passage many worried they might fall victim to malaria. For the first of many occasions to come, I cursed the tropics.

Maneuvering the ship through the canal presented quite a challenge. A special ship pilot came on board and stood on the deck, remaining there during the entire passage. As the Odenwald slowly pushed its way to the Pacific, I remember passing lush green mountains that seemed so close that we needed only to stretch out our hands to touch them.

Once we were through the canal, just three days of travel now separated us from the conclusion of our sea voyage, the port city of Buenaventura in Colombia. This final stretch flew by with amazing speed, such a stark contrast to previous weeks that had rolled along at a snail's pace. We arrived in the port at eight o'clock in the evening, too late to pass through customs. We spent one last night on the Odenwald, eager to finally plant our feet upon the soil of our new home, eager for a new start in life.

Perspective: The Panama Canal, 1956

An engineering marvel of the late nineteenth and early twentieth centuries, the Panama Canal is a forty-eight-mile waterway that includes three sets of locks and several artificial lakes. Traversing the Isthmus of Panama in Central America, the Panama Canal has greatly facilitated the movement of cargo and passenger ships between the Pacific and Atlantic Oceans. Before its completion in 1914, ships traveling from one ocean to the other had to sail around Cape Horn at the southern tip of South America. Not only was this route hazardous, but it also added another eight thousand miles to the total length of the journey.

Although building the canal presented major engineering hurdles, the most formidable obstacle standing in the way of its construction was a tiny little insect. The present course of the Panama Canal was once covered by dense jungle inhabited by indigenous people. Such terrain provides the perfect breeding environment for the *Anopheles* mosquito and its cousin, the *Aedes Aegypti*. The female members of these species pack a very potent sting, one far deadlier than that of any of the snakes found in this area. The first transmits malaria, the latter yellow fever. In 1881 the French began initial construction work on the canal but abandoned the project after some 22,000 workers succumbed to these diseases. When the Americans took over the construction work in 1904, priority number one was controlling the reproduction of the Anopheles mosquito by clear-cutting sections of jungle, removing sources of standing water, dispersing pesticides, and even introducing natural predators into the insects' breeding areas.

Among the engineering triumphs of this project was the Culebra Cut. Involving the removal of 100 million cubic yards of earth, the Americans created an eight-mile artificial valley through the Continental Divide, connecting Lake Gatún with the Pedro Miguel locks on the Pacific side. The cut lowered the terrain from a maximum height of two hundred feet above sea level to forty feet above sea level.

CHAPTER 3

Colombia, 1956-1966

Colombia and border countries, South America.

Our Arrival in Buenaventura, Colombia, 1956

It was now April 16, 1956. The sun rose, and for the first time we could gaze out upon the pier that had beckoned us during the night with bright lights and the dancing shadows of palm trees swaying in the wind. In our imagination we had expected this harbor to look exactly like the one we had visited in Curaçao. How wrong we were! Disbelief and disappointment—those were our first impressions. Rather ironically, Buenaventura, literally translated, means "good adventure." As a city it did not live up to its name.

Dilapidated warehouses lined one side of the pier. Called *bodegas*, these structures were in wretched condition. Rats as big as a cat darted from one trash can to the next right before our very eyes. On every corner we saw a suspicious character or two, leaning against the wall, standing there like a mannequin in a storefront window, while their eyes followed every piece of freight offloaded from the ships. Beggars sat on the streets, not moving a single muscle until someone strolled past, at which time an arm stretched out, hand extended, palm up. While they sat, they protected themselves from the sun with shields made from cigarette cartons taped together.

Terrified, I grasped Barbara's hand firmly and thought of only one thing: *how in the hell do I get out of here?* Obviously, at this moment I was questioning whether I could really endure life in South America. One thing was for certain—my feelings toward my husband could not be described as warm and endearing. Anyway, I regained my composure and made that first step. Indeed, we were past the point of no return. We headed for the customs house. As crude as it may sound, Buenaventura was a real cesspool. Around 30,000 people lived in the city, spread out around the harbor. The houses must have been very colorful at one time, but now they stood in an awful state of disrepair, and many lacked indoor plumbing. A huge water tank nicknamed *la pelota*, meaning "the ball," dominated the skyline.

Life on the street seemed to be a theater production, with kids playing everywhere, small groups of men and women huddled together, and others carrying loads carefully balanced on their heads. Many of the women looked like prostitutes, and many of them probably were employed in this sector of the economy. One thing I had not expected was to see so many people of African origins, the descendants of slaves brought to this region many years ago.

At the customs house I noticed that the offices were dirty, and some sort of stale odor wafted through the air. Instead of chairs, we sat down on old leather sofas that lined the walls. I suspect these sofas belonged to the colonial era, before Simón Bolívar liberated South America. The Colombian customs officials looked at us as though we were crazy. Perhaps they wondered why these Europeans would come here in the first place. Our amazement was just as intense. Could these people be our future neighbors?

For quite a long time, we tried to communicate with the customs officials without any success. Perhaps it would have been helpful if we spoke Spanish. Anni, our friend, finally arrived along with a woman from Bavaria. I never imagined I would be so happy to see another German. Anyway, I lost my self-composure and could not help but give her a bear hug right in front of everybody. Since Anni spoke Spanish, she was able to help us with the language barrier. Gently pushing me to the side, she spoke to the officers, and finally the customs process started rolling. It seemed as though they were negotiating some sort of international treaty. The "talks" consumed half the day, and then finally they released our luggage.

My nerves were frayed, and after a long ocean voyage and the negative first impressions of my new home, my patience was pretty much exhausted. As we were searching through our belongings, a young man walked up behind me and snatched my genuine German *Kuchenglocke*—he was trying to steal my plastic bell-shaped cake cover! I was filled with outrage. Did he have any idea how many shops I'd had to visit in Berlin just to find this cover? Well, anyway, I wasn't about to let some punk kid steal my Kuchenglocke, even if he was well-built and several times my size. Besides, with all the insects around, in this country a cake cover was a necessity. Immediately, I leapt forward and tore after him, waving my arms and screaming in German, "Give that back! That doesn't belong to you! Give that back right now!"

The young man looked terrified. He froze. Not a muscle moved. He made no attempt whatsoever to defend himself. Never before had a crazy German-speaking gringa chased after him, I imagined.

I reached out and ripped the *Kuchenglocke* right out of his hands. "Mine!" I exclaimed. I was still irate and continued to scold this idiot. Finally, the young man put his tail between his legs and slowly crept away, occasionally looking behind him with a worried look on his face. Now there are certain things you don't do in life, and one of them is steal Irmtraud's cake cover!

Besides recovery of my cake cover, this whole affair had a hidden bonus. Suddenly, the customs officers became far more cooperative. Perhaps they also were afraid of the German-speaking gringa. The time it took to finally rid ourselves of those customs officers seemed ridiculous. Later I found out that a little money under the table would have expedited this matter in record time—another lesson I had not yet learned.

Buenaventura was a giant sauna—the heat and humidity were stifling and made me feel claustrophobic. The city had definitely not made a good impression. Atop piles of garbage, the odor of rotting vegetables and fruit filled the air. Stagnant ocean water from the Pacific splashed against the pier, and even the harbor itself was one giant trash container. I found all of this disgusting. I still recall the intense odor of human sweat and how it made me sick to my stomach. Barbara clung to me, remaining silent while staring with astonishment at all that paraded before her. We still had not reached our destination. We needed to travel by road through the jungle and over the mountains to Cali—and during the night, no less!

Only four of us were to continue on to Cali—Barbara, Anni, the Bavarian woman, and me—while Georg remained in Buenaventura to take care of some unfinished business with our container. He planned to join us later, hitching a ride with someone working for Hapag-Lloyd.

Our taxi seemed to have fallen on hard times. I noticed that the tires lacked any tread, something I could not change. At least the large taxi could haul all of our carry-on luggage, items that we needed for the first day until we got our big boxes with our belongings to start a new household. I climbed into the taxi and noticed the knots in my stomach, a pain that had tormented me for the last couple of hours. The smell inside the taxi made me feel even more ill. My hands shook, and a cold sweat broke out on my forehead.

Barbara looked at me nervously and whispered, "Are you okay, Mommy?" What was I supposed to say? My nerves were completely shot.

We drove through the tropical night, our surroundings pitch-black, with the headlights barely piercing the darkness ahead. I noticed the thick vegetation alongside the road and how it even concealed much of the moonlight. Our driver must have raced cars in a previous life. He drove like a Formula One race car driver, accelerating hard between the turns, which followed fast one after another on that narrow, twisting road. From time to time he had to ford a stream, busting through with such force that water penetrated the interior. Horrified, we screamed and held hands, but our "experienced" driver could not have cared less. Unfazed, he pressed on as the luggage rattled violently. Now and then he was forced to stop while I vomited. Maybe it was carsickness, or maybe it was a stomach virus or just stress, but "miserable" sums it up well.

We went around another curve, and suddenly the unexpected happened. Our driver actually used the brakes! We stopped at a roadblock and handed over our papers to the police for inspection. It was definitely time for a short break, a chance to stretch our legs and grab some fresh air.

Grinning, our driver pointed to a row of stands near the roadblock and said, "*Comida! Bebida!*"[1]

At the stands, colorfully dressed Colombians sold a variety of foods and drinks. My stomach was now empty and despite the dizzying ride, I was feeling better. The four of us needed something to eat. For the first time in my life, I sampled empanadas, a local specialty prepared before us in an open-air kitchen. Served with a spicy sauce, the empanadas were a kind of turnover made from a cornmeal dough and filled with sour cream, meat, vegetables, and

---

1   "Food! Drink!"

herbs. I found them delicious, and perhaps this was the first positive impression of my new home. As we ate, everything was illuminated by a bare lightbulb held up by a crumpled piece of wire. The wind blew, and the light swayed gently, casting shadows everywhere as the unusual *bambuco* music played on the radio.

Our driver approached with a glass, motioning for me to drink from it. I took a cautious sniff of this strange concoction, and a powerful odor climbed up into my nose. "Aguardiente, aguardiente," he kept saying. "Señora, esto es bueno para el estomago. Tómelo, tómelo!"[2] This strange, mildly anise-flavored liquor was supposed to ease my jittery nerves. It worked astonishingly well. By the time I climbed back into the car, I felt almost normal again.

We reached the Lobocarrera, the highest point on the road. From here, on a clear night you can see the lights of Cali, a city the locals call *la Sultana del Valle*.[3] However, the view is often obscured by fog, formed by cold mountain air that hangs over the jungle below. After a few more sharp curves, the road finally opened up, becoming a wider highway. Later our driver stopped a second time to let us enjoy the view. Cali, a large city in the Andes, greeted us with a spectacular light show. The remainder of our journey passed quickly. We took the other passenger, the woman from Bavaria, to her house. As we helped unload her luggage, I noticed that the *Odenwald* had brought her some Bavarian beer, a commodity almost as rare as French champagne in this region. The next stop was our hotel. I can't remember what happened past this point. I don't remember how we got inside the hotel or whether we took a shower to dissolve the caked-on dirt that we had accumulated during that day. I can recall only that we were completely and totally exhausted. We sank into our bed and fell into a deep slumber.

This was a new start in life in a very foreign country. It would make me more mature and wiser, bringing to the surface abilities I never knew I had.

---

2   Meaning something like "firewater," *aguardiente* is an anise-flavored liquor made from sugar cane. "Lady, this is good for the stomach. Take it, take it!"

3   "The mistress of the valley."

If You Wish for Something with All Your Heart... 1956

I opened my eyes. Bright colors danced on the ceiling above me. Noise flooded my ears, so foreign, so strange. I had to ask myself where I was. Finally, I got out of bed and slowly came to my senses. Memories of the thrilling adventure from the previous night filled my head. I cautiously pulled back the curtain and looked out the window. Before my eyes stood a busy city street. The cars that drove past honked constantly, while the locals mingled about, hawking their goods and services from the edge of the road. I remember the ear-piercing singsong call of those offering a shoeshine, who's jabbering not even the locals understood. Not far from our hotel was the central market, an open-air venue where colorfully clad women balanced baskets of fruit on their heads, while others squeezed past with a live chicken tucked underneath an arm.

My first opportunity to bond with this strange and unfamiliar culture occurred that first day in Cali inside the bus that would take Barbara and me to our friend's house. Before climbing aboard, we counted out the bus fare, which we held firmly in our hands while the remainder of our money remained well hidden. It was another day and, once again, another exhausting journey. Cali lies at an altitude of 3,271 feet, and daytime temperatures ranged from 80 to 100 degrees, something to which we were not accustomed, especially after having just spent several weeks at sea.

We arrived the house where Anni and Enricas lived, feeling quite proud of ourselves for mastering the bus transit system on our first try. They were such great hosts. Georg had arrived during the middle of the night. I remember this day as the start of our attempt to adjust to life in South America.

No matter where you go in life, you must contend with bureaucratic paperwork. We had to appear in person at the local immigration office, located inside an old house in downtown Cali. Anni accompanied us to this meeting. Cucaracha Street, which ran past this government office, probably derived its unusual name from the insects that infested the houses in this part of town. The dwellings stood so close to each other that when one house was fumigated, the insects simply made their way up to the roof and crossed over to the house next door.

Inside the government building, steel bars replaced window glass and curtains in the small, stuffy offices. The immigration officer on duty scrutinized my passport photo, determining that it matched the face before him. He then stated that my name was something unusual in this town. "*Eso es un nombre muy raro. No existe aquí.*"[4] The officer grumbled and mumbled, trying to pronounce Irmtraud, my given name, only to twist his tongue in knots. He took another hard look at my passport while I sat there, about ready to lose my temper. Finally, he looked up, stretched for a second, and said, "We are in a Catholic country. You need a Catholic name. I will register you as Franziska. If you don't like that, go somewhere else."

Did I really have a choice? With a few strokes of a pen on a government form, my name instantly changed from Irmtraud Franziska Katharina Stein to Franziska Irmtraud Katharina Stein. It seemed that along with a change of name, I also received a new personality.

We returned to the hotel and talked about the events that had just transpired in the government office. Georg decided that he also wanted to be included in the act, partly to show solidarity with me, his wife, and partly because he also wanted a name that the locals could pronounce. We stopped calling him by his German name, Georg, and started to call him George, his given name in English. Then we enrolled Barbara in a German-speaking school where she received a crash course in Spanish.

After about ten days in the hotel, we decided to accept Anni and Enrique's invitation to stay with them until we could afford our own apartment, and that would require us to get jobs. Soon it was May. As the school year came to an end, plans were drawn up to celebrate with a dance for the students and their parents at the school. Anni, our very generous host, insisted we attend. She thought this would present a good opportunity for us to make new friends. I must admit, when

4   "This name is very rare. We don't find it around here."

I look back on these first few months of our new life in Colombia, I found the very generous support of so many people awe-inspiring. Our friendship with Anni opened so many doors for us.

When I first arrived at the dance, I remained shy and reserved, but then I noticed a change in my personality. The courage to leave the safety of our nest in Berlin and find a new life in South America had created a momentum that could not be contained. Many years before, I had thought the university could teach me everything I needed to know in life, but the war had closed that door forever. Now I was infected by a new spirit of adventure. Once again, I thirsted for knowledge. I wanted to hear, see, taste, smell, and touch my new home; I wanted to experience this new environment with all five senses. The bridge behind me collapsed, and now the only direction was forward. I seized the initiative, boldly confronting the challenge before us, now ready to take on any opportunity handed to me. I had confidence in myself. I knew what I wanted. I was prepared to make it happen.

George also changed. He now spent most of his time with Enricas, visiting local farms in the hills around Cali. They rode horses together and later drank *cerveza* and *aguardiente*. Gradually, our personalities diverged, moving farther and farther apart. George maintained a poor attitude, always seeing the problem and never the opportunity. Instead of taking initiative, he found solace in the bottle. Thus, began a lifelong struggle with alcoholism that hurt our marriage.

Was I an overbearing wife? I can't really say, even today. When I look back, it seems the move to South America reversed the roles we played in our marriage. It was not easy for George to accept this. The problems we faced then, as well as those to come, belonged to both of us. I always tried to be part of the solution, whereas I think George hoped these problems would disappear on their own.

By sheer coincidence we met the director for the branch office of Hoechst, a German company. We also met his wife, and right from the start, we liked each other. It was nice to talk to her. Both of us had just arrived in Cali. We discussed our experiences and problems in making the transition. In passing I told her that it would be nice to find a job.

A few days later, through Anni, she contacted me. We met for tea at Anni's house and thrilled to see me, she said, "My husband would like to speak with you. He has an opening!" Then she winked her eye, and I knew exactly what this meant. She had dogged her husband constantly until he had come up with something for me. Suddenly, I was employed! Not only did I receive a decent salary, but also one of my coworkers offered to give me a ride to work each day. This was a stroke of luck for me because the office was located some distance outside the city in an office park, and we didn't have a car.

At times the heat became suffocating. The clothes we brought from Germany had been manufactured for another climate and were not suitable for Cali in early summer.[5] During the evenings I sat at my old sewing machine and sewed and sewed and sewed—some new clothes for me, some for Barbara, and occasionally a shirt for George. While I sat on the balcony with the clattering monster, Anni's cook, Abigail, babbled nonstop. Subconsciously, I acquired quite a bit of Spanish vocabulary from her. Often, I tried to pronounce a word or two, but what came out of my mouth sounded very different from what I had heard. At first, she placed her hand over her mouth to conceal the giggling, but the laughter overpowered her. Then she followed me around in the kitchen, repeating the Spanish words I had just mangled.

Through other connections George received a head receptionist position at the *Hotel Tequendama* in Bogotá, one of the first grand international hotels in South America.

Me and George in Colombia in 1956 or 1957.

---

5   Though Colombia is in South America, most of it is in the Northern Hemisphere.

The Gray City, 1956

George's new job separated us. He lived in Bogotá, and we stayed in Cali. I sometimes thought of our ordered life in Berlin, when George had come home in the evenings and, together, we had picked up Barbara from school. Now hundreds of miles separated us. Serendipitously, not long after George got his job in Bogotá, I met the local director for Bayer, another German company operating in Colombia. Through the grapevine he had heard that I needed a job in Bogotá. "I am looking for a secretary who can speak German. If you want the job, you will have to relocate to Bogotá," he said one day while we met with friends.

At first, I was speechless, and then I warmed up to the idea in record time: executive secretary for *Químicas Unidas*, the Bayer subsidiary in Colombia. At the job interview my heart pounded wildly. I probably took on more of a job than I could really manage. But I felt I didn't have a choice.

I found it astonishing that during the Second World War many German companies had sought to protect their assets in South America. By 1939, when war seemed probable instead of possible, companies such as Bayer and Hoechst had already formed foreign subsidiaries in Latin America. Local businessmen of German ancestry managed these ventures. The chief executive officer of Químicas Unidas was from a family that had emigrated from Germany just a generation prior.

Now I sat directly outside the office belonging to the owner of the company. I worked until my head spun. Never in my life had I had to handle so many tasks at once. On top of that, I learned Spanish in the evenings. My job responsibilities required me to have a certain command of the language in order to reserve hotel rooms, purchase airline tickets, and even change pesos into dollars. Back then, rapidly fluctuating exchange rates meant you could never guess the value of currency. Also, there was no such word as "stress" in the common vocabulary; however, I certainly felt it.

We had an apartment in a beautiful section of Bogotá. This area reminded me of the suburban neighborhoods found outside many

English cities. I had not ever been to England, but I had occasionally seen pictures of these areas inside a newspaper or magazine.

Bogotá was cooler than Cali, and the temperature rarely exceeded 75 degrees. I remember the cold, moist air during the evenings and mornings. The sun rarely broke through the thick layer of clouds that constantly blanketed the city. For this reason, I called my new home the "gray city." At an altitude of around 8,500 feet, the city was bordered on one side by tall mountains and by savanna on the other.

Truth be told, I hated Bogotá. Even the locals always seemed to be depressed, which infected us newcomers. I almost got homesick for Berlin. When the fog rolled in during the evenings, the homeless, mostly *indios*, often retreated to entryways and wrapped themselves in *ruanas*, a type of poncho. With the *ruanas* they even concealed their faces, and this, combined with the fog, frightened me, as though I was seeing something out of a B-grade science-fiction film. I avoided leaving the house after dark, partly to avoid any contact with this depressing street scene.

When I wasn't working, I was depressed. George and I barely spoke to each other. We retreated to our own separate caves to lose ourselves in our own thoughts, to reconcile the events of the day, and to gather up the courage to face another. What bothered me greatly was that George started to have second thoughts about coming to Colombia. After all, he had brought us here in the first place, wanting to cast aside the constraints of Germany and find a new beginning. Now the guilt he felt, for what he had done to Barbara and me, destroyed him. He became more and more withdrawn.

When George was not working, he mostly sat around in the apartment. After a short time, his never leaving the apartment started to drive me crazy. Even if confronted by depressing, gray surroundings, I could not give up hope that surely there must be a way out of this rut. It was time take in some of the local flavor. Over time we made friends with other Europeans. They took us on road trips through the surrounding area outside of Bogotá. What a difference from the depressing city. Like a well-guarded secret, the countryside offered us a pleasant diversion.

I don't know where to start. Zipaquirá, a salt mine, was quite interesting, an underground cavern inside a mountain where the locals had built a cathedral out of salt. I also loved Lake Guatavita. According to the legend of the Golden One, or El Dorado, the Chibcha Indians and their ruler, the Zipa, allegedly sank a boat loaded with treasure here. We also ate at several excellent restaurants offering local cuisine, something we should have sampled much earlier.

Bogotá lies in the Department of Cundinamarca, a region teeming with the artifacts of ancient Americans, some of which still manage to surface centuries after the Spanish conquest.[6] As a reminder of the *conquistadores*, all over Colombia, even in the smallest of villages, one finds statues of the area's most renowned Spanish explorer, Sebastián de Belalcázar.

The Colombians are aficionados of music and dance, part of the razzle-dazzle ingrained into the street scene. Around Christmas the bullfighting season began, a spectacle that commenced right after Sunday Mass. The season brought many joyous celebrations fueled by dancing to the rhythm of *bambuco*, the colorful native music, and massive quantities of the local beer. Once we took time to experience some of the local culture, our attitude toward the city changed. We no longer felt so depressed.

Barbara had remained in Cali to continue her education with a summer school program. We made arrangements for her to stay with some friends, a decision that was painful for us. I worried about how she might feel, being left alone in a foreign country, attempting to adjust to a new culture and its customs. The time apart made it a little easier for George and me to furnish our apartment, but we missed our daughter greatly. Shortly before the start of the new school year, near the time when Barbara was supposed to finally join us in Bogotá, a large explosion rocked the area around the central train station in Cali.

On a hot August day, a military convoy of seven trucks carrying dynamite and gasoline had parked outside the central train station, a

---

6   The term "department" denotes a political entity, somewhat like a state or province.

densely populated part of the city. The trucks were parked overnight, the drivers sleeping in the cabs intending to go on to their final destinations the next day. Somehow a spark or a cigarette left in the wrong place ignited the explosives shortly after midnight. The ensuing explosion, complete with a horrific fireball and concussion, leveled forty city blocks. Within a few seconds, human remains and rubble littered the area around the train station.

The death toll in this heavily populated area was high—about 4,000 lives were lost, and more than 10,000 more were injured. The blast left a crater fifty meters wide and twenty-five meters deep and triggered an earthquake registering 4.3 on the Richter scale. The authorities could never determine whether someone had deliberately triggered the explosion or whether the explosion had been a tragic accident. Terrorism like we know it today was not present then.

When I first heard about the explosion, I had to sit down. My second reaction was to call Barbara. I dialed the number only to discover that phone service had been interrupted. After several hours the phone on the other end finally rang, and soon I spoke to Barbara. "Get yourself on the next plane and come to Bogotá immediately." Essentially, I was giving her a direct order, probably stricter than the situation required.

"But, Mommy…" she replied.

"No excuses," I said. "The next flight, you understand?"

I left no room for negotiation. She whined, but it was pointless. Several hours later, she climbed out of the airplane in Bogotá. An incident at the airport only added to her unhappiness over the rushed departure. We had just finished loading the luggage into a car I had borrowed from my boss when a young man slipped past us, grabbed Barbara's book bag, and bolted, stealing her much-cherished stamp collection. This time pursuit would have been senseless. What can I say? Colombia wasn't exactly the safest place in the world, and such incidents came with the territory.

We placed Barbara in a private school run by nuns—*El Colegio de Santa Clara*. She was less than enthused about the decision. When my company offered to foot the bill for tuition, George and

I felt both relieved and privileged. In many ways we had a lot for which we could be thankful. In a short period of time, George and I had obtained good jobs, and Barbara had begun attending a well-respected school. Yet something gnawed at me in the back of my mind. Was there anything about Bogotá that I found appealing?

Now we spent our first Christmas in South America. To the extent possible, we attempted to maintain the same holiday traditions that we'd had in Germany. I decorated the apartment with angels and tinsel that I had brought with us. I put in the full effort to prepare a traditional Christmas dinner, which we served to several young Germans who also worked for Bayer. Like us, they also missed the holiday traditions from home. For the holidays we also received tons of mail from Germany and an occasional book.

I found a German friend, Ulla, whose daughter was a year older than Barbara. Ulla and her husband possessed an absolute treasure—an old Mercedes—and together with them, George and I explored the countryside around Bogotá, which helped us slowly adjust to our new home. We spent quite a bit of time with Ulla and her family, which was like a breath of fresh air. What particularly impressed me about Ulla was her attitude. Often, when I spent time with other Germans, I heard nothing but constant complaining about how terrible it was to live in Colombia. Every minute of the day, they regretted not being home. After a while I had no interest in socializing with them. Ulla was different. She made a sincere effort to appreciate the culture and to adjust to a new way of life.

Our life in Bogotá slowly took shape. Almost without noticing, we adapted to the local customs, slowly making the transition to exile. Those who decide to settle in a foreign land often experience a sense of euphoria about their new surroundings, infected by a sense of adventure and a sense that life in their new country is better than in the old. Invariably, the same people then go through a period where they hate the new country, where everything is worse than in the old. Finally, hopefully, one can simply accept that the new county and the old are merely different; one country is no better and no worse than the other. As I made this transition, I certainly never forgot where I came from or, most importantly, my upbringing in

Bohemia. Yet as I bonded with the culture, I could never become used to the weather in Bogotá. I found the gray overcast sky and constant lack of sunshine simply depressing.

For our daughter the onset of puberty came rolling in like a juggernaut, and it was soon obvious that Barbara had all the classic symptoms of teenager syndrome: rebelliousness, anger, sullenness, defiance, sassiness, and apathy. I felt I lacked the necessary preparation to deal with this change in my daughter's life because I had never really had a chance to be a teenager myself. During the war I'd had to make an overnight transition from girl to adult. Also, in our situation I think the stress of adjusting to a new home in another country had compounded the tension normally encountered by parents and teens.

George felt disillusioned by our new life, but he had made the decision to come here, and as far I was concerned, he could accept the consequences. Colombia represented the epitome of machismo, the worship of all that is masculine, a disease that soon infected George while we lived in Colombia. The fact that I earned more money really ruffled his pride. What can I say? I became quite adept at networking among the other German expatriates in Colombia, and this skill paid off nicely. George had been able to obtain employment because he was European, a characteristic favored by the Swiss director at the hotel. Because of this, he faced harassment from his coworkers. On top of that, as a receptionist he constantly had to deal with disgruntled guests, which became even more burdensome because of shift work and the resulting lack of sleep.

Like many unhappy men, George dealt with the disappointment of his work by cooking up one fanciful scheme after another. This became old. I already had enough uncertainty and danger in life. It was now time to settle down, to plant roots somewhere. George seemed to thrive on the idea of constant change, despising the everyday routine but rooted firmly in it. Reality bored him, but independent action scared him. I also think George wanted to be like me, but he could not. I seriously worried about whether I could depend on him.

The cynicism with which George saw life surfaced when he tried to pick fights with me. As if this were not enough, the war injury came back to haunt him. As a receptionist he was constantly on his feet. Now the war-injured foot became inflamed, and he had to rest in bed for a week. Clearly, George needed to find another job.

Since I tend to be proactive, soon after George started experiencing problems with his foot, I contacted the German embassy and requested some financial compensation for my disabled war veteran. We desperately needed the money. How naive of me! If the German bureaucracy was slow and cumbersome at home, why should it expedite a claim for a citizen residing in another country? This process took more than a year and involved the intervention of the Foreign Ministry several times.

While we adjusted to life in Colombia, West Germany rebuilt its armed forces, a decision to which the Western Allies gave their consent and perhaps even encouragement. In newspaper advertisements the German defense minister promoted the new army, trying to encourage young men to enlist. I found this outrageous. I quickly fired off an angry letter to the defense minister, asking how he was supposed to find the money to pay these young recruits when the government could not scrape together enough money to support its disabled veterans from the previous war. Then I sent a copy of the same letter to several of West Germany's leading daily newspapers. Did I ever obtain results! Shortly thereafter, we received a favorable response to our petition, and about two months later, George finally received some compensation. Moreover, the West German government started to take its obligations toward its disabled veterans a little more seriously.

Another life-changing moment occurred when I received a phone call from someone I knew in Cali. "I am going back to Germany. Would you like to take over the pension?"[7]

There were discussions, then deliberations, then consultations with friends, and then mathematical calculations, and eventually, we reached a decision. We were going into the hotel business! Now we had to scrape together our startup capital. Our friend Anni loaned us

---

7 A type of guest house or boarding house, typically providing room and board in a less formal environment than a hotel. Often pensions are family-owned establishments.

some money. A Colombian bank also gave us, rather unexpectedly, a line of credit. When I left my position at Bayer, I also received some extra compensation. So, we packed our household goods and made our way back to Cali. When Barbara heard we were moving, she cheered and jumped for joy. I also had to cheer. Now we could leave the gray city.

The Move to Cali—La Sultana del Valle de Cauca, 1957

I spent the last two weeks in Bogotá alone. The apartment had to be turned over to the new tenants, and I wanted to train my successor at Bayer. When I left the company, I cried a little, but I also departed on very good terms with my coworkers. I had enjoyed working for the company. Many of my colleagues had become good friends.

I still remember the day I departed Bogotá. It was a Sunday. About the only luggage I had was a large expensive radio. It was very heavy, and I thought it would tear my arms off as I carried it on board the airplane. At that time the main airport in Bogotá was called El Techo. This small airport lacked many of the comforts that we have grown to expect in modern airports. We had to carry our belongings quite a distance across the airfield, in the open air. I remember the wind blowing through my hair as I lugged that monster of a radio.

The flight path to Cali took us between mountains that towered more than 15,000 feet on both sides of our airplane. Our view was not obstructed by any clouds. Seeing the rocky slopes of these mountains so close to our airplane gave some of the passengers religion. Frightened, many fired off a quick prayer to heaven. "Dear God, if we are going to have an accident, don't let it happen here." Their prayers must have been answered because our flight managed to land in Cali. I noticed again a couple of dusty palm trees that swayed in the afternoon wind amid the lush surroundings. I had missed these trees during my stay in Bogotá.

The afternoon quiet was disturbed only by the occasional porter stomping across the airfield to retrieve luggage. I had flown to Cali with Avianca, the Colombian airline, which had been founded by a group of German pilots after the war.

Self-Confidence and Change, 1957

I arrived in Cali wearing my best wool outfit. Within minutes sweat started rolling down my back. Obviously, my attire was not suitable for tropical weather. My heart pounded with excitement. I filled myself with hopeful expectations of what this new venture would mean for me and my family. But I also needed to constrain myself and attempt to be realistic about the future endeavor because it was not going to be easy.

George was waiting for me at the terminal. I knew he would need my strength and hard work to build a successful business. This new endeavor required me to change directions overnight, from secretary to hotel director. It has always seemed strange to me that happiness comes with strings attached. Even this new venture troubled me. It would have been nice to have time to decompress before running my own business, perhaps just enough time to take in a deep breath. But that did not happen. As soon as one adventure ended, the second began. George counted on me to make all of the serious decisions that running a small business required. So, I rolled up my sleeves, threw caution to the wind, and got down to work.

Our new "castle" was relatively large, and we could offer eight large guest rooms, each with a bathroom. The building also had two interior courtyards. However, the small kitchen made it difficult to prepare my European specialties for the guests.

In a certain way, running my own business was thrilling. Before I arrived, George had already rented a few rooms and had even taken some reservations. This was a positive start, but on the other hand, we needed to fill even more rooms, a goal we were not meeting because we did not have any kind of marketing strategy. Unless we started to rent more rooms, we ran the danger of defaulting on our business loan.

Every day I went to the central market, the only venue for buying the produce we needed. My jaw dropped when I saw papayas the size of soccer balls. Often. I sorted through strange fruits and vegetables that I had never seen before, let alone eaten. In an elaborate roundabout way, an old market woman explained that the oranges were green here, sometimes with small yellow dots. Then she explained that the limes and lemons were also green.

At the central market, I always bought from this one seller named Soledad, whose name implied being alone. When I found out that she had nine children, I just had to smile. With nine children she could not have been alone too often. A wonderful woman with a small and wiry frame, a dark face, and dark hair, Soledad talked nonstop as she continuously rearranged the fruit on her counter. She patiently explained to me the best way of opening and serving the various types of fruit. From her I also received numerous recipes, which I first tried out in our small kitchen. She lived somewhere in the mountains above Cali. One day she gestured with a couple of hand signals that I should peek underneath her counter. I pulled back the plastic tarp and dropped it immediately. Laughing uproariously at my terrified reaction, she said her pet snake slept there coiled up during the day, waiting for the trip home in the afternoon, and as I found out later, she used him to keep away thieves.

I purchased beef, veal, and pork at other stands. For hours on end, the meat hung above the counters on hooks, while the flies crawled and buzzed about. My favorite butcher was a Jewish refugee from the Wedding section of Berlin. His wife looked like a character from a drawing by Heinrich Zille, a famous German illustrator from the late nineteenth and early twentieth centuries. I remember her red-colored hair and fingernails, her ankle socks, and how she wore high-heeled shoes. The familiar Berlin dialect spoken by the butcher brought back a piece of Germany to me. He specialized in lamb and goat, which he sold from an open-air stand that had a bit of Middle Eastern flair, perhaps like something you might have found in biblical times. Several years later, I helped him and his family return to Germany. He was among the many former German "nomads" living in Colombia for whom I was the catalyst for change, helping them reconnect with their roots, even while mine remained forever severed.

Perspective: The Political Climate in Colombia

The Spanish conquered Colombia in the early part of the sixteenth century. This new territory became a Spanish colony, part of the Viceroyalty of New Granada. Under the leadership of Simón Bolívar, in 1819 New Granada gained its independence from Spain. Following years of political upheaval, the current political boundaries of Colombia emerged in 1903.

Colombia has had a stronger democratic tradition than the other countries of Latin America. Nevertheless, its history has been plagued by numerous civil wars and the occasional military coup d'état. Colombia's inhabitants, 75 percent of whom live in cities, represent varying racial and ethnic groups, including Africans, Asians, Europeans, indigenous Americans, and mestizos, people with mixed ancestry. Those who live outside the large cities, in the countryside, are among the country's poorest citizens, many of whom survive below the subsistence level.

Despite the civil unrest, Colombia's economy in the 1950s remained strong by South American standards, surpassed only by Chile.

When George and Franziska moved to Colombia, the country was in the midst of a ten-year long civil war known as *"la Violencia"*. At the time of their arrival, Colombia was governed by President Gustavo Rojas Pinilla, a general who came to power during a military coup in 1953. About four years later, he stepped down under pressure from the National Front, and the era of la Violencia came to an end in 1958. The National Front represented a coalition of moderate conservative and liberal factions who agreed to share power over a sixteen-year period. During the eleven years the Steins lived in Colombia, five different heads of state came and went, each one as corrupt and horrible as the last.

Exact measurement of La Violencia's humanitarian consequences is impossible as a statistical record does not exist. Scholars, however, estimate that between 200,000 and 300,000 lives were lost; 600,000 to 800,000 were injured; and almost one million people were displaced. La

Violencia directly or indirectly affected 20 percent of the population.[8] Moreover, la Violencia did not acquire its name simply because of the number of people it affected; it was the manner in which most of the killings, maimings, and dismemberings were done.

Jubilation, 1957

One day I saw people running through the street yelling, "*Se cayó! Se cayó!*" This meant "He fell!" They danced jubilantly, celebrating the demise of President Pinilla. It was definitely time for a new government. Yet for the ordinary citizen, a change of government meant only a change of face. Much-needed reform never materialized. Pinilla's successor, President Gabriel París Gordillo, carried out the same system of plunder, filling his own pockets while his fellow citizens went hungry, an injustice that seemed unnecessary because Colombia has abundant mineral and agricultural resources.

Residencia Stein, 1957

Early on, we employed only one maid at the hotel. Our financial situation was tight. We had to pay back our business loan while too many rooms remained vacant. Nevertheless, failure was never an option. This could happen to others, but not to us. I was always searching for new ways of boosting business while George, it seemed, merely went along for the ride. His charm sometimes managed to cheer me up, but I questioned whether the hotel business really suited him. Our married life remained difficult. He remained withdrawn, lost in his dreams, thinking of the next scheme. He suffered from constant pain, some of it real and some of it, I think, imagined. Often, I found myself wanting to grab him by the shoulders, to shake some sense into him, to let him know that he also had a role to play in this new life of ours.

---

8   *Bailey, Norman A. (1967). "La Violencia in Colombia". Journal of Inter-American Studies. Center for Latin American Studies at the University of Miami.* **9** *(4): 561–75.*

During this time, complications from his war injury in 1942 became very severe. He lived with excruciating pain. His metatarsus and heel bones never let him forget, not even for one minute, what he had experienced. In the years immediately after the war, we could not afford to obtain a proper pair of orthopedic shoes for him. There were more basic needs to fill. Yet with regular shoes, he could not walk properly. In 1957 we finally bought the shoes he required, which we ordered from Germany.

The war injury also came back to haunt George in other ways. Occasionally, pieces of bone fragment worked their way to the surface of his skin, which resulted in open wounds that sometimes required surgical care. The years of mobility problems also caused muscular atrophy in parts of his legs. After spending some time in the hospital in Cali, George had to move about on crutches for a while. The healing process, which also included the psychological recovery, dragged on for an eternity. The doctor prescribed exercises for him to strengthen his leg. But George ignored these instructions, finding denial easier than action.

The situation forced me to become a nurse, and I forced him to do the exercises. But this meant spending too much time away from the hotel, which also required my attention. Yelling at George and slamming the door, I told him that he would have to hire a nurse. "Oh, Mother, he said, don't get so upset." That's how he reacted.

During this time in our marriage, I refused to fetch things for him. When he asked, I said, "George, if you don't want to get it yourself, then you probably don't need it." Today, I am sorry for having said that. I can't possibly imagine how the war injuries made him suffer.

Despite the trouble in our marriage, something always remained that prevented me from walking away from the relationship. He was sarcastic toward me; often he said things that were hurtful. But sometimes he could be absolutely charming, and there were beautiful moments that I still cherish. George often sat with the guests for cocktails. As I entered the room, he would always glance in my direction with a sparkle in his eyes and say, "It is truly a pleasure to see you." I, in turn, radiated the warmth back in his direction, soaking up this extra attention like a sponge, saving it for when times became difficult between us.

My relationship with my daughter improved considerably following the move to Cali. She made a better adjustment here than she had when we lived in Bogotá. Right from the start, she made friends with other German-speaking girls. She stayed busy, with typical teenage energy that sometimes pulled her in directions that did not please her parents.

The quest for happiness and contentment always remains elusive. Sometimes I built a wall around myself. I often grew impatient with the routine of life, failing to heed the principle that progress often comes in small strides. Anni became my best friend, and only with her could I sort through the difficulties of expatriate life in Colombia.

Encounter with an Unusual Man, 1958

A considerable number of Germans had settled in Cali, many of whom we met over the course of several months. One of them was Don Martin, with whom Anni brought us together one day. During the First World War he had been a fighter pilot, assigned to the same squadron as the Red Baron. The German military hand-selected these warriors of the sky from the battalions of hussars, an elite cavalry unit. Like George, Don Martin came from West Prussia. As soon as the two men met, they became inseparable. They formed an instant friendship, spending many hours talking about religion, world events, imperial Germany, the Kaiser, the war, and horses.

Don Martin was a sales manager for a German company that imported rice hullers, machines capable of removing the husk from grains of rice. The business meetings usually took place at his farm, where he hosted dinners for his customers. Yet his passion in life was horse breeding. To defray the costs of this hobby, he offered riding lessons to countless gringos. Despite his age, he still retained the military bearing he had acquired as a young man. This wiry and disciplined man galloped across his farm every day wearing a riding outfit. I remember one time, when he had to attend a reception, how disgruntled he became about having to wear normal clothes. Don

Martin got along very well with Theresa, his second wife, a former kindergarten teacher and a few years younger than he. She appeared to be a perfect match for him, a woman with an unusually short hairstyle and an athletic build. This couple spoiled their hunting dogs, which they also bred on the farm.

Pompillo, their farmhand, came from somewhere in the mountains of Colombia. His face was dark brown and beset with numerous deep wrinkles. His dark brown eyes beamed whenever he stroked his curved hands over the broad backs of the magnificent horses. He also showed great patience when a clumsy European struggled to climb into the saddle. I never saw him without the old, worn-out hat that he used to wear, one given to him as a gift by Don Martin. Similarly, nobody could ever separate him from his poncho even though it was full of holes.

Looking like something you would see in a Hollywood western, the flat-roofed adobe buildings on the farm might have been one or even two hundred years old. Each had a small window with a long ledge. Instead of flowers, the buildings were decorated with small clay sculptures, pre-Colombian art Don Martin had collected on his many trips throughout Latin America. The veranda before the entrance of the main building consisted of a giant terrace. Tiles handmade by Indians formed the floor upon which colonial-style wood furniture had been placed. Colorful bougainvillea grew like a waterfall, stretching from the balustrade to the brown floor below.

On Wednesdays and Saturdays, Don Martin gave us riding lessons. An accomplished horseman, he seemed rather gruff, and sometimes crude, to those he trained. I remember that Barbara refused to climb into the saddle and how Don Martin growled disapprovingly. She simply was not interested in this sport. Of course, the large horses on his ranch were intimidating and difficult for people of small stature, like me, to ride. I still remember the problems I faced during the first couple of lessons. George, of course, was a natural, an experienced rider who once had broken young horses from eastern Prussia while serving in the military. He enjoyed going for rides with Don Martin. Despite the pain, George could not resist galloping through the hills, the wind blowing in his face.

Over a period of several weeks, the German consul paid regular visits to the horse farm. He brought his wife with him, a woman of noble birth. Upon returning to Germany, she intended to show off the finely-honed equestrian skills that she had acquired in Colombia. Don Martin could not have cared less. He treasured the horses far more than the wife of some bureaucrat. Not exactly a featherweight, this woman began to parade around sidesaddle. At first Don Martin tried to ignore this behavior, but this eccentric noble, who rode more like a sack of flour, finally made him burst at the seams. "Damn it!" he said. "Move your royal ass to the proper position and stop mistreating that poor animal."

You could hear a pin drop as all eyes turned first to Don Martin and then in unison to the woman with the royal buttocks. Still sitting sidesaddle, she dismounted the horse in as dignified a way as possible. Making a beeline to the house, head held high, cheeks red, she gathered her belongings without saying a word and made a hasty departure with her husband in tow. The following Saturday, the couple reappeared for another riding lesson. From that moment on, the noblewoman followed Don Martin's instructions without protest.

After we finished our riding lessons, we always groomed the horses and led them to their stalls, where they were fed. Now we could relax as Doña Theresa entertained us with a delicious meal inspired by a local recipe. Exhausted, we sat on the veranda around a large table made of unfinished wood. As the sun disappeared behind the mountains, hurricane lamps hanging from the roof provided illumination. For dessert we indulged in a glass or two of aguardiente, which was often accompanied by music that Pompillo conjured up on his *tiple*, a type of guitar that the indigenous Colombians played. Our faces began to glow while the moon floated overhead. One of many simple but unforgettable moments in Cali, our new home in South America.

Through the riding lessons at Don Martin's ranch, we met other displaced Europeans. I can remember the discussions we had together over drinks and tapas prepared by Doña Theresa. I felt a special kinship with them, people just as friendly and helpful as the locals. In my new surroundings I began to feel safe; I felt as though one could seek refuge here. Everything about the new culture, including the language and the scenery, inspired me.

The relationship with Don Martin not only improved my riding skills but also helped bring in more hotel guests. He introduced us to so many people who recommended our business to their friends and business partners. Soon we filled most of our rooms on a regular basis. In 1975 I had a chance to visit with Doña Theresa one last time. She was ready to sell the farm in Colombia and return to Munich. Don Martin had died several years prior in a manner befitting an old cavalry officer: he fell from his horse and was fatally injured. Doña Theresa wiped the tears from her eyes and whispered to me, "That's what he always would have wanted, to die while riding one of his horses."

We spent one last evening on the terrace after eating a meal of local specialties. Sipping glasses of aguardiente, we reminisced about old times and how taken we had been with the scenery and culture. Then I realized what a force for change Cali had been in my life, how this experience had shaped me as a person. I am convinced this experience made me a better human being, opening my eyes and mind to new possibilities, lifting my self-esteem. Then we said goodbye to each other. Our hearts were heavy for we both knew we would never meet again.

Panta Rhei—Everything Is in a State of Flux, 1958–1959

One day we received a letter from the owner of our hotel building. He needed a change and wanted to sell the property. Just when our business had started to become successful, we had to find a new location. Since we were in this situation anyway, it only made sense to find a larger building in a better area. The long search became nerve-wracking, but eventually we found the optimal house not far from Cali's city center. Located on a hill, the new building acted like a sail, catching the cool afternoon breezes from the ocean, which provided much-needed relief when the weather became warm. But we had to take the good with the bad. Anni now lived further away, and we could not see each other as often.

During the day our new hotel remained surprisingly cool because the outside heat did not seem to penetrate the walls. The charming colonial-style house had an interior courtyard and a large garden that furnished us with fruit, including papayas and avocados. Purple, red, and pink bougainvillea covered the walls around the garden and interior courtyard. In one of the yards stood an unusual tree, one that I had never seen before. Though it was certainly not among the best examples of Mother Nature's beauty, this imported cananga tree emitted a wonderful odor, especially after it had rained.[9]

After finding a new location for our hotel, we didn't waste much time and moved into the new building as quickly as possible, with guests in tow. Finally, I had a large kitchen where I could prepare something special for the guests. The beautiful veranda offered a terrific view of the city. On top of that, I enjoyed seeing the tremendous variety of wild birds that flocked to the property. George soon built a birdhouse, and every morning our feathered guests greeted us with lots of chirping.

George, an accomplished handyman, busied himself day and night with the interior renovation. He hammered and sawed up a storm to refit the rooms to suit the needs of our guests. In the meantime, I supervised the staff, making sure the laundry was washed, the dishes cleaned, and the kitchen stocked with food. The extra work that the new property required seemed to have placed our marital problems on the sidelines for a while.

Barbara attended a German high school, a school she loved, and slowly became a remarkable young woman. Surrounded by many friends, she stayed active by swimming, playing tennis, and of course, dancing. Barbara was still too young to have a boyfriend. Nevertheless, she had a secret admirer. Half-Colombian and half-Swiss, the boy was the son of a cattle rancher. The lad tried every trick in the book to impress Barbara. Lack of money was no obstacle. He even sold his motor scooter to hire a group of musicians, called *conjuntos* by the locals, whose assignment was to stand outside Barbara's room and serenade the young lady at night.

---

9   Also known as *ylang ylang*, this is a tropical tree native to Asia

At the time our guests included several Austrians who worked for Simmering-Graz-Pauker, one of Austria's large industrial conglomerates. This firm was building a mountain railway from Buenaventura to Cali. One of these guests, a particularly crass engineer by the name of Josef Ü., had to add his two cents when he heard about the sale of the motor scooter. "Well, it looks as though the boy finally got rid of that crotch rocket." With that, he let out a laugh and slapped his knee, thinking himself quite funny. Herr Ü. did not know why the sale had been necessary until a short time later. At first the guests did not seem to mind the serenades. However, the music prevented Barbara from obtaining a full night of sleep, and she was too tired to attend school. George and I also woke up exhausted, something we could not afford with all the work to be done.

Either the boy ran out of money, or George put his foot down. In any case, three weeks after their debut at the Residencia Stein, the *conjuntos* were playing somewhere else. Finally, everybody could have a bit of peace and quiet at night. This did not seem to bother Barbara in the slightest. Obviously, she was indifferent to this one-sided love affair. Our Austrians returned to their favorite pastime, chasing the young ladies and taking shots of aguardiente, an activity they called *katzen und schnapps* in their Austrian dialect.

We had adjusted to our new lives in South America. Running a successful business consumed much of our time, leaving little time to reflect on the past and our previous life in Europe. Then came some sad news from Berlin. Grandpa Max had died. We knew that he had been sick for quite some time and that for the most part he had endured this illness alone. Ulla, George's sister, ran a tailoring business. For reasons not entirely clear—perhaps she lacked either the time or the interest—Ulla had let her father fend for himself. Erna, his second wife, had refused to provide the nursing that her very sick husband needed. He attempted to manage things as best as he could, yet his illness eventually took a turn for the worst. Max went to the hospital and passed away.

I really do not believe that Max Stein was ever happy, not for one day of his whole life. From the first time I met him, life always disappointed him. He felt his family did not appreciate what he had provided them, which was probably true. I do not know what he expected from life or why he hated his children. Material possessions meant everything, whereas human relationships meant little. Out of fear of the unknown afterlife, he attempted to buy his way to heaven. The silver goblet he gave to Senorina's convent for crucifixes was one example, but this represented just one of his smaller donations to the church. During the requiem Mass held in his honor, everyone was surprised to learn of Max's very generous gift toward furnishing the church with a new roof. The priest praised Max Stein and offered his gratitude for this donation. I wish I could have seen the expression on Ulla's face.

Upon reading the letter informing us of Grandpa Max's death, I was overcome with emotion. Tears streamed down my cheeks as I recalled how he had hardly any friends or close bonds with his family. The last few years of his life must have been very lonely. It still bothers me that he never found inner peace. I still have the last letter Max wrote to us. In it he suggested indirectly that he would like to see us again. Why had family become important suddenly? Did he want reconciliation with his family, knowing the end was near? Today I want to believe that in between the lines he wanted to say, "I love you." How unfortunate it was that he went to his grave without repairing the strained relationship with his children.

When George learned that his father had died, he did not show any signs of grief. I found that odd, but then again, George never shared his feelings with me. His strict Prussian upbringing and a childhood lacking in parental affection and warmth, and the security that these provide, came back to haunt George when he was an adult. What had happened when he was a child and later during the war had hurt him profoundly.

Most of Max Stein's estate remained in Berlin. Before we left Germany, I had received a steel engraving of Voltaire and a picture of Frederick the Great, as well as several old maps. In a reflection of Max's anger toward his son, George did not appear in the will. However, Max willed one of the houses to Ulla and the other to Barbara.[10]

---

10   In Germany, many residences are structured like co-ops in the United States, with separate ownership of units within a single building. In this case, the

As with most inheritance matters, the division of Max's estate produced a mixture of envy and resentment among those who survived. One factor was that we never received an inventory of the family heirlooms. We knew of some Dutch paintings and a big bronze sculpture, among other items, that we thought should have been ours, but our attempt to determine what exactly remained was met with evasive answers from Ulla.

Once she asked if we wanted several heirlooms from the estate. A couple of crates were haphazardly thrown together and shipped to his. When they arrived, I found an incomplete set of Margarethe's china, the family silver I had smuggled out of Karlsbad, two Japanese Imari plates, and a small painting. Everything else from the estate disappeared without a trace. George should have fought for what rightfully belonged to him, but he absolutely refused to become involved with the matter. He wanted nothing from the old man with whom lifelong enmity had existed.

The Temp Job That Lasted Forty Years, 1959

"I need a room. Do you have something available?" the man asked over the phone.

I scratched my head, clueless as to how I could find a solution to this man's problem. Unfortunately, every one of our rooms had been taken, but I wanted to help him. He had a friendly voice, and I never wanted to turn away a German. "Give me a bit of time to find something. Can you call back in about two hours?" I asked him.

It must have been a miracle—just then a guest approached to inform me that he regrettably had to check out. That is how Rolf Zieschang came to be an important part of my life. A young lawyer from Berlin, he was now in Colombia to help Jewish immigrants file claims for compensation from the German government.

When we first met, he could not speak a word of Spanish. As a matter of fact, one of the first questions he asked was whether I knew

---

style of the building was like a side-by-side duplex, with Max's daughter, Ulla, getting one unit and Barbara the other.

anybody who could help him with the language. Then other questions followed. "Do you know anybody who can fill out these forms? You wouldn't happen to have a typewriter, would you? Perhaps you know someone who could type a letter for me?"

The first and third questions were rather straightforward. "Yes, I speak some Spanish. And I can loan you a typewriter." The second and fourth questions required some thought. After some hesitation I finally responded. "Um, well… I can fill out these forms, and I suppose I could type something for you."

My fate was sealed from that moment. For over forty years, I was his loyal secretary, his representative in North and South America. How could either of us ever have predicted the avalanche that would eventually bury us in compensation claims? We had no idea. In fact, he planned to stay only a week, enough time to deliver a speech to the local Jewish community. Zieschang (I always called him informally by his last name) thought perhaps he would receive a couple of claims before moving on to the rest of South America. By the middle of each week that followed, he found himself needing to extend his stay by yet another week. The stack of paper on the temporary desk I had set up grew taller and taller.

It was as though someone had opened the floodgate. The number of people who attended the presentations surprised us. We knew that Cali had a sizable Jewish community, yet we had not really comprehended how many had joined the community after fleeing Nazi Germany. Furthermore, after fleeing to Colombia, many had married locals and as a result were no longer active in the Jewish faith.

The immigration of German Jews to South America had peaked right before the start of the Second World War. To emigrate from Germany, these migrants were forced by the Nazi regime to forfeit most of their assets to the government. Taking what little money remained, many booked passage on a ship destined for the New World. Many countries in the Western Hemisphere, including the United States, refused to admit those fleeing from Nazi persecution. Colombia, on the other hand, remained very tolerant and gave them sanctuary.

When the Second World War finally ended, a new wave of immigration to South America began—including Jews who had survived the concentration camps, as well as those who had emerged from hiding, displaced peoples, and economic refugees. Many of them suffered from malnutrition and the psychological scars that their mistreatment had left behind. For a while the United Nations Relief and Rehabilitation Administration cared for them, but eventually they had to fend for themselves.

One fact that should not be omitted is that some of the Germans arriving in South America had been key figures within the Nazi government and had even participated in war crimes. Officials within the Swiss government, the Red Cross, and even the Vatican aided their escape from justice. Many immigrated to Argentina, Brazil, Paraguay, and other South American countries. Luckily, we never encountered any of them, at least that I know of. Moreover, they were barred from receiving any kind of compensation from the German government.

Many of the German expatriates living in Colombia and South America desperately needed compensation. Having lost all that they owned, they now lived in extreme poverty at the basic subsistence level. For many, the key to survival in Europe had been their education, something that did not necessarily bring them much of a reward in their new country. Moreover, German children missed many years of school between the war and emigration, and public schools were very weak in Colombia. This meant as young adults they were not good employment prospects and their families suffered as a result.

The daily routine at the hotel included planning the menu, supervising the maids, shopping, and taking care of the guests. Working for Zieschang was something interesting, a much-welcomed diversion. In certain respects, this work became a means of coming to terms with my past. I often read the case histories, which allowed me to learn the fate of so many people. Even George found these stories interesting. As he read the reports, his face reflected the homesickness that tormented him.

Finally, Zieschang had to depart. People all over South America were awaiting the assistance he could provide. He requested that I accompany him. "Your help is indispensable," he said.

Somewhat embarrassed, I had to decline the offer. I could not abandon George and our hotel. However, he persuaded me to continue to service the existing clients in South and Central America. Some weeks later, this entailed a trip to Ecuador, Peru, and Central America to build up the business within the Jewish communities there.

My duties at the hotel and the work I performed for Zieschang consumed most of my time. Soon customers stood in line seeking help with their compensation claims. I never would have thought so many former refugees lived so close to me. Many had problems with the legal terminology and could not provide complete answers to questions on the forms. Often, they lacked the necessary documentation to support their claim for compensation.

Over the course of forty years, I worked on these claims, sometimes very intensely and sometimes less. Over the years new legislation was passed or amended that made more victims of the Nazi persecution eligible for compensation. The hundreds of case histories detailing the ways our clients had suffered often became heart-wrenching for me. Most of those who emigrated had lost everything they owned, and many had lost family members. Quite a few of our clients had escaped from the concentration camps. Of course, many of the clients were reluctant to tell me about these tragic events. However, I noticed something interesting. After clients overcame their initial hesitation, the narration of these terrible events became cathartic. Once they started, they were eager to recount what had happened. I became not only a legal secretary but also a grief counselor who patiently listened to their stories.

For years I maintained copies of the many petitions for compensation that I reviewed over the course of more than three decades. In 1991, when we returned to Germany, I destroyed most of the files, taking only the open cases to Germany with me. Today, when I see how this era is often portrayed, I regret that I didn't attempt to save these claims. Many of the eyewitness accounts detailed in these personal histories contradict what is dramatized or sensationalized in films and books and would bring a whole new perspective to the Holocaust. Often the media-driven stories are based on hearsay, shoddy research, ignorance, and even fantasy. For whatever reason, the story these immigrants had to tell never received the attention it deserved. Often, descriptions of the Second World War detail how the Nazi regime inflicted suffering on other Europeans but somehow overlook the fact that they also inflicted immense suffering on their own people.

Working with the past became an experience that was exciting and interesting, but I also had very real tasks in the present that required my attention. Our small hotel, the Residencia Stein, prospered. We managed to keep our rooms booked and often had to turn potential customers away for lack of a vacancy. The upturn in business required us to hire more staff. When we first went into the hotel business, we employed only one maid, and now six were on the payroll, along with two laundrywomen and a houseboy.

One of our maids, Chavela, was a jack-of-all-trades. Skinny and hardworking, she possessed the secret knowledge of Colombian witches, which sometimes became rather annoying. "¿Señora, puedo ayudar a usted?" she constantly whispered when I looked over the booking sheet. "Yo soy de capaz de arreglar este problema."[11]

At first, I wanted just to get rid of her. She constantly interrupted me as I juggled guests and rooms. Then one night, when everything had gone wrong and I was on the verge of losing my sanity, I gave into her ceaseless pestering. I was desperate to accommodate a new guest, but I simply had no room left. After a short cackle, she grabbed the broom, sprinkled some sort of magic liquid potion on it, and set it behind a door with the handle end down. "That will help," she said assuredly.

The next morning one of the guests announced he would be checking out because he had found a house for himself and his family. I couldn't believe what I heard him say. The problem from the previous day was solved, and I had a room for rent. Everyone was happy.

Chavela practiced her magic whenever possible, always managing to achieve a miraculous outcome at the last minute. One time I was suffering from gastrointestinal problems. Eventually, I went to the

---

11   "Ma'am, can I help you? I have the ability to solve this problem."

doctor. He explained that some sort of amoeba had gotten inside of me, a condition that was fairly common in the tropics. The cure consisted of a medication containing arsenic, which was just as toxic as the amoeba. Soon I suffered from severe swelling and constant nausea. After a week of this, I still felt awful. I had finally had enough and was ready to try something new, if not radical. Chavela sent me to Negra Maria, who practiced her magic in the marketplace. Her craft inspired both admiration and fear. This time the cure consisted of taking a morning glass of aguardiente with salt on an empty stomach. Afterward, I had to eat a large slice of fresh pineapple. Within a few days I felt an improvement, and shortly thereafter I was cured. I had no further problems with the amoeba.

But it would have been foolish to put all our trust in Chavela's magic. We simply needed to find a way to offer more rooms to potential customers. Unexpectedly, the house across the street became available, which we rented and converted into space for additional rooms.

Our business success brought us a status symbol—a car. At that time, it was against the law in Colombia to import a car. This limited our choice to a used car and, on top of that, an old-timer. The vehicles we saw on the roads of South America had been taken off the highways of Europe and the United States many years ago. At an auto market we found a magnificent icon of American culture—an old Cadillac. We liked the interior, but to be on the safe side, we asked a mechanic to look things over.

The mechanic, while scratching his ear, finally remarked, "Señor, este coche tiene verdaderamente mucho motor."[12]

Now we had wheels. Our car served us well. Overloaded with groceries from the market, our Cadillac nearly ran out of breath as it crawled over the mountains. With our new chariot we took guests to the airport, floating over the potholes on the badly maintained streets. We kept the car in service for many years, selling it when we finally found a better car.

---

12   "Sir, this car has a huge engine."

Confession and Separation, 1959

Two years earlier a handsome German man named Otto Kollman had stayed in our hotel with his fiancée. Now, at the beginning of 1959, he walked through our door a second time. I looked deeply into his green eyes and *bang*! I remembered him immediately, recalling how he had introduced me to his fiancée. But this time he was alone. The intense look he gave me, I returned with equal intensity.

Later I found out more about this woman, who had never become his wife. "I could not stand her any longer, so I sent her back to Germany," he said. Then he asked me if I believed in love at first sight. What I felt that day came close. Maybe it was love at second sight. Now in addition to the stress of running our own business and the squabbles that arose from my troubled marriage, I had another problem. I felt a strong attraction to this man—a rather difficult situation, since I had a husband and a half-grown daughter, things in life that you avoid losing.

I was not sure about my feelings. Again, and again, I toyed with the possibilities in my mind. I thought about my mother and how she had raised me to be a good wife and mother. When I was a girl, extramarital affairs had existed only in novels and dreams. Yet I could not suppress the desire inside of me. I was a woman, a real woman, one who had experienced a sexual awakening, which now remained buried under a mountain of worries, strains, and privations. Now I wanted to live, live, live—I wanted to love and be loved, to feel once again the butterflies in my stomach, to feel once again the closeness of a lover. I wanted to thank God for each day that I would awake to see him next to me.

George and I occasionally had time for intimacy, but it was never carefree, and the genuine, spontaneous affection that accompanies true love had long since disappeared. In Colombia, the power of attraction had gradually cooled between us. The strain of everyday life became almost unbearable. Life was supposed to have become easier, but instead life with George had become more difficult and complicated. Again, and again, I scolded Max Stein in my thoughts for not ever showing affection toward the ones he should have loved.

In all honesty, life with George ran almost the same way, with a lack of feelings between those who should have loved each other. To avoid conflict, we had clearly delineated areas of responsibility in our lives. I made the decisions and planned for the future; George entertained the guests.

I desperately needed a change. Life had too many responsibilities, there was too much work, and I had no time for myself. Now suddenly, I had found Otto, and somehow, I was pulled to him like nobody before. Whenever possible, we spent time together, just talking. We had so much in common. Both of us came from an area once under the rule of the Austro-Hungarian Empire. Otto was born in Brod, a city in the former Yugoslavia. He owned an apartment in Cali and made a living as an engineer. Along with two German partners, he owned a garage and repaired heavy motors. Outside of Cali, in Pichinde, the three of them owned a small farm and coffee plantation called a *cafetal*. On the property they had horses. Together we rode horses throughout the hills that surrounded the farm. We became closer to each other, and the attraction was magical. However, we kept our physical distance. When the first kiss came, it was redemption, a long-overdue revelation. Faster than a flash of lightning, he became a part of my life, throwing me for a loop. Without saying a word, he offered me protection and his devotion, which I soaked up like a sponge.

I could see clearly the problems George had with himself and with life, the terrible childhood and the dreadful experiences during the war. With Otto I could just dream and fulfill my own needs. I felt the caterpillar inside me changing into a butterfly. Otto needed me just for me, and my wings took on a vibrant color. Yet I knew that a butterfly does not live for long. At first it was platonic love, but the feelings inside me became more intense. I needed him.

Over and over, I said to my husband, "George, we need to talk." He ignored me and continued with whatever task was at hand, such as the gardening. He must have noticed, even if he tried to deny it. George no longer played first violin in my life. Of course, he saw what was playing out, but he could not or would not do anything about it.

I needed distance from him and his moods. I needed my own space. I needed time to find myself. Otto was the catalyst that led me to make important decisions and develop in ways I never would have imagined. Because of George's coldness toward me, I stepped out into unfamiliar territory. Perhaps we would come back together, but not yet.

A letter from the government floated across my desk around the time of the crisis in our marriage. Fate had struck once again. We were being offered an opportunity to manage a hotel under construction in the San Agustín Archaeological Park. Within the international community in Colombia, we had made a good name for ourselves. Now the government wanted to utilize our experience. Initially, we declined the offer. But after the government failed to find someone else, they tried their luck a second time. Impulsively, George seized the opportunity, which meant a way out from the dark storm clouds that had settled over our marriage. He would be responsible for organizing a grand opening, for marketing, and for training a manager, a journey into the wilderness that would last for several months.

It was a done deal. For different reasons we both welcomed this new diversion. We climbed into our VW bus, which we had purchased in addition to the Cadillac. Together, George and I set out for the archaeological park to assess the condition of the hotel. This difficult journey would take us to a remote area in southwestern Colombia.

Heading south by southwest out of Cali, and after crossing the Cauca River, we reached the city of Puerto Tejada. This city had become infamous during colonial times for the slave trade that was conducted there. Many of the large *fincas* (plantation estates) and *rancheros* (cattle ranches) around this area are still in existence from the colonial era.

From Puerto Tejada the road widened and rose in elevation as we traveled to Popayán, a beautiful city founded in 1537 and the former capital of the Department of Valle de Cauca. Colombia and its neighbors are prone to severe earthquakes, and in 1983 one registering 5.5 on the Richter scale struck near Popayán, destroying much of the city and killing at least 250 people.

Known as the "White City," and at an elevation of 5,770 feet, the city of Popayán looks on the snowcapped Puracé volcano, one of the most active volcanoes in South America. Our destination lay on the other side of the volcanic mountain chain, and we headed out of Popayán toward the Puracé volcano pass. As we neared the summit, the unpaved road became very narrow. The car crawled its way up and over the volcano's pass and descended the other side, on what seemed an even worse unimproved road, into the Magdalena River basin. We crossed the Cordillera Central, a mountain chain, and eventually reached San Agustín. Along the way we saw one coffee plantation after another, which seemed to thrive in the year-round spring-like weather found in this region.

The spring weather outside stood in stark contrast to the cold, winterlike atmosphere inside the car. We spoke to each other only when it was necessary. Time seemed to last for an eternity, as one hour of silence followed another. When we finally reached the park, George had to stop the car and study, for a moment, the sign at the entrance. "Est es el fin del Mundo."[13] We took in a deep breath and drove the remaining stretch.

The hotel was still under construction. Certainly, the government had spared no expense with this prestigious project. As soon as George saw the hotel, he could not wait to take on the challenge. He almost thawed out as he strode enthusiastically toward the building site. This project fed his ambition. He wanted to prove to himself and others that he had the ability to put a hotel into operation. Over the same punishing roads, we returned to Cali so that George could prepare for an extended stay at the hotel, a stay that would last at least three months. Without saying a word to George, I sensed that our marriage hung in the balance and that we would have to assess things during this period of separation.

I remained behind in Cali and now ran our business alone. Not much had changed, except that my husband now lived ten hours away by car. Now nothing hindered my attraction to Otto, who felt the same attraction to me. The inevitable came next. Our bodies

---

13   "This is the end of the world."

knew what they wanted, and what had been mere fantasy now became reality.

Otto stood by me. Having already spent thirteen years in Colombia, he showered me with advice and useful suggestions. For the first time in quite a long time, I had someone to lean on, someone with whom I could discuss everyday problems and setbacks. A ton of weight had been lifted from my shoulders. I worked hard, and the business flourished, but now I did not have to contend with arguments or someone scolding me at every turn. I almost felt happy.

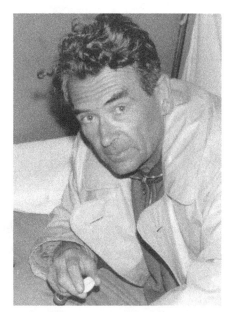

Otto Kollman, 1960.

Otto corresponded to my picture of the ideal man, exceeding by far the standard I had set in my youth. I would describe him as adventuresome and protective and as a sensitive lover and educated speaking partner. Otto was a knight in shining armor, the kind a young girl imagines while gazing at the full moon on a star-filled evening. He sparked in me a hunger for culture, a topic I could discuss with him for hours on end, enthralled by the history and fed by my never-ending curiosity. He set me free.

The tropics change people, especially those who were not born there. Virtue and vice are amplified. Self-discipline diminishes. The heat saps your inhibitions, leaving little strength to adhere to previous standards of behavior. Even I was powerless to resist. Perhaps even George was having an affair with a Colombian. It did not matter now.

The Land of the Gods, 1959

Despite all the work that needed to be done, and perhaps also because of the need to take a break from the hard work, I began to explore different parts of Colombia. It is a land with much diversity, with snowcapped peaks, hills covered with coffee plantations, and plains formed by meandering rivers, where the climate ranges from cool to hot and humid. In many areas of Colombia, the land is very fertile, and farmers can harvest three crops in a year. I enjoyed the diversity of the flora and fauna of this country, a feast for my hungry eyes.

Far from home and European civilization, those in Colombia's expatriate community were faced with a choice: either obtain a basic command of the Spanish language or languish in social and economic stagnation. I learned Spanish.

During the many years that Otto had spent in Colombia, he had delved into the history and culture of this country and its people. He preferred to visit attractions that told a piece of history from hundreds of years in the past. This was something he wanted to share with me.

We also made frequent trips to Don Martin's ranch, where we saddled up the horses and took long rides through the hills, the cool wind blowing in our faces. We could speak for hours at a time, exchanging thoughts and ideas about topics ranging from extraordinary world events to the most mundane details of everyday life. As one word followed another, I felt liberated; I felt that finally I had found the intellectual and emotional stimulation that I had craved so desperately.

George called once a week. Things seemed to be going well for him. Or perhaps I was just imagining things. Several weeks after he departed, I promised to visit him. He needed supplies and my help for the grand opening of the hotel. "By the way, I'll need to use Otto's car," I added. This meant that a man would be coming to the hotel with me, something that did not faze George a bit.

The Grand Opening at the Hotel Yalconia, 1960

Since we were making our journey during the school holiday, Barbara could accompany us, and my daughter insisted on bringing one of her friends. The four of us rode in Otto's VW minibus, an adequate but far from luxurious vehicle. At least it was relatively new and could be trusted to get us there without breaking down.

In a way I felt like a little kid setting off on his or her first trip, but in the back of my mind, I felt uneasy about entrusting the care of the Cali hotel to someone else. For several months I had been training Carmen, one of the housekeepers, and now I would find out how well she could run the business in my absence.

We took the same route that George and I had taken before, but with time on our side, we decided to spend the night in Coconuco, a little past Popayán up in the hills, because we didn't want to try to make our way over the Puracé volcano in the dark. At the hotel in Coconuco, we enjoyed a refreshing bath in a hot mineral spring warmed by the volcano. We sat in a bathtub carved from natural stone in the open air under a star-covered sky. The sweet fragrance of the wild mint bushes that proliferated in this area combined with the sulfur fumes from the mineral springs to yield a strange, almost intoxicating odor. Tall bushes around us gently swayed in the cool evening breeze, and soon we felt relaxed, forgetting the strenuous day in the car.

I thought about the elegant spa resorts from my childhood, and this simpler retreat in the Western Hemisphere, where one could just as easily enjoy the genius of Mother Nature, certainly did not disappoint us. The quiet and the seclusion, along with the hot mineral water, refreshed both body and spirit. Finally, we had to brave the cold night air and make our way to our hotel rooms. I snuggled up with the girls in a giant bed and fell fast asleep.

The next day, as the motor howled and strained, we drove over the narrow gravel road to the edge of the Puracé crater. The heavy fog around the volcano surprised us, so thick that you could cut it with a knife. Very slowly, we pushed our way through the clouds, watching for the occasional cow that might wander out in front of the car. Small bushes lined the road, growing among the ever-present *frailijones*, flowers that reminded me of the much-beloved edelweiss flowers of Europe.

Soon we reached the summit, which provided a breathtaking view of a distant lake. Having already traveled for several hours, we could not resist going for a hike to this lake, whose mirrored surface reflected the sky and mountains. "Who's jumping in first?" I yelled, springing from the car.

We were certainly inexperienced with what Mother Nature had to offer. An hour later, straining at elevation to pull in the next breath of air, we finally reached the shore of the lake, where we collapsed onto the grass, totally exhausted. The strenuous hike had killed any desire to take in a beautiful view, and now we had to concern ourselves with returning to the car, hoping our lungs would survive the ordeal.

The fog started to roll in as we made our way through a small patch of forest. At a clearing we noticed a house surrounded by a barn and several shacks. It seemed someone lived there. We knocked on the door to ask for a cup of water.

The door opened, and a blind woman stood before us. "What can I do for you?" the occupant asked in German.

We looked at each other in amazement, having expected Spanish. German immigrants, in fact, lived on the property. Three generations shared the house. The grandfather had worked for the German Foreign Service during the Second World War. His daughter, who was blind, lived there with her husband, a war veteran, and they had three children. In all likelihood, the grandfather was once a member of the Nazi Party; otherwise, he would not have been a diplomat during the war. However, the present concerned me more than the past, and he seemed to be a nice, although rather helpless, old man. Confined to a wheelchair, he depended on his daughter's family to take care of him. The family intentionally lived in seclusion, in conditions that I would describe as nearly primitive. They did not have electricity or a telephone, grew most of their vegetables, and baked their own bread. From time to time, we would have subsequent visits with this family, before finally losing contact several years later. I did not know then how our lives would be linked again in the future.

Back in the VW minibus, our journey continued, descending from the mountains to the Magdalena River, which we followed for fifteen or twenty miles and whose valley captured the oppressive tropical heat. As we ascended back into the mountains, we could rid ourselves of the heat, exchanging it for the more pleasant temperatures of the higher altitude. Before we knew it, our journey to San Agustín ended.

San Agustín takes its name from a small Spanish settlement founded here in the early seventeenth century. Here, traditions of the old world collide with those of the new, producing a unique mixture of cultures. On market days the Indians arrived from distant fields and settlements to sell fruits and vegetables, whose variety paid tribute to the diverse climatic conditions found in this region. The women wore colorful handwoven dresses. Many of them also carried a baby on their back. Looking at the bustling marketplace, I had to wonder how long this tradition could survive in a land plagued by social and political unrest.

For us Europeans, the archaeological heritage remained far more important than events in the town market. Here, people can experience some of the best pre-Columbian art, some of which was produced over 2,500 years ago. Since the early nineteenth century, scholars have been particularly impressed by the numerous large statues standing guard over the graves of indigenous peoples. After this area was accidentally rediscovered in the eighteenth century by a Franciscan friar, rumors soon circulated that the area offered artifacts just as unique as those found in areas inhabited by the Olmec and Mayan cultures. After all the study of these statues that has taken place, there is no definitive conclusion as to the origin of these figures. Is there a connection to the Tierradentro, another significant archeological site just over 150 miles away that is filled with pre-Columbian figures and pictoric patterns similar to those in San Agustín? Or to the Kogi Indians of the Caquetá area? No one knows.

As more and more people visited this park, the area became unsafe because of *bandoleros*, bandits looking for easy money. Although crime was a problem when I first visited the park, the explosions of robberies and kidnappings that later followed eventually made travel in this region hazardous for foreigners.

We knew none of this while crossing over the small bridge that took us onto the hotel property. Tired and stiff, we climbed out of the van and stretched a bit before encountering the first of the locals who ran out to greet us. Together we unloaded the groceries, which had been packed in dry ice. Finally, we brought in our luggage, which included a couple of tennis rackets because we thought the two girls could play tennis on the large patios.

The sign for the Hotel Yalconia at its opening in 1960.

George slowly made his way out to where we had parked. When I saw him, a guilty conscience began to torment me, ruining what should have been a happy moment. The cold look he gave me did not help matters all that much. However, George was overjoyed to see his beautiful daughter. Perhaps my arrival also made him happy after all. Instead of wasting time by talking about the separation, we spoke about everyday matters and plans for the grand opening. Our body language indicated that a connection still existed between us. A relationship that had lasted as long as ours could not disappear after a couple of months. As bad as things were between us, it surprised me to see how cordial he was toward Otto, the man who was having an affair with his wife.

We planned to stay for about a week, enough time to take part in the grand opening and see some of the local attractions. I had told George that I would lend him a hand. Politicians, members of high society, and businessmen, some

Inner courtyard of the Hotel Yalconia when it opened, 1960. Later, amenities such as a pool and garden were added. Barbara and her friend played tennis on these patios.

from Colombia and others from abroad, had agreed to attend the festivities. Of course, I also had selfish reasons for coming in the first place. I wanted to visit the archaeological park and see as many of the artifacts as time permitted.

Despite the lack of staff, the hotel ran surprisingly well. Staffing problems stemmed from the fact that very few experienced people wanted to work in this remote region of Colombia. The hotel mostly hired people who lived in the area, which posed a problem because many of them had not received any formal education and were illiterate as a result.

We planned the celebration meal with what we could obtain locally and prepare it in the local style. Using some imagination, we were able to fashion some rather tasty dishes using the local herbs and vegetables to go along with the chicken and pork roast. But then again, we had our limitations, and this was something visitors to this area would have to accept.

I had to give George credit when he said rather firmly, "We are not a gourmet restaurant but rather an archaeological park. If you want luxury, you won't find it here."

As soon as time permitted, I strolled through the park, visiting the excavation sites and talking with a few of the archaeologists. Before my very eyes stood some of the most significant remains of pre-Columbian history. This area is vast, and the archaeological work continues today.

Perspective: Colombia's Geography

The geography of Colombia is rather complex. Because of variations in altitude and rainfall, climatic conditions can vary dramatically from one region in Colombia to another. Five natural regions define Colombia: the lowland rainforests of the Amazon basin shared with Venezuela, Brazil, Peru and Ecuador; the Andean region with snowcapped mountain peaks more than 18,000 feet above sea level, the jungles and swamps of the Pacific lowlands, the interior tropical plains and the deep-water ports of the Caribbean coast.

The western third of the country is dominated by three mountain ranges, or *cordilleras*: the Occidental, the Central, and the Eastern Andes. The ranges run the entire length of the country and converge in southern Colombia in a section known as the Colombian Massif, an area filled with volcanoes and faults and the origin of nearly seventy percent of Colombia's drinking water.

The Magdalena River, whose headwaters are found in the Colombian Massif, runs northward and eventually empties into the Caribbean Sea near Barranquilla. The San Agustín Archaeological Park is in southern Colombia, near the start of the river. Indigenous peoples first inhabited this region around 15,000 years ago, perhaps to escape the oppressive heat found at lower elevations. Later they took advantage of the fertile soil and began to cultivate a variety of crops, including corn, sweet potatoes, and beans.

Around 1,500 to 2,000 years ago, indigenous Americans living near San Agustín began to carve statues to mark the tombs and burial mounds of their ancestors. Standing out from the eternal green of the region, some of these statues are more than twelve feet tall. Chiseled from solid stone without the benefit of iron tools, most of the statues depict human forms. The bodies, however, are compressed, and the faces have menacing characteristics, like the hideous and frightening facial

Sign at the entrance to the San Agustín Archaeological Park, Colombia, in 1960.

features found on the religious idols of the Mayan culture, only these are more colossal. Sometimes the statues depict people with features borrowed from predatory animals to represent the sun. Statues of animals also have meaning; the eagle symbolizes light and power, the snake fertility, and the turtle rain and earth.

Even today, very little is known about those who carved these statues. They were created over a period of nearly one thousand years, with the newest dating to around 1200 AD. The United Nations Educational, Scientific and Cultural Organization, more commonly called UNESCO, declared this area a world heritage site in 1995. [14]

San Agustín Archaeological Park, Colombia.

Archaeologists at work in 1960, San Agustín Archaeological Park, Colombia.

---

14   For those interested in learning more about the San Agustín Archeological Park, I recommend Gerardo Reichel-Dolmatoff, *San Agustín: A Culture of Colombia* (New York: Praeger, 1972). See also www.whc.unesco.org.

A San Agustín figure, a mother with child.

San Agustín figure that I found intriguing for its almost happy or hopeful demeanor. So many of them show angry or menacing expressions.

San Agustín

The day after we arrived in San Agustín, I rode a horse through the park. Surrounded by enormous and frightening statues, I felt as though I had entered the realm of the supernatural. Essentially, I had trodden onto a cemetery. Those who were buried here now expected reverence, and even the wild animals remained silent. Perhaps they also feared the statues, which stood as sentinels to protect this sacred ground. In the stillness I could almost hear them speak, paying homage to the ancient Americans. Stunned, I quietly rode through the park under a clear blue sky. The ground underneath my horse was soft and muffled every step. Carefree, I inhaled the cool, refreshing air and looked around at the lush vegetation that seemed to grow before my very eyes. Suddenly, the sky turned overcast, and in the distance, I saw wisps of dark clouds that stretched down to earth like black finger smudges on a pane of glass. Now I had to seek shelter from the approaching storm. I turned around, gave the horse a kick, and galloped back to the hotel.

Riding in San Agustín. Note the ruggedness of the animal.

Numerous plants in the New World contain mind-altering chemicals. Sometime after the ride, I learned something interesting about the many leguminous (pod-bearing) trees that I saw in the park. The pods on these trees secrete a resin that produces a narcotic effect when dried into a powder and inhaled. Indigenous peoples often incorporated this mind-altering drug into their religious ceremonies. Considering the trancelike state I found myself in after returning to the hotel, I can only wonder whether I was exposed to the narcotic effects of this tree.

On another day we decided to take a tour of the Río Caquetá, a tributary of the mighty Amazon river. George and a guest from our hotel in Cali, a German teacher, joined me for this adventure. We bumped through the jungle in a four-wheel-drive vehicle. We stopped briefly to stretch at a small village, and we talked for a while with the small children and their teacher at a one-room school. I remember the joy of the children in seeing the car and meeting such exotic people.

One of the guests at our hotel in Cali was a German schoolteacher, shown in this photo wearing a hat, and he came to the grand opening of the Hotel Yalconia. During a tour of the area around San Agustín we visited this school. Cities like Cali were modern, but the rural areas were very poor and primitive.

We traveled a bit further by car and then we had to trek through the thick vegetation on foot. I can still remember the knee-high boots we wore along with jeans and long-sleeved shirts, collars turned up, our heads protected by a scarf and a brimmed hat. The river tour was by canoe, and our goal was to visit an Italian-Catholic mission a couple of hours away. Often the tree branches and bushes extended out over the surface of the water, which we noticed only when it was too late, when we rubbed against them. Spiders, mosquitoes, and midges clung to these branches; insects that could make life very miserable for humans. I sometimes imagined that a colony of ants was marching over my entire body as though it were a multilane superhighway.

Two or three weeks later, I saw a doctor about an area of red, inflamed skin around my waist, which became very painful when my belt rubbed against it. He determined that I had been stung by numerous very small biting insects who sought my blood and had found a way in at my waistline. He treated the inflammation with a petroleum oil mixture (yes, motor oil!) and then after a few days lifted a layer of skin from the wound. Finally, I started to heal. I seriously questioned whether it was worth going through so much trouble just to see a frog no bigger than a thumb. Sadly, because of habitat destruction, hunting, and disease, most species are designated as threatened or endangered in many areas, and some have been lost to extinction.

George, wearing sunglasses, is shown here getting into the canoe for our tour of the Río Caquetá.

The next day, at the Hotel Yalconia, I visited with the cook for a while. I admired the way she prepared the evening meal. She cooked with the same skill as a conductor of a renowned symphony orchestra, rhythmically moving from one pot and pan to the next, performing flawlessly the execution of her duties. My technique, in comparison, was awkward and clumsy. The cooking skills possessed by the indigenous women are an art passed from one generation to the next. If only I were so fortunate.

The food was both delicious and unusual. What I found particularly appealing was the herbs and spices they utilized, cooking ingredients of which I had never heard, not even in Cali. After the outstanding meal, our day came to an end, and we took one last final look at the park. The half-moon barely illuminated the mysterious hills out in the distance. Several dogs barked as we heard voices penetrate the darkness. Somebody slowly strummed a *tiple*, its gentle sounds mixing with the wild atmosphere. Tomorrow would be our test, the opening was upon us.

After a lot of preparation, we were finally ready for the grand opening. Around sixty guests were expected to attend this event. Slowly, they arrived, one after another, some in chauffeur-driven jeeps. Surprisingly, they all came! Among our guests were businessmen from Neiva, Bogotá, and other large Colombian cities. *Hazendados*, owners of large cattle ranches, joined the celebration. Even the German ambassador came with his wife from Bogotá for the party.

The guests mingled with each other, exchanging pleasantries and smiles and engaging in small talk. Speeches followed, along with a toast to the success of this project, everyone drinking a festive cocktail I had created with passion fruit, limes, and rum. We catered the event with locally obtained meats and produce. For dessert we served a mango cake based on a similar recipe for German apple cake. Our guests enthusiastically helped themselves to these delicacies, while we fueled them with plenty of beer and aguardiente. Our celebration lasted until the wee hours of the morning.

After grabbing about three hours of sleep, I was up bright and early to prepare our guests a breakfast, many of whom suffered from a hangover. Soon they departed the hotel and headed back to civilization, and we actually felt relieved when the brake lights finally disappeared in the distance.

During my stay I had an opportunity to make the guest rooms a bit more comfortable and inviting. At the local market I purchased handwoven blankets made from natural fibers and colored with natural dyes. The designs had a striking similarity to those found in blankets made by the Hopi and Navajo Indians of North America.

I would have gladly stayed longer, but I had to return to our hotel in Cali. In late 2017, the Hotel Yalconia celebrated its grand reopening after a major renovation. Based on the photos on their website, it looks very similar now to how I remember it. I would love to go back and visit it once again.[15]

The park attracts only a small portion of the adventurers who seek to discover more about the cultures of ancient America. Interest in this area pales in comparison to the interest in the archaeological remains of the Aztecs and Mayans in Central America or in the lost city of the Incas, Machu Picchu, in Peru. For me, San Agustín tops all of these places, most likely because it retains its secrets.

Another plant that grows in abundance in Colombia, especially in the area around San Agustín, is the coca shrub. For hundreds of years, the Indians have chewed the leaves of this plant with lime, which releases a chemical that gives them greater stamina at high altitude. While in Colombia I saw only Indians, and never any white people, chewing this plant. Cocaine is derived from the very same leaves through several chemical processes. I never would have imagined that these harmless-looking leaves would cause a many-decades-long drug war.

Perspective: The Violence after La Violencia

Certainly, the fear of crime has hampered the tourist industry in Colombia, a country that has a lot to offer, in terms of both natural beauty and ancient culture. By European or American

---

15   The hotel website is www.hotelyalconia.com.

standards, lawlessness seems to be a persistent characteristic of life in this country. Two years after George and Franziska immigrated to Colombia in 1956, the era of La Violencia officially ended. Yet among the country's coffee and coca plantations, criminal organizations resorted to violence to control part of this trade. During the 1960s several guerrilla organizations, often espousing a Marxist ideology, waged an armed conflict against the government and landowners. At the end of this decade, the hippie movement popularized the use of recreational drugs in North America and Europe. Colombia became a major supplier of cocaine and heroin to these markets. In the mid-1980s, two rival drug cartels, one in Cali and another in Medellin, controlled around 75 percent of Colombia's illegal cocaine exports. Attempts by the Colombian government to control the illegal drug trade have often resulted in the assassination of leading political figures. Today both cartels have lost much of their former influence through arrests and prosecution. In many cases, drug traffickers are extradited to the United States to be tried under American law.

The homicide rate remained very high in Colombia. Some of this violence can be attributed to terrorist organizations active in the country, most notably the United Defense Force (AUC), the National Liberation Army (ELN), and the Revolutionary Armed Forces of Colombia (FARC). All three organizations are funded through the drug trade. The AUC consists of numerous paramilitary groups that have taken the law into their own hands. At times they engaged in combat with Colombia's other two terrorist organizations, and at times they exacted vigilante justice. Besides homicides, robberies and kidnappings also remained problematic. The reasons for so much lawlessness are complex and include poverty, an ineffective system of justice, government corruption, drug trafficking, and the fact that Colombia still has many remote areas that are not easily administered.

A peace agreement between the federal government and the FARC was negotiated in 2016 after five decades of fighting. The agreement was not approved by voters in a referendum as it did not include any punishment for the terrible crimes committed against civilians by the FARC. A second agreement was ratified in November with approval from both houses of the Colombian Congress that addressed these concerns while also promoting reconciliation.

The Road to Cali

At the Hotel Yalconia I met a professor from the university in Cali who had profound knowledge of the archaeological sites in Colombia. The two girls wanted to stay longer, and he agreed to bring them back to the city. Now I sat alone in the car with Otto, watching the Hotel Yalconia disappear behind us. We did not say much. It was nice just to be close to each other. The weather turned stormy, and it started to pour. Driving conditions were hazardous. Not only did we have to take care on the slippery road, but we also had to be on the lookout for cattle that occasionally wandered out in front of us. Often, they just stood idly in the middle of the road, stoically chewing a bit of grass, before leisurely moving on at their own pace.

When we reached the volcano crater, it was already dark. Otto told a joke, and I was laughing uproariously when he suddenly stomped on the brakes. Out there in front of us, two luminescent dots moved. We sat still, surrounded by a dark forest on a muddy road, hearing occasional drops of water splatter on top of the car. Slowly, a figure emerged in the beam of the headlights. Before us, in the middle of the road, sat an ocelot, a beautiful wild cat found in South America. It was certainly astonished, and we felt the same, for it is rare to see these animals; they are exceptionally shy. We waited patiently for the ocelot to move out of the way, not wanting to startle him any more than we had already. In a flash, he finally jumped over the bushes alongside the road and disappeared into the darkness.

Sometimes, Negative Impulses Rejuvenate the Soul, 1960

During my absence everything had run well at the Residencia Stein. Carmen did not disappoint me and took good care of our customers. However, the day-to-day struggle with finding enough rooms to meet the demand continued. Moreover, I still don't quite understand how we lived then. We did not live in our own apartment; instead, the hotel was our home. Like nomads, we moved from room to room in search of a bed. Most of the time, I could not claim a guest room for myself and was forced to sleep in the laundry room.

Cali was booming. Companies from Europe and North America had invested in Colombia and decided to establish a branch office in Cali. Managers and supervisors from abroad were brought in to train local personnel in the business practices of their multinational companies. Luckily, we had already taken over the house across the street, which gave us five additional rooms to rent. But the demand always seemed greater than our ability to meet it.

Several days after I returned from San Agustín, George returned to Cali, bringing the two girls with him. "I have to take care of a few things," he said to me with a cold look on his face.

Somehow, I felt he had become lonely in San Agustín, out there at the edge of the world. He stayed for only a few days, enough time to buy a new motor for our VW bus and enough groceries to fill the vehicle. Not once did we speak about the state of our marriage, nor did he sleep next to me.

It never really occurred to me that we should discuss this matter. My days were filled with work, work, work. After dinner, once I had checked the inventory for the next day, I would sit at my desk and start my second job. For the lawyer in Berlin, Zieschang, I reviewed the petitions for compensation, a task I found fascinating. The routine chores around the hotel became the obligation I had to fulfill before doing the work that I liked. Sometimes tears rolled down my face after I read one of the personal history statements. What I experienced in these stories was far different from what one would ever read in a book or see in a movie.

How I Learned to Love Colombia, 1960–1961

The Rockefeller Trust, along with Harvard University, funded a research project exploring tropical diseases in Colombia. This brought several professors and students to Cali, all needing a place to stay. Due to the reputation of our hotel, these visitors took our rooms first before seeking lodging elsewhere. Again, we didn't have enough room to house them all, but it was nice that other businesses also received a piece of the action. No matter where these academics stayed, our hotel became their social center. During the evenings they gathered in either our lounge or our garden, and together Americans and Colombians talked shop. Sometimes the conversations were quite lively.

For a long time, a lady from America by the name of Mrs. Robinson stayed with us. She was a teacher at the local American school. She was a very lovely and lively extrovert, and she would arrange a daily cocktail hour. She would mix the drinks and facilitate the conversation amongst the guests. She was a real ambassador for international relations, always looking for the positive angle in an argument.

As a good businesswoman, I had to adjust our menu to suit the tastes of our distinguished visitors from America. This is how the hamburger came to Colombia. Every evening, ground beef sizzled on the grill. To say thank you, and sometimes because they needed a translator, the researchers invited me to accompany them on some of the weekend projects in the field. Anyone who knows me knows I would never pass up such an opportunity. My thirst for adventure and exploration was insatiable. Although I sometimes wanted Otto to come along, he rarely participated in these adventures.

During the first of these field trips, we traveled to Pasto, the capital of the Department of Nariño, a region in the southernmost part of Colombia, on the border with Ecuador. About 80 percent of the inhabitants were Indians. I remember going to the local market and finding the typical fruits and vegetables for sale. However, I also recall potions and cure-alls that had been prepared by sorcerers and witches, clear evidence that local customs and traditions prevailed here and that the government in Bogotá and

An Indian Territory in the Valle de Sibundoy near the border with Ecuador in 1962. Note the hats and ponchos worn by the natives.

the protection of its laws were hundreds of miles away. I saw several cooking fires where the natives were roasting one of their favorite delicacies—guinea pig. It tastes like chicken!

Another one of our field trips was to an Indian territory (similar to a reservation in the U.S.) in the Valle de Sibundoy. The people who lived there followed centuries of tradition, according to their spiritual beliefs and living off what the land provided them. In the 1950s, the Colombian government and some well-intentioned global relief agencies tried to change their way of life, believing that their diet was inadequate. For example, the children drank a sugarcane-based drink instead of milk once they were weaned from their mother's breasts. The children were healthy and thrived on this, but it wasn't milk. The community received cans of powdered milk from the United Nations Relief Agency (UNRA) and with that they painted their houses. The houses were a beautiful milky white as a result, and the best part for the households that got the milk was that the cans could be repurposed to carry water or to cook dinner.

The bus we took to Quito in 1962. While waiting at this stop I talked with some of the local people.

The adults of the Indian community chewed coca leaves to boost their energy and stamina working in the fields. They didn't get high really, it was as if they had drunk a strong cup of coffee. Later, once refined cocaine was discovered, Colombia's remote areas were overrun with drug cartels growing coca everywhere it could be planted, and a new kind of violence erupted. But at the time of our visit, the coca plant was still considered something only the indigenous people used.

Introduced through somebody that one of the professors knew, we visited with an immigrant family that had settled in this remote region; the husband was from Switzerland and the wife was from Holland. In this unique cool, moist climate they cultivated mint plants for cosmetic and pharmaceutical companies. In stark contrast to what was found in the local shacks, or even the international hotels in Bogotá, they furnished their house with valuable furniture acquired in Holland and Indonesia, where they had lived for several years. Prior to moving to Colombia, they had moved to Indonesia, a country they had to leave after the war, when they were no longer welcome. Purely by chance, they had followed a recommendation given to them and settled in the Valle de Sibundoy, a narrow strip of land on Colombia's border with Ecuador. There the husband could continue his trade, agronomy, and cultivate rare plants.

Until the early morning hours, we sat together talking about God and the world. We were certainly an international bunch, representing the United States, Colombia, Switzerland, Holland, Germany, Yugoslavia, and Russia. Meanwhile, the indigenous servants gracefully slipped in and out of the scene, bringing us food and drink, knowing full well that they, and not we, belonged here. I recall how beautiful the women looked with their dark faces and braided hair. The male servants seemed proud, something transmitted to us in the way they stared at us, the epitome of machismo. I was struck by the contrasts found in this house, the elegance of Europe and the untamed wilderness of South America.

I found Hetty, the lady of the house, to be an interesting and highly cultivated woman. She looked after the entire house and the servants in a quiet yet determined manner. On their property lived a Russian assistant who helped the husband with his scientific work. The assistant also had a second job as Hetty's lover. Several years later, Hetty visited with me in Colorado. She told me that she had left her husband and now lived in San Francisco with the Russian assistant. Talk about international relations!

The next morning an airplane waited for us at the airfield in Pasto. The airport was notoriously dangerous for pilots who landed or took off from there. According to rumor, these death-defying pilots had a special relationship with the Almighty. Before landing or taking off, they made the sign of the cross and fired off a quick prayer to heaven. The entire airfield was about the size of a postage stamp, with a steep drop-off on all sides. When the pilots landed, there was little room for error. They had to line up perfectly straight with the runway while paying constant attention to the speed and height of the aircraft. When taking off, the pilots had to rev the engines to full power to attain enough acceleration for the aircraft to become airborne before exhausting the entire length of the short runway.

Another field trip took us to the rain forests of Chocó, a region in the northwest corner of Colombia on the Panamanian border. There I became very familiar with the Spanish word *agreste*, a term describing rough and inhospitable terrain. The climate in this region is very tropical, and often a misty haze covers the land because of the huge amount of precipitation and heat. Furthermore, the West Andes, also known as the Cordilleras Occidental, separate this area from the more populated areas of Colombia.

Along the bank of the San Juan River, prospectors once panned for gold, but they had long ago disappeared by the time we arrived, leaving behind abandoned shacks. I had to smile when I thought of the paradoxes this region presented. The area swam in gold and platinum yet remained poor and undeveloped because of the difficulty in extracting these minerals from such a remote, disease-infested area. Those who came here had to contend with malaria and yellow fever and a complete lack of infrastructure, including improved roads. This area was so inhospitable that anyone breaking a trail with a machete soon learned that the cut vegetation grew back within a day, obscuring the way out. Despite these problems, a few successful mining ventures remained in the region. Even more interesting, some of the miners were Germans.

I remember a visit to the town of Andagoya. Many of the houses had been built on stilts because of regular flooding caused by the nearly constant rainfall. Every month of the year the area experiences at least twenty inches of rain, and the wettest month, May, averages over twenty-five inches. Tin roofs covered these structures, and the walls were made from unfinished wood. Hardly any of these homes were built from brick or stone.

The students had a keen interest in the poison dart frogs found in the Chocó region. Very interesting creatures, when threatened they secrete a liquid that is poisonous to many animals. The Indians used to rub their darts and arrows on the skin of these frogs to make their weapons more lethal. In the early 1960s some scientists thought this poison could be beneficial to humans, perhaps a cure for some disease.

An elderly Swiss man now living in Cali accompanied us on this field trip. For many years he had cultivated *anturios* (anthurium) flowers, work that also allowed him to study these frogs. When he heard about the academics holding meetings at my hotel, he could not resist barging in to talk shop with them. One word led to another, and soon the Americans had a frog consultant. The poison dart frogs had been detailed in many publications, but much more needed to be learned about these amphibians. Otto accompanied us on this field trip as well.

I slowly got to know Colombia and its people and culture. Over time I fell in love with them. We had been in this country for five years, yet it seemed like much less time to me. So many things had happened, so many experiences I had enjoyed, and I was reborn with a new name and a new outlook.

The Way Back to a Spouse Begins by Finding Yourself, 1961

George came back from San Agustín. During the several months that he had lived there, he must have been lonely, something about which he never spoke. To distract himself, George had developed a keen interest in growing coffee beans at a nearby plantation that belonged to the hotel owner. He learned everything one needed to know about cultivating this plant, from harvesting to storing the beans. Then something occurred that quelled any desire whatsoever to continue living in this area. One day bandits killed the man who oversaw the coffee plantation for no apparent reason. Perhaps they were attempting to extort money from the man and murdered him when he could not pay. This incident shocked George deeply, and soon he returned to Cali for good.

This was a difficult time for everyone. Now I had to decide between my marriage and my affair, between duty and love, between George and Otto. The fact that George started with biting sarcastic remarks upon returning certainly did not help the situation.

This time I resorted to confrontation, screaming at him, "You know, George, you never accomplish what you set out to do!"

He turned as white as a sheet. His parents had told him the exact same thing.

Then I continued. "It's not going to be business as usual between us. I want a separation, at least for a while."

He turned even whiter. "Mother, we have to keep trying. A separation means the end. I know we can work things out. Please, don't throw our marriage away."

What could I say? The affair perhaps represented a failure in our commitment to each other, and regardless of whether anyone was to blame, it had not helped our marriage. However, the way George looked convinced me to stay. In his eyes I could see both loneliness and despair. Despite all that had happened during the last few years of our marriage, I decided not to leave him. It was time to let Otto know.

"I am staying with George," I told him. "Otto, please understand. Honestly, he needs me more than you."

Otto was shocked. He tried to change my mind even though I had already made my decision. I explained to him that I could not simply throw everything away. Then I told him that Barbara was at a difficult age and that perhaps later I could consider a separation. As we spoke, not once did the word "divorce" enter my head. Since my childhood, the mere thought of this word had filled me with terror, bringing to mind horrible images of what happened to children when parents went their separate ways. I shuddered to think of the consequences for myself. As a woman, it would be unthinkable to live in Colombia by myself.

Otto and I had several long conversations on this topic, in which we weighed the pros and cons of my staying with George. As we argued, we exchanged feelings, accusations, and assertions of love, but at some point, I'd had enough of talking. It had become physically and emotionally draining. Finally, I let him know once and for all that I intended to stay with my husband.

Otto needed several days to recover, but finally he came to terms with my decision. What could he do? Although our affair had lasted for two years, the connection to George remained stronger. One day I saw George and Otto engaged in a serious discussion in the garden, and I knew the affair had officially come to an end. My relationship with Otto changed. With one exception, from that time until his death, he remained just a friend. I will tell you about that exception later in my story.

It took a while for us to get used to the new situation, but once again I had a husband! George started to treat me better, much better than in recent years. I noticed that he wanted to be a better husband and was trying to make changes. After a two-year absence, once again George stood at my side, and Otto remained on the sidelines. Life continued in Cali, even for Otto. Occasionally, he dropped by to take care of some business at the hotel, but the way we encountered each other was far different than before. Now we just shook hands and discussed everyday matters.

Barbara did not seem to favor her father over Otto or have a special attachment to either one. While George was living in San Agustín, Otto had become something of a father figure for her. Now that her real father had returned, George assumed his rightful place in her life.

A family photo on the patio of the Residencia Stein. I think our expressions suggest the tension we all felt over our marriage, our teenage daughter's moods, and my affair with Otto.

The daily routine of running a business left little time to worry about our situation. Supervising the hotel staff and caring for our guests demanded our full attention. While managing to keep all our rooms booked, we also gave our daughter the parental support she deserved. However, we lived without any privacy, as though in a fishbowl. In a hotel such as ours, there were no secrets. The staff heard every word we exchanged. I worked hard and suppressed the storm raging inside of me.

Now, years later, as I write about what transpired next, it seems a little strange. George had left several personal items at the hotel in San Agustín, and we had to go get them—there was no way to have them shipped to us. In Huila and Cuaca, two regions that we had to pass through to reach San Agustín, the situation had become very dangerous for travelers. Mafia wars, burglary, and robbery prevailed; crimes committed by young men who had chosen to become hardened criminals rather than earn an honest living. Human life in Colombia had become cheap, no more valuable than the life of a chicken slaughtered at the marketplace. We took the precaution of hiring two security guards to make the journey with us. If we were to go through the trouble of filling the car with George's belongings, it made no sense to let everything fall into the wrong hands.

But feeling uneasy about the danger of the trip even with the guards, George asked Otto if he would go with us. Much to my surprise, Otto agreed to join us. It was a strange and tense journey, but I was comforted to have them both with me purely for the strength in numbers.

During the journey we decided to visit the German family living near the crater at the Puracé volcano. When we drove up to the farmhouse, we saw several police cars parked outside the building. Sensing the worst, we got out of our vehicle and talked to one of the uniformed officers. He regretted to inform us that the lady of the house had been shot sometime during the night. We stepped inside the house to talk to the family. During the night the blind woman had heard something coming from the yard. Due to her disability, she had an enhanced sense of hearing. As she opened the door to step outside, she surprised a group of bandits attempting to break into the house, and one of them shot her, fatally wounding her. The bandits then fled.

We attempted to bring the family some comfort. However, nobody could understand this senseless tragedy. The woman and her husband had survived a terrible, inhumane European war, and now another war on the other side of the planet was exacting its revenge.

Finally, we had to go. Our hearts went out to those who survived. We promised to notify the German embassy of what had happened. The embassy officials urged the widower and his three children to move away from the Puracé volcano and live in a more populated area. The uninhabited regions of Colombia had become unsafe, especially for children. The man finally gave in to the pressure and moved. Now that his wife was gone, the widower made other arrangements to provide his children an education. A Swiss family in Cali took in the oldest girl. She returned to Germany several years later. The youngest son also found a home with a family in Cali. Since the youngest daughter wanted to become a nun, she was sent to a convent in Popayán.

The widower now lived alone. Shortly before his wife was murdered, his only other adult family member, his father-in-law, had passed away. In my first visit with the family, I had mentioned to him that he should file a pension claim with the German government. He now asked me to help him fill out the forms. Together we completed the paperwork, and in the process, I read his personal history statement. I was crushed to learn how he had suffered. During the war he. had fought on the eastern front. Afterward he had been taken into custody by the Soviets and sent to Siberia. His experience there left behind deep physical and emotional wounds. Little by little, disgust and a collapsing worldview replaced the respect and enthusiasm he once had for the *Führer*. When he finally was able to return home, this man of humble origins had absolutely nothing. Years later he met his wife, who had been blinded by an injury.

As soon as the couple could scrape together enough money, they left Germany, a country that did not offer them any future. They immigrated to Colombia and moved in with her parents, who had already lived there for several years. Disappointed by Bogotá, they eventually found the means to buy a parcel of land near the Puracé volcano. Nev-

This is the house of the German family that lived on the Puracé volcano – the man on the left standing with the child is the father from the family. I am standing on the right with a scarf on my head and a Belgian engineer stands next to me.

ertheless, they had merely exchanged a miserable life in Germany for a life of poverty in South America. On their property they resigned themselves to living in seclusion, having as little contact as possible with the outside world.

After reading the personal history statement, I wondered whether some people naturally attract misfortune. It seemed this family could neither run nor hide from their destiny. Eventually, the man returned to Germany. Like so many in postwar Europe, happiness eluded him. Adding another insult to his long story of tragedy, before he could sell his property at the volcano in Colombia, bandits had set fire to the farmhouse and stolen his cattle and horses, essentially stealing what little wealth he had.

This was the ugly side of Colombia, a land with wonderful, gentle people, deeply entrenched in a belief system that incorporated both native superstition and Catholicism. Somehow this had not yet lived up to its potential on the world stage. Instead of harvesting its abundant natural resources, the country became a worldwide supplier of illegal drugs. The political system never committed itself to providing the prerequisites for economic development, which would have required not only improvements in infrastructure but also political reform. Perhaps this had been the intent of politicians all along, for it was certainly much easier to exploit the poor and uneducated. Exploitation was an area where the government and the drug lords shared common ground. Perhaps the agreements between the government and the FARC rebels ratified in 2017 will bring a new era of prosperity to Colombia.

At the beginning of the 1960s in Neiva, the capital of the Department of Huila, some thugs kidnapped Señor Lara, one of Colombia's wealthiest landowners and businessmen. When George lived in San Agustín, Señor Lara had often visited him. For hours they had discussed their knowledge of agriculture. Señor Lara worked for Caterpillar, an American company that manufactures farm and heavy construction machines. As the company's chief representative for Colombia, Señor Lara became quite prosperous. This was enough to make him the target of a kidnapping. These abductions mostly ran according to plan: ransom demanded, ransom paid, hostage released. However, Señor Lara suffered from a severe form of diabetes and depended heavily on his medication, without which he would die. Certainly, he must have told his captors about the medication, asking that they arrange to have it delivered. Anyway, when the ransom money was finally paid, time had run out for Señor Lara.

Thus ended the San Agustín chapter in our lives, a chapter that left behind a bitter aftertaste. The archaeological treasures, the breathtaking scenery, the kind people of Indian heritage—all that means nothing if you don't feel safe.

We could see that Colombia was becoming more and more dangerous. Nevertheless, we decided to stay. One could say that after having been driven from one place to the next for so many years, we had finally decided to plant our roots in Cali. There was so much I loved about my new home, especially the language, the customs, the traditions, and the unique mix of geography. Meanwhile, in our marriage we did what we had to do, but the relationship started again to fall to the wayside.

The compensation claims and applications for government pensions continued to pile up, both in Cali and in Berlin, where Zieschang had his office. One day I received a letter from him containing an urgent request that I fly to Berlin to get some instructions about new laws.

Because of the difficulty in getting a reliable telephone connection to Europe, long discussions by phone were impossible—the only way I could get this training was in person or possibly by reading, but often legal texts are unintelligible to those without full legal training. Thus, the best and fastest way to get up-to-date on the new laws was to go to Berlin.

"Why don't you take some time off?" George suggested. "Perhaps that would be for the better. I promise to work on myself. I can clear my head and make a change. When you return, you will not recognize me." I knew George dreaded the thought of my leaving him. Despite his efforts to be a better husband and to help me more, he was still prone to cruel comments and a poor outlook.

As I packed my things in preparation for the trip to Europe, I did not leave any instructions behind. Those who remained, including George, could figure things out for themselves. Thinking about all that was going on in my life, including the hotel, the work for Zieschang, and raising a daughter, I wondered where I found the energy that drove me every day. George knew that without me he would be in deep trouble. On the one hand, he was jealous and envied my strength and energy. On the other hand, he could not make it in Colombia without my skills. He constantly attempted to attack me verbally. On the surface he was a man capable of expressing himself with a certain natural elegance, but the verbal abuse was a facade for his lack of self-confidence.

Despite how unhappy I was with my marriage, and even though George was my opposite in almost every area, I could not see myself leaving him. Whatever had brought us together formed a bond that could resist arguments, suffering, or even an affair.

The Berlin Wall, 1961

I had to prepare myself mentally for the trip to Europe. This would be my first overseas flight. Although international flights are routine today, in 1961 passenger airline service between South America and Europe was relatively new. Only a handful of airlines flew this route. I managed to obtain a seat on a Varig Airlines flight departing from Bogotá and bound for Amsterdam. Almost like riding the city bus, I would have to make several stops during the journey, including Curaçao, the Virgin Islands, Madrid, and Paris. I left at the end of July.

The flights were so fancy it was as though everyone flew first-class, including those in coach. The food was excellent, the seats were wide with plenty of legroom, and the stewardesses were friendly and helpful. Of course, the cost of the flight was well beyond the means of mere mortals. Mr. Zieschang paid my travel expenses. Considering all the clients he had, I knew this would not cause him too much of a hardship.

On board the Varig airliner I enjoyed the special attention. I dreamt I was some empress on her way to Europe to make an official state visit. Once I was on European soil, the illusion suddenly evaporated, and I felt like a stranger. I could not believe what I saw with my own eyes. What had happened? In the six years that I had been away, Western Europe had made a miraculous recovery from the devastation caused by the war. This economic boom stood in stark contrast to the situation in South America, where very little if any economic development had occurred since my arrival in Colombia.

The flight from Bogotá ended in Amsterdam, but the journey to my final destination continued. I still had a few days before I was expected in Berlin, so I chose to tour southern Germany and then go to Austria. I caught a connecting flight to Munich. As I exited the plane and stepped out into the terminal, standing there to my complete astonishment was none other than Otto! He had obtained my itinerary from mutual friends. The longing to be with me had driven him to come to Europe; it was, he said, something he could not resist.

After ending our affair, I'd had little contact with him, and now he stood right before me. My first instinct was to run away as quickly as possible, to get back on the airplane. However, within seconds my feelings switched to unending joy, as well as fear that I would be drawn into a new and dangerous adventure. This situation raised again a serious dilemma, one that I had never resolved, for in Colombia I had simply buried my feelings for him under a mountain of guilt. Like embers remaining from a bonfire the night before, the fire had never been extinguished, and the sight of him waiting for me was the gust of wind that inflamed those feelings once again.

I told Otto of my plans to visit relatives in Vienna. "Good," he said. "I'll accompany you."

Sitting next to him in the car as we drove on the Autobahn to Austria, I felt the pain of a guilty conscience. Yet as mile after mile of beautiful scenery rolled past us, the love we had once shared rose again to the surface. I wanted to enjoy the moment. I wanted to give in to impulse. I could deal with the consequences later, even though it would be hurtful to those I had left behind in Colombia. Perhaps I was careless, but sometimes obligation has its limits and fails to constrain what you feel from the bottom of your heart.

Turn around just once, and the centuries roll past—this saying came to me as we wandered through Vienna, the city where my mother was born. Everywhere I still saw signs of the once-mighty Habsburg Dynasty. Again, it simply amazed me to witness the transformation of postwar Europe. When we left Germany just five years earlier, the task of rebuilding had just begun. Now I saw the change with my very own eyes.

In Vienna I remembered the ceremonies surrounding the ratification of the Austrian State Treaty and smiled. I recalled the concert that the Vienna State Opera had performed for the first time since the end of the war. In their inaugural performance they had played a unique work by Beethoven, his opera *Fidelio*, the only opera he composed. I remembered sitting in front of our radio in Berlin mesmerized, listening to the performance and commentary provided by Hugo Portisch, the leading Austrian reporter of his time, known for his raspy voice. The moment was so moving that tears had started rolling from my eyes.

Since the treaty, the Austrians had embarked on a major renovation project, through which they had been able to win back the beauty and charm of Vienna's past. Now I strolled through this beautiful city with Otto at my side. It was so unreal. My complicated existence had not allowed me to lead the life I once dreamt.

We could not resist a side trip to Venice, a city built for lovers with its famous bridges, canals, and plazas. Napoleon once had an expression for hopeless love: "As soon as it catches up with you, the only cure is to flee." I had no way out of this trap. With childlike enthusiasm, we explored this city. One day we boarded a water bus, called a *vaporetto* in Italian, and traveled to Murano, a small island where glass is still made by artisans blowing air through a metal tube. After watching various demonstrations of this craft, I understood why glass making is called the art of long breaths in the Orient.

The northern Italian scenery was beautiful, full of rich vibrant colors and small peaceful villages, some of which still bore scars from the war. In the Dolomite or Apennine Mountains, near Gran Sasso, stood the Campo Imperatore Hotel. We visited this area, walking around the grounds, and restored ourselves with the crisp mountain air.

I recalled that just eighteen years earlier, Mussolini was imprisoned at this hotel on orders of King Victor Emmanuel III and then later rescued by a small band of paratroopers acting on direct orders from Hitler. Visiting this grand hotel in these magnificent mountains you could forget there ever was a war. But even here there was a war story.

Otto and I toured the Swiss, Italian, and Austrian Alps, taking in the beautiful scenery. Along the way Otto's gaze caused me to forget all my problems. Colombia seemed light-years away. However, life is not always a fairy tale with a happy ending. Now it was time to return to Vienna and fly to Berlin, where a mountain of paperwork and intense training waited for me.

One difficulty I had to overcome was that only a few passenger airliners flew into this political island. After a long search I found a flight to Berlin that landed at Schönefeld, one of Berlin's three airfields and the only one that served the East German capital. There I was greeted by rude customs officers who asked about my ultimate destination and the purpose of my visit. Yet none of that bothered me for I still had fond memories of a wonderful, affectionate man.

Then I made my way from the airport to Zieschang's office, which was in West Berlin. As I traveled there on the bus, I passed through several miles in East Berlin, a very depressing sight. It still lay in ruin, looking much like the Berlin I had left behind. In contrast, once I crossed the border into West Berlin, a new city greeted me, largely rebuilt and well on its way to becoming a modern city with all the amenities. But my vacation was over, and it was time to turn my attention to the work at hand. When I finally arrived at the office, I opened my suitcase and got down to business, trying to make some progress with the work I had recently neglected.

Early in the morning on August 13, 1961, the wail of sirens woke me out of a sound sleep. East German police and soldiers began closing the border to West Berlin, stringing concertina wire as the first of many forms of what would become the Berlin Wall.

Perspective: The Exodus and the Wall to Keep People In, 1961

During the Second World War, Allied bombs also fell on Vienna, damaging much of the city. After the war, Austria also was divided into four occupation zones under the control of the United States, Great Britain, France, and the Soviet Union. Like Berlin, Vienna became a divided city, having four sectors under the control of the Allies. On May 15, 1955, the Austrian State Treaty went into effect under which the four occupying powers agreed to create a democratic and sovereign Austrian state. On October 25 of the same year, the last of the occupation troops left.

On June 4, 1961, President John F. Kennedy of the United States and Premier Nikita Khrushchev of the Soviet Union held a meeting in Vienna, Austria, known as the Vienna Summit. The leaders of the two superpowers of the Cold War era discussed numerous issues in the relationship between their countries. Importantly, this discussion included the Berlin crisis, in which 2.7 million East Germans had moved from East Berlin, the Soviet sector, to West Berlin, the Allied sector, between 1945 and 1961. Not all of them stayed in West Berlin, choosing a final home in West Germany or elsewhere, but the point of contention was that they were leaving East Germany.

The leader of the GDR, President Walter Ulbricht, argued that the large number of emigrants leaving East Berlin threatened the existence of the GDR by diminishing its population. In the early months of 1961, Ulbricht pressured Khrushchev to close the border between East and West Berlin. Khrushchev understood Ulbricht's concern but feared that a potential intervention from Western powers would destabilize East Berlin further. It was the position of the United States that West Berlin continue to be occupied by the Allies, for strategic value and to uphold the commitments made to the West Berliners during the airlift.

In August 1961, at a secret meeting in Moscow with other members of the Warsaw Pact, Ulbricht obtained permission to build a wall to seal off West Berlin from East Germany. Every month many thousands of East Germans voted with their feet and entered West Berlin to escape political oppression and to seek better economic conditions. This mass exodus of citizens threatened to undermine what little sovereignty the Soviet Union had given the communist regime in East Germany. Moreover, many of those fleeing were skilled workers, citizens East Germany could not afford to lose.

The agreement with the Warsaw Pact was so secret that most members of Ulbricht's own political party, the Socialist Unity Party of Germany (SED), were unaware of his plan to build a wall. He entrusted the execution of this plan to Erich Honecker, the head of the SED defense committee and a future East German head of state. In the early morning hours of Sunday, August 13, 1961, about 10,000 East German police officers and soldiers, supported by armored vehicles, converged on the border to West Berlin. All border crossings were closed. Train and subway service no longer connected East and West Berlin. East German workers began to rip out the paving stones along the border, over which they place barbed wire. A few days later they began to replace this temporary barrier with a concrete wall, which they call an "antifascist protection barricade."

When East Germany closed the border, more than 50,000 workers in East Berlin could no longer travel to their jobs in West Berlin. Moreover, the border closing separated East Berliners from their friends and relatives in West Berlin. The situation became even more desperate on August 23, 1961, when West Germans were required to have a visa before entering East Berlin. Many East Germans attempted to flee before their government erected the more impenetrable concrete wall. East German border police were given authority to use deadly force to stop anyone attempting to flee. On August 24, 1961, twenty-four-year-old Günter Litfin became the first victim of this new policy.

Over the next twenty-nine years, East Germany expended a considerable amount of its resources to build, improve, and guard a wall covering ninety-six miles long around West Berlin. On their side of the border, the East Germans eventually erected a concrete wall that was twelve feet high and two and a half feet thick. A border zone extended up to a mile away from the wall to further restrict access to the border. Those residing in houses along the border were given a few days to leave. The East German government then confiscated the houses and filled in the windows and doorways with brick and mortar. Later, these buildings were removed altogether. In the border zone, the wall was further protected by secondary fences, barbed wire, vehicle barriers, land mines, and guard dogs. Armed police, watching from more than three hundred towers or bunkers, used lethal force against anyone found within the border zone, the so-called death strip.

In the twenty-nine-year history of the wall, more than one hundred people were killed while attempting to escape. One of the more disturbing shootings occurred when eighteen-year-old Peter Fechter and his friend Helmut Kulbeik attempted to climb over the wall in August 1962. Kulbeik successfully scaled the wall but Fechter was shot in the pelvis by the East German police. He became entangled in the barbed wire in front of the wall. Over the course of an hour, he slowly bled to death while his desperate pleas for help were ignored by the East German border guards. West German police and American soldiers on the other side of the wall witnessed the shooting but were afraid to cross the border to render aid to the young man.

Despite the risks involved, East Germans developed many elaborate schemes to escape to the west, including jumping from windows, hiding in the engine compartments of automobiles, swimming across the waterways along the border, building elaborate underground tunnels, and even floating over the wall in hot air balloons. Despite the human ingenuity, the wall managed to stop the exodus from East Germany.

Governments throughout the world condemned the East German decision, but many Germans felt that this token gesture was insufficient. On August 16, 1961, Willy Brandt, the mayor of West Berlin and future West German chancellor, sent an angry telegram to John F. Kennedy, the president of the United States, demanding more action. The Americans did not interfere with the building of the wall on East German soil. However, the American government made it clear that it intended to protect West Berlin from any Soviet or East German invasion. Furthermore, the United States insisted that East Germany adhere to existing agreements that allowed American military observers and diplomats unrestricted access into East Berlin.

East German attempts to interfere with this right of access were met with a show of American military might on October 26, 1961. Several American tanks were positioned in front of Checkpoint Charlie, the border crossing between the American sector and East Berlin. The Soviets countered by positioning several of their tanks on the East German side of the crossing, and for twenty-four hours the situation remained tense, while each side waited for the other to shoot first. Eventually, both sides withdrew their tanks, yet Berlin remained on the front lines of Cold War brinkmanship between East and West, a test of which political system would prevail, communism or democracy.

For many in West Berlin, the most obvious symbol of a divided city was the Brandenburg Gate, a magnificent city monument now located directly behind the concrete wall that divided their city. President Kennedy delivered a stirring address to the citizens of this besieged city on June 26, 1963, at the Berlin City Hall in Schöneberg. In his speech Kennedy dared anyone who believed in a communist system to come to Berlin. He pointed out that democracy, though not perfect, never requires a wall to prevent its citizens from leaving. Kennedy assured the crowd that the United States remained committed to a democratic and united Germany. Citing history, he told the crowd how people were once proud to call themselves Roman citizens. Kennedy then told them that those who aspire to be free can, with equal pride, call themselves citizens of Berlin. He closed the speech by saying, "All free men, wherever they may live, are citizens of Berlin, and, therefore, as a free man, I take pride in the words—*Ich bin ein Berliner!*"

A Rescue of Sorts, 1961

In the beginning of the 1960s, television had limited influence in the mass media in Europe. Not many households owned one of these expensive devices, and even fewer still had color TVs. A few photographs of the events unfolding in East and West Berlin made their way into the newspapers, but for the most part we used our ears instead of our eyes to keep informed. The main source for information was radio broadcasts. I found it very disturbing to learn how people living along the boundary dividing East from West were being evicted from their homes with little notice. The same thing had happened to me in Czechoslovakia. Many of these homes had belonged to families for several generations, and now the inhabitants were suddenly uprooted.

With mounting fear, I wanted to finish my work as quickly as possible and say a final farewell to this city. The struggle here did not belong to me. Any connection I'd had to Berlin had been severed long ago, when Grandpa Max died. His daughter, Ulla, now lived in Florida. Some of Opa Max's distant relatives lived in East Berlin but reaching them was completely out of the question. I also could forget about catching a flight out of East Berlin's Schönefeld Airport.

Only one passenger airline, Pan American, flew into West Berlin, and it used the same air corridors that had been used during the 1948–1949 blockade. Obtaining a ticket would be nearly impossible given the current political situation and even if one were available, its price would likely be prohibitive. Things seemed to be spinning out of control when I heard that Soviet fighter jets were now harassing passenger aircraft flying out of West Berlin, coming so close that the pilots could sometimes see each other. I started looking for other options to leave this city and make my way to West Germany. I ruled out renting a car as too expensive and too risky given that I would be traveling alone, and I was not a skilled driver. Then I considered using the inter-zonal train, but this would be unreliable because passengers were often forced to exit the train to wait for a connection that might or might not arrive.

My employer and lawyer, Zieschang, was not in a position to help me. When the East Germans closed the border, he was in Luxembourg on a business trip, and now we were both just as stranded. I felt like a caged animal in a zoo. I wanted out of here—the quicker, the better. Then I came up with perhaps one of my more promising options. I could take one of the transit trains, but first I had to obtain a visa.

I went to the government office that issued these visas, expecting something different from what I found. An uncountable number of people filtered through the hallways and waiting room, waiting for a turn to inch a little further up the queue. My attempt to find the right room was met with unnecessarily snide and unhelpful remarks. I played the waiting game with some degree of patience since I had been in this situation too many times before. The persistence paid off, and eventually I had a visa in my hand. But this visa-getting experience did not bode well for the trip ahead.

I remember how the stores in Berlin were packed with people attempting to hoard the necessities of everyday life, anticipating another blockade of the city. Since everyone in Colombia expected me to return with something from Germany, I had to come up with a plan to accomplish my shopping. *Okay,* I said to myself, *I am almost out of here. I'll just visit Aunt Marie in Nuremberg, and certainly the well-stocked stores there can provide all that I need.*

Although I had a visa, I had no ticket, so I continued to wait. The situation intensified by the hour. As badly as Zieschang wanted to return, I wanted to leave. Neither of us had any idea how to accomplish either goal. I sat in the office, my packed bags sitting next to me, waiting for a phone call telling me that a seat was available on the train or airplane. In the meantime, East Germany tightened its noose around West Berlin. Finally, the phone rang. On the other end was Otto. Of course, he knew about the events unfolding in Berlin, he and about fifty million other Germans. He was worried to death about me. Otto told me that he had purchased an airline ticket to Berlin and two additional return tickets so that he could fly out with me. God only knows how he managed that!

I never asked.

I gathered my things. As soon as I hung up the phone, I was out the door. I made my way to the Tempelhof Airport in West Berlin as fast as my legs and public transportation could take me. There, I waited for Otto's plane to land. When he finally arrived, we embraced without saying a word. Never had I been so happy to see him. We didn't bother to leave the airport. Several hours later, we climbed aboard the Pan Am flight, and the troubled city soon disappeared behind me. My heart still pounded, yet I was relieved that the nightmare was over and was grateful for the man sitting next to me, a man not my husband. Oh, Otto.

Otto took me to Munich and invited me to travel with him to Allgäu in southern Germany, where I could relax with his family for a few days. There, I met his mother as well as his two half-grown daughters, whose mother had divorced Otto shortly after the end of the war. Otto had never remarried. He had once been engaged, but after seeing me in our hotel in Cali, he'd called off the wedding. He'd fallen in love with me then even when there was no us. And I too had fallen in love with him. Although I was greatly relieved to be out of Berlin, being with Otto troubled me. I was torn between love and duty, and now I had to decide between the two of them. He did not make this decision easy for me. But I knew deep in my heart, that the right answer was to return to Cali as soon as possible.

I continued to listen to the radio broadcasts. The wall in Berlin was nearing completion, and on both sides of this political island, heavily armed men stood face-to-face. West Berlin received moral support from governments throughout the world. President Kennedy affirmed again, "We shall protect West Berlin."

The victims of this inhuman act were the citizens of East Germany. Almost daily, someone died trying to escape to the west. Today one can see their names engraved on a memorial plaque. After the wall fell in 1989, former political figures in East Germany faced criminal prosecution for the shoot-to-kill order. Archived records that surfaced confirmed the underlying reason for construction of the wall. The East German leadership linked the survival of their state to stopping the mass westward exodus. They lost.

My departure was difficult for Otto and just as difficult for me. For many hours I sat on the airplane lost in my thoughts. Finally, my plane landed in Panama for a long stopover. Now I placed the experience and memories of my adventure in Germany behind me and focused on resuming my life in South America.

Many years later, several years after Otto died, I wrote to his daughters, attempting to explain what he had meant to me.

Dear Inge and Heide,

Memories are a paradise from which you can never be driven. You can also say that forgetting is like when the soul faints.

This is a story about love between your father and me. I first met the two of you during the summer of 1961. The meeting was somewhat overshadowed by embarrassment for at the same time I also met your mother. With her female instinct she could sense that I had a relationship with your father. In the sixties the stigma of divorce still existed, which brought with it a certain shame at having failed. Today one can push those feelings aside and accept that former spouses will look elsewhere for companionship.

I met your father in the late fifties in Cali. It was a tender affair, one in which we shared a great deal of affection for each other. However, we lived in Colombia, which meant we were at the mercy of the small expatriate community.

I was in my late thirties. In these years, women experience a new sense of excitement and search for a new direction in life. Like so many other women, I belonged to a different generation, one that was betrayed by history. Happiness was rationed in tiny portions, and the struggle to survive left little time to enjoy life. Despite being a poor country, Colombia was a paradise. Nobody could restrain my boundless energy, and the encounter with your father swept me off my feet. He radiated the peace and calmness I searched for, to balance out my boundless energy. I remember the lively exchange of thoughts and ideas, and your father and I were happy together. Perhaps the words of the Emperor Hadrian could better express how we felt:

"Each bit of happiness is a masterpiece that erases the smallest mistake, extinguishes the smallest doubt, and lets you joke about the most minor act of foolishness. Happiness consists of that inner peace that enhances both your life's work and the moments of contemplation and represents the greatest gift of love between two people."

I knew I could not expect this happiness to last forever. Contentment is never a happy ending. I enjoyed the time with your father, a child of nature, a cross between Luis Trenker and perhaps Reinhold Messner.[16] He opened a new world for me and accepted me for who I was. At the time my husband lived in San Agustín. He wanted to give me time to find myself. Your father wanted to have a more permanent relationship with me, and I could not. I am not sure if it was out of duty for my family or just cowardice.

We met once again in Europe. I was not aware that someone had told him about my travel plans. That is how we met in Munich. We wanted to experience once again the passion of our relationship in South America, yet we both knew it had to come to an end. We traveled throughout Europe, visiting acquaintances. We enjoyed visiting the opera house in Vienna. For us it was like a "grand finale."

With a heavy heart I flew back to Cali. Your father returned several weeks later. I was not exactly received with open arms by the German expatriates, who never forgave me for kidnapping their most eligible bachelor.

After this trip we occasionally met in secret, but the fire was extinguished.

In 1966 I left Colombia, but on my return trips to South America we met with each other. The romantic relationship developed into a deep friendship. Your father even visited me in Colorado. I saw him for the last time in February of 1978 in Cali. He seemed troubled and I felt he was looking for a way out. Nothing appealed to him anymore. He was not a man to speak about what bothered him. His former business partners had already returned to Germany. He did not have any friends. He no longer went horseback riding. His health was

---

16   Trenker was a famous Austrian actor and Messner a famous Austrian mountaineer.

failing. He told me that nobody cared about him anymore. As he walked out the door, he dragged his injured foot behind him, with his shoulders lowered, looking as though he had given up on himself.

Your father was not any easy man to understand. He loved both of you. Often, he told stories about his grandchildren, and of course, about you.

There are so many details I could tell about this man who unconditionally gave his heart to me, which I rejected.

It has been seventeen years since we last met. We have all become older, much wiser, and even grateful for what we have experienced. Life is a gift. What matters is how you wrap it.

With love,
Franziska

In 1961 the airport in Panama had all the charm of a dilapidated South American airfield, with a myriad of flies and mosquitoes, as well as a filthy floor. On one side of the terminal, a local swept the floor at a snail's pace. On the other end of the terminal, I saw a mother with a screaming child. In this unventilated building, the temperature hovered around 105 degrees with 100 percent humidity—an extreme environment, just as extreme as Berlin. On the bright side, I was no longer dwelling on what had happened in Europe, events that had raced back and forth in my mind over the last several hours. Finally, I heard the boarding call and was grateful to step onto the aircraft for the final stretch of my journey. The last several weeks had been simply nerve-wracking. Now I looked forward to returning to a normal routine and perhaps even to retreating to a quiet corner for a while.

Cali had not changed. The same dusty palm trees swayed in the breeze to greet my arrival. The airport was still disorganized. The customs officers still remembered to "confiscate" some of the gifts I had brought back with me, standard procedure for foreign visitors. Nobody waited for me, which was to be expected because I had not informed anybody of my arrival time. Nevertheless, a part of me would have liked to have seen George or Barbara standing in the terminal to extend a warm welcome home. Alone, I made my way to our hotel.

There, I received my warm welcome. All were excited to see me home safe and sound, especially after this eventful time in Germany. Barbara gave me a bear hug. Then we tore open my suitcase and distributed the gifts I had brought back with me. I was so happy to be home. However, George's behavior toward me did not let this feeling last for long. From acquaintances he had learned that Otto and I had traveled together while in Europe. The international community in Cali was relatively small, everybody knew each other, and everybody knew someone in Europe. Somehow the news of my adventure had made its way back to the Residencia Stein. George just stood in front of me with an angry look on his face. Disappointed and hurt, he had run the hotel in my absence, and now he gave me the cold shoulder. For several days we did not say one word to each other.

Miguelito, 1961

One evening not long after my return from Europe, an old Colombian man, Miguel Liscano, sat on our veranda. We had met long ago when I worked in Bogotá. He owned several large leather factories and tanneries. Miguel looked like a typical Native American Indian— dark skin, no facial hair, wiry frame—and was always very friendly. His wife reigned as the matron of their household, using her time to organize church events and receiving guests at her home. She lived according to the principle that a woman's place is in the kitchen. Miguelito, as he was affectionately known, enjoyed staying at our hotel in Cali to avoid his wife's parties. He always called me "*Panchita*." This was an endearing way of saying "Franziska" in Spanish.[17]

"*Panchita*," he once said to me, "even if I have to sleep underneath the stairs, it will be okay, because it is so beautiful and relaxing here."

Before the war he had owned just one tannery, and the business provided him with a modest income. He imported the chemicals he

---

17   For men named Francisco, the equivalent nickname was *Pancho*.

needed for the business, manufactured by Hoechst in Leverkusen, from Germany. One day he told his secretary to order several month's supply of the chemicals he needed for tanning hides. For whatever reason, she ordered several-hundred times that amount by mistake.

Panicked, he cried to the secretary, "How can we possibly pay for that? We are ruined!" But something completely unexpected occurred before he went bankrupt: the Second World War started in Europe. He received the last shipment of tanning chemicals that would come from Germany until long after the war had ended. Soon Miguelito possessed the only sizable stock of these chemicals in all of Colombia and Ecuador. Just like that, his problem was over, and he was able to reap a huge windfall. During and even after the war, he had a monopoly on the tanning business, which made him a wealthy man.

Now he sat at our hotel in Cali conversing with the other guests. Later we were able to join him. Out of the blue, he said, "Would you be interested in taking over a large house? Not far from here, I own a large house, and I do not know what to do with it. If you rent it from me, you will have a free hand and can do whatever you like with the place."

A Huge and Demanding House, 1962

As soon as we received the offer, we did not hesitate to take over the house, which seemed more like a small palace. We had dreamt of finding a larger building for our hotel, and suddenly the opportunity had been handed to us. Of course, the new building would require some renovations to suit our purposes, such as the construction or teardown of walls and installation of several more bathrooms. The swimming pool also needed to be cleaned, a task far more difficult than it sounds.

The renovation of the new building for the hotel was entrusted to a carpenter from Ecuador and an architect from Bogotá. Part of the exterior facade and much of the interior woodwork consisted of mahogany. The lightly colored stonework contained numerous reliefs inspired by Indian artwork. Unfortunately, the floorboards tended to become infested with woodworms, and for this reason we often had to replace them. Sometimes I helped female guests who stood before me with bare feet, after their high-heeled stiletto shoes had punctured a hole through the worm-infested floor and become stuck. Luckily, nobody was injured. This was life in the tropics!

When we moved from our old hotel to the new hotel, we did not close our business. Somehow, we managed to pull it off with style, a major feat of logistics. This entailed quite a bit of planning. George oversaw the construction of the new bathrooms and much of the electrical work in the new hotel, while I ran the existing hotel. My staff and I also arranged to have the furniture and guests moved. When the new hotel was finally ready, we set the plans in motion.

During this hectic time, I received a letter from Mr. Zieschang in Berlin. He asked that I travel as soon as possible to Ecuador, to help potential clients fill out application forms for compensation. He closed by saying that they desperately needed my help and to let him know when I could depart.

Now how could I possibly manage that? It was time to sit down, take in a deep breath, and come up with a plan. I felt like everyone was tugging at me from all directions. The crisis with George and Otto, caring for our guests, supervising our employees—it was all too much. Now Zieschang needed my assistance. Actually, his clients needed the help. How could I be fair to everybody? I closed my eyes and saw myself at the intersection of two roads, with weathered and crooked signs pointing in different directions. *Should I stay, or should I go?* I wondered. *Do I pack now and run off to Ecuador? Can they manage the move without me?*

I decided that the move had priority, and then I could tackle the assignment given to me by Zieschang. Our guests cooperated with this endeavor, mostly through moral support. We planned to make the move during the night. At the old hotel we served dinner to the guests. Afterward we packed them and their belongings into some waiting cars and drove over to the new building. As they slept in the brand-new beds, through the night we continued to work on setting up the hotel. In the morning the guests were able to eat breakfast in our new dining room. Although George, the staff, and I ran around like lunatics in the insane asylum, we received nothing but praise from the guests for the smooth transition.

Next on the agenda was Ecuador. Again, air travel in the early 1960s paled in comparison to what one finds today, where several airlines fly jumbo jets from one major city to the next and service the smaller towns with commuter planes, filling the skies with endless miles of contrails. At that time just one airline company flew from Cali to Ecuador—Avianca. And this one was on strike! Well, I am not someone who lets others tell me that something is impossible. Instead of flying, I decided to take the bus. This journey would take two days, which I would spend squeezed between locals who often spoke incomprehensible Spanish. Moreover, this was a *chiva* bus, or rural service bus, meaning it might include farm animals as well as people.

George offered to look after the hotel in my absence, so only final duty remained: I prepared as many desserts as the refrigerator could hold. Fortunately, I could depart knowing that Barbara would be among the least of my problems. She now attended an English-Colombian business school. She wanted to improve her command of the English language, so she could later study in the United States. I sent word of my impending arrival to Ecuador, and then I was out the door and on the bus.

The Journey to Ecuador, 1962

I am certainly not the bravest person in the world, and I very much welcomed the chance to have a travel companion for the journey to Ecuador. A young Austrian au pair, Inge, came often to our hotel with her sponsor and the children, and she had a few days of vacation available, so she agreed to come with me. She worked for the director of the Rockefeller Foundation in his household. We were indeed a perfect match for each other. Like me, she had no desire to travel alone, but she very much wanted to explore. The bus left Cali early in the morning and managed to cover a lot of distance that day. Soon we rolled through Popayán, a city that almost felt familiar to me after the visits on the way to San Agustín. Besides us and an American student, the passengers on the bus were locals.

At dusk we reached Pasto in southern Colombia. The transition from day to night came very fast, which is typical for the tropics. We managed to find a room for the night in a hotel. Exhausted from the long journey, we sampled local cuisine, but soon the need for sleep overtook us, and we went to bed. At four in the morning, we climbed aboard the bus, and the journey continued south into Ecuador. When we made our plans for the day, we decided to spend the night in Ibarra rather than travel all the way into Quito.

Just after we crossed the border into Ecuador, we came to Santuario de Las Lajas, a basilica church, near the city of Ipiales. Located on the Rio Guáitara, the present church was built in the first half of the twentieth century in the Gothic Revival style. As much as the basilica impressed me, I found the surroundings even more spiritual. The women who stayed at the basilica, praying much of the day, brought a deep serenity to the air.

Around noon we stopped in a small village, which was more of a settlement formed by several houses. The houses looked very much like those found in southern Africa, round buildings with straw roofs. The similarity with Africa made sense when one considered that this area had been founded long ago by the descendants of African slaves. I remember seeing tall, thin people with dark skin living among the dry and dusty surroundings, which had been bleached

This statue was outside the basilica church near Ipiales. I was struck by the wildness of the terrain and the stark contrast of the Angel.

white by the relentless sun. A few hours later, we finally reached Ibarra, our destination for the day.

Ibarra, a provincial city that retains much from its colonial past, lies about four hours south of the Ecuadorian–Colombian border. There we found monuments to Simón Bolívar, who led New Granada in its struggle against Spanish oppression. With his fighting spirit, tactical skill, and energy, he prevailed, forcing the Spanish to surrender their South American colonies, achieving the impossible. Bolívar became a hero to South Americans, attaining almost godlike status. He spent quite a bit of time in this area since his mistress lived in Quito, the capital of Ecuador and our destination for the next day.

We stayed in a hotel built in the colonial style. However, the interior decor was influenced by Indian designs and art. The hotel pampered the guests with a local variety of the unmistakable beat of South American music. The next morning, we climbed onto the bus to complete the rest of our journey. In Quito I planned to hold a series of meetings with potential clients. We twisted our way up and down the hills and over highways that ranged from heavily damaged to well-maintained. During the journey we traveled on parts of the Pan-American Highway, which spans 19,000 miles, from Alaska to Tierra del Fuego at the southern tip of Argentina. In South America, sections of this highway follow routes initially used by the Spanish conquistadores. Over the years the Pan-American Highway has been improved constantly, but in the early 1960s, the stretch upon which we rode was simply punishing, especially in an old bus with worn shock absorbers.

During the journey we crossed a very important line that circles the earth—the equator. The driver stopped the bus so that we could cross over this symbolic geographical division on foot. From here we had a wonderful view of Chimborazo, a stunning, snowcapped peak surrounded by other snow-covered mountains.

Nowadays we live in an era in which speed is of the utmost necessity. We thirst for what is larger and more exciting. Extreme mountain climbers tackle the highest peaks just to brag about conquering a tiny piece of nature. In those days, as I made my way to Quito, traveling was a true adventure. Even the simple things impressed us, and nature was a beautiful masterpiece waiting to be appreciated. We just drank it all in.

In the morning, from Ibarra, we continued South towards Quito. We stopped briefly in Otavalo, a city famous

On the equator in 1962.

for its market of locally crafted weavings. I was not there on the big market day, but I remember speaking with a native woman who proclaimed herself a witch and a healer. I also spoke with a man selling firewood from his donkey.

The market in Otavalo.

This spirit of adventure certainly infected the German scholar Alexander von Humboldt, who explored South America between 1799 and 1804. He managed to catalog some of the flora and fauna, while one of his companions drew sketches of what was recorded. Humboldt's work would inspire others to examine South America's prehistoric past, which revealed to astonished Europeans that the indigenous Americans had lived in a remarkably advanced culture at a time when Europe was still wallowing in the stone age.

Our legs were stiff from riding in the bus all day. At sunset we finally arrived in Quito. We exited the bus station and made our way through the crowd of people that pushed past us on the street. After this long journey, our hotel was a real disappointment. It lacked anything of aesthetic value—very stark, just offering minimal comforts, and featuring nothing of the cultural tradition of South America.

Quito lies about eight thousand feet above sea level, about the same as Bogotá, yet the climate is more agreeable, almost an eternal spring. The inhabitants seemed much happier in this city, which seemed to put on a bright smile every morning. In the old section of town were old homes with beautiful interior courtyards, along with well-maintained gardens displaying a stunning variety of plant life. Churches, reflecting the architectural styles of different eras, and buildings from the colonial period added to the city's unique character. However, many of the cultural treasures were in desperate need of restoration. The excessive use of candles had left behind a layer of soot on many paintings, causing extensive damage. Everywhere, it was impossible to escape from the smell of musty air, which joined with the smoke from mouthwatering food cooked outdoors at every corner to produce an unforgettable odor.

Everywhere we saw people of Indian ancestry, recognizable by their distinctive facial features and the blue ponchos that they carried. Women often wore colorful skirts. Many carried a baby on their back. The men, and many women, wore a unique hat, similar to English bowlers.

The day after our arrival, I met with one client after another, Jews and Christians, representing all points on the socioeconomic spectrum. Some had found success in South America; others struggled to survive. Many suffered from homesickness yet returning to Germany was completely out of the question, either out of principle or because of the lack of money.

All those with whom I met sought a pension from the German government. I particularly remember a man named Karl. In South America he went by the name of Charles. During the Second World War he had worked for Universum Film AG, Germany's principal film studio. His wife had danced in ballet films. After the war it had become difficult for them to find work. In this destroyed and devastated country, nobody needed artists, even those who had never belonged to the Nazi Party. They saw no future in Germany and were not about to spend the next several years cleaning up the rubble, living from the occasional project thrown their way. They decided to emigrate and try their luck in South America. In Ecuador they founded a dance school, which brought them some success. The entrenched expatriate community wanted to impart some of the old traditions to their children. For this reason, many sent their girls to the school to learn waltzes and ballet.

Each of my clients was grateful. I helped them produce complete applications that incorporated all the proper legal terminology. Without a doubt, we could reach only a fraction of those entitled to some sort of compensation. We found it particularly difficult to contact people living outside the major cities. Zieschang or someone else was able to assist a few of them, yet I found it disturbing that many never had any idea that they could file a claim. Consequently, many forfeited their legal right to compensation.

Perspective: Nazis in South America

Not a single country in South America remained unaffected by the wave of European immigration before and following the Second World War. However, some of the South American countries had a closer diplomatic relationship with the Nazi regime than others. Argentina, for example, made a deliberate effort to seal its borders against Jewish immigration. Toward the end of the war, Argentinean officials, with the support of some within the Catholic Church, helped several leading Nazis and war time collaborators escape justice. These fugitives were provided with falsified identity papers. Then they were smuggled through other European countries and given sanctuary in Argentina, Brazil, Chile, and Paraguay. During a 1947 visit to Europe, Eva Perón, the wife of the Argentinean dictator, lent her support to organizations that aided these fugitives from justice. The Argentineans were interested in promoting the immigration of those with technical skills, especially in the areas of aviation and rocketry. For example, Hans-Ulrich Rudel, a highly decorated German fighter pilot during the Second World War, became an advisor to the Argentinean air force. They were also interested in the plundered wealth these men brought with them.

Three of the more notorious Nazi fugitives who immigrated to South America were Joseph Mengele, Adolph Eichmann, and Klaus Barbie. Mengele and Eichmann found sanctuary in Argentina and Barbie in Bolivia.

Mengele, known as the Angel of Death, conducted inhuman medical experiments on prisoners at the Auschwitz concentration camp. Unfortunately, he was able to escape justice. In 1979, while swimming off the Brazilian coast, he suffered a stroke and died. Mengele was buried under the name of Wolfgang Gerhard, but forensic experts later established his correct identity.

Eichmann was responsible for facilitating and managing the logistics of the mass deportation of Jews to ghettos and, later, to extermination camps in German-occupied Eastern Europe. In 1960 the Mossad, the Israeli secret service, determined that Eichmann was living in Argentina under an assumed identity. In a daring undercover mission, Mossad agents kidnapped Eichmann in front of his home in Buenos Aires and secretly flew him to Israel for trial. In 1961 an Israeli court found him guilty of crimes against humanity. The following year he was hanged.

Barbie headed the Gestapo unit in Lyon, a city in France, during the German occupation. Known as the Butcher of Lyon, at times he personally tortured members of the French resistance movement. Historians estimate that Barbie was directly responsible for the deaths of more than 14,000 people.

After the war, Barbie became an agent of the US Army Counterintelligence Corp (CIC) (predecessor of the CIA) as the

US was worried that France had become infiltrated by communists. Sadly, the CIC was also interested in learning what he knew about interrogation techniques. The British were also using former SS Members to this end.

The French later learned that Barbie was in US custody and sentenced him to death in absentia for war crimes. Rather than hand Barbie over to the French authorities, the CIC arranged safe passage to Bolivia with the help of a Catholic priest. Barbie continued to work with the CIA in anti-Marxist activities while living in Bolivia. In 1983 he was finally extradited to France and stood trial for crimes against humanity. Barbie was convicted and received a life sentence in 1987. He died of cancer four years later.

Managing All My Fulltime Jobs, 1962

I was happy when the meetings in Ecuador finally came to an end. Of course, I was glad to help these people, but their stories also made me very depressed at times. The ability of the human spirit to endure the seemingly limitless cruelty and most deplorable conditions described in their stories never ceased to amaze me.

Squeezed into a bus packed with women, children, pigs, and chickens, we traveled northward in the direction of the Colombian frontier. You can only imagine my shock when I saw an Indian woman breastfeeding a piglet!

We started our return trip on a Saturday, which allowed us the perfect opportunity to visit Ottovalo, a small town with a famous open-air market held every Saturday. When we arrived, the Indians had already begun to cart their goods and wares away, but still there was much to see. I remember a frail old lady with a heavily weathered face. She approached me to seek a *lismona*, Spanish for alms. At first, I felt a little apprehensive, but I warmed up to her when she grinned and led me to a bench. Taking my hand, she briefly studied my palm before looking deep into my eyes. "*Permíta me adivinar que le vaya bien*,"[18] she said.

---

18   "Let me see if it is going well for you."

While mumbling something to herself, she removed a handful of sacred herbs from her pocket. Then with a high-pitched voice, she uttered a mixture of Spanish and Quechua while looking into the depths of my soul. I did not understand most of what she said, yet it seemed she gave me some sort of a blessing. A very special aura radiated from her, and I was very moved by this encounter. Whenever I think of her, the following words from the Native American author Mourning Dove come to mind: "Everything on the earth has a purpose, every disease an herb to cure it, and every person a mission. This is the Indian theory of existence."[19]

The next day, before our bus departed, we had time to attend Sunday Mass. Inside the Catholic Church countless lit candles decorated the altar, their flickering glow faintly illuminating the frescos as well as the silver and brass ornamentation. A thick cloud of smoke from burning incense and candles partially obscured the light, making the ceiling beams appear darker. The odor of incense made us light-headed. Our spirits rose in more than one sense of the word.

On board the bus the punishing journey continued, bouncing us side to side, up and down, over heavily damaged roads. By the time we rolled over the Colombian border into Pasto, enough was enough. We decided to put our lives in God's hands and fly home from there. The Pasto airfield is infamous because of the terrain surrounding it. One prayed feverishly that the pilot had built up enough speed on the short runway to clear the mountains at the opposite end. The airport was located on a plateau only fifty meters wide, leaving little room for pilot error. In addition, the airport was plagued by strong crosswinds. I remember one landing attempt here a few years later that was aborted at the last minute, forcing us to fly back to Popayán without any success. But on this day, as we rolled down the runway, I surely felt the truth of the following expression: "The good Lord must have surely blessed the Colombians. Their pilots have all the luck."

I must admit to enjoying these excursions into remote areas immensely. Finally, I could distance myself from the things that

---

19   Mourning Dove, or Christal Quintasket (Okanogan), was a Native American author in the United States best known for her 1927 novel *Cogewea the Half-Blood: A Depiction of the Great Montana Cattle Range.*

usually bothered me, such as deadlines or the fights with my husband. Nevertheless, I carried a knapsack of guilt with me wherever I went—the people I disappointed with my absence, the hotel work I neglected, the hurt I caused both Otto and George.

On this trip I remember that I felt just awful about overextending my stay in Ecuador. Just before my departure, we had moved into the new hotel building. While in Ecuador I still had a lot of unfinished work in Cali. Yet when I returned home, my work for Zieschang continued to demand much of my evenings.

Zieschang wanted to know immediately how the meetings had gone. Then the applications had to be reviewed and ultimately sent to the German government for a decision. To make things worse, we faced a deadline for submitting the claims. With the time short, every minute of my day became precious. I had to adhere to a very tight schedule, meticulously organizing all the events of my day to accomplish all that was expected of me. George now ran the hotel. Thankfully, Barbara remained a diligent student, and I could trust her to stay out of trouble.

I often tossed and turned in bed, trying to deal with one concern after another. Although George now ran the day-to-day operations of the hotel, this was just an interim solution. For the business to succeed, he needed my drive and ideas. The tone of our conversations became mostly confrontational.

Of course, I could not let the frustration get the best of me. I was responsible for not only myself and my family. Many other people also depended on me. If we had to dismiss an employee, the consequences would be devastating, a return to the most bitter poverty. Good-paying jobs were rare for the locals and there were no unemployment benefits. Many supported their families on just one income. Then I had to worry about our customers. Who would care for them if I stepped into the background?

In my opinion, among the essential strengths of women is their ability to resolve problems through compromise and consensus. Men, on the other hand, tend to be assertive and confrontational. This style of problem solving is probably the result of social pressures and expectations that men will protect and take care of women. Certainly, young women take advantage of this tendency. In all honesty, who doesn't appreciate a strong shoulder on which to lean? But we women must realize that our ability to resolve problems through compromise and consensus is indeed a gift—and often the preferable response in many situations.

The person I had become was shaped by the traumatic events surrounding the Second World War, events that had deprived me of a smooth transition from child to teenager and finally adult. For me, as well as millions of other ethnic Germans, May 8, 1945, the day the war ended, will forever be remembered as *Nullstunde*, meaning zero hour. From this moment on, our world spun in a completely new direction, and like millions of others, I was pulled into the whirlpool of social and political change, swimming with the currents of renewal, fighting constantly to keep my head above water.

The Characters of Residencia Stein, 1962

Most of our guests came from either the United States or Europe. Almost every evening, we had a full dining room. Our cuisine enjoyed a very good reputation and was much sought after because Cali did not possess very many fine restaurants serving cuisine in the Old-World style.

A growing business, such as ours, demands attention to detail and extensive planning. Five days a week, we visited the outdoor market to purchase meat and produce and stock up on whatever we needed. We planned our menu a week in advance and closely supervised our hotel staff.

The outdoor market in Cali was unforgettable. In the morning the vendors hung meat on hooks, shaded from the blistering sun by only a thin cloth awning. As the day grew longer, more and more flies swirled around the hooks and pieces of meat that had not been sold. The stench of fish, meat, and cheese, which became ripe in the sweltering afternoon heat, could be overwhelming. Without a doubt, this required a strong stomach. Sometimes when I arrived home after a visit to the market, I had to pour myself a small glass of aguardiente to keep myself from gagging. At least we didn't have to carry our purchases home. Plenty of day laborers loitered around the market, willing to perform the work for little pay.

By that time, we had a houseboy. He carried suitcases for the guests and performed other chores, such as helping with the shopping at the market. His name was Edgar, and he was a small, wiry Indian, very kind and goodhearted. Edgar had a pet rooster who lived with him in a shack at the end of our property. During the week Edgar was available to help us at any hour of the day, but on the weekends, he was often unavailable. On Saturdays and Sundays, he would take his rooster to the cockfights to earn a little pocket money.

Our American guests usually arrived with an ample supply of whiskey, which they shared generously with the other guests. One of our American guests, an older man who always dressed in a very sharp black suit, taught political science in Cali on behalf of the University of North Carolina. His colleagues kept calling him "OB." After this had gone on for a while, and after I had failed to guess what name these initials might represent, I finally asked for an explanation.

"Doña Franziska," a man answered, with a smile on his face, "that means Old Bastard."

Considering the environment, our German guests must have looked rather exotic. Perhaps they had read in some travel guide that European ladies at the Residencia Stein required formal or chic attire at all times. Who knows? Anyway, many arrived wearing outfits totally unsuitable for the climate, such as designer clothing made from silk. I remember how they perspired heavily while sitting on our porch in the sweltering heat.

For a Christmas party at our hotel, one of the Americans we knew ordered a pound of caviar from Macy's, which was delivered in a large can. We opened the can and made it the centerpiece of the buffet we had set out, one befitting the director of a major company. About two in the morning, the American pulled me aside and whispered into my ear, "What in the devil happened to my caviar?"

Looking at the buffet table and the empty can, I shrugged my shoulders in regret, unable to offer any explanation.

The next morning, after I had been asleep for maybe a couple of hours, Carmen shook me awake. Very agitated, she said, "*Señora*, come quickly. Something has happened to all our plants and beautiful flowers. They have been attacked by some kind of insect."

Still half-asleep, I tromped behind her out to the swimming pool. Suddenly, I burst out laughing. In the flowerpots and around the garden plants, instead of some parasite I found numerous tiny pearls of that black gold from the previous night. It turned out that many of the Colombians had never heard of caviar, and when they sampled it, the taste did not agree with them, so they spat it out into the plants.

Over the many years that we operated the Residencia Stein, I had an opportunity to meet many people. Most of them were guests who stayed with us, and as one can expect in a business such as ours, we formed just short-term relationships. We said goodbye when the taxi to the airport arrived and then never heard again from the person who the night before had been our best friend. Nevertheless, I was able to develop a long-term friendship with one of the guests, Richard C. Hessert, the manager of the First National City Bank's (the original Citibank) Cali office. Years later, when I was traveling from one place to the next in search of adventure, I saw him several times in airports in the most unexpected locations.

People were not the only guests at our hotel. When George returned from San Agustín, he brought back "Miko", a small marmoset monkey, who made himself right at home with us. His name was taken from a children's book popular at the time about a little monkey that lives in the forest with his family. Another permanent guest was Patricia, a yellow and red parrot

Miko, on the terrace. For reference, he is holding onto a camera case. He wasn't much bigger than an adult human's hand.

capable of mimicking several words, which she uttered with a terrible squawk. God only knows where she learned the swear words. With her in the house, we never required a weather forecaster. Whenever she became very talkative and began to fling herself toward the window, we knew it was about to rain. Our garden became a bird paradise. They arrived every day to feast on the bananas and fruit we set out for them. We were especially fond of the hummingbirds. They constantly buzzed around the feeders that we filled with sugar water and hung out for them. I should not forget to mention Resi, our dachshund. She had a phenomenal memory and easily recognized all of our guests.

Jesus, our gardener, maintained our English-style lawn and cleaned the swimming pool. A very conscientious employee, he arrived every morning on time, ready to start work. Humble and friendly, he made his way from one end of the garden to the next, greeting guests he encountered along the way. When he worked for us, Jesus was already an old man. During my time in Colombia, he was one of the few I saw chewing coca leaves. Perhaps the drug gave him the stamina he needed in his old age to work all day in the garden in the intense heat.

Years after moving to the United States, I returned to Cali for a visit. As I made my way on foot to our former *residencia*, Jesus and I bumped into each other, something completely unexpected for both of us. He was a wonderful part of my past, and I had never forgotten how he smiled when I paid him his wages. We purchased a few bottles of cola at a *tienda* and then found a table and spent an hour reminiscing about old times.

Colombian Bambuco, 1962–1963

The colorful and often demanding lifestyle of Colombia had cast a spell over me even though I still clung to the memories of my former life in Europe. My list of friends and acquaintances grew longer and longer. Whenever possible, I enjoyed visiting with our guests as they sat out on the veranda during the evenings. Many became dear friends. Occasionally, some of the guests stayed for an extended period, up to three years in a few cases, particularly after being transferred to Colombia by an employer. They obtained temporary housing at our residencia, and finding our hotel very pleasant and comfortable, some never bothered to look for an apartment.

For many I became someone to turn to when life became difficult, a shoulder to lean on, someone who would listen to their problems. Often the conversations were prefaced by "Franziska, do you have a moment?" or "Let's go for a walk in the garden."

I heard it all—problems with a spouse, a girlfriend, or a boyfriend; difficulties with the language barrier; struggles to get along with the locals or with the foreigners; problems with the boss or with staff; or just the need to let off a little steam. For the most part, hearing these problems really did not affect me. On the other hand, what could I say to someone with tears in his eyes who told me about an employee who was stealing from the company? The problems faced by expatriates were certainly complex.

Besides dealing with the concerns of my guests and the work I received through Zieschang in Berlin, I often received forwarded inquiries for compensation or a pension from the German consulate, calling for my response. The paperwork stacked up on my desk, keeping me busy late into the night as I prepared one document after another using an old typewriter.

The case histories I prepared were especially troublesome, leaving me depressed after long nights and even causing nightmares as I slept. I asked myself the same question over and over again: "How much can a person take?" Then I was reminded of my own personal tragedy, having been driven from my home in Karlsbad when a new regime rose to power. After turning us into the enemy in the eyes of our former neighbors, the new government had taken everything we owned and sent us into exile to live in unfamiliar surroundings, where we often lived in poverty. And I was lucky—so many others had lost much, much more.

One of my favorite books is *Letters from the Black Sea*, written by the Roman poet Ovid after Emperor Augustus sent him into exile, to a remote corner of the Roman Empire near the Black Sea. Ovid had written a book about passion and love. Some speculate that Augustus found the book offensive and for this reason banished Ovid from Rome. Ovid's impressions and experiences far from home were a stark reminder of the personal history statements.

I typed every night, stories that detailed the fate of so many unfortunate people. Exile means you may never get home again; it means a separation from your roots, culture, and kin, a cruel and barbaric punishment both in ancient times and even in the modern era. I thought of my former home in Karlsbad, a separation that had now lasted for many years.

We were certainly fortunate to have a friend like Anni. She had helped us immensely in finding a new start in Colombia, selflessly opening many doors for George and me. During the winter of 1981, I visited with Anni in Costa Rica. She lived in Cartago, the former capital of that country, where she cultivated orchids with her husband. They had recently lost most of what they owned in Colombia. Because of the growing worldwide demand for illegal drugs, the raw ingredients were often transported from a place of cultivation to production centers over set trade routes. Unfortunately, Enricas' sawmill in Rio Hacha lay on one of these trade routes, which the drug lords protected with brutal force. Over time the area around Rio Hacha became uninhabitable for "normal people." Anni and Enricas were lucky to escape with their lives and some of their belongings. Of course, they did not receive any compensation for the loss of their business.

Enricas and Anni, along with their three daughters, then settled in Costa Rica. Enricas found work with an Austrian company in Panama. The three daughters grew into adults. Their oldest daughter moved to West Germany, where she married. The middle became an actress and lived in Berlin. Their youngest daughter joined a religious cult, much to the chagrin of her parents.

Enricas came from Lithuania, a country that had disappeared after the Second World War and that reappeared after the collapse of the Soviet Union. He was a nice man and was committed to his wife. But marital fidelity had a different meaning within the tropical lifestyle. Anni told me that over the course of several years, he'd had an affair with a Colombian singer, with whom he had fathered two children. Shortly after the birth of the second child, the singer disappeared and abandoned her little ones. Anni, who coped remarkably with the ups and downs of everyday life, brought the children to her home and raised them as her own. She had a generous heart, and she made the world a better place for those of us who were lucky enough to have crossed paths with her.

That visit would be the last time that I saw Anni. I think of her often, for the many great gifts of her friendship over the years.

Hard work seemed to help our marriage. Sometimes I wondered whether we were a real married couple. Yet what is a real couple? Sexuality never played much of a role in our relationship. Perhaps George looked for this outside the marriage. I did not know, nor did I ever want to know. Even today, when I look back on our life in Colombia, it is difficult to assess the situation. All day long, I remained as busy as a bee, supervising the staff, purchasing supplies, planning menus, and settling disputes. Only in the evening, when the heat of the day eased, and the cool breezes blew in from the ocean, could I finally relax and take an hour for myself. I often sat on the veranda, watching the tropical sun as it set rapidly on the horizon. Flowers would unfold and release their fragrance, and sometimes the faint sounds of a tiple would fill the air, competing with the night calls of birds in the garden. Tension would flow from my body, and occasionally, my thoughts would wander through my past, or I would just stay in the present, on the chair on the veranda.

Then my personal time would end, and the work would take over. Our guests would gather for dinner, and once the dinner service was over, they would entertain each other with conversation. I would take my exit then and begin tackling the huge pile of paperwork on my desk. During these moments to myself, I tossed various ideas back and forth in my head, thinking about what I wanted out of my life and the future.

Now it was Christmas 1962, and I was turning forty. Anyone with a birthday during the holiday season knows that this personal celebration often becomes part of the larger family holiday. In many ways this big-O birthday was just another routine day at the hotel. Our guests expected a traditional European holiday celebration, which we delivered. Then we managed to find time for a small birthday celebration for me. While serenaded by *conjuntos*, Colombian musicians, we popped open a bottle of French champagne purchased on the black market and raised a glass in my honor.[20]

At the beginning of 1963, Zieschang contacted me from Berlin with a personal request. Several weeks before, he had made arrangements to have a Volkswagen car (the well-known Beetle model) sent from Hamburg to Buenaventura. While in Colombia he needed reliable transportation. Soon the car would arrive at the harbor. Now he wanted me to negotiate with the customs officials to get the vehicle released from the impound yard. I just had to sigh and roll my eyes in disbelief. It was illegal to import an automobile. How did he expect me to clear the vehicle through customs?

Soon we received word that the car had indeed arrived at the port. Together with someone we knew quite well, George and I drove to Buenaventura. Since we planned on staying for several days, we booked a room at the Hotel Estación, the only decent hotel around the port facility. Built several years before the war, the hotel was supposed to offer all the comforts of home for weary travelers who had endured a long voyage at sea. Among the amenities was a swimming pool. However, nobody had bothered to clean it since the grand opening. As much as we wanted to take a refreshing swim, we were not about to jump into the thick green broth now inhabited by frogs.

The balcony railings were rusted because of the high humidity and salty air. Walking through the large dining room, we noticed plain, worn wicker furniture that probably had not been replaced since the hotel was built. Contrary to original expectations, those just coming into port would not have found the hotel all that inviting. The British novelist and playwright Somerset Maugham could have used this place as the setting for a terrific story.

---

20   Colombia had very strong importation restrictions because of currency issues and high sovereign debt obligations. We could get anything produced within the borders, but exotic items such as scotch, bourbon, and French champagne were not legally imported. Most things could be obtained on the black market, however.

The tropical nights cast their own spell upon this port city. Sailors who were here for a short stay celebrated with the locals. Heavily influenced by African heritage, the music of Colombia saturated the air: bambuco, bolero, merengue, and cumbia. Out on the ocean, the dark waves of the Pacific shimmered under the silvery glow of the moon. Above, a star-filled sky formed a roof over the dirt and decay of the city below, whose filth was all too conspicuous during the day. This nighttime atmosphere brought a whole new perception to the establishment. Old candelabras in the dining room, combined with the lit candles that illuminated the terrace, created a fairy-tale land through which one had to tiptoe. At night our hotel had a certain flair, like an enchanted palace. I called it the "Mistreated Lady of Buenaventura."

On the beach in Buenaventura, in 1963. This is on the Pacific coast.

When George went to the kitchen for a snack, this illusion suddenly came to an end. As soon as he opened the swinging doors, a large rat jumped out of a pot of rice that had cooled on the stove. George stood there terrified as the rat disappeared behind the shelves. Letting the doors slam behind him, George found that he had lost his appetite completely. After this incident we avoided eating in the hotel. Yet in all honesty, the hygiene in Buenaventura's other restaurants was probably not any better.

Through friends in Cali, we learned of a small island just a short boat ride from Buenaventura that sounded like a fun adventure. Our friends highly recommended a fish restaurant there that we wanted to try. The island was charming and featured native-style houses, made of bamboo and featuring roofs made of leaves. We located the restaurant and were pleased to find that the fish and rice were freshly prepared, deliciously flavored with local herbs and spices indigenous to the area. As we looked for a restroom before starting our return journey, we discovered that the restaurant didn't have running water.

At the back of the kitchen was the "dishwasher." An older native man sat on a chair next to a large plastic pan filled with dirty dishes and a bucket of water. He would dip a cup into the bucket, fill his mouth with the water, and then spit it out in a steady, thin stream onto the dish in his hand as he rubbed a dishcloth over it. It was so comical that I was not even the least bit squeamish—to this day it just makes me laugh.

After a few days we finally had an opportunity to look at the VW car that had just been offloaded from the freighter. "*Scheisse!*" George said angrily. "Someone broke the vent window and stole the radio!"

He yelled at the customs officials, but they were indifferent to his issues with the condition of the car. Unfortunately, they were also indifferent to our mission, and our effort to retrieve the car from the impound yard failed. We returned home without the new car.

When Herr Zieschang arrived at our hotel, the first words out of his mouth were "I assume you parked the car out on the street."

We told him what had happened, and he was not happy. He threw a tantrum while standing in the entrance hall.

"No wonder they call this place the third world. Well, I intend to go to the top and show those idiots down at the dock who the boss is around here." That evening we discussed the matter further and decided to obtain the assistance of the Automobile Club of

Colombia. To get this organization and its influence on our side, we had to visit the club's office in Bogotá.

While sitting in the office in Bogotá, we were advised to return to Buenaventura. Handing us a document, someone from the organization gave additional instructions for speaking to the customs officials. "Calmly read aloud what is stated in paragraph one. Demand your rights. That should be sufficient."

It worked! Within an hour of arriving at the port, we had the keys to the car and a permit valid for three months, after which the vehicle had to be taken back to Germany or to some other country in South America. We never let these petty rules and regulations stand in our way, particularly when we needed reliable transportation. Persistence pays off, especially in a country that operates according to the "*mañana* principle": why do today what you can delay until tomorrow? We also became used to this aspect of life in South America.

Canary-yellow and brand-new, the car stood out like a sore thumb. Whenever we stopped at an intersection or were stuck in traffic, people just stared in amazement and envy. Several auto dealers attempted to buy the car, but that was against the law. Later we sold the vehicle to someone we knew, someone who had connections and was able to fabricate all the necessary documents. From rumors that floated our way, we knew that the car survived for at least another fifteen years, taking one happy owner after another up and down the many mountains of Colombia, as well as across its lowland plains.

Twelve years after selling the Volkswagen, we lived at the foothills of the Rocky Mountains in Colorado. There, one of the most unusual encounters of my life occurred. A group of South American students who attended the nearby University of Colorado held a birthday celebration at my restaurant. During the course of the evening, I began talking to a young man in the group. He was interested in hearing about my life in South America, and I expressed interest in his academic major. He had studied economics at the university in Bogotá but had been raised in Cali.

During his studies, he'd had an opportunity to research unsolved smuggling cases. He was very proud to have solved all but one of these cases, one that involved a woman who smuggled a Volkswagen into the country. According to his research, the woman obtained a permit to drive the vehicle for three months and was supposed to notify the authorities when the vehicle left Colombia. Here the paper trail ended. The documentation failed to indicate who the woman was or whether she had taken the vehicle out of the country. Slamming his fist on the table in frustration, the young man concluded, "And she probably sold it for a ton of money!"

Briefly stunned, I smiled and then began to laugh. I was about to solve this mystery for him. Placing my hand on his shoulder, I said, "You need not look any further, my friend. The woman you are searching for is sitting right across from you!"

With a straight face, he listened to my version of what had happened, and we laughed together. Wanting to be part of our funny discussion, his friends then joined us. I will always remember this event, the high point of a birthday celebration at the base of the Rocky Mountains, where the Colombian case of the smuggled Volkswagen was finally solved.

Suspiros Que Se Van—Sighs That Depart: Our Daughter Leaves Colombia, 1962–1963

Barbara had grown into a beautiful woman. Very popular and with many friends, she attended a party almost every weekend. Although George found it annoying at times, he took her to these celebrations and picked her up afterward. As our daughter became a woman, she probably made some of the same conclusions as I about Colombia. It was difficult for a woman in this country to realize her full potential in life. Machismo was so deeply embedded in this culture that the only freedom most women ever experienced was when they were girls and still innocent enough to play with the opposite sex.

After our daughter completed high school, she dedicated herself to finding a way to study art in the United States. While in high school Barbara had learned English, a skill she perfected by talking to our guests, many of whom were native speakers of the language.

In the summer of 1962, she met Bill, a young American teacher from Denver, Colorado. He taught English in a business school in Cali, and Barbara happened to be one of his students. It must have been love at first sight between the two of them. After just a couple of weeks, he proposed, and she accepted.

As much as I liked the young man, I hesitated to give my blessing. Barbara was still quite young, only eighteen years old, and she still depended on me for guidance and direction in her life. Furthermore, Bill had not yet received his university degree and he didn't have a trade skill, which brought up a very important question: how were they going to make it? Yet when children make up their minds, the objections of their parents often seem senseless.

Barbara and Bill at the tennis club, 1962.

Colombia offered hardly any incentive for Barbara to remain there. As a young teenager, she had decided that she wanted to study art in America, and it was a dream that only grew bigger. To ease our apprehension, Bill told us, "There's a terrific university in Denver where she can study art." Later, we found out that Bill was referring to the Art Institute of Colorado. Although not a university in the traditional sense of the word, it still presented an opportunity to learn commercial art.

Soon my daughter would leave the nest. This turning point in my life was difficult, as it is for many other parents. I attempted to prepare myself mentally for this important day and found it somewhat disturbing that George remained unemotional about the whole matter. "If it is okay with Mother, then it is okay with me," he said. I became absolutely enraged whenever he made comments like this.

In May 1963, Barbara left home and moved to Denver. I missed her terribly. Of course, we had our

George and Barbara in 1962, dancing at the tennis club where she had been crowned club queen.

mother–daughter conflicts, but nevertheless she was the greatest gift I had ever received. After she left, I felt so empty inside. Nothing replaced the void that followed. The most fulfilling part of my life came to an end.

Certainly, I wallowed in self-pity for a while. I then rededicated myself to working hard, to distract myself from having to worry about Barbara and whether it was going well for her. During my free time, of which there was very little, I began to read the most diverse variety of books, the foundation of my later interest in the esoteric, which I would explore in greater depth while living in America.[21]

Barbara's new life in the United States did not always run smoothly. She had to find her own way and overcome one challenge after another. We waited impatiently for her letters, which we

---

21   The esoteric is a collection of traditions including alchemy, astrology, gnosticism, gnosis, magic, mysticism, Rosicrucianism, and secret societies and their ramifications in art history, history, literature, and politics.

answered immediately. It was still difficult to arrange reliable telephone conversations. The operator had to connect us, and our conversations could be interrupted at any time. Bill's aunt offered Barbara a place to stay until the wedding. Although the 1960s brought about many social changes in America, the norms in Denver in 1963 were such that men and women did not live together before marriage. That would be simply too scandalous, especially for the young lady. Barbara kept herself busy by studying, helping out in the household, and planning her future with Bill. Amid all of this, she managed to obtain a driver's license.

It never seemed to fail—just when I started to settle into a routine, I once again received a letter from my employer, Zieschang, at the worst possible time. With his usual sense of urgency, he said that he desperately needed my help in Berlin. What was I supposed to do? Oh well, I could use this trip to Berlin as an excuse to see my daughter on the way back from Germany.

Shortly before my departure, a German immigrant managed to find me. He worked in the gold mines near Andagoya in the Department of Chocó, the same area where the Rockefeller Trust searched for the poison dart frogs. The difficult working conditions and the extreme climate had ruined his health. Through the German consulate in Colombia, he had learned about the possibility of receiving a pension. That is why he came to see me.

Along with numerous other Germans working in the gold mines, he once had belonged to the youth movement of the German Social Democratic Party (SPD). When the Nazi regime came to power, many of them had been forced to flee Germany. Some, like Willy Brandt, fled to Norway. Others made their way to Sternberg in Czechoslovakia. Meanwhile, the Christian Committee in England looked for ways to help these young men and purchased some land from the Colombian government. Shortly before the war began, some members of the SPD youth movement managed to settle on this land in Colombia. The Department of Chocó is located close to the Pacific Ocean, much of it is swampland infested by mosquitoes and other insects. The need to make a living forced many of them into the gold mines, including the man standing before me.

Now I had to tell him that the deadline for filing a claim had expired. He was devastated. Tears welled up in his eyes, and his chin started to quiver. Moved by his account of human misery, I decided to find a way to help him. "There is still a possibility. We need to talk to the SPD or someone in the German parliament." Then I gave him a reassuring slap on the shoulder and prepared for my trip to Berlin.

In Zieschang's office in Berlin, I discussed with him the matter involving the gold miner in Colombia. Frustrated, Zieschang responded, "My hands are tied, and nothing can be done. Do you realize that I have a whole stack of claims just like this one on my desk?" He started to walk off, and then suddenly he turned around and said, "I tell you what. I will give you the name and address of someone I know. He is a member of the SPD Party, a member of the Bundestag, and a lawyer like me. With his influence we might be able to help these forgotten people."

So, I met with the man and was very impressed by his open-mindedness and willingness to listen. He, in turn, arranged a meeting with Willy Brandt, who was then the mayor of Berlin and who would later become the West German chancellor.

Brandt quietly listened to my story. Finally, he reached for the phone and called several very influential people who were able to help. I then returned to Zieschang's office. To the total amazement and disbelief of my employer, within one day I had obtained permission to accept these applications and begin the process of awarding compensation to around twenty-five forgotten gold miners.

I felt the same satisfaction as when someone saves the life of another. The forgotten Germans working in the Colombian gold mines often married local women and raised their families in poverty in the most squalid of conditions. With a German pension they could send their children to school in the city, and armed with an education, those children could pursue a better life for themselves.

This victory had a bittersweet ending. Obtaining permission to accept the petitions was far easier than coming up with the funds for compensation. It took a long time for the payments to begin, and in the meantime many of the forgotten gold miners died. At least their children and widows could live a better life from the small fortune that eventually came their way.

I finally finished my work in Berlin. In Munich I visited with some friends for several days. Barbara and I managed to speak to each other on the telephone. "Mother, guess what? Bill and I have picked a wedding date—November 15, just before Thanksgiving. We decided just a couple of days ago. We've already spoken with the church and ..."

She's pregnant! I immediately thought. I could not help but wonder why they were in such a hurry to marry. But to my relief, she wasn't pregnant. After Barbara explained the reason behind this rash decision, I just had to laugh: they were coordinating their wedding plans with their vacation schedules. Moreover, my daughter made the point that they could save money doing things this way. By going on vacation right after the wedding, they could delay moving into the new apartment and save a month's rent. That was my daughter! Always the practical one, even when deciding to get married.

During my last day in Munich, I walked through the city and purchased material for Barbara's wedding dress. Overloaded with fully packed luggage, I flew to Stapleton Airport in Denver, which was undergoing a transformation from a small regional airport to an international one, reflecting Denver's growth from a rough mining and cattle farming town to a sophisticated city.[22] Cowboys did not fly, especially across the ocean to foreign destinations, but business people surely did.

I was nervous. I had known Americans in the past—the GIs in Berlin and the students and professors in Cali—but now I would meet them on their home turf. Then I found Barbara, her fiancé, and the prospective in-laws all expecting me and welcoming me to Denver, the Mile-High City. Bill's father and mother, along with his aunt and her family, gave me a very warm welcome. They were very nice people who placed all my fears of America to rest. America made a wonderful impression on me. I could see that everything was going well for Barbara. She was so fortunate to be marrying into

---

22   In 1964 Stapleton Airport became Stapleton International Airport.

such a nice family. They also treated me as if I were a member of the family. It had been such a long time since I had felt such warmth from people.

Unfortunately, I could not stay in Denver for the wedding. George needed me back at the hotel. I was sad to say goodbye to everyone. This would be the last time that Barbara belonged to me. Soon she would be married. Like every mother, I prayed for a happy marriage, one that would last forever and an eternity, filled with love. At times like this, you think of your own marriage and hope for the best for your child, that all the bad and unpleasant moments may never occur. The wedding took place in November 1963, shortly before President Kennedy was assassinated in Dallas.

Marriages Are Made in Heaven, but We Still Have to Live on Earth, 1963

The women of my generation were still raised according to Victorian standards and morals. Since we married young, women from my generation entered married life lacking any real-life experience and the maturity that such experience brings. Consequently, maturity often came with a heavy price. Our mothers had finally gotten a small taste of an emerging feminist movement when many countries granted women the right to vote. However, in postwar Europe the women's movement stood on the sidelines while most struggled with basic everyday survival. Many of the same women now had to fend for themselves. Millions of husbands never returned home from the war. This, in turn, empowered women with a new identity, which led to demands for social equality. Women no longer viewed themselves as dependent on men, but rather saw themselves as equal partners.

I accepted the marriage of my parents as a social institution and not a union between man and woman, bonded by companionship and sexuality. My first taste of romantic love was with my major. This relationship, however, remained very tender and innocent. My relationship with George finally changed my perception of love, the fairy-tale image of a knight in shining armor who was supposed to conquer my heart. However, George also remained a symbol of the past, a time shaped by war. I was always puzzled as to why George wanted me. I was so young and inexperienced. Perhaps he saw me as someone who would look up to him and admire his strength. He thought I could adjust and make him a good wife. The fact that I agreed to marry him probably gave him the self-confidence he needed at a point in his life when he needed it the most.

George married me when I was just nineteen years old. Though an adult in the legal sense of the word, I certainly lacked maturity. Without a doubt, the strong and independent woman I became in South America was a totally different person from the very shy and reserved girl that George married in 1942.

George's personality started to change after the second combat injury, when he almost lost his foot and was paralyzed for several months. All that he experienced during combat traumatized him for life. The constant fear of pain and death became too much. In such circumstances you must wonder what prevents a human being from becoming an animal or, even worse, a beast. Once the carnage is over, how does such a person reintegrate into "normal" society? George, like his fellow soldiers, was bound by that oath sworn to the *Führer*. Desertion was punished with death—those who hid in a barn, an attic, or the forest lived in constant fear of discovery.

After the war millions of people needed mental health counseling to recover from the wartime experiences, but the destroyed land had other problems. The scars always remained. That was our beginning! Those of us who survived eventually had to simply bury the tragedy and move on with life, discovering in the process that it is impossible to flee from your past, for it follows you everywhere.

Fantasy Is the Kite That Soars the Highest, 1965

Another year, another revolution. That was life in South America. Civil unrest and government corruption were ingrained into the culture, hindering any chance for social and economic progress. George and I were at a point in our lives when we needed to think about retirement. The value of the Colombian peso fluctuated wildly, meaning money we saved could become worthless overnight. On top of that, we retained our German citizenship, meaning we didn't enjoy what little legal protection the Colombians might have had. Nothing prevented the next dictator from seizing everything we owned.

Zieschang offered me an opportunity to manage his branch office in Paris, which served Jewish clients who had recently immigrated to the area from countries behind the Iron Curtain. This seemed to be an attractive offer. I had always connected Paris with elegance and cultural greatness. "Let's give it a whirl," I said to George.

During my next business trip to Europe, I stayed in Paris for two weeks and worked at the branch office. Afterward, I decided that this was not an alternative for us. I did not feel at home in this city. The work was frustrating and stressful. Most of the refugees showing up at our office could not speak one of the four languages I spoke, Spanish, German, English, or French. Instead, they mostly spoke Russian or Yiddish, which meant we had to work through interpreters, a slow and laborious process.

Furthermore, we worked in an old run-down building in a rather seedy part of town. My potential coworkers were stuffy and conservative, not a good match for someone like me, who was still relatively young and full of energy. Lastly, I realized that obtaining a work permit would be more difficult than I had previously imagined.

I sometimes wonder what would have become of George, a grumpy and unhappy man whose health was not the greatest, if I had accepted the position. I do not think he could have waited all day in some Parisian apartment for me to finally come home. Anyway, we had to cross Paris off the list.

What about America? Barbara and her husband now lived in Denver, and we could join them. Surprisingly, when we inquired about immigrating to America, we received a positive response. After the experience in Paris, the path before us was crystal clear. We made this decision together, knowing that in order to build our retirement nest egg, we needed to live in a country relatively free from civil unrest and corruption. So, George and I completed the paperwork for a green card and sent the documents to the US embassy in Bogotá.

After a few weeks, we received a response. My heart started racing. Excited, I tore open the envelope and found the following words: "Dear Mrs. Stein, your application for an immigration visa has been approved. Please obtain your work authorization in Miami, Florida."

Terrific! But where was the letter for George? Within a couple of days, we received another letter from the US embassy. "Dear Mr. Stein, please report to the United States Embassy for an appointment … to resolve certain discrepancies surrounding your application for an immigration visa." Period! No other details were contained in the letter. What could it be? We had filled out the applications together. What made his application different from mine?

We had a meeting with the American consul, a man we knew well from the time he'd stayed at our hotel, shortly after he first arrived in Colombia to accept his assignment there. As soon as we walked into his office, it was obvious that we had not traveled all this way for a pleasant chat about old times.

"Take a seat, Mr. Stein," the consul said tersely. While two armed military police officers stood at the door, the interrogation began. "You were an officer in the German Army?"

George nodded his head.

"Did you parachute behind enemy lines in the Soviet Union?"

"Huh?" said George.

The consul continued. "Did you spend time in Norway and Italy?"

"No," said George, confused.

"Do you speak Norwegian and Italian?"

"No," George replied again.

"Okay now. Do we have this straight? Your name is George Stein, and your parents are Max and Margarethe Stein …"

George was absolutely stunned. What was all this business about parachuting behind enemy lines and being in Norway and Italy? The interrogation continued, and only later would everything start to make sense for us.

After we submitted our applications for immigration visas, the FBI had conducted a routine background check, and the name George Stein had raised some flags. According to documents that had fallen into the hands of the US military, a secret agent by the name of George (Georg) Stein had engaged in various acts of espionage during the Second World War.

The reader may recall that during the Battle of the Demyansk Pocket in 1942, George was injured, his foot shattered by an enemy bullet. The Soviets took him prisoner, and a short time later, the Germans rescued him. George was taken to the hospital in Lötzen, where he nearly died of a severe infection caused by the injury. None expected him to survive. The German military had used the identities of fallen officers to create fictional identities for its secret agents. Since they thought George had died or would die, a secret operative assumed his identity to conduct espionage all throughout Europe. As the reader of this story knows, George survived and returned to active duty. However, Germany never corrected the service records. Consequently, the US government could not determine whether the real George Stein had been a spy during the war. After I had already been in America for six weeks, the American embassy in Bogotá finally resolved the matter, and George received his immigration visa.

Before I left Colombia, we sold the Residencia Stein to a Swiss woman, Mrs. Annamarie Frei, following a brief negotiation. Our friends and the numerous farewell parties made the departure difficult. Just like so many other decisions in my life, this one was painful.

Many of the residents of the hotel who worked for well-known, prestigious companies wrote letters of reference for us to help us get a new start in America. These letters were invaluable for obtaining credit to start our new business in the United States. Then, as now, whatever credit history one has established in their current country did not transfer to the next, making it near impossible to obtain loans without recommendations from well-situated people. These are the letters I still have in my files:

Cali, August 1965

TO WHOM IT MAY CONCERN,

Since 1958 I know Mr. George and Mrs. Francisca [sic] Stein as Managers of their "RESIDENCIAS STEIN" in Cali.

As KLM Manager I always recommend my clients to their Hotel/Pension as the best one there is in Cali.

In every respect their Pension/Hotel is managed in an excellent – way and a stay is always a pleasant one as both Mr. and Mrs. Stein are very attentive to their guests and provide an efficient service with an especial [sic] personal touch.

I am very glad to recommend them as hotel operators, in every part of the world.

KLM ROYAL DUTCH AIRLINES
District Manager for the South of Colombia

Harry L. Win

KLM-CIA. REAL HOLANDESA DE AVIACION
AGENTES GENERALES DE VIASA

Bogotá:	Teléfono	435-070
Barranquilla:	"	12-566
Cali:	"	76-233
Medellín:	"	23-505
Bucaramanga:	"	39-31
Cartagena:	"	13-346
Pereira:	"	57-77

KLM

Cali, August 1965

TO WHOM IT MAY CONCERN,

Since 1958 I know Mr. George and Mrs. Francisca Stein as Managers
of their "RESIDENCIAS STEIN" in Cali.

As KLM Manager I always recommended my clients their Hotel/Pension
as the best one there is in Cali.

In every respect their Pension/Hotel is managed in an excellent
way and a stay is always a pleasant one as both Mr. and Mrs. Stein
are very attentive to their guests and provide an efficient service
with an especial personal touch.

I am very glad to recommend them as hotel operators, in every part
of the world.

KLM ROYAL DUTCH AIRLINES
District Manager for the South of
Colombia

Harry L. Wins

CALI

CONSULTE NUESTRA COOPERACION CON IBERIA Y VIASA

- 365 -

August 13, 1965

TO WHOM IT MAY CONCERN,

Mr. Georg and Mrs. Franciske [sic] Stein are well known in this community and very well acquainted with the various nationalities in this area. They are an efficient and reliable couple who manage a surprisingly clean and well organized boarding house with the name of Residencias Stein.

I do not hesitate to recommend the Steins as far their honesty, ability and efficiency are concerned.

William Proskauer

District Traffic & Sales Manager,
Pan American Airways

PAN AMERICAN AIRWAYS

August 13, 1965

TO WHOM IT MAY CONCERN:

Mr. Georg & Mrs. Franciska Stein are well known in this
community and very well acquainted with the various nationalities in this area. They are an efficient and reliable
couple who manage a surprisingly clean and well organized
boarding house with the name of Residencias Stein.

I do not hesitate to recommend the Steins as far as their
honesty, ability and efficiency are concerned.

William Proskauer
District Traffic & Sales Manager

WP/nrd

CALLE 12 No. 5-11 - CALI, COLOMBIA

March 1, 1966 Cali, Colombia

TO WHOM IT MAY CONCERN:

This is to introduce GEORGE AND FRANCIS STEIN whom personally I have known in Colombia for over four years. I do not hesitate to recommend them to you as being wonderful people, honest and trustworthy and intelligent and industrious as well.

I hope that their residence in the United States will be a long and happy one and trust that their future endeavors will be successful.

Albert V. Bauer

General Manager,

Quaker Products

productos Quaker, S.A.

APARTADOS:
AEREO 2074
NACIONAL 368

CALI - COLOMBIA

TELEFONOS
41001 - 41002 - 41003
41004 - 41005
CABLES: "KWAKER"

T O   W H O M   I T   M A Y   C O N C E R N:

This is to introduce GEORGE AND FRANCIS STEIN whom personally I have known in Colombia for over four years. I do not hesitate to recommend them to you as being wonderful people, honest and trusworthy and intelligent and industrious as well.

I hope that their residence in the United States will be a long and happy one and trust that their future endeavors will be successful.

Albert V. Bauer
General Manager

AVB:pde

March 1, 1966

August 17, 1965 Cali, Colombia

TO WHOM IT MAY CONCERN:

It affords me great pleasure to give this testimonial of the excellent character and reputation of my friends Georg and Frederika [sic] Stein.

Until we found a house of our own in Cali, I and my family stayed for one month at the Residencias Stein and both Georg and Frederika [sic] did a wonderful job of making us feel at home. They were hosts par excellence. Everything we had heard beforehand about Residencias Stein proved to be an understatement. The accommodation was most comfortable and the meals left nothing to be desired. This speaks well of their organizing ability, for such an efficient attention is most difficult, if not impossible, to come by here.

We shall always remember with gratitude how well they cared not only for us but for all their guests, and we wish them well wherever they may go. With their personality any venture they go into cannot fail to succeed.

R.M. Ireson

Manager,

Royal Bank of Canada

The Royal Bank of Canada

Cali, Colombia

August 17, 1965

R.W. Ireson
~~M. ST. GODINEZ~~
MANAGER

TO WHOM IT MAY CONCERN:

It affords me great pleasure to give this testimonial of the
excellent character and reputation of my friends Georg and
Frederika Stein.
Until we found a house of our own in Cali I and my family
stayed for one month at the Residencias Stein and both Goerg
and Frederika did a wonderful job of making us feel at home.
They were hosts par excellence. Everything we had heard beforehand about Residencias Stein proved to be an understatement.
The accommodation was most comfortable and the meals left
nothing to be desired. This speaks well of their organizing
ability, for such efficient attention is most difficult, if
not impossible, to come by here.
We shall always remember with gratitude how well they cared
not only for us but for all their guests, and we wish them
well wherever they may go. With their personality any venture
they go into cannot fail to succeed.

August 21, 1965 Cali, Colombia

Dear Mr. Stein,

By means of this letter we are pleased to confirm in writing that the undersigned and his family stayed at your residence when we first arrived in Cali.

The service and food served while we were there was most satisfactory, especially taking into account the difficulty of operating this type of business in an area such as this.

The undersigned is pleased to highly recommend Mr. and Mrs. Stein whom have been known to us personally and as bank clients, and we consider them to be capable people of a very good standing in this community and completely worthy of confidence.

Very truly yours,

Richard C. Hessert

Manager, First National City Bank
(affiliate of Citibank)

FIRST NATIONAL CITY BANK.

APARTADO AEREO 123

CABLE ADDRESS "CITIBANK"

CALLE 11 No. 3-50

CALI - COLOMBIA

IN REPLY PLEASE QUOTE

RCH:hsg

August 21, 1965

Mr. Georg Stein
Ave. 4 Norte #4-01
Cali

Dear Mr. Stein:

By means of this letter we are pleased to confirm in writing that the undersigned and his family stayed at your residence when we first arrived in Cali.

The service and food served while we were there was most satisfactory, specially taking into account the difficulty of operating this type of business in an area such as this.

The undersigned is pleased to highly recommend Mr. and Mrs. Stein whom have been known to us both personally and as bank clients, and we consider them to be capable people of a very good standing in the community and completely worthy of confidence.

Very truly yours,

Richard C. Hessert
Manager

March 9, 1966 New York & Cali

TO WHOM IT MAY CONCERN:

I have known Mr. and Mrs. George Stein for the past six years during which they have maintained an excellent "pension" that has been used from time to time by our staff and families during the process of getting settled in, and departing from, Cali. Without exception, the staff who took advantage of the Stein's hospitality have been extremely satisfied with both the living arrangements and the cuisine, and happy with the atmosphere created by the owners.

Guy S. Mayes, M.D.

Assistant Director, Rockefeller Foundation

THE ROCKEFELLER FOUNDATION
NEW YORK

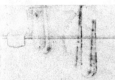

FUNDACIÓN ROCKEFELLER
APARTADO AÉREO 6555
CALI, COLOMBIA

CABLES: ROCKFOUND
CALI (COLOMBIA)

March 9th, 1966

TO WHOM IT MAY CONCERN:

I have known Mr. and Mrs. George Stein for the past six years during which they have maintained an excellent "pensión" that has been used from time to time by our staff and families during the process of getting settled in, and departing from, Cali. Without exception, the staff who took advantage of the Stein's hospitality have been extremely satisfied with both the living arrangements and the cuisine, and happy with the atmosphere created by the owners.

Guy S. Hayes, M.D.
Assistant Director

GSH/glc.

My former hotel, now called the Hotel Stein Colonial, is still in business.[23] In April 2006, I flew to Cali to celebrate the fiftieth anniversary of its founding. Heinrich "Enrique" Frei is the current owner, having taken over the business from his mother. During my visit, he and I delivered a speech in Spanish to the Cali Society, describing the history of the hotel.

Residencia Stein, Cali, Colombia in 1965

Brochure cover from the fiftieth anniversary of Residencia Stein, later known as Hotel Pension Stein, and now called Hotel Stein Colonial, in Cali in 2006.

---

23   The website is www.hotelsteincolonial.com.

At the Hotel Pensión Stein's anniversary celebration, I am speaking about the founding of the hotel while the current owner, Heinrich Frei, stands next to me.

CHAPTER 4

Lyons, Colorado, United States, 1966-1990

Northern Colorado, United States

The First Months in Colorado, 1966

I went to America alone in March while George waited in Colombia for his visa. In Miami I obtained my green card, and then I flew to Denver. In Colorado I noticed a drastic change in the weather. I had finally become accustomed to a tropical climate, and I asked myself whether it would now be possible to endure long, cold winters again.

Would our marriage improve in America? At this point it seemed as though things could not become any worse between George and me. Cynicism shaped our married life. We were like two match heads close to each other, where one could ignite the other in a split second. While George waited for his immigration visa, he stayed in Colombia with our friend Nadja and her family. Although I wrote several letters to George, he never responded. Later, Nadja told me that George had taken a turn for the worse during those final weeks in Colombia. He spent a lot of his time at parties and drank heavily.

After I arrived in Colorado, I went shopping and bought myself some winter clothing. Once again, I owned a warm winter jacket. From time to time, I thought of my former life in Cali. I also thought of the plans that we had made and how we had not yet acted on them. Clearly, I had way too much time on my hands and needed to find something to keep me busy, something active so that I wouldn't wallow deep in thoughts of doubt.

One of the few diversions I could find was translating for the honorary German consul in Denver. Through this work I obtained new clients for Zieschang. Some of the new clients had fled Germany in 1940. They had made their way through Russia and had eventually settled in Shanghai, one of the few Chinese cities willing to tolerate refugees. In 1949 the communists under the leadership of Mao Zedong took control of mainland China. The living conditions for foreigners residing in Shanghai deteriorated, and in the early 1960s, many immigrated to the United States.

The Rocky Mountain West became my new home, which in the 1960s was relatively unspoiled and uninhabited.

Perspective: Colorado

Colorado is characterized by majestic mountains, old mining towns, modern cities, oil wells, fertile farmland, and ranches with enormous herds of cattle. Its capital, Denver, started out as a small mining settlement, when gold was found on the banks of the South Platte River in 1858. Known as the Mile-High City due to its elevation, 5,280 feet above sea level, Denver lies on the Great Plains of America, at the eastern edge of the Rocky Mountains, a mountain chain that stretches from the northernmost part of British Columbia in Canada to southern New Mexico in the United States. Before the arrival of the white settlers, tribes of Native Americans passed through Colorado in search of bison, millions of which roamed wild on the great American prairie, a vast grassland.

In 1970, Colorado had 2.2 million residents. The largest city, Denver, had a population of a little over one-half million. Boulder, home of the flagship campus of the University of Colorado, was a city of 66,870. Due north sixteen miles, lay Lyons, a town of 958 people.

On January 26, 1915, President Woodrow Wilson signed the legislation that created America's tenth national park, Rocky Mountain National Park in Colorado. During the Great Depression, men from the Civilian Conservation Corps built Trail Ridge Road to facilitate the movement of visitors through the park. Among the highest paved roads in the United States, Trail Ridge Road is usually open from late-May until late-October. The rest of the year a huge blanket of snow covers the road. Although maintenance crews start to remove the accumulated snow in mid-April, sometimes the road is not passable until the beginning of July. The main road through Lyons leads from the flat plains through the rolling foothills and then winds its way through steep mountains to Estes Park and the eastern entrance to Rocky Mountain National Park.

Reunion, 1966

After three years of separation, I could finally spend time with my daughter. She was now an adult, and it took a while to adjust to this version of her, in her home, married. And she and Bill had to adjust to new housemates as they had graciously agreed to let us stay with them while we found our new home.

At the end of April, George finally came to Denver. But before George could leave Colombia, the government required him to obtain a certificate showing that he had paid all of his taxes. For three days he roamed from one government office to the next in an unsuccessful attempt to obtain the necessary document. As George was about to leave yet another government office, now in a state of total despair, a minor bureaucrat spoke up and asked, "How much would you pay if I were to issue the certificate right now?" It was plainly evident that the bureaucrat did not possess the legal authority to issue the document. Nevertheless, George approached the counter and laid out several 1,000-peso banknotes.[1] Within a half hour he had the certificate in his hand, which had cost him a lot less money than if he had obtained the document the legal way, which would have meant paying the outstanding tax liability.

It took George only a few days to fall in love with Colorado. "*Wunderbar*," he said. "This is what I call easy living," he said, putting to use a new phrase he had picked up somewhere.

Before determining what to do with the rest of our lives, we decided to take a long vacation in Europe, something we had earned after eleven hard yet beautiful years in South America. This would be the first true vacation we had taken together since the journey to Austria in 1943. George and I would have to get used to spending time together without work to unite us. The money I earned by working for Zieschang provided the means through which we could afford this trip, a real luxury for us. George especially looked forward to spending time in "his city"—Berlin. We made our grand tour of Europe, visiting Copenhagen, Hamburg, Berlin, and Vienna. I finally felt compensated for the many lean years that had followed the war.

Twenty-one years after the end of the Second World War, West Germany had won back its rightful place in Europe, leading a

---

1   The exchange rate at that time put the value of each note at about 30 US cents. He paid less than $10 for the document.

phenomenal economic recovery. The businesses were well-stocked with goods, offering anything you could ever want to buy. In total awe, I strolled along the sidewalks, window-shopping and gazing at the luxury items that were totally unattainable in Colombia. Of course, I could not resist spending one German mark after another in the department stores. Throughout West Germany, unemployment was extremely low. In fact, the West German government had to invite guest workers from other countries to fill an acute labor shortage.

Perspective: The German Miracle

Between 1949 and 1973, the West German economy made a dramatic recovery. Germans refer to this period as the *"Wirtschaftswunder,"* meaning "economic miracle." The United States contributed to the postwar recovery by providing the Germans with economic assistance through the Marshall Plan, a debt the Germans later repaid. The currency reform of 1948 also spurred economic growth. When West Germany was created in 1949, Chancellor Konrad Adenauer and his economic minister, Ludwig Erhard, adopted a social market economy, which balanced the best of capitalism with social justice. The new West German government also wrestled with Lastenausgleich, a word that is difficult to translate into English, but which implies an obligation to share the burdens of war, particularly compensation. Legislation was passed to compensate Germans who had lost property during the war, compensation funded by those who had not lost property during the war. This legislation helped all Germans benefit from the postwar recovery.

Finding the Place to Hang Our Hat, 1966

When we returned from our vacation in Europe, we still had no idea what we were going to do with the rest of our lives. Staying with Barbara and Bill was nice, but it was a temporary solution and we needed to get out of their hair. The Colorado lifestyle was calming. Here you still found the character of the Wild West, much like what we had seen in films, including men who wore western-style shirts, cowboy boots and hats, and blue jeans, while walking bowlegged with a thumb tucked in their waistband.

We started to search through the real estate listings for restaurants and hotels. To be fair, we could not really judge the value of a listing because we had not yet become accustomed to the American way of life. I remember how we overlooked ads for properties in towns such as Vail and Aspen. We certainly missed out on an opportunity to make a huge windfall from these vacation destinations, which had just started to become popular. Aspen, for example, is now regarded as the American equivalent of St. Moritz. But in the mid-1960s, Vail did not even have paved streets. Today, in these popular resorts that draw the rich and famous, you would be lucky to buy a doghouse for under a million dollars. Another factor that limited our property choices was the fear of taking out a large business loan and being tied to the bank for an eternity.

During this time of social and political turmoil, when the United States sent thousands of its young men to fight in the jungles of Vietnam, a ray of sunshine entered our lives. Barbara was expecting a baby! This newest citizen of our world was due at the beginning of February, about the time of year when the groundhog Punxsutawney Phil would look at his shadow to determine how many weeks of winter remained.

We obviously wanted to live near our daughter during this important time in her life. Fortunately, we were able to buy a restaurant in Lyons, Colorado, about an hour's drive northwest of Denver. This town stands at the edge of the Great Plains as a gateway to the Rocky Mountains. Highway 36 connects Lyons with the city of Estes Park and Rocky Mountain National Park, two very popular tourist destinations. During the summer months it is obvious that this highway was never designed for the traffic it now carries.

As we planned the move to Lyons, cooler autumn weather set in, and with that, the aspen leaves changed colors. It was a spectacular time of year, with mountainsides aglow with shades of green, yellow, orange, and red.

Like every new beginning in my life, this one too was plagued by growing pains. Daily routines—the security of knowing that when you wake up, everything will be almost the same as yesterday—are highly underappreciated. George and I were now middle-aged adults, a time in life when it is not that easy to begin anew. We attempted to adjust to the new culture as best as we could, even in the smallest ways, like how we combed our hair and what we wore. For us, it became important to return to a normal everyday routine. Over time we made the adjustment, adopting many of the habits and customs of our new neighbors.

Many Coloradans regard autumn as the best time of year. By early October the majestic mountain peaks are once again covered by snow, and in the mountain meadows, the rut is underway, announced by bugling bull elk that can weigh over seven hundred pounds. The high-pitched mating call can be heard miles away and is a warning to the other bull elk to keep their distance because this bull intends to protect his territory and his harem of cows. When an intruder bull challenges the dominant bull, a dramatic spectacle takes place where these massive animals lock antlers and try to assert their dominance. During this time of the year, I could sit and listen to the bulls bugle for hours—nature, pure and simple.

Lyons, found in the narrow mouth of the St. Vrain Valley, is surrounded by sandstone cliffs. There we purchased the Cliffside Café, named after the sandstone cliffs directly behind the restaurant. In fact, many of the buildings in this town, including our new restaurant, were constructed from sandstone, mined from nearby quarries.

Perspective: Lyons, CO, 1966

The city of Lyons is named after Edward S. Lyon, who in 1880 purchased 160 acres of land, upon which he intended to start a cattle ranch. He found a large sandstone deposit on his property and decided it would be more lucrative to sell sandstone slabs to Denver, an expanding city that needed sandstone to construct sidewalks. Swedish and Finnish immigrants flocked to Lyons, as well as the nearby towns of Beech Hill and Noland, to work in the sandstone quarries. Extracting the sandstone was a laborious and dangerous process. To remove the slabs, workers scored the sandstone where the cut was to be made. Then workers drilled holes every six inches with a metal punch. Wedges were then placed into the holes, which finally produced the cut.

By 1905 many of the quarries near Lyons had closed because Denver had begun using cement to build sidewalks. The Lyons quarries received a much-needed boost in 1918 when Charles Klauder, an architect from Philadelphia, met with George Norlin, president of the Board of Regents for the University of Colorado. Klauder presented a plan for constructing future university buildings in Boulder using an architectural style found in Italy, one that incorporated sandstone slabs in the exterior walls. Norlin and the regents endorsed the plan and left behind their architectural legacy at the University of Colorado's Boulder campus. Today several quarries still operate near Lyons to supply building material for the construction industry. [2]

In the days of horse-and-buggy travel, Lyons had been a popular resting point for people heading into the mountains. Even earlier, before the arrival of white settlers, Native Americans of the Ute tribe lived there. They were the last tribe to be forced onto a reservation by the US government, pushed out of Colorado in 1861 and settling in eastern Utah. By the mid-1960s, however, local Indian artisans had returned to the area around Lyons and established a following among collectors.

The Grand Opening, 1966

Of all the property listings we considered, the Cliffside Café best suited our needs; it was relatively close to our daughter and near the mountains, and it had a garden and even a small house. Nevertheless, Lyons was not exactly the most exciting place to live. This rural working-class town of around nine hundred inhabitants, lacked the cultural diversity we had encountered in Colombia and the cultural traditions we had in Europe.

---

2   Ironically, in 1969 Lyons became home to a large cement plant, founded by the Martin Marietta company and now operated by Cemex Corporation.

Long before the war, this building had belonged to a man of Native American descent who sewed moccasins by hand. In one of the rooms, the floor consisted of slate tiles that, over the course of many years, had become highly polished and uneven by the boots of the people who worked there. This caused the floor to become slippery and even dangerous in spots. Later, the Loukonen brothers bought the property and turned it into a diner. They also owned a large redstone quarry in town and other land. These hardworking men became our good friends.

At first, we had no interest in renovating the restaurant. Priority number one was to accept things as they stood, even if some of what we saw appeared rather tasteless. We simply wanted to work, to do something useful. It felt good to be gainfully employed. But we soon realized that we had to make at least some changes to make this a workable enterprise, and the plans that we tossed back and forth, as well as the hard work, did our marriage good. We got along better than we had in many years. Our new endeavor required that we concentrate on the immediate future. We divided between us the work that needed to be done. George bought the new furniture. Together we drew up plans for a new bar. I planned the renovation project.

Right from the start, everything ran smoothly. We opened early in the morning for breakfast, and before the door a crowd waited impatiently for their pancakes. It was now late autumn, the beginning of hunting season in Colorado. I buzzed from one table to the next, taking care of men who spoke enthusiastically about their hunting success. I found it both exciting and perhaps even romantic.

Our new home seemed to be made of money. During the day the locals came to drink coffee and gossip. In the evenings the restaurant filled with people from Longmont, Boulder, and other nearby cities, including Denver. They expected a gourmet dinner or at least what they thought a gourmet dinner should be. Eventually, we decided to change how the restaurant looked, to renovate completely, offering something new, unique, and stylish. The first step was to find a new name.

Again, fate struck in the best way. Through my work with the honorary German consul, I was able to meet a man who had organized an exhibition in Denver on behalf of the city government in West Berlin. "Wow," he said. "Your restaurant looks terrific! Just like something I would find in Berlin. The only thing missing is the bear."

He was referring to Berlin's mascot for hundreds of years, a black bear, which is depicted on the city's coat of arms. His remark made me wonder, *could we use Berlin's bear as our mascot?* Why not? It was no sooner said than done. After his return to Berlin, our newfound friend sent us hundreds of small stuffed bears and other promotional materials. We expanded the restaurant and spruced up the interior. That is how the Black Bear Inn was born.

Our English left much to be desired. But we managed to cope with the everyday spoken English, adapting to the western accent that had a certain rural quality, with a definite air of cowboy twang. Since I am not a native speaker of English, I often maintain a clear recollection of the moments when I am introduced to new colloquial expressions. One day, after I returned from a shopping trip in Denver, one of the waitresses approached me.

Black Bear Inn, Lyons, Colorado, in 1967.

"A woman was looking for you, Mrs. Stein."

"Who then?" I said.

"I didn't ask," she replied.

"How old was she?" I asked.

"Ida know. She's an old bag, like you."

Now in German "an old bag" simply means an old bag. Of course, you find at least two different meanings in English. I never determined who was looking for me, and I learned that "Ida know" was her way of saying "I don't know."

The waitstaff we hired always seemed to have a colorful background, which while typical for the restaurant business in America, our staff seemed blessed with an extra dose of eccentricity. Another one of my waitresses came from Germany. She was a blond, tall, beautiful woman who had real restaurant experience, and she helped me keep my sanity.

Another memorable one was a student at the University of Colorado. She was a double-size lady but always pleasant. She was from Texas, and in some ways, she reminded me of the women of *Dallas*, a popular TV series during the 1980s. One day I asked what she studied at the University of Colorado. "Well, I don't exactly know," she said, "but I sure like my professor."

While organizing a party for a group of Japanese businessmen, I asked her to type the menu from handwritten notes I had given her. While proofreading her work, I noticed that she had typed "Oysters-Rock-a-fellow." "You were supposed to type Rockefeller!" I yelled.

"Aw, Mrs. Stein," she answered in her long southern drawl. "In Texas we don't need any Rockefellers."

The dealings with the staff had overwhelmed me at first. In Colombia it had been much easier, and I certainly did not have the burden of so much paperwork when I hired somebody. Now I paid a variety of employment taxes and had to contend with a minimum-wage law. In what seemed to be a crash course, I soon learned all the legalities of operating a business in Colorado.

One morning after I opened the restaurant for breakfast, a tall cowboy walked through the door, so tall he had to duck his head at the entrance. It was like meeting John Wayne, or at least his twin brother. He stepped over to the counter, sat down, and said, "A stack with coffee."

I gave him a puzzled look, not understanding what he meant by "a stack." "What was that?" I asked.

With a chuckle, he said, "Lady, four pancakes with maple syrup. You must be new around here."

That's how we met Ray "Sticks" Palmer, the Boulder County water commissioner. Throughout the growing season farmers may have to rely on irrigation to water their fields because of insufficient rainfall. He made sure that everyone received his or her fair share of the water from the reservoirs, which helped agriculture thrive in this region.

The pancakes we served to Sticks must have been quite good because he frequently came back for more, sometimes with his wife. After a while we became good friends, and through this friendship we met many people not only in Lyons but also in nearby Longmont and Boulder.

At the new restaurant I had to set aside the style of cooking I had acquired in Cali and learn how to cook all over again. Colorado was beef country. Lots of cattle in the fields meant lots of beef on the plate.

Lyons was typical small-town America. The nicer houses stood along the main street, behind which stood small and less well-maintained houses painted in a variety of colors and packed close together. It was like a Potemkin village. This area was certainly different from Cali, yet Lyons had a certain charm. Somehow one felt safe among all those tiny houses and the friendly neighbors.

It was not very practical for us to shop in Lyons. The town had only a very small grocery store and numerous shops that catered to the tourist industry, some of which sold carpets, T-shirts, and ice cream. Some of the other shops sold American Indian artwork and artifacts.

Lyons was another world for us. In Cali we had lived among the upper class in a vibrant city, but now we were among the working class in a sleepy working-class town. Although I enjoyed the simplicity of this town and its people, I sorely missed our maids in Colombia, who were available whenever we needed them. The mountain area around us featured large houses and ranches, but the workers and civil servants lived in town. After a while we met many interesting people and learned much of the history of the Rocky Mountains and the stories of some old-timers.

One of the more unusual features of Lyons was the "laundry." This business had not only washers and dryers for clothes but also showers for the men who worked the stone quarries, a dirty job to say the least. Few houses affordable to the quarry workers possessed a bathtub or shower, so it was necessary to provide the quarrymen a means of washing themselves. During the summer these men often bathed in the St. Vrain River, which was also the public swimming hole for the kids.

On Saturday evenings Lyons came alive. Inside the gymnasium at the local school, square dancing took place. The women wore wide skirts with lots of tulle, white blouses, and flat shoes. Their men wore western-style shirts, cowboy boots, and of course, Stetson hats. As they danced, pairs changed partners according to the instructions of an announcer, who also called out the steps. While the band played, those who danced showed their enthusiasm by yelling and whistling. It reminded me of some of the dancing in Europe in the beer halls.

George and me in front of our restaurant soon after our welcome signs were installed in 1969. Note the Colorado red rock used as parking barriers and as bricks on the façade of the building.

From Lyons a hiking trail led to

Noland, an old ghost town. At one time as many as 1,900 people had lived there. The town once had provided a dance hall as well as saloons, where gamblers and other adventurers could try their luck. When I walked through Noland, it seemed like I had once seen the same town in some western film. I noticed that some of the buildings were still very much intact. The stillness that now replaced the hustle and bustle of city life seemed strange and lonely. At the end of town, I found a cemetery. As I looked at the gravestones, I noticed that many had died young, in an era without modern medicine, when diseases were often fatal and when the smallest injury was potentially deadly due to infection.

I often walked to Noland during the lull between the lunch and evening business. Sometimes I stood in the middle of the deserted street, and after closing my eyes, I tried to imagine how life must have appeared here, women wearing long dresses, men with dusty trousers, screaming children running up and down the street as someone played the piano inside the saloon. It was a fantasy, surely, but it entertained me.

Perhaps too often, I wondered why I had exchanged an exciting life in Colombia for a boring life in Lyons. Now I was stranded here, and my only remaining choice was to make the best of the situation. Anyway, Lyons had one special reward. I could soon spend time with our happily anticipated first grandchild, a gift that compensated us for the lack of daily adventure. Slowly, we sank our roots into the hard Colorado soil.

With our new business, one of the hurdles we had to overcome was Colorado's restrictive alcohol laws. Since a liquor license would mean increased sales, we hired a lawyer to help us. As in many places, there was a distinction between a beer and wine license and a liquor license that allowed businesses to sell whiskey and other hard alcoholic beverages. With the Lawyer's help, we soon obtained a beer and wine license to complement our attractive new menu, but not the license to sell cocktails.

We watched with envy as a nearby restaurant, the Foothills Inn, did a booming business because it had a full liquor license. The establishment was able to draw in the crowds that attended the University of Colorado football games and other events.

But the serving of alcohol had an unpleasant side too. Inside the only western bar in Lyons, fights and brawls occurred at least once a week. It seemed rather strange that we had to fight tooth and nail for a license for our restaurant, a business that did not attract the riffraff like the bars. Repeatedly, our application for a full liquor license was rejected. The official reason was the "nearby" University of Colorado, about fifteen miles away in Boulder. They didn't want to encourage underage drinking.

One evening luck rained down on us again when an older couple came to the restaurant for dinner. They ordered a double bourbon on the rocks. We had plenty of rocks but not a drop of whiskey. "What?" the man said, looking surprised. "You can't pour us bourbon? Well, we are not going to stand for that. I tell you what—I'll call Andy."

It turned out that Andy was the secretary of state for Colorado, and we later learned that the customer was the state treasurer. On the Monday that followed, we received a call from his office. We were told to expect a visit from somebody important. Somewhat nervous, we hoped this new development would be a step in the right direction. That very afternoon, two chauffeur-driven vehicles arrived in Lyons, bringing the secretary of state and his entourage. His first order of business was to inspect our restaurant and to get some of the details from our attorney about our many applications for the liquor license. Then he told our lawyer to call the mayor of the City of Lyons and demand that he come to the restaurant immediately. When the mayor arrived, Andy simply said to him, "Give these people the license."

It seems the mayor was the reason we were being denied, for whatever his reasons. A couple of handshakes among men wearing cowboy hats, and the deal was concluded. Two days later we had the license in our hands, much faster than the usual waiting time of four to six weeks for those who managed to qualify for one or, in our case, to be rejected for one as we had been previously.

At the beginning of the Christmas season, we proudly presented our new German restaurant, with an elegant menu, a wine list, and a fully stocked bar. Several companies held their holiday celebrations at our restaurant, a huge windfall for us. We now employed a chef along with several other employees, but I truly missed our loyal maids in Colombia. Although our restaurant specialized in German cuisine, the new grill we bought proved indispensable. We could cook the much sought-after steaks to perfection, and our customers were happy.

We celebrated Christmas Eve with Barbara and Bill, and together we looked forward to the approaching birth of our first grandchild, a new life that would bless our family. I had already gone shopping in Boulder and Denver and bought baby clothes and shoes. I loved to do such things. How wonderful it was to visit all the specialty shops or even a large department store, where I could match a dress with a pair of shoes within the same building. Never had I imagined that it would be so easy to equip a baby with all that he or she would need. Before Barbara was born, we had to make all of her clothes ourselves, from whatever material we could find.

January brought one snowstorm after another. Almost every morning, George had to shovel out the car. We just hoped our car would start when we needed to go somewhere. The winter scenery looked very beautiful. However, the warm pullover I had bought proved inadequate against the bone-chilling temperatures. After so many years in the tropics, winter weather was a rude awakening. On top of that, for the first time in our lives, we had to learn how to drive on icy roads to avoid sliding into the ditches. Of course, we had never encountered such conditions in Cali. And although it had certainly snowed in Berlin when we shared the car with Grandpa Max, when the roads were iced over, we simply parked the car and waited out the storm.

Opa Max's Legacy, 1966

The house inherited by Barbara had been placed under the control of a trustee, to be released when she reached her twenty-first birthday. One day in 1966, we received a letter from the trustee informing us of some sort of wheeling and dealing on the part of George's sister Ulla and her husband: shortly before Barbara turned twenty-one years old, the house had been sold without our permission for well below market value.

George refused to become involved, even though he should have to protect the inheritance of his daughter. I attempted to take matters into my own hands and contacted a lawyer. Unfortunately, I could not accomplish anything alone because I lacked legal standing. George and I should have fought together to protect the inheritance, or at least George could have given me power of attorney. I just cannot understand why he was so disinterested in obtaining a favorable outcome for his daughter.

For her part, Barbara was happy to receive the money that she did get, so that she and Bill could buy a new, modest house for themselves. She had no context for the value of the large house from Opa Max or the potential it had to grow in value and set them up for a life of security.

So ended the great dream of Max Alexander Stein, a man who had worked hard to protect what he had acquired in this world. Even when he was an old man, the large double house had symbolized his values. He had hoped this house would leave behind a legacy among his descendants. This dream went to the grave with him.

Amy, 1967

In February 1967, my granddaughter Amy was born. According to Indian belief, her birthday is the first day of spring. She certainly seemed like a sign of spring.

She was born with a full head of hair, enough to make a ponytail for her first photo. Those tiny fingers grabbed at anything that passed before them. I carefully held this small miracle in my arms just hours after the birth. I was so nervous because she seemed so fragile. And that is how it happened: the birth of a child into a multinational family. According to the saying, the gift of happiness belongs to those who unwrap it.

George was overjoyed. He adored his grandchild, loving her almost as his own daughter. Whatever anyone could say about George, and despite all his faults, nobody could ever deny that he was a devoted grandfather.

During Amy's first weeks of life, I was somewhat jealous. Often, I could not leave the restaurant, yet Bill's parents had lots of time to spend with our granddaughter. Even George got to spend more time with the little one. As soon as Amy could walk, she became a regular guest at the Black Bear Inn. I tried my best to spoil my granddaughter, giving her all the things that I had not been able to give Barbara. Life had given me a second chance to accomplish what had not been possible after the war.

The first signs of spring appeared in the Rockies. Thousands of very loud geese flew overhead in a V-shaped formation on their way back to Canada. Then the pleasant temperatures in March surprised us almost as much as the heavy snowstorm that followed in April. Life in Colorado certainly had a learning curve. Our neighbors, the wild animals, were far different from anything we had ever experienced, much like the new climate. One Sunday a brazen raccoon darted into the restaurant through the back door, wanting to make off with some of our groceries. George chased after the little rascal and sent him back outside, where he belonged. These raccoons became a real nuisance. They constantly rummaged through the trash containers, attempting to find something to eat, and in the process, they made a real mess.

When Amy was two, she had a bad encounter with a skunk. Around Easter time we told our granddaughter about the Easter Bunny and what he brought the little boys and girls. In hindsight, we should have shown her some pictures of this animal. On Easter Saturday, Amy was playing outdoors when she saw a skunk directly in front of her. Impulsively, she wanted to pet the "rabbit." After all, the Easter Bunny was nice to children. She started to run toward the skunk with her little arms outstretched. The skunk, who felt threatened, sprayed Amy with a direct hit. When she got a whiff of what the "Easter Bunny" had done, she started screaming, and of course we came to the rescue. We had to burn her clothes. Trying to remove the scent from her skin was another matter. One of the neighbors suggested a remedy, and within a half hour, Amy sat in a bathtub full of tomato juice. Ever since then, I think she has had an aversion to Easter.

Our restaurant flourished. I devoted endless hours of work to creating a menu that would steer our customers away from the traditional steak dinners.

In April 1967, George sat down to have something to eat. After swallowing a spoonful of soup, he was overcome with pain. The ambulance rushed him to the nearest hospital, and the doctors determined that he was suffering from a peptic ulcer. They operated on him immediately. George remained in the hospital for three weeks. After he was discharged, he needed several more weeks to fully recover. For years he had suffered from heartburn. The excess coffee, cigarettes, aspirin and alcohol, as well as his bad eating habits, had finally taken their toll.

Barbara, Amy, and me in 1969.

It bothered me to see how George suffered. To distract myself, I worked long hours in the restaurant. During this time of crisis, the outpouring of help from friends and family was very touching. Bill and Barbara came over quite a bit, helping in the restaurant even though they already had a lot going on in their own lives.

The Cold War Touches Lyons, 1968

One of the regular visitors to the restaurant was Dr. Thomas Riha, a professor of Eastern European history at the University of Colorado in Boulder. He often brought students or colleagues with him. Professor Riha was born in Prague, and we had much in common. Whenever possible, I joined him at the table, and often we talked for hours about our shared experiences.

A few times he invited us to his house for dinner or for a party when a special visitor was in town. I met his brother-in-law, Dr. Jiři Červeny, an attorney from Prague on one occasion.

Early in the summer of 1968, he flew to Eastern Europe and Asia to spend time with colleagues and relatives. During this journey he spent time in the Soviet Union, in Moscow and Samarkland, which is now the second-largest city in Uzbekistan. The relationship between us had become so friendly that he found time to send us some postcards. At the beginning of September, he walked into the restaurant with Hana, a young student from Czechoslovakia, now his fiancée.

Walking into the restaurant, he yelled out to me. "Franziska, I want to hold our wedding reception at your place." Then he took me aside and whispered in my ear. "Perhaps you know someone who can help me. I have a nephew who just escaped from Czechoslovakia. Now he's living in Vienna. I am sure you know how he must feel. I want to bring him here. Is there anyone who can point me in the right direction?"

What could I say? I really was not a person of influence and certainly was not someone with political connections. However, many of our guests had such connections. I promised the professor that I would try my luck. The next day around noon, two lawyers were eating in the restaurant. I approached them and laid out the facts of the matter as best as I could. After listening carefully to what I had to say, one of them responded, telling me that they might be able to do something. I then introduced them to the professor. A week later, a woman by the name of Galya Tannenbaum came into the restaurant. She was very muscular, looking almost masculine.[3] I'd hardly had a chance to seat her when she told me, "I heard there is a Czech professor who has a nephew in Vienna. When can I meet him?"

"I'm not his secretary. He is probably busy planning the last details of his wedding coming this Saturday," I told her. She got up and left immediately.

I was taken aback by her rudeness and aggressive attitude. But I soon forgot about the encounter as I had business to attend to.

As the professor's wedding day approached, I spent most of my time preparing for the reception, which left little time to take care of anything else. Then the big day finally arrived. The guests were an interesting mixture, including intellectuals from different areas of Eastern Europe and colleagues from the University of Colorado. Everyone appeared to have an enjoyable time as the couple mingled with the guests at the reception.

Then Ms. Tannenbaum showed up. I had no idea she would crash the wedding reception. She demanded to meet Professor Riha right then. They went into the barroom, which we had closed for the reception, so they could talk in private. They sat in there for over an hour talking while the wedding guests grew more and more impatient. The bride was certainly not happy about her new husband's absence during their wedding celebration. The professor finally returned, and Tannenbaum disappeared. But the mood was gone, and the party ended quickly thereafter.

After the wedding, Riha and Tannenbaum would meet every few days in my restaurant. They would talk for an hour or two at a time,

---

3   Tannenbaum used several names, among them the first name Galya and Gloria and the last names Tannenbaum, Forest, McPherson, and Scimo. People called her "the Colonel."

sitting close together, speaking quietly so they wouldn't be overheard. I don't know what they discussed, but their body language did not seem warm the way two friends might meet over lunch.

Over the next several weeks, the professor spent a lot of time at the restaurant, sometimes meeting with Tannenbaum and sometimes arriving with his wife. I noticed that the relationship between him and Hana had soured considerably. They lacked the togetherness you normally find with newlyweds. Completely absent was that gaze of mutual attraction. Though I didn't know why, something seemed odd about this couple.

About two months after the wedding, Riha's nephew, Zdenek Červeny, landed in Denver. Not long after that, he began coming frequently to the Black Bear Inn alone with Hana. Moreover, they had the look of mutual attraction that was now missing from Riha's relationship with his new wife. Their closeness was certainly too intense for a newly married woman and a single man. But it wasn't my business, so I never said anything to them or Riha about what the others were doing.

Over the course of 1968, I paid close attention to news reports about the civil unrest in Czechoslovakia. I was horrified by the events that unfolded in there. It seemed to me as though I had lost my home a second time. I certainly felt for the people of Czechoslovakia, regardless of their ethnicity. The Soviets were vicious.

Perspective: Prague Spring, 1968

In January 1968, Alexander Dubcek became the leader of the Communist Party in Czechoslovakia, replacing the unpopular Antonin Novotny, whose economic policies caused the people of his country considerable hardship. Dubcek sought to retain the communist system but instituted a series of political and economic reforms that he called "socialism with a human face." His government tolerated freedom of the press as well as freedom of speech. Soon the reform movement grew. In what became known as the "Prague Spring," thousands of people participated in demonstrations held throughout Czechoslovakia. Many demanded an end to the

Communist Party's monopoly on power and free elections. Other Warsaw Pact countries were concerned that the Prague Spring would spread beyond the Czech borders, something that would undermine the other communist governments behind the Iron Curtain.

On the night of August 20, 1968, tanks and soldiers from the Soviet Union and members of the Soviet Bloc—Bulgaria, Poland, East Germany, and Hungary—invaded Czechoslovakia. Dubcek was arrested at gunpoint and taken to the Soviet Union. The Czechs met the invasion with passive resistance instead of armed confrontation. Still, seventy-seven Czechs were killed, and more than one thousand were injured. Meanwhile, the Soviets forced Dubcek to rescind his reform program. They give him one of two options: either institute "normalization," or Czechoslovakia would become a Soviet colony. The Soviets planned to make Bohemia and Moravia a protectorate of the Soviet Union, similar to what Hitler did, and Slovakia a Soviet Republic.

Dubcek returned to Czechoslovakia and remained the leader of the Communist Party until April 1969. The Soviet Union stationed 100,000 soldiers in Czechoslovakia, where they remained until 1991. Soon after Dubcek's return the Czech government censored the press and banned public protests. On January 16, 1969, Jan Palach set fire to himself in Wenceslas Square in Prague to protest "normalization." He became a national hero.

Citing Czechoslovakia as an example, in November 1968, Leonid Brezhnev, the general secretary of the Soviet Union, proclaimed what is known as the Brezhnev Doctrine, announcing that the USSR would use force to prevent any Warsaw Pact government from straying too far from the communist standard set by Moscow. Twenty years later, a future leader of the Soviet Union rescinded this doctrine, an act that ultimately led to German reunification.

The Cold War Touches Me, 1969

At the beginning of 1969, I made another journey to South America. Like in previous years, I spoke with clients and accomplished some essential tasks on behalf of Zieschang. When I returned, George waited for me at the airport. I saw a strange look on his face. "What's going on?" I asked him. "Did something happen at the restaurant?"

George answered, "The Czech professor you know has disappeared. The FBI now wants to talk to you."

The next day, two FBI agents appeared at the restaurant. It's funny how in moments like this, certain things remain embedded in your mind. I remember that they drove a beige car with huge antennas on the trunk.

They asked some rather basic questions—what I knew about the professor, where he might be, whether I had ever been to Prague, what his family was like, and so on. I really could not help them in this matter. I saw and spoke to the professor only when he came to the restaurant. Before leaving, the agents confiscated some photos I had, which showed the professor inside the restaurant with friends.

Slowly, the events surrounding the disappearance unfolded in press reports. One night, about a month after Professor Riha had filed for divorce, neighbors saw Hana screaming for help from the window of her and Riha's house. She insisted that Tannenbaum had attempted to kill her. Neighbors who came to the aid of the young wife noticed the strong odor of ether inside the rooms. Hana reported that she had heard whispering voices inside the house. Shortly thereafter, she left Boulder and settled in New York City.

The Boulder police investigated the incident and interviewed both Professor Riha and Tannenbaum. Inside the house they found a container with ether in it. Five days later, Professor Riha failed to appear either in class or later at a meeting he had scheduled with friends. Nobody could find him, and soon the police became involved in the disappearance. A short while later, the police arrested Tannenbaum and accused her of falsifying bills of sale for Professor Riha's house and car. On top of that, she was accused of forging a check for a charter aircraft flight.

The police did not have enough evidence—namely, the body of Professor Riha—to charge Tannenbaum with his murder, but they were able to obtain a conviction on forgery and burglary. Tannenbaum pled not guilty by reason of insanity and was committed to a state mental hospital, where she died several months later after committing suicide with a cyanide pill.

Even today, the circumstances surrounding Professor Riha's disappearance remain a mystery. The FBI questioned me several more times, but I could not give them any new leads in the case. We were asked to cooperate with the investigation, and on one occasion, George accompanied the lead detective and his partner on a search of Tannenbaum's house. They went from room to room through the house, looking for any clue regarding Riha's disappearance. While in the basement, George found Riha's wallet and passport. It indicated that Riha did not leave of his own accord but did not lead to much because they had no way to know how it got there.

Even though I often saw the professor talking to Tannenbaum, I never knew what they said to each other. Later I testified in court and provided testimony about the property Tannenbaum might have taken from Professor Riha's house, but that was it.

In the early 1970s the *Denver Post,* one of Denver's daily newspapers, took a special interest in this story and ran several articles about the disappearance on the front page. Perhaps this disappearance involved Cold War intrigue between East and West. Such a conclusion is supported by reports that the disappearance severely damaged the working relationship between the FBI and CIA.

Was this professor a secret agent or even a double agent? The newspapers reported that a year after the professor disappeared, he was seen in Moscow and Czechoslovakia.[4] But I never saw him again and have often thought about him and what might have happened to him.

In November 1970 I visited relatives in Vienna. While planning this journey back in Colorado, I had looked forward to a calm and relaxing vacation in Central Europe. Things turned out differently when Professor Riha's nephew, Zdenek, asked me to make a side trip to Czechoslovakia. I agreed to visit with some of his relatives

---

4   For additional information refer to David Wise, *The American Police State: The Government against the People* (New York: Random House, 1976), 261–73. Also see Eileen Welsome, *Cold War Secrets: A Vanished Professor, A Suspected Killer, and Hoover's FBI* (Kent: The Kent State University Press, 2021).

in Prague, including his father, Jiři Červeny, whom I had met the one time. He asked me to bring back some of the professor's books and jewelry and a few other personal items.

I found Prague terrible, as though someone had turned back time. The government had started to arrest opponents of the communist regime. Everyone feared the Soviet military. Professor Riha's relatives in Prague invited me to a small party. A young couple sat in a corner of the room, looking very inconspicuous. While the rest of us talked, the couple quietly disappeared. Later, someone in the party noticed they were missing, and we began to look for the young couple in the apartment. The only place they could be was the bathroom, and that door was locked. After pounding on the door and calling for the couple to come out, we forced our way in, only to discover the young couple next to each other on the floor. They had extinguished the flame inside the small hot-water heater and died of asphyxiation when gas flooded the room. We were absolutely stunned. As the police and ambulance crew walked through the apartment, we discussed among ourselves what could have driven this young couple to take their lives. Perhaps they belonged to the protest movement and feared arrest and torture, or worse, a life a bleak existence under the oppressive communist regime.

This event ruined the rest of my stay in Prague. The deceased couple were about the same age as Barbara. The gray November weather made everything even more depressing. I thought about the expulsion order that had forced me to leave Czechoslovakia in 1945. As the result of ethnic cleansing, I had become a nomad in the West. In the process I had found a better life than many of my former Czech neighbors, something Beneš never would have intended.

In my luggage I packed the books and other items for Professor Riha's nephew as well as the requested jewelry. I decided to take the night train to Vienna, so I would not have to spend another night in Prague. On board, inside my sleeper cabin, I began to think about crossing over the border into Austria, which grew closer and closer. Surely, the Czech border police would want to question me about all the jewelry in my luggage. After all, I was a foreigner and, on my way, back to the United States. Perhaps they would throw me in jail for a while and conduct a lengthy interrogation.

I came up with a plan. Right before we arrived at the border, I put in my hair curlers and applied a thick layer of facial cream to my forehead and cheeks. A few minutes later the border police started to walk through the cars, and one of them knocked on my door. I opened the door and looking at him as innocently as possible, I asked the policeman in English, "What can I do for you?"

Embarrassed, he quickly apologized in German, closed the door, and continued his rounds.

In Lyons I met with Zdenek and presented him with the things I had brought back from Czechoslovakia. I was happy to have this whole affair over with, and I hoped that I would never again see up close how the Cold War affected individuals, squashing their hopes and stealing their lives.

The Great Flood, 1969

Soon our second winter in Lyons was over, and within a short period of time, the standing snow had melted giving way to green grass and spring flowers. A storm came on May 4 that parked in the mountains north of Denver, raining continuously for four days. The usually unremarkable St. Vrain River became a raging torrent. The water level climbed over the banks of the river and flooded the highways cutting off access to many mountain communities. The flooding destroyed homes and businesses. The water supply for Lyons was also destroyed. Government officials considered issuing an evacuation order for Lyons, and many people were stranded by raging waters. After 86 hours, the rain stopped, having deposited nearly twenty inches across the northern front range.

Slowly, the waters receded, and life returned to normal. The Black Bear Inn did not have any damage and we saw a little uptick in business from many of the relief workers and gawkers that came through town. The water treatment plant was soon back up and running, so we no longer had to boil the tap water.

This flood spurred state and local government officials to develop a better flood-control strategy, regulating development near rivers that would be harmless if not for human settlement. With development, the wild untamed landscape that greeted the first pioneers in the St. Vrain Valley has disappeared.

The attempts at better flood control from this time were later undone both by poor zoning that allowed many homes to be built very close to the river over time and by the wrath of Mother Nature. In September 2013, another massive flood hit the canyons of the front range of the Colorado Rockies. By the time it was over, more than half of the Lyons population had been displaced by damage to their homes and to the roads, bridges, water supply, and power lines, and 20 percent of the homes were destroyed. The St. Vrain River charted a new course in some places, moving as much as a mile from its original path in one area. The Black Bear Inn also was damaged, even though it was not on the river, with more than a foot of sludge left by the waters that had come through town.

Remembrances of the Black Bear Inn, 1970–1971

The glamorous and progressive side of America was thousands of miles away. Lyons remained a part of the western frontier. Denver, the twenty-seventh largest US metro area in 1970, had a downtown with two high-rise buildings, several steak houses, and numerous saloon-style bars. It had not yet undergone the transformation that would make it the great, modern city that it has become. The most recognized building in Denver then was the Brown Palace Hotel, which reminded me of the Hotel Adlon in Berlin. The city also had several museums with remarkable collections, but the buildings that housed them then were unimpressive.

Whenever a snowstorm blew in, I felt cut off from the rest of the world. I remember sharing these feeling of isolation with George. He looked at me, shrugged his shoulders in resignation, and gave me some sound advice. "Mother just close your eyes and say the following words: '*Lyons-sur-Mer*.'"

"Lyons-by-the-Sea." I have to give George credit for putting a romantic spin on the new surroundings, even though the nearest beach was over a thousand miles way. I was stranded here for a while, and the only thing I could change was my attitude. In a book about Lyons, I once read the following words by Walter Mason:

If I had the tongue of Bryan

I'd give that tongue no rest

In boosting Lyons

The jewel of the West.

Though it might not be a glamorous jewel, Lyons still had its redeeming qualities. We adapted to life in Colorado, a state famous for skiing in the winter and hiking in the summer. One activity I could never endure was fishing. I was far too impatient to stand for hours at the edge of a stream or sit on the banks of a lake, not saying a word to avoid frightening the fish. But like South America, Colorado also offered plenty of opportunities for horseback riding, something I really did enjoy.

In January 1970 I made another one of my working trips to South America. This time I spent more time in Guatemala than in the other countries. Thinking back on this adventure, I must shake my head in astonishment and wonder whether I was crazy. I rented a car and drove through the countryside, a dubious decision as bandits frequently attacked cars traveling through that area, robbing them and in some cases, kidnapping the occupants for ransom. I wanted to travel to Antigua, the old capital city. Located in the mountains, the city was home mostly to descendants of the Mayans. There you could find exquisite huipil dresses and colorful scarves, which were a regional specialty.

On this journey, I attended Sunday Mass in Chichicastenango in an old church built by the Indians. In this primitive structure I found the sermon uplifting. As I looked around, the interior appeared rather plain, but those who worshiped here looked very colorful in their native attire. It seemed that all members of each household attended Mass, including the pigs and chickens. Outside, a semicircular staircase led from the church down to a small open-air marketplace. There a lively exchange of goods took place, complete with the typical South American odors. As the sun started to set, I felt hungry, and I found a small restaurant nearby. I sampled the local tortillas filled with meat and local vegetables and enjoyed some herbal tea while a cat sat on my lap. In the interior courtyard a woman played a very moving folk melody with a marimba. She wore the traditional Indian dress and an unusual piece of cloth wrapped around her head, which reminded me of the turbans seen in India.

Soon after I left Guatemala, a revolution took place, one that ravaged the land and ruined the textile industry around Antigua, destroying the old looms that once wove colorful fabrics. Many people fled to bordering countries to escape the bloodbath, and a centuries-old cultural tradition suddenly came to an end.

Before I returned home, I thought about my marriage. Sometimes we experienced a lot of tension and sometimes less, depending on George's moods and health. However, I was bound to him by the ring I wore on my finger. Why did I stay? Was it fear? A sense of duty to the expanding family? Or maybe it was to set an example for Barbara, whose own marriage had started to deteriorate. Was it my destiny to be chained to George until "death do us part"?

George desperately needed me in Colorado. He continued to suffer from his painful stomach ulcer. When I returned, his condition had deteriorated to the point that he now spent most of the day in bed. This lasted for several more weeks before he was finally able to recover well enough to move about on his own. It seemed like George took longer to recover from his illnesses than other people. Over the years he had lost much of his stamina. Of course, as he often confessed, George made his medical problems worse by not following the advice of his doctors, particularly with his excessive drinking. No doubt he drank to wash away the memories of his loveless upbringing, the terrible things he witnessed in the war, and the heartless rejection he faced from his family on his return from the POW camp. But the mental scars that George carried were beyond the ability of anyone to cure.

Amy frequently visited us in Lyons. No matter how busy I was in the restaurant, the weekends always belonged to her. By the time she turned four or five, Amy could peel potatoes, peel and devein shrimp, and garnish the plates with a sprig of parsley. I remember how the busgirls would play with her, which made it impossible to send her to bed.

In the spring of 1971, as business started to pick up after the winter lull, the state widened the highway in front of the restaurant. Though we welcomed the road improvements, working around them was just another hassle I didn't need.

The summer brought lots of tourists to our restaurant and Lyons. I always felt like there were not enough hours in the day for me to take care of everything. To obtain supplies for our restaurant, we had to travel to Denver, which meant at least two hours on the road in addition to the time spent doing the shopping. We often hired staff without any experience, mostly students who needed some extra pocket money. Rarely did an experienced cook or waiter apply for a job at our restaurant. Those with experience had no desire to move to a small town like Lyons. The inability to hire experienced employees reminded me of the situation we had encountered in San Agustín. At least our staff in Lyons could read and write.

Good professional dishwashers were hard to find in this part of rural Colorado. Although we had a dishwashing machine for the tableware, we washed the pots and pans the old-fashioned way, with a sink full of hot soapy water and elbow grease. Don, our dishwasher at the time, arrived an hour late for work one day. When he came through the back door with a box underneath his arm, he uttered a quick "sorry." Then he placed the box on the desk in my small office and started to tackle the huge pile of dishes stacked up for him. An hour later I made a quick phone call in the office and noticed something was moving inside the box. Whatever it was I didn't want it loose in my office, so I didn't open it.

"Don," I yelled to him. "What exactly do you have in the box?"

"Ah, don't worry," he said. "It's just a couple of rattlesnakes."

It was more like ten rattlesnakes, which was about eleven too many. I looked at him without saying a word because I was too stunned to speak. From my walks around town, I knew you could often find snakes around the cliffs, where they liked to coil up and warm themselves in the sun. That was fine, but I sure was not about to tolerate any of them in my restaurant. Boiling mad now that I had collected my thoughts, I pointed the way out the door with my thumb. That was the end of Don's employment at the Black Bear Inn. Then I stepped up to the bar and poured myself a double brandy.

For each captured rattlesnake, a person could receive a reward of ten dollars, not a bad side job for a dishwasher.[5] A company in Estes Park extracted the venom to produce an antivenin, a serum doctors gave to help those bitten by rattlesnakes. Even I benefited from this serum. Next to our restaurant stood a small shed where we stored garden furniture during the winter months. The shed was positioned directly underneath the cliffs, an area where snakes took in sun during the day. At the end of September, I started to place furniture in the shed, and with all the noise this caused, I did not hear the rattle. I saw the snake only when I was bitten. Fortunately, the weather had already turned cold, and the snake was somewhat lethargic. Consequently, he could not deliver a full dose of venom into my ankle.

George took me to the hospital immediately. The doctors forbade me to sleep for twenty-four hours to lessen the danger of cardiac arrest. I had to keep moving, despite the pain in my foot, which had swollen to twice its normal size. For three days the doctors kept me in the hospital, where I was administered the lifesaving serum, perhaps from Don's snakes.

These and many other stories remain buried deep inside the treasure chest of my mind, which I open occasionally to rummage around inside. Lyons has certainly changed, though it is still a charming rural town. Today it is considered chic to live in the snake-infested hills above Lyons (forever *Sur Mer* to me).

---

5   Roughly $65 in 2018 dollars.

There Are No Saints without a Past nor Any Sinners without a Future, 1971

The Vietnam War changed American society. Young people became politically active and protested the war. Along with the peace movement came a desire to break free from the social norms of the previous generation and its middle-class values. This was the birth of the hippie movement, a phenomenon of the 1960s, the counterculture that sought an alternative lifestyle. On the positive side, they strove for peace and nonviolence, yet they also popularized the use of dangerous recreational drugs, such as LSD, heroin, and cocaine.

As I read or listened to media reports of the Vietnam War, I recalled hearing the same lines before, reports of a distant war taking the lives of many soldiers, who were part of an army that could not lose the war, in a conflict whose real progress was heavily censored. Often these reports filtered down to me in Lyons through a black-and-white television set instead of a state issued radio, but the story was the same.

Amy was four years old. I can still see her right in front of me with her baby blanket in one hand and two fingers from the other hand stuck in her mouth, something like Linus from the *Peanuts* cartoons. Whenever she visited the restaurant, she made a beeline for the kitchen, where she yelled, "Good morning!" at the top of her voice. The cooks and waitstaff then yelled back, "Good morning to you!"

At the end of March 1971, another trip to Colombia and Central America stood on the agenda. On short notice I decided to add another destination to my itinerary, the Yucatan Peninsula in Mexico. When I arrived at the airport in Merida, I looked every bit a Colorado girl, wearing winter clothes and boots. I inhaled the refreshing tropical air, wanting to relish this moment. Then reality caught up with me, which usually happens at the worst possible moment. The airline had lost my luggage.

I was not happy. Standing there in my winter clothes, I wondered how I could buy tropical clothing on a day when the stores were closed because of a holiday. I was devastated because I thought I had now lost my chance to visit Chichén Itzá and Isla de las Mujeres. Two young men noticed my frustration, and I became even more upset when they approached me. I calmed down a little when they generously offered to take me to both destinations.

"Why don't you ride with us tomorrow? We'll pick you up at your hotel." Both looked nice. Moreover, I wanted badly to reach Chichén Itzá the following day to observe a rare event that occurs only on the vernal and autumnal equinoxes, when the setting sun casts a figure of a snake on the Castillo, a Mayan temple.

"Tal vez," I told the young men, which means "maybe." I was torn between desire to go the temples and concern that going with two strange men might not be a good idea.

In the hotel I started talking to two women from the United States, and as soon as I explained my misfortune, they took pity on me. They loaned me a bikini, a pair of Bermuda shorts, and a rather long T-shirt from their own luggage. The maid then suggested that I try my luck at the open-air market, where I found a *huipil*, a native dress made from colorfully embroidered white muslin. I also bought a pair of *huaraches*, the traditional sandals worn in this region. After climbing into my new outfit, I felt like a new person, like one of the natives. That evening I did not think of the two Romeos from earlier – *Surely their offer was not serious*, I thought. Instead, I studied the bus routes and schedules, trying to determine how I could reach my destinations using public transportation. Later I drank a margarita with the two American women who had loaned me their clothes.

At about nine o'clock in the morning, the receptionist woke me out of a sound sleep. "Your companions are waiting for you in the lobby."

I sprang out of bed, and even though I was still half-asleep, I managed to throw on my clothes and gather up the few things I had with me in a bag. After inhaling a cup of coffee in the reception area, I looked outside at our transportation for the day: a Mercedes cabriolet. What luck!

With a smile and pointing to my dress, one of the young men jokingly asked, "Are you the same woman from yesterday?"

On the road I found out that of one of them made a living as an archaeologist. The other man, Octavio, worked as a business consultant for an American company. I found both men very charming and kind.

What an adventure! Here I was at age forty-eight in a remote corner of Mexico, racing down some bumpy road in a convertible with two men at least twenty years younger than me, both of whom I had just met yesterday. Octavio looked very European, not having the dark hair and complexion shared by many Mexicans descended from the indigenous people. During our drive I found that he was a very courteous man and had impeccable manners.

The tropical heat became almost unbearable when we finally reached Chichén Itzá. This temple complex had become a center of Mayan influence in the region between 600 and 1200 AD. Many of the visitors to this site have a keen interest in the Kukulcan Pyramid, often called El Castillo, Spanish for castle. Kukulcan was the Mayan equivalent of Quetzalcoatl, an Aztec god and the most important of the creator gods, depicted in religious art as a feathered serpent. The Kukulcan is a step pyramid. Nine separate layers are stacked on top of each other, with each layer smaller than the one underneath. On all four sides, a staircase ascends to the top of the pyramid. The Mayans designed this structure to cast a shadow on the northern staircase at sundown on the vernal equinox. Following the movement of the setting sun, the shadow of a diamondback snake winds its way down the northern staircase, terminating at a statue of the feather serpent, depicted with its mouth wide open.

We climbed to the top of the Kukulcan Pyramid, where we enjoyed a fantastic view of the complex and caught a refreshing cool breeze, a bit of relief from the oppressive heat. From this vantage point we saw small groups of tourists arriving and leaving. The surrounding forest concealed many of the ruins, which extended far across the valley. Later in the afternoon, the shadow finally appeared on the pyramid. A shiver ran down my back, as though I could feel the presence of the Mayans who had been here thousands of years ago.

After sunset we drove in the direction of Isla de las Mujeres and took the ferry across the water to the island. At that time, it was impossible to find luxury accommodations there. We had to settle for something more basic—perhaps you might even call it rustic. Despite the long day that had filled my senses, I still was not tired. I eavesdropped on the conversation between my companions and some of the locals, who joined us for a simple meal. Around midnight I decided to end this day by taking a refreshing swim in the warm water. As I relaxed, the tide brought gentle waves that rolled over me, soothing my skin.

I said goodbye to my traveling companions and the next day caught a bus back to Merida. There at the hotel I saw the American ladies and thanked them for their generosity as I returned the clothing they had lent me. My suitcase had finally arrived just in time for me to continue my journey.

From Merida I flew to Guatemala, where I met my son-in-law, who just happened to be in the country on a business trip. He was working for Pan American Airlines leading travel tours around the world.

Octavio often wrote to me, but I never responded to his letters, thinking he wanted something from me that I could not give. He often sent me postcards from places he visited. Once I received a piece of jade from Taiwan. Another time he sent me a book, which found a permanent home on one of my bookshelves.

Many years after my journey to Mexico, while I was standing in the kitchen of my restaurant, one of my employees approached me. "A man came in earlier today looking for you. I told him you were not here, and he said he'd return."

That evening the man walked into the restaurant with his family. I recognized Octavio immediately. "Franziska," he said, "it was not easy to find you!" He then introduced me to his wife and children.

Later that evening, I opened a bottle of champagne in honor of the occasion. While we sat together, his wife mentioned something that embarrassed him a little. "You know, Franziska, he has always talked about you. Octavio even told me that he would always remember you."

I offered him a warm smile. Indeed, I would always remember this gentleman and our adventure at Chichén Itzá. The ancient

Mayans must have written a blessing for us in their hieroglyphs, so that we would never forget each other and what we had experienced there.

The Disappearance and a Separation, 1971

From the age of four, Amy often stayed at the McGraw Ranch with George. She inherited her love of horses from him. In fact, "horse" was among the first words that she spoke, a word she used to describe anything with four legs. At a very early age, she would make her way to the horse stable whenever possible. George was especially pleased that his granddaughter had developed such a keen interest in horse riding. His granddaughter, whom he deeply loved, fulfilled his dream of having someone to whom he could pass along this special interest, one that he had acquired over the course of a lifetime. During the long and terrible war on the Russian front, the horses sometimes had given him the companionship he needed and the strength to endure the separation from home and loved ones.

The McGraw Ranch, a rustic dude ranch, was located high in the Rocky Mountains, north of Estes Park.[6] It consisted of a main house surrounded by several small cabins that had been built on the property over a period of many years. There was a barn for the horses and their equipment and a bunkhouse for the staff. A river ran through the property, which fed an ideal pond for trout fishing. Fish caught during the day were grilled outdoors the same evening while the guests enjoyed a sundowner, the six o'clock cocktail. Here George found his paradise. Once he was there, we had a hard time getting him to leave nature and the quiet life and come home again.

The journey to the ranch presented somewhat of a challenge, a drive over winding roads and through Devil's Gulch. Once we left the confines of this valley, we saw open range where cowboys roamed over rough terrain, just like in the westerns.

---

6   The ranch was established in 1884 and was a working cattle ranch until 1935, when it was converted to a guest ranch by the McGraw family, who operated it until 1973. The McGraw Ranch is now listed in the National Register of Historic Places and is part of Rocky Mountain National Park.

None of the horses at the ranch were fast or fancy; they were cattle horses, little sturdy quarter horses. They were reliable on the trail and had good sense—and they needed every bit of it because some of the visitors were not usually experienced horse people, and more than a few were just plain stupid. Each guest was held responsible for the horse assigned to him or her. In the mornings, after saddling their horses, the guests rode with a guide into the nearby mountains. There they enjoyed a picnic among the rocks before returning to the ranch in the late afternoon.

One evening I received a phone call and learned that Amy had disappeared. I was scared to death and drove immediately from Lyons to the McGraw Ranch. There I scolded George for being so careless and not looking after her. The evening before, she had attempted to feed bubble gum to one of the black bears that spent most of the evenings and nights stalking trash cans. On the plus side, nobody had heard the scream or roar of wild animals, but still we were about ready to panic as we made our way in between and around the buildings, yelling out her name. Finally, the ranger came to help, and we spent the night searching for her in the mountains on horseback.

When the sun started to rise, we returned to the ranch exhausted and distraught. During the night I had kept thinking about how Amy loved horses, and something told me that this little tidbit of information might be the clue that would solve her disappearance. Just before I could call Barbara to give her an update, the stable boy walked up to us with a smile on his face and motioned with his arm. We followed him into the stable. Snuggled up in the corner on a bed of straw, our little angel slept soundly. The horse next to her looked at us with his large dark eyes, as if to say, "Just let her sleep." Gently, George picked her up and carried her to bed.

Those days in the great outdoors formed an unforgettable part of Amy's youth. To this day I am so grateful that we could give this little girl something we had not been able to give our own daughter. Amy's interest in horses continues to this very day. In the past she has taken part in large horse shows, returning home with a dirty face and buckets of ribbons. Riding has given her a sense of direction in life and has built character and self-esteem, and just like they did for her Opa, the horses have given her companionship and comfort when she has needed it most.

We had seen the signs earlier, but now it was official. Barbara's marriage came to an end. On Valentine's Day, Barbara called us to say that she had just been served with a letter from a lawyer. The letter stated that Bill wanted a divorce. Even though we had known the marriage was in trouble, the letter shocked us deeply. In the fall of 1972, the divorce became final. Barbara seemed relieved, happier than she had been in months.

Shortly before Thanksgiving in 1972, while Barbara was walking behind the restaurant after business hours in the dark, she tripped over a root protruding from the ground and hurt her ankle badly. We took her to the hospital immediately. The doctors determined that she had a compound fracture of the ankle. They performed surgery, and Barbara remained in the hospital for several weeks. Around Christmas she came home. Still, she had to wear a cast around her foot for another six weeks. This situation was complicated for everyone. George stayed with Amy and Barbara in Denver while I looked after the restaurant in Lyons. Fortunately, business had fallen off during the winter, and the more leisurely pace made this arrangement manageable. Caring for her during the busy summer season would have been unthinkable.

My old car, an Opel, finally bit the dust. I bought myself a new Audi, or rather George bought the car for me. The model we purchased turned out to be notoriously unreliable, plagued by numerous mechanical problems. In America these cars became known as "Hitler's Revenge." For one of these problems, I made an appointment with a repair shop in Denver and used the opportunity to visit Amy.

On occasion, when the business in the Black Bear was slow, a young Colombian woman named Dolly who worked for us would watch Amy when she needed a babysitter. On this day, when I arrived at the house, I found Amy and Dolly sobbing. According to Dolly, they had been talking about their families and about how Amy's mother worked and didn't have a husband anymore. Inspired by their discussion, the five-year-old had gone to the phone and dialed 911. The dispatcher was a woman, so Amy hung up. She dialed again, and again, never getting a male dispatcher. Soon a squad car arrived with lights flashing.

"Daddy moved out, and Mommy is lonely," she told the officer. "Mr. Policeman, would you like to meet my mommy?"

The police officer looked down at Amy and scolded her. "Young lady, that is not a good reason to call 911. That's a naughty thing to do." Then he drove away, leaving Amy extremely disappointed.

The young woman did not really understand all that had just happened as her command of English was still developing. Yet when Amy started to sob uncontrollably, she was also moved to tears. The following week, a short notice appeared in the local newspaper's police reports, describing a "juvenile" who had made a prank phone call to find a date for her mother. Amy just wanted to take control of her own life and help her mother find someone to love.

Dolly was the daughter of an engineer at a gold mine in Chocó. He had been a restitution-claim client of mine and we had been successful in getting compensation for him. His dream was that his daughter would go to America, and I needed the help. So, she came to live with us. We converted the little storage shed next to our house into a room for her. The shed was made of cinderblock with a solid roof, had electric power, and we made it cozy by installing carpeting with padding on the floor and wood paneling on the walls. She had to walk the ten feet to our house to use the bathroom, and as primitive as it might sound, it was a nice room.

Dolly worked for us for many years, learning the restaurant trade inside and out. She met a Slovak man, Rudy, and after they married, opened a café in Boulder serving breakfast and lunch. She worked hard, and the café was successful for over twenty years before she retired. We remain friends to this day.

The Greatest Sin Is Complacency, 1973

George traveled to Germany once a year to take a series of spa treatments to help with his war injuries and to restore him, yet his health continued to deteriorate. He had let himself go and depended on me to make all the decisions for him. He suffered chronic back, leg, and stomach problems, and his excessive drinking and smoking were surely not helping him.

When he flew away in June 1973, a major construction project was underway at the Black Bear Inn. We had been successful with the restaurant and wanted to live in a nicer home than the little house afforded—it was only about eight hundred square feet in size, and we were feeling stifled by it. So, we took the plunge. In Cali we'd had to renovate two different buildings to suit our needs, but the project in Lyons occurred on a much grander scale. Two months later, a spacious apartment for us had been built above the restaurant. It didn't change our commute much, given that we just walked down the stairs instead of across the yard, but the space was like a ray of light, releasing the burden of closeness imposed by the old cottage.

Business continued to thrive, with many of our clients booking large parties and bringing friends who became repeat customers on their own. We met many very interesting people, which helped keep my energy up. I devoted many hours to studying various cookbooks, attempting to create unusual dishes and desserts. I worked nonstop to fulfill the obligations of a perfect host.

It was the middle of January on a cold winter evening. Shortly before closing time, a handsome man still sat at the bar. Then a married couple from Lyons walked into the restaurant for a warm cup of coffee. Midnight was approaching, and the liquor laws were very strict about the serving of alcohol after this hour—not one drop more could be poured after the clock struck twelve.

I had a bad cold and just wanted to sleep. Before going upstairs, I asked one of the waitresses, Dottie, to lock everything up after the last guest had left. I also made it clear that she was not to serve the cowboy at the bar any more alcohol after midnight.

Several days later, we received a summons in the mail, a notice to appear at a hearing in Denver. We had not violated any laws or regulations. Why this summons? Paul, our lawyer, accompanied me to the hearing, and Dottie and several other staff, who also had been summoned, were with us too.

After arriving, we looked through a window into the courtroom and saw another hearing in progress. Suddenly, Dottie became as white as a ghost and leaned on me to regain her balance. "Oh my God, that's the man at the bar from a couple of Sundays ago."

Black Bear Inn in Lyons, Colorado, in the early 1970s, after the addition of the apartment above the restaurant and the party room off to the right.

"So, what?" I said. "We didn't do anything wrong."

She started crying and slowly told the entire story of what had happened. Dottie had found the cowboy handsome, and the two had flirted with each other. Two legal double bourbons before midnight had been followed by two illegal double bourbons after midnight. Now I understood why I had received a summons.

In the courtroom I saw the cowboy, who also happened to be

a state liquor inspector. When I was allowed to speak during the hearing, I asked if the drinks had in fact been served after midnight. The inspector replied that when he left, he looked at the clock over the bar, and it was two o'clock in the morning.

Then I said, "Sir, we don't have a clock over the bar." Looking calmly at the inspector, I continued. "On top of that, after drinking four double bourbons, I'd be surprised if you remembered much of anything."

When questioned by the judge, the inspector revealed that he had indeed forgotten many details from the night in question. Finally, the judge had had enough. He suspended our license but also suspended the suspension. Perhaps the judge felt that the liquor inspector could have prepared a better case, and for this reason he was lenient. Outside the courtroom I breathed a sigh of relief, happy that this whole episode was now over and that we had not lost our liquor license, which would have been devastating. I learned a very important lesson from this ordeal: never trust a waitress, especially one looking for a husband. Moreover, never trust a handsome cowboy at the bar.

Strange Times and Best Friends, 1973

The peace movement of the later 1960s and early 1970s sometimes brought strange and even dangerous people onto our property, such as drifters high on one or more of the recreational drugs that had become popular in this era. Moreover, many resorted to crime to support their addiction.

The view of highway 66 from the balcony of our apartment. This would have been in the early 1970s.

During this period, many, including the Beatles, searched for an alternative lifestyle and became interested in Eastern religion and philosophy. The flower-power generation rejected American military involvement in Southeast Asia, a war that belonged to another generation. For this generation, peace became ingrained in the alternative life that they sought. The hippies are the most recognized symbol of this movement. They often moved from place to place, seeking out odd jobs for survival while rejecting social norms that required commitment to spouses, homes, and work. I was rather surprised that something like this could arise in puritanical America, but it sure seemed like most of the region's hippies found their way to the area around Lyons.

Several of the more levelheaded members of the flower-power generation found employment in our restaurant in Lyons. I will never forget Lenny, a young man of German heritage from Chicago. He had received some culinary training but was not all that interested in steady employment. A convert to Buddhism, after working three days straight he would retire to his room inside the small house he rented in town. He meditated while sitting upright, legs folded, on top of a round cushion called a zafu. Sometimes I broke free from the restaurant to visit him, to learn something about the art of meditation.

One day I asked him, "Lenny, what do you think of when you sit there and meditate?"

Turning his head in my direction and talking in a very calm and peaceful voice, he said, "Mrs. Stein, you would not believe all the crap that fills your head over the course of a week. I come here to clear my mind, to be able to fill my head with something new. That is what happens."

Not even our little corner of the world could avoid social change. Lyons lies about fifteen miles from Boulder and the University of Colorado, where you find a great deal of tolerance for alternative thinking and lifestyles. Starting in South America, I had developed an interest in holistic medicine, the power of the mind and nature to heal. I never reject out of hand another person's view of the world but always try to consider other opinions and beliefs, and sometimes I adapt them into my own way of life. Among my more redeeming qualities is a lifelong love of learning.

During the rare moments of free time that came my way, I buried myself in books written by leading freethinkers of this era, including Timothy Leary and Ram Dass. I discovered a whole new dimension to life. I find the world between reality and fantasy rather intriguing. Through this experience long-forgotten events returned to me, events that influenced my daily life in the present. In response to this newly redeveloped interest, Barbara and George would just roll their eyes, convinced I was nuts.

During this time of social change, I met Olga Seybert, an unusual woman who might be best described as resembling Yoda from *Star Wars*, in both appearance and wisdom. One day she was traveling through Lyons with a friend from Denver. The pair had just spent a wonderful day in the mountains and now wanted to enjoy a cup of coffee at the Black Bear Inn. As often happened with our guests, I soon started talking to them. Our discussion led to a long-term friendship that lasted until Olga's death in April 1990.

We had many of the same interests. Olga was born in 1909 and had spent the formative years of her life in Vienna. After the First World War she left the city with her mother and sister and moved to Paris. Lisette Model, Olga's sister, studied in Paris and later immigrated to the United States. She became a famous photographer, and her work was regularly featured in the prominent magazines of her time. Lisette later taught at the New York School for Photography. Today several museums still exhibit her work.

Olga studied at the Pasteur Institute in Paris and specialized in forensic photography and documentation. The world of art and philosophy attracted her. A friend of Gertrude Stein, Olga managed to spend a lot of time in art studios and in the process was able to meet several prominent artists, including Picasso. She also met GI Gurdjieff, an Armenian-born mystic and writer who authored several books on the esoteric, an attempt to introduce Eastern thought into Western culture. In New York and Paris, he founded groups that taught and spread his theories. Olga attended these meetings, and later she moved to Denver to found her own group. I attended the meetings she held in Denver, which inspired me, bringing a new perception of culture and a new way of thinking.

Olga and I got along with each other very well. One element of the Eastern belief system is reincarnation and rebirth. If these concepts are true, then Olga and I surely must have known each other in a past life. I could tell her almost anything. She always had the right answer. Her enthusiasm and interest in art fueled my previous interest in this subject. In short, Olga helped quench my thirst for knowledge! Shortly before George and I left Colorado in 1990, Olga's health took a turn for the worse. Three weeks before we departed, she died. I often think of Olga. I remain grateful for the wonderful experiences and all that I learned from her.

Through Olga I met Paul von Lobkowitz, a priest of the Sovereign Order of Saint John of Jerusalem, Knights of Malta, and a prince of the Austrian monarchy. We became fast and best friends immediately. Like me, he was born in Bohemia, and unlike me, his ancestors were among the nobility. Father Paul, as we affectionately called him, had studied medicine before becoming a priest of the Order of Saint John. In 1977 Father Paul founded the Hospice of Saint John in Denver, the second hospice in the United States and the first to offer services to gay men suffering from AIDS. He also founded other hospices in Russia and India. It was a great honor for our family when Father Paul came in 1996 to Berlin to lead the Holy Mass for George's funeral. He also officiated at my granddaughter's wedding in 1998.

Father Paul frequently came to the restaurant and later visited us in our house in Hygiene, Colorado. We discussed the politics of Europe, especially regarding our for-

One of the photos of Amy taken by Olga Seybert.

Photographer Olga Seybert, early 1980s.

Paul von Lobkowitz, a priest of the Sovereign Order of Saint John of Jerusalem, Knights of Malta and founder of the Hospice of St. John in Denver, CO.

mer homeland. He also educated me about the inner workings of the Vatican. He was born a rebel and had a quick sense of humor. He originally had been a Roman Catholic priest, but finding the politics of the Vatican too absurd, and chaffing at their rules, he left the Catholic Church to join the Russian Orthodox Church. He often joked that he looked good in a nun's habit, commenting on the vestments of his new faith. Although he was critical of church doctrines and leadership, he never wavered in his commitment to helping the poor and especially the sick or to his spirituality and faith in God.

When he was in Russia for the first time, sometime in the early 1980s, he was traveling from eastern Russia to Moscow with another young priest. His traveling companion wanted to visit the grave of Lenin, which was not something Father Paul had on his agenda, but he agreed to the detour. The guard at the tomb asked what the purpose of their visit was, and Father Paul responded, "To make sure he is dead." That is how I remember Father Paul's sense of humor and disdain for authority. To me, he was a real gift from heaven.

Thinking about the Next Step, 1974

In 1974 Barbara remarried. A few months prior, she had moved from Denver to Longmont with her soon-to-be husband.

Over the years the Black Bear Inn had improved, like a good bottle of wine. Apart from the winter evenings when snowstorms swept over the region, making the streets impassable, we were constantly booked.

I decided to apply for American citizenship. George would never do this for he was a true-blooded German. As a prerequisite to citizenship, I had to take a short course dealing with American law and history. On the same day that Nixon resigned in 1974 due to the Watergate scandal, I took the written exam for citizenship, which I passed. The following January I took the oath of citizenship. This was my third citizenship, after Czech and then German. Once a friend asked me to which country I belong. I responded by saying, "I am a citizen of the world."

It seemed like yesterday that we had moved to Lyons. George was now sixty, and I was fifty-three years old. I felt as fit as a fiddle. My only health problem was burnout syndrome, which sounded like a sort of clinical diagnosis. The doctor told me to take a long vacation, the standard course of treatment for that malady. George, however, continued to suffer from poor health. He had undergone a complicated stomach operation and suffered from weakening of the bones as a result of the injuries he received during the war. The yearly treatments in Germany helped, but only for a short while.

We desperately needed a change. We agreed that we would soon sell our restaurant and pursue a less hectic life. For me, it would be difficult to slow down, yet I wanted to try something completely new. George and I spent too much time together, which is not good for any relationship. Moreover, his constant health problems became overwhelming at times, a load my narrow shoulders could not bear. Through these difficult times I counted on the support of a few close friends.

During the summer of 1974, following the advice of my doctor, I decided to take several days off and travel to New Mexico with my granddaughter. After packing her things in the car, Amy and I traveled along Interstate 25, heading south to the "Land of Enchantment." I remember the sagebrush that grew alongside the road and the distinctive fragrance that filled the air. The sunset was spectacular, a trademark of western living, with its vibrant display of orange, red, and yellow light out on the horizon.

We stayed at the Kachina Lodge in Taos, a resort town in New

The mural that we had painted on the east wall of the apartment in 1973. The patio and garden were installed years later by the subsequent owners.

Mexico. The word "kachina" refers to religious dolls used by the Hopi Indians of the southwestern United States. These religious icons are carved from the wood of the cottonwood tree and then painted and decorated with feathers and other materials. The Hopis use these icons to pass their religious tradition from one generation to the next.

That evening we strolled through Taos and noticed the adobe construction of many of the homes. We walked past the house of Nicolai Fechin, a famous Russian painter who left his homeland after the communists came to power. He combined Native American art with the Russian artistic tradition, a true example of the Old World meeting the New World. Most of the people we saw on the street were Native Americans, many of whom wore ponchos to keep warm. Although daytime temperatures can hover around one hundred degrees in the summer, the nights in the desert are often cold.

After we ate dinner at a local restaurant, I needed to crawl into bed, to recover from the long journey. When we returned to the hotel, torches illuminated the round interior courtyard. Young men started pounding on drums while others started to perform traditional Indian dances. Amy was beside herself. We forgot about going to bed. We had to take in this new experience. One dance followed another. Then some of the spectators were invited to participate in the dancing, including Amy. To the rhythm of beating drums, she stomped around on the ground, enthusiastically chanting and clapping.

Several years later, I returned to Taos with George for a visit. Once again, the Indians performed their traditional dances while we watched. Suddenly, one of the dancers approached me, a handsome young man. "Excuse me," he said. "Would you happen to be Amy's grandmother?" Unbelievable! After all these years, Amy was remembered; her rendition of the eagle dance had left behind a lasting impression.

Dancers from the Taos Puebloan Tribe.

During our stay we made one excursion after another. I will never forget the tour of the Taos Pueblo. This settlement, a UNESCO world heritage site, has been continuously inhabited by the Pueblo Indians since at least 1400 AD and is arguably the oldest community in the United States. We saw cube-shaped adobe houses stacked on top of and next to each other. Red Willow Creek flows past the settlement. I remember seeing numerous stoves in front of this creek, which the Indians used to bake their bread.

Another excursion took us to the D. H. Lawrence Ranch, named after a famous British author of the twentieth century. During the early 1920s, Lawrence lived in Taos and became part of a writing colony in this area. While living in Taos, Lawrence met Mabel Dodge Luhan, a wealthy patron of the arts from New York City. According to rumor, Lawrence acquired the 160-acre ranch, known then as the Kiowa Ranch, from Luhan in exchange for a manuscript. He lived at the ranch for about two years, producing such works as the *Feathered Serpent* and *St. Mawr*. Lawrence was also an accomplished painter, and you can still admire some of his works in Taos.

The Move to Hygiene, Colorado, 1976

After her move to Longmont, Barbara helped me in the restaurant, which allowed me to catch my breath. George and I decided we wanted to leave Lyons and find a place outside of town in the countryside, something that would afford us some privacy as well as some peace and quiet, the way life ought to be. Purely by chance, in Hygiene, just a few miles away, we found exactly what we wanted. One day as I was driving, I noticed a brick house at the edge of a large lake. Even better, a for-sale sign stood next to the mailbox at the end of the driveway.

It was love at first sight. I drove back to Lyons, picked up George, and returned. On the spot we decided to purchase the property. Both the dining room and the living room offered a spectacular view of a small lake and the mountains, including Longs Peak, Mount Meeker, and the Twin Sisters. Near the house, cows grazed in the pasture. It was everything we had ever wanted.

The house had a positive effect on both of us. I was no longer tied to the restaurant twenty-four hours a day, seven days a week, there to handle every minor problem that surfaced. In Hygiene I could put my feet up and relax. George was thrilled to have a garden, which he tended with devotion. He possessed a green thumb, and all the plants thrived under his care, yielding impressive results at harvest time. The constant pain that had previously afflicted him suddenly disappeared. Now he felt better and was not so temperamental.

To help Barbara out and to test whether we could keep the restaurant in the family, we invited her to move into the apartment above the Black Bear Inn. She continued to work in the restaurant, and she got free rent, utilities, and food as well as a small salary. Although she was a good waitress, her interest in management left a lot to be desired. More troubling, however, was the complete lack of support we got from her husband. Whenever I asked him to help us, whether in the restaurant or in our home, he would say, "I don't work here. I only live here."

The final blow came on Mother's Day 1977. I had been in the hospital for a few days due to a heart condition, and they had performed a test that involved inserting a wire into my artery from my leg to my heart. I was feeling tired and bruised from the procedure, but I dragged myself into the restaurant to help wherever I could because Mother's Day was one of the busiest days of the year. I came in to find that we had half the staff we should have—nobody had thought to do the schedule while I was in the hospital.

Barbara said to me, "It's Mother's Day, and I'm heading out now to spend the day with my family." And out she went.

I was so shocked I nearly fainted. By the time I could form a coherent thought, they were already gone. Then panic set in. How could I make this work? I called some of the staff, one of whom was an employee named Ruth. She was the first to step in, and she quickly took control of the situation. I thought I was going to die that day, from the stress of the work and from the heartbreak of my daughter doing that to me. I was certain that her husband had put her up to it, but that didn't make the pain go away. I decided at that moment to sell the restaurant to someone else.

We sold our restaurant in Lyons to a European couple, a transaction that involved relatively little paperwork. The family owned and operated the Black Bear Inn until the summer of 2015, its forty-ninth year of operation, when they sold the property. It now houses a quilt shop.

With the restaurant sold it was time to fade to the background and relax. Olga arranged a three-week visit to Rancho La Puerta, a well-known spa and fitness resort near San Diego, California. Through this spiritual experience I learned the hidden abilities of my mind and body.

When I returned to Colorado, I felt rejuvenated, ready to take on the next adventure. I felt far too young to just sit at home, to have nothing in my life other than the garden and my marriage. I loved the area around Hygiene and its tranquil surroundings, yet a tiny voice inside my head kept saying, "Franziska, you are too young to stop learning."

I was still energized from the stay at Rancho La Puerta when I received a phone call from the curator at the Denver Art Museum.

Olga, who had photographed some of the pre-Columbian collection for the museum, had introduced us. The curator asked if I could assist him with the office work.

A New Challenge, 1977

With the help of a gardener and our neighbors, George took wonderful care of the garden. He lost himself in this hobby, and with that, his problems faded into the background. Sometimes I could convince him to attend special events at the Denver Art Museum with me. He never found this sort of thing interesting, but I still appreciated the fact that he accompanied me.

Three days each week, I drove from Hygiene to the museum, a distance of fifty miles each way. At the museum I was technically an office assistant, but I also received training to give lectures and tours. I got drawn into different assignments. For example, I often led groups of children on a tour of the "new world collection" when they came to the museum as part of a school field trip. Sometimes the kids asked a question for which I did not have an answer. This gave me an incentive to learn more about the museum's art collections. I often attended special presentations at the museum to acquire this knowledge and even attended some courses at the University of Colorado.

I often catalogued incoming works of art and attempted to determine their origin and provenance. Our department had an extensive collection of pre-Columbian and colonial art. The curator, who reminded us of Indiana Jones, was an excellent teacher. I accompanied him once to Hungary to examine a restored art collection and another time to Mexico and Guatemala to visit excavation sites.

From time to time, I helped the curator organize large art exhibits. One of these exhibits was a selection from the art collection of Baron Hans Heinrich Thyssen-Bornemisza, who at the time of his death in 2002, had accumulated the largest private collection of art in the world. Another large art exhibit that we organized was part of the collection of Armand Hammer. These exhibits gave me a moment of fame. The *Longmont Daily Times Call*, a local newspaper, published a picture of me with one of the more spectacular paintings from the collection, Gustave Moreau's *King David*.

At the beginning of 1977, I was planning yet another journey to Central America. This time Costa Rica and Honduras were on the itinerary. When I finally arrived in Costa Rica, what I saw impressed me. On one hand, Costa Rica had managed to retain many of its cultural traditions; on the other hand, this country, the so-called Switzerland of Latin America, was progressive and had a stable government.

Before leaving for Latin America, I had attended a series of presentations at the museum featuring pre-Colombian art of Central and South America. Through the curator I met several art dealers and scholars in this field. Among them was a lawyer living in San Jose, the capital of Costa Rica. When I arrived in San Jose, I called him. To my complete surprise, he invited me to have lunch at his house. In this part of the world, people usually did not invite strangers into the privacy of their home. When I arrived, the only other person in the house was his daughter. We ate, and then he gave me a tour of the home. He opened a huge wooden door, and I could see a shed in the interior courtyard. Inside the shed he showed me an impressive collection of artifacts, which included several items of silverwork. On a large table also lay several books, perhaps reference guides pertaining to the pieces of art stored there.

"How did you acquire this?" I asked, examining the silver pieces.

"Well, someone has offered to sell this to me. When a friend of mine found these in the local marketplace, I couldn't resist." He laughed nervously and continued to further explain what he thought the history of this treasure was.

"Now you know," the lawyer said. "I am particularly interested in the silverwork. Was this produced during the colonial period, like the guy says, or is he taking me for a ride? I need your help because I can't take this out of the country to have it examined. That would mean filling out customs declarations, which means the government would confiscate the silver, as we are not allowed to export or trade in colonial items. Is there something you can do to help me?"

"I tell you what," I said. "Let me take some pictures. I'll show them to the curator at the Denver Art Museum. He'll be able to tell you if the silver is from the colonial period. But to be completely honest, I doubt that it is."

Once I returned to Denver, I showed the photographs to the curator. "Let's make one thing perfectly clear, Franziska. This wasn't produced during the colonial period. It belongs to the British monarchy, to Queen Victoria, I'd say." One of the pieces was a baptismal font that Queen Victoria had given each of her grandchildren, a specially designed piece.

After the First World War, Prince Sigismund of Prussia, a great grandson of Queen Victoria and nephew of Kaiser Wilhelm II, immigrated to Costa Rica and founded a coffee and banana plantation. In 1976 or 1977, thieves ransacked his home, stealing many of the Prince's personal possessions. The thieves probably did not know that they had stolen one-of-a-kind items from a relative of the British monarch. Otherwise, they would not have sold these objects in the marketplace for the same price as locally produced art.

Though I don't know what channels were used, whether legal or illegal, the silver eventually made its way to a New York City auction house. It is possible that the Denver Art Museum curator alerted authorities, or they simply found out on their own, but solicitors working for the Queen of England were at the auction house on that day. Before the auction could start, two experts from the British embassy examined the silver, which had been set out for display. They then demanded to speak to whoever was responsible for the auction and confiscated the silver, with a court order, on behalf of the British Crown, the rightful owner.

After visiting Costa Rica, I made a trip to Honduras based on a suggestion from a colleague at the Denver Museum of Art. I wanted to learn more about the cultural history of the area. To fly into Honduras, I had to catch a flight at Tocumen International Airport in Panama. I could not believe what they had done to the airport since my last stopover in 1961. Now I stood in an ultra-modern airport, with lots of glass and, best of all, air conditioning. From Tocumen I had to book a flight to Santa Rosa de Caban, my destination in Honduras. At first, I thought I would be waiting a long time for the next flight. Only two passenger flights a week flew to this remote region. Then I noticed a large crate containing a generator with the words "Santa Rosa de Caban" written on it. *That must be a desperately needed generator*, I thought to myself. Anyway, it seemed to me that the pilot could take both the generator and me to this area. I suggested this to a friendly member of the ground crew, who was surprised by the request. My plan required a stop in Tegucigalpa, Honduras, before delivery of the generator to Santa Rosa de Caban, and the crew were open to the idea.

A wave of disappointment hit me when I saw the pilot, who looked more like an auto mechanic than a skilled pilot, clearly hungover and reeking of stale cigarettes. I had serious doubts about going but other options didn't exist. Anyway, he managed to deliver both me and the crate to Santa Rosa de Caban without any problems. Once we landed, I wondered how I could keep this guy sober until after the return flight later in the day. "Look," I told him, "if you can refrain from drinking, I'll buy you a huge bottle of rum once we land in Tegucigalpa."

The pilot nodded his head, grinning ear to ear. As he waited for me, I visited a few of the archaeological sites and took several photographs. This area was once an important center of Mayan culture. The plant diversity found in this region was particularly impressive. All too soon, I had to go, but this short tour has stayed detailed in my memory to this day.

Life in the Slow Lane, 1980–1987

In about 1982 Barbara's second marriage started to unravel. I offered my opinion about the relationship, which caused serious tension between us, something that occurs frequently between mothers and their daughters. In our discussions I told her that the marriage would come to an end, but Barbara could not come to terms with the mistake she had made. During one of our more positive discussions, we talked about the old Victorian house I had purchased in Longmont several years earlier. The business space on the first level of the building had remained vacant. We had converted the rest of the building into apartments. Anyway, Barbara came up with an idea: to utilize the vacant first floor to open a café. She needed my financial backing and organizational skills, but I was happy to help her and hoped that she would be successful. We planned to open Café Vienna later that year, and when an apartment on the second floor became available, we decided to convert it into a small art gallery, F&B Gallery.

I took care of the refurbishing and getting the necessary licenses for our grand opening. Barbara could not quit her job to help me because her husband was unemployed. Because her marriage was already strained, and because he and I were not getting along, he did not help us get the restaurant in shape. During this time, I worked part-time at the art museum and also had responsibilities in Hygiene, where George needed as much attention as the house we shared. As he grew older, he became more and more dependent on me.

In the meantime, the attorney I worked for in Berlin retired. When he handed control of his law firm over to one of his partners, I must have been on the property inventory list. Just when I thought I could retire, I found myself buried in work and attempting to open a new business in Longmont.

Even today, I probably do not fully comprehend all the personal difficulties that Barbara encountered during this time. While attempting to open a café, she also was raising a teenage daughter and dealing with numerous marital problems. This lack of understanding on my part probably contributed to the conflicts that occurred between us. On the other hand, I think Barbara could not forgive us for selling the Black Bear Inn in Lyons. The Black Bear had generated a very nice income for George and me, but every dollar had been earned with my labor. Barbara and her husband had benefited from our success but had not vested themselves in the business and had no idea how hard it was.

Unfortunately, Barbara expected similar success with the café we opened in Longmont, not realizing that such success usually took time. She failed to account for the fact that you cannot build a customer base overnight. Moreover, we had to repay a business loan, and the economy in Colorado was less than stellar at this time.

Barbara's second marriage finally came to an end. Amy retreated to the sanctuary of the barn and her favorite pastime, being with her beloved horses.

Barbara became involved with another man, which would eventually lead to her third marriage. I felt obligated to share my advice with her about this new relationship, and this eventually caused a rift between us. This estrangement became so severe that at one time we maintained the appearance of a mother–daughter relationship only for the sake of Amy.

Differing opinions about personal lives affected our business venture. We agreed that Barbara would pull out of our agreement and that I would run the café alone. This made my life even more stressful. Today, when I look back on this time in my life, I am sorry about everything. How could this estrangement occur between us? Why did we wait so many years to settle our personal differences? Every year that loved ones remain apart is a wasted year. Our life on this earth is so limited, and it seems foolish to let pride stand in the way of spending time with family members.

Suddenly, I was working once again in the hospitality industry, jumping in with both feet while working part-time at the art museum. Zieschang's office in Berlin also kept me busy. Now we had a new type of client, Poles and Russians who had immigrated to the United States. Many of them had been slave laborers during the Nazi era. True to their reputation for efficiency, the German firms that employed these workers also had made payments on their behalf to the pension fund. Now these former slave laborers wanted the compensation to which they were entitled. In the Denver metropolitan area, I was the only one who knew how to complete the necessary forms for the pension money. Despite all these responsibilities, I managed to open an art gallery on the floor above the café, where I advised local businessmen and bankers on the type of art they should purchase for their businesses.

Today I no longer know how I accomplished everything. Eventually, I concluded that I was no longer fifty years old. Gone with my youth was the boundless energy that had enabled me to make the most of a twenty-four-hour day. The beautiful home we

In F&B Gallery, the art gallery I opened above Barbara's restaurant, Café Vienna, in Longmont, Colorado. This photo is from 1984.

owned in Hygiene had become too much for us. George no longer wanted to tend such a large garden, nor could I find the time and strength to take care of a husband and a plot of land in addition to my three jobs. Although it was a very difficult decision, at this point in our lives it was necessary to downsize.

In 1987 we sold our house in Hygiene and moved into a smaller rental house in Longmont, not far from the café. We decided not to buy a house since the economy in Colorado was in a recession caused by the oil and gas bust. We needed to keep our options open in the event we had to move again.

The rift between Barbara and me, which lasted nearly eight years, was a tremendous burden to all those concerned. I often saw her on the street or inside one of the local businesses, and she would turn her head and keep moving. Pride kept both of us from making the first step toward reconciliation. This conflict also affected George, who could no longer drive because of his failing health. Perhaps he suffered more than I from the strain that this falling-out caused.

Perspective: The Iron Curtain Falls, 1989

History books often speak of an Iron Curtain, a geographic and ideological boundary that separated Western Europe from Eastern Europe after the Second World War. After the war, Eastern Europe fell under the control of the Soviet Union. Poland, East Germany, Hungary, Czechoslovakia, Romania, and Bulgaria had no other choice but to adopt a communist system of government. However, these communist governments lacked popular support among their citizens. To help the various communist regimes in Eastern Europe survive, the USSR provided substantial economic and military assistance, which imposed a huge financial burden.

In 1985 Mikhail Gorbachev became general secretary of the Communist Party in the Soviet Union. He observed that his own country had missed the economic and technological revolution that had occurred in the West. He sought to correct this deficiency and embarked upon a reform program that attempted to achieve openness in government (glasnost) and economic restructuring (Perestroika).

By 1988 Gorbachev let word leak out that the Soviet Union would no longer enforce the Brezhnev Doctrine, meaning that the USSR would no longer use military force to intervene in the political affairs of Eastern Europe. Soon various reform movements swept through the countries behind the Iron Curtain. In Poland, for example, the Solidarity labor movement achieved free elections in June 1989. This spirit of reform spread to Hungary. During a summer in which border enforcement became increasingly lax, Hungary effectively disabled its physical border defenses with Austria in August. After this, more than 13,000 East Germans escaped into Austria via this route. East Germany responded by disallowing travel into Hungary.

The leader of the East German Communist Party, Erich Honecker, was determined to resist the calls for reform that were occurring in his country. In October 1989 Gorbachev paid a state visit to East Germany to observe the fortieth anniversary of the founding of the German Democratic Republic. During his visit tens of thousands of protesters took to the streets, with the largest demonstrations held in Leipzig. Honecker ordered the East German military to use deadly force against the demonstrators.

But before such violence occurred, Egon Krenz, then Politburo member in charge of security, flew to Leipzig on Oct. 9 and canceled Mr. Honecker's order, allowing the protesters to march freely. Honecker was forced to resign within ten days after suggesting such a terrible action, and Egon Krenz became the new party chief on October 18, 1989.[7]

During those days in October 1989, hundreds of East Germans waited patiently in front of the German embassy in Prague (the former Palais Lobkowitz[8]) for permission to leave for the west.

---

7   A nice summary of these events is "How the Wall Was Cracked - A Special Report; Party Coup Turned East German Tide; CLAMOR IN THE EAST" by Craig R. Whitney, David Binder and Serge Schmemann, *New York Times*, November 19, 1989.

8   This property was formerly part of the noble family from my friend

Finally, after the crowds had waited for days, the foreign minister, Hans-Dietrich Genscher, appeared, and amid great rejoicing, he delivered the message that the people could leave the east and will be welcomed in West Germany. "The trains are standing by."

After weeks of unrest in East Germany, the East German Politbüro met and decided to revise the travel restrictions policy. On the evening of November 9, 1989, Politbüro member Günter Schabowski held a press conference to announce the new reforms to travel restrictions that would allow East Germans to leave the country. He had not been present during the deliberations on the policy and was reading from the script given to him shortly before the press conference began by Egon Krenz. The press conference was broadcast live on international television and carried on radio stations on both sides of the border. A reporter asked when the changes were to take effect. Schabowski paused, studying the piece of paper before him with a furrowed brow. Then he stumbled through a partially intelligible answer, telling reporters, "It takes effect, as far as I know ... it is now ... immediately."

Later, when asked whether the new regulations also applied to travel between East and West Berlin, Schabowski looked at the text again and discovered that they did. When Daniel Johnson of the Daily Telegraph asked what that meant for the Berlin Wall, Schabowski sat frozen before giving a rambling statement about the Wall being tied to the larger disarmament question. Though not the intent of the Politbüro, Schabowski's repeated confirmations on the new policy that the borders were now open changed the course of history.

Within hours, thousands of East Berliners converged at border crossings at the wall, and the border guards soon allowed them to cross over into West Berlin. Throughout the night celebrations took place in Berlin. Some even danced on top of the wall. After forty-one years, Berlin was no longer a divided city. Indeed, as the entire world focused once again on Berlin, it was abundantly clear that the Cold War had come to an end.

Many in East Germany were not interested in reunification with West Germany, but rather, they wanted to reform their existing

---

Father Paul von Lobkowitz.

government. The West German government, on the other hand, had sought a reunified Germany ever since the founding of East Germany in 1948, a goal enshrined in the country's basic law. In November 1989 the East German government had essentially collapsed, leaving nothing for the East Germans to reform. This provided Helmut Kohl, the West German chancellor, a perfect opportunity to announce a ten-point plan for German reunification.

The four victorious powers from the Second World War—the United States, Great Britain, France, and the Soviet Union—insisted that they must approve any German reunification agreement. In May 1990, Two-Plus-Four talks began in Ottawa, Canada. An acceptable agreement was reached among the East and West German representatives, as well as the four Allies. On October 3, 1990, the German reunification agreement went into effect. Willy Brandt, the former West German chancellor, provided perhaps the best commentary on this momentous occasion: "Now grows together what belongs together."

Leaving Again, 1990

I remember this time vividly not only because of the euphoria of the reunification but also because of the people I knew. I had met Willy Brandt when he was the mayor of Berlin, when he helped get benefits for the miners in the jungles of Colombia after the statute of limitations had expired. He seemed to me to be the consummate public servant, not just a politician. He died soon after the reunification agreement went into effect, fulfilling for him, I think, a lifelong wish that his city would be whole again.

For several years George had been homesick and longed for the city he called home—Berlin. Once again, fate struck. George, upon seeing the fall of the Berlin Wall, knew it was time to return home. He made his decision on the spot, and I had little choice but to give my consent. Like before, when George said it was time to go, it was time to go.

Before leaving Colorado, we needed to sell the café, something that delayed our new adventure. On my sixty-seventh birthday I received a call from Texas. Someone was suddenly interested in buying the business, and after some long and difficult negotiations, we finally sold Franziska's. I was happy to be relieved of this burden.

Until a week before I left Colorado for Berlin, I worked for the Denver Art Museum. I also was still working on compensation claims in the lead-up to our departure. As I mentioned earlier, by this time Zieschang had retired, but I had been conveyed along with his other staff and cases to the new lawyer who had taken over his office. I remember a sudden upsurge of business from the many people seeking compensation. When word circulated that I was leaving town, many decided that their final opportunity to file a claim would soon expire. The new lawyer from Berlin, Mr. Blankenhorn, came to Denver to personally meet with some of the clients. He came during the spring, when the Colorado weather can turn from pleasant to nasty within hours. Indeed, as we drove through the northern suburbs of Denver, we suddenly encountered heavy snowfall. The temperature plunged with the onset of the storm and caused the water on Interstate 25 to turn into black ice. I wanted to pull into the shoulder lane to wait out the storm. Unfortunately, other cars already occupied the highway shoulder, and this was not possible. Soon I found myself involved in a forty-vehicle pileup. My car was totaled.

Sitting there in the middle of all this wreckage, I turned to Blankenhorn, who now leaned against the door unconscious. The adrenaline pulsed through my veins as I waited for the police and ambulance crew to arrive. Fortunately, the accident had occurred near a hospital. Blankenhorn emerged from the accident almost unscathed, but I suffered from a bad case of whiplash, which required several weeks to fully heal. It was time to leave Colorado!

After the Iron Curtain fell, many Eastern Europeans traveled west to reestablish family ties and to admire the variety of consumer goods found inside the well-stocked businesses. The increased demand for used cars, apartments, and groceries caused the prices of these commodities to skyrocket. An expression soon circulated whenever German shoppers wanted a special grocery item that was sold out: "Sorry, already in Poland." As we planned our move to Berlin, one question at the back of our minds was whether we could find housing. Around the time when George left Colorado, we received an offer that would allow us to rent a furnished house for several months in Berlin. This took us completely by surprise. It was exactly what we needed! For once we could move and not worry about finding a roof over our heads.

My life in Colorado ended with a series of farewell parties. On top of that, one of the local papers ran a story about George and me, discussing our plans for a new life in Berlin. The departure was painful. But I found comfort in knowing that our lives have a destiny. Barbara attended the goodbye party we held at our neighbor's house. I was glad she came, but there still existed a large distance between us. As I look back on our departure, perhaps my only regret is that my daughter and I were not on the best of terms with each other.

By the end of May 1990, George had already begun his new life in Germany. I remained behind in Colorado for several weeks to dispose of what we had accumulated over the course of twenty-five years. Carefully, I sorted through all that I had, throwing some items in the trash, giving other items away, and arranging to take the rest to Germany with me.

CHAPTER 5

Germany, 1990-2011
and Virginia, 2011 and beyond

December 2011, Great Falls National park, Virginia.

First Steps into a New Life, 1990

Finally, it was time to fly to Berlin. It was a beautiful day at the end of June when I said goodbye to the Front Range and to Colorado. The famous Colorado sunshine greeted me as the airplane turned to the east. I departed without hearing from my daughter, and this was painful for me. Tears welled up in my eyes. However, I still held a faint glimmer of hope for reconciliation sometime in the future. George had become lonely during this brief separation, and when I arrived in Berlin, he was overjoyed to see me again. Once there, I felt dead tired, partly from the long flight and partly because of all the stress surrounding the move. The house we rented represented an interim solution, and clearly, we needed to find something permanent.

Finding housing in Berlin was problematic. Many people from East Germany were moving there along with those anticipating the relocation of the reunified nation's capital from Bonn to Berlin. Furthermore, the housing stock in East Berlin was in terrible shape. While engaging in some small talk with one of the neighbors, I mentioned that we needed an apartment. Again, we were in luck. She knew someone who had a vacant apartment and arranged a meeting for us. As it turned out, we knew the owner of the apartment from our time in Berlin after the war. We signed a lease, but before we could move in, the apartment had to be renovated, which George supervised. Our new apartment received a new coat of paint, the contractors installed a new bath, and badly needed electrical work was completed. The house in which our apartment was located had been built in the early 1930s, and each floor of the three-story structure was an apartment. We occupied the top floor.

I kept busy and worked four days a week for Blankenhorn. I had brought all the open cases I had in Colorado with me to Berlin. Despite having lived in Berlin during the 1940s and '50s, once again I had to become acclimated to life in this city and to its unique attitudes. In many ways this city had become different, something to be expected after such a long separation. One thing remained the same—the bureaucracy, which waited for us every time we moved. Another thing that remained the same was the beauty of Brandenburg, the

German state surrounding Berlin. Tree branches often hung over stretches of road in the countryside, forming a cathedral-like roof through which rays of sunshine penetrated, casting mysterious shadows on the pavement below.

Perspective: Potsdam, Germany

Magnificent palaces and country estates, as well as the historic city of Potsdam, add a certain charm to this area. Many of the castles and old manors were badly neglected by the communist regime in East Germany, which had neither the interest nor the resources to repair the war damage and subsequent deterioration that occurred. After reunification, a massive effort was undertaken to restore the historically significant buildings and estates around Berlin. Sanssouci Palace in Potsdam was among the first to be restored.

Sanssouci was the summer palace of Frederick the Great. In a large ceremony the remains of the famous and controversial king were returned to their original resting place to find eternal peace. Even his beloved greyhounds were reinterred next to him. During the war his remains had been taken to another location in the southern part of what became West Germany for safekeeping. Only after reunification could they be once again reunited at his favorite home.

The New Palace, which Frederick the Great built after he lost Silesia in a war with Austria, was built using borrowed money. He was ridiculed for this folly and for putting the country in debt. But the structure was a great success and still today, following the reconstruction, is a beloved venue for concerts and other cultural events.

During the Cold War, the Glienicke Bridge, spanning the Havel River and connecting the Wannsee district of Berlin with the Brandenburg capital Potsdam, was primarily used by Allies as a link between their Berlin sections and the military liaison missions in Potsdam. It is named after nearby Glienicke Palace and was also the location used to exchange spies between East and West Germany, gaining the nickname "Bridge of Spies". One such exchange was depicted in the 2015 movie called *Bridge of Spies* starring Tom Hanks. It is a scenic place, surrounded by parks and forest, leaving no obvious traces to the history made there.

In the summer of 1990, Iraq invaded Kuwait, thrusting the world into a precarious situation. Moreover, civil war raged in the Balkans. Large candlelight demonstrations against these conflicts were held in Berlin, a city all too familiar with the senselessness of war and its aftermath. The communist regimes of Eastern Europe fell overnight. Although many countries adopted democratic governments, long-standing ethnic divisions remained. Czechs and Slovaks, for example, parted company in January 1993, forming the Czech Republic and Slovakia.

Settling In but Not Staying Put

Our beginning in Berlin started out rather strange. Almost immediately, George left to take a spa-treatment vacation, and I returned to Colorado, now as a guest. Legislation recently enacted in Germany had provided Blankenhorn's law firm with additional clients because more people qualified for compensation. In Colorado I visited with some of my friends, but for the most part this was strictly a business trip. The rift between Barbara and me continued, and during my stay we did not meet with each other.

I returned to Germany on October 3, 1990, the official date of German reunification, a date I shall never forget. Before landing at Berlin's Tegel Airport, the pilot announced on the intercom, "Ladies and gentlemen, we have a special passenger on board. His Holiness the Dalai Lama is flying with us to Berlin. He wishes all passengers peace and happiness." Before the airport stood a long row of taxis from former East Berlin. Reunification meant they could now pick up passengers at the Tegel Airport, located in the western part of the city, something that filled them with pride.

By this time, the renovation project on our home had come to an end, and we could move into our new apartment. Since George was still at the spa resort, I could furnish our home undisturbed.

Now that the wall had fallen, Berlin embarked on a major campaign to improve its infrastructure. When East Germany erected the wall, subway and rail service along many existing routes had been severed, and suddenly it became necessary to reconnect these routes, sometimes using sections of track that had not seen rail traffic in almost three decades. Berlin also utilized buses to provide public transportation to all corners of the reunited metropolis. Getting around town was easier every day, and I liked the adventure of seeing what changed from one day to the next.

On a gray November day, George and I visited the Schloss Rheinsberg. This jewel of Prussian architecture, mixing baroque and romantic styles, lies on a beautiful lake in the Havelland region. Here, Frederick the Great, then the Crown Prince of Prussia, enjoyed the company of Voltaire for several months. Frederick's philosophical inspirations are manifested in his letters to Voltaire that followed over the years. Early in our marriage I received a gift from my father-in-law, Max, a steel engraving dating from about 1760 depicting Voltaire and Frederick the Great walking through a hall of Sanssouci. Through everything I have managed to keep this heirloom in my possession.

I felt rather lonely during our first Christmas in Berlin. I missed all the gatherings with friends and family that took place in Colorado. Now we sat by ourselves in the small living room of our apartment. We received a boatload of Christmas cards from America, Colombia, and Germany. I pinned them on the door frames to remind me of all those who were thinking of us on this holiday. I especially remember the card I received from Amy as well as the one from her father, which included a picture of his daughters. Some of George's high school classmates, members of Virgilia, also spent time with us. Like so many people, I fell victim to a winter holiday depression. The Christmas Mass lifted me out of this depression, at least temporarily, when I heard the Don Cossacks, a choir from Russia, whose powerful voices in the darkened church comforted my soul. Finally, and perhaps mercifully, the holiday season ended, and with that I regained my self-confidence and courage. Once again, a multitude of plans and ideas ran through my head, a sign I had finally returned to my normal self.

In spring 1992 I joined the Berlin International Women's Club (IWC). The IWC exists in many capital cities of Europe and brings together women from around the world who now live in and around these cities. The purpose of the club is to foster mutual understanding and tolerance through cultural exchange, friendship, and support. The Berlin IWC draws its membership from sixty countries, and its members all speak English. I met some of my best friends through this club.

Through outings with the Berlin IWC, I saw famous historical places, attended the inauguration of the New Synagogue in Berlin, and heard many exhilarating lectures on politics, history, and music. Members of the club served as hostesses when President Clinton visited in 1994. When the Hotel Adlon Kempinski, located on Unter den Linden, the main boulevard in the Mitte district of Berlin, was newly renovated, members of the Berlin IWC got a grand tour. This hotel is one of the most elegant in Berlin, and during its grand history it has hosted national and international nobility, state leaders, and celebrities. The roaring 1920s gave the hotel a special spark as a meeting center, and later the Nazi Party used it for their meetings. It was bombed during the last few days of the war, and most of it was destroyed. Forty-eight years later, it was brought back to its former glory.

Once again, spring came to town. The birch trees lining the boulevard near our apartment had already blossomed. It had been many years since I last saw them. I could not help but think of a line from a poem by Rilke: "Let me see just once a birch tree on a cold day in spring." How I love these trees—with their speckled bark and small leaves.

To relax I attended a course dealing with autogenic training. During one of the lessons, I met Martha, a wonderful and gentle woman from Uruguay. She soon became one of my closest friends. Because of her I felt less lonely in this world.

The Unification Treaty of October 3, 1990 had declared Berlin the capital of the reunified Germany. However, the actual movement of the German government from Bonn to Berlin would happen incrementally over several years, culminating with the movement of the legislature, the Bundestag, to the Reichstag in 1999. One of the more disturbing political issues that surfaced was the question of compensation for those whose property had been confiscated by the former East German government. I found the lack of concern by many of the bureaucrats to be shocking. I cannot tell you the number of times a petty civil servant told me, "There's nothing we can do."

When Berlin became capital of a reunited Germany in name, seemingly overnight the city became one large construction site. Daniel Barenboim, the famous conductor of the Berlin Philharmonic, used this setting for an unusual concert. Beethoven's Ninth Symphony was accompanied by the choreographed movement of large construction cranes—a unique event to see and hear. However, I barely noticed any of this for my entire world consisted of either getting my home ready or working through the mountains of paper at the office.

The departure of the Allied troops was the last of the major events in the reunification of Berlin and the two Germanys. Throughout the summer of 1994, parades and parties celebrated the service of the occupation armies. With some controversy, the British, French, and American leaders decided not to include the Russians in their parades and festivities. However, they did permit the Russian troops to march through the Brandenburg gate in their final parade.

On August 31, 1994, Boris Yeltsin came to Berlin to bid a final farewell as the last of his Russian soldiers left the city and Germany. A week later, the last of the Allied soldiers vacated Berlin, leaving behind only NATO troops in the reunified city. The final stage of the end of the Cold War was completed.

During the planning and execution of the troop withdrawal, we witnessed things that gave me pause. Although the economic miracle had enveloped West Germany and West Berlin in the 1950s and '60s and continued to the 1990s, Russia and its allies had seen little economic progress and a lot of poverty, violence, and deprivation. After the wall came down, Russian troops stationed in East Germany and East Berlin got a small taste of the prosperity that we had in the West and could fully embrace it. Now they faced a return to a homeland that was still in shambles, to a life devoid of comforts and even simple luxuries, such as toilet seats.

A Berlin newspaper, *Tagespiegel*, featured the headline "In a Bitter Goodbye, Russians Leave Germany." A Russian officer was quoted as saying, "We are leaving because we are under orders to leave, but none of us wants to go home." The officer was in his mid-forties and said that after his thirty-six-hour train ride to Moscow, he would not have a place to live. "The Germans killed millions of our people, and we are being kicked out like dogs."

The Russian troops took with them everything they could remove from their apartments in Berlin—the appliances, the pipes, the toilets as well as the toilet seats, the bathtubs, electrical fixtures, everything. They even stole from people on the streets—muggings were common at this time, especially in the border area between East and West Berlin. I knew what it was like to go to an uncertain life with only what you could carry, but I had never once considered what it would be like knowing that not even a toilet would be available on the other end of the journey.

Our Golden Anniversary, 1992

Old age had been good to me. Despite a touch of gray hair and the loss of some of that twinkle in my eye, I still felt like a young woman. My marriage with George had been very much like a roller coaster ride, and now the relationship had taken a turn for the better. Often, he held my hand and said, "I am so happy to be here again," meaning Berlin. "I just can't tell you how much." That made me happy. These short fleeting moments are burned forever in my heart. As our fiftieth wedding anniversary approached, we tossed ideas back and forth about how to make the most of this milestone in our lives. The idea surfaced of repeating our wedding vows in Karlsbad, the city where I was born, baptized, and married, where Barbara was born and baptized, the city from which I had been expelled after the war.

No sooner said than done. For the first time since 1945, I returned to the city of my origins to make the necessary arrangements for our anniversary. My memories of this place had gathered dust in the attic of my mind, and now I witnessed how difficult life behind the Iron Curtain had been for Czechoslovakia. As we rolled through one village after another on the train, the conditions I saw were very disturbing—the dilapidated buildings, the peeling paint, the bad roads, the visible poverty. To be on the safe side, every so often I reached inside my jacket to make sure that my American passport was securely tucked away in the inside pocket. Every small village we passed through brought me closer and closer to Karlsbad. Soon I was afflicted with a case of déjà-vu. Then I suddenly realized something. The railway still had not fixed the heating in the train cars!

Finally, we arrived at the main train station in Karlsbad. Before I could feel astonishment, anxiety, or disgust about the condition of the train depot, I found myself in the arms of Gerda, my former classmate and best friend. I had not seen her for so many years. Tears ran down her cheeks and mine.

Gerda and I took a stroll on the promenade. I noticed that a layer of soot covered almost every wall in the city. I also noticed that nobody spoke German or English, and my Czech had become somewhat rusty. Most of the German-speaking people, whose ancestors had lived here for hundreds of years, were now gone. Many had been expelled, like I had been. The rest either had died or were now confined indoors because of poor health. I suspect some refused to speak German to avoid persecution. Communism had just ended in Karlsbad, and many perceived the newly acquired freedoms as tenuous. Of course, under the communist regime the schools had no longer taught German. Instead, children had learned Czech and Russian.

Gerda was overjoyed to see me again. While living in Colombia, I had reestablished contact with her, and over the years we had periodically exchanged letters. She learned about my many overseas adventures, and I learned about Gerda's four children, as well as her grandchildren. I often sent her parcels containing clothing, vitamins, and medication, but I hadn't realized from our letters just how much the years behind the Iron Curtain had taken their toll on her. She now suffered from poor health due to a lack of proper nutrition, a lifetime of inadequate medical and dental care, and the long-term effects of physically difficult work. One thing had not changed, though—my friend had maintained her lovely personality and sense of humor.

During this beautiful reunion with the city, I could find reconciliation with the past and all that had haunted me since the expulsion order. As Gerda and I sat across from each other in the hotel restaurant, it was difficult for both of us to find the words to explain what had happened in our lives. Eventually, we started from our common childhood experiences. Then the words flowed more freely.

Reunited with my childhood friend Gerda in Karlsbad in 1992. It had been 47 years since I had last seen her.

Though I was excited to be back in Karlsbad and to enjoy Gerda's company again, I had a mission: to plan our anniversary celebration. The next day I began all the preparations, attempting to reconstruct as much of the original wedding as possible. We wanted a priest to say the Mass in German, and the city was very helpful in finding one who spoke the language. We also wanted to have lunch in the very building where we had held the wedding reception fifty years prior.

As we made our plans, Karlsbad emerged from its winter hibernation. Many of the inhabitants began to spruce up their homes and businesses. With every step, I wanted more and more to embrace the city of my birth. Moreover, as I talked with those who lived here, I was touched by the gratitude and pride extended to us for choosing to celebrate our fiftieth anniversary in Karlsbad.

Those attending the celebration of our golden wedding anniversary received an invitation to have cocktails with the mayor.

The city's director of tourism picked everyone up and took us on a sightseeing tour. Although I had lived here during the first twenty-two years of my life and thought I knew the city like the back of my hand, there were still treasures to be explored—including, for example, the Emperor's Bath, named after the Austro-Hungarian emperor. What splendor! The private bath of Empress Elisabeth contained frescos in the baroque style, and the bathtub contained gold fittings. I was surprised to learn that even after the plundering over the last fifty years, many historical relics still remained. We also saw a royal waiting room adorned with magnificent sculptures.

Almost everybody we invited showed up for the big event. Amy flew in from Virginia, my relatives from Munich and Nuremberg came, and Aunt Mitzi from Vienna also attended. Even some fellow expatriates from Colombia, who now once again lived in Germany, made the journey to Karlsbad. This meant so much to us. Of course, a little rain fell on our parade. Someone had turned my favorite café into a pub that played loud music. Perhaps this was done to introduce the youth of Karlsbad to all the Western decadence they had missed during the forty-five years of communism.

March 15, 1992, was cold and sunny, just like on our wedding day fifty years prior. I looked at myself in the mirror and tried to imagine the person I was in 1942. I remembered a shy and reserved girl, a girl who had dreams and knew what she wanted from life, a girl who eventually would become a woman who took destiny into her own hands. The reflection in the mirror now showed a woman who had worked hard her whole life, one who had experienced her share of the good and bad. Without a doubt my life had been an adventure. I thought about George, a handsome and assertive man fifty years ago, now a very tired man.

We made our way to the Church of St. Mary Magdalene which had been built by Kilián Ignác Dientzenhofer, architect of Empress Maria Theresa, in the classic Austrian baroque style. The evening before, it had snowed. Our priest, who was coming from a nearby town, arrived late with a blast of cold air and a thousand German apologies. Within a short period of time, we forgot all of that. He delivered a beautiful Mass. His homily included a discussion about the expulsion of ethnic Germans from Czechoslovakia in 1945. Then something embarrassing happened. When he attempted to retrieve the communion chalice from the tabernacle, the door would not budge, possibly because the lock or hinges had frozen due to the cold air and humidity. After several unsuccessful attempts by the priest, the daughter of one of our friends approached the altar and managed, with her youthful strength, to open the tabernacle. The priest looked at her gratefully and distributed Holy Communion.

Renewal of our wedding vows on our fiftieth wedding anniversary in Karlsbad (Karlovy Vary) in 1992. The priest sang a lovely German hymn as his gift to us. The mass was held at the Church of St. Mary Magdalene.

This priest was very poor, but he gave us a most generous and valuable gift. Blessed with a rich tenor voice, he sang us a song, a German folk song played at our wedding fifty years ago. It reached deep inside my soul, and it also moved our guests. There wasn't a dry eye in the church when he finished. Some of the best gifts come unexpectedly. The priest had grown up singing in the choir and had continued his musical education in the priesthood. When the communists came to power, they forced him to work in the coal mines. There, he continued to sing. They couldn't take that away from him.

Following the ceremony, we made our way to the church's front entrance while the organist played a traditional wedding march with the huge church organ. Once we were on the street, the bells of St. Mary Magdalene Church rang to mark the occasion.

My only regret on this day was the absence of my daughter. During the reception the chair next to me remained empty. Over and again, my thoughts drifted to her. I am sure she thought of us.

Life in Berlin returned to normal. Now I worked for two law firms, one in Berlin and another in Spain. After making several journeys to Spain, I decided it was simply too much. I did not want to admit it, but old age has a way of sneaking up on you. I had to learn to take smaller steps. I decided to retire from my work on the restitution cases after nearly forty years. I had helped thousands of people get their rightful compensation, often lifting them from poverty and giving them a glimmer of hope for their family's future, but now I had to help myself.

Many years earlier, I had met Muna Fischer, an adventurous woman from Vienna who traveled through several of the world's deserts. For several years she had lived on one of the remote Greek islands. Now she invited me to travel with her to visit the Greek island of Ammouliani, to rejuvenate both my body and my soul. I accepted. We reached the island by ferry and crossed the sea over the Xerxes Canal. When we arrived, Muna was greeted by several older ladies, all dressed in black. Muna had returned to them with a *xenia*, a stranger—me. For two weeks Muna and I swam in the Aegean Sea. I gave the clouds above us names, and late at night the moonlight cast a spell on us. During the evening we watched traditional dances at the marketplace. I sampled Retsina, a wine aged in pine instead of the now traditional oak barrels. Unfortunately, such a life cannot last forever. After leaving the island, I met George in Vienna, and we returned to Berlin together.

Near the end of her life, Muna sent me a small collection of her poems, all beautifully written, about Ammouliani. Here are the opening lines from one of them that I want to share with you:

Olive Tree

In the center the old olive tree stands,
It doesn't bloom anymore, only in my dreams.
Only the bell—it doesn't exist anymore—
Nowadays the announcements are different made.
I was missed by someone—it shows in many kisses,
and by me too—as said in greetings …

—Charlotte "Muna" Fischer, 1998

The winter in Berlin was cold and gray, made bearable by the vacation in Greece, where I had filled up on sun. George, on the other hand, fell into depression. I celebrated my seventieth birthday with friends from Colorado and new ones from Berlin. During our conversation, I recounted all the places where I had celebrated the decades of my life, sometimes in another country and sometimes on another continent.

In the former Yugoslavia, religious and ethnic differences led to bloodshed and civil war. The ethnic cleansing that occurred there was disturbingly similar to the Final Solution in Nazi Germany. In Berlin candlelight vigils were held to remember the victims of this violence. Psychologists have extensively studied human aggression, attempting to understand humans' inhumanity against their fellow humans. Some say humans sympathize with those who exterminate other people, perhaps realizing that what infected them to commit these atrocities could become contagious. Perhaps it is time to examine our performance-driven society and ask whether this has extinguished what remains of our humanity. Ignorance and the lack of any desire to comprehend the cultures and religions of others breeds intolerance, which breeds hate, which becomes war.

On my seventieth birthday I received a present that could not have been any nicer for me—a hand-embroidered pillow from Barbara. I think Amy had something to do with this gift, a possible peace offering and first step to repairing our relationship. In 1993 I flew to Colorado. Barbara and I had a meal together, and the conversation between us was very pleasant. Yet we never discussed the reasons behind our estrangement.

Bad News and a Farewell, 1993–1996

It was spring in 1994. My darlings, the birch tree blossoms, appeared once again, the snow bells that greeted the end of winter. I made another trip to the United States on behalf of Blankenhorn to work on more cases. During my business trip in America, George took his annual spa treatment. He did not feel well at all, something very much his own fault for not following the advice of the doctors. George smoked like a chimney and drank too much alcohol. Without any success, I had attempted to convince him to make a change for the better. It had become difficult to see him slowly self-destructing before me. To escape from this, I buried myself in my work. Even as an old man, George never really came to terms with the past and never could embrace the present as I did. He had thought the return to Germany would present an opportunity to make a change, but soon he had become disillusioned by all that had changed around his beloved city.

While in a meeting with clients in Denver, I had to call our office in Berlin to forward some information. Soon I was on the line with Blankenhorn. After I had passed along the information, he forwarded some distressing news from my husband. "Franziska, there's something I have to tell you. George has been diagnosed with lung cancer."

I was devastated. Although I stood in a warm office and the sun shined through the windows, I felt cold. Standing there stunned, I felt as though my whole world was starting to collapse in on me.

Finally, I gathered enough strength to say "okay" into the receiver, at a loss for what else to say. I slowly hung up the phone and returned to my meeting. Only during the evening could I further reflect upon the tragic news. I was deeply concerned about George and wondered how he was taking this diagnosis.

George met me at the airport in Berlin, tears filling his eyes. I think he appreciated the gravity of the situation, but at the same time, I think he was trying to suppress the fact that it actually had happened to him. Maybe he expected me to work one of my miracles—definitely a tribute to my strength, but not realistic in this situation.

Our family doctor sent George to Berlin's largest hospital for respiratory diseases, Heckeshorn. This hospital, built on the bank of the Wannsee before World War I, now served to combat diseases of the lung with the best that modern medicine had to offer. Our doctor wanted to delay surgical intervention as long as possible and prescribed an extensive treatment program for George. He stayed in the hospital for several weeks.

I visited my husband every other day, and despite my best effort, I could not get him to kick the smoking habit. "George," I said to him, "you've got to stop smoking!"

He ignored me, waving his hand in my direction as though I were crazy. To his credit, he did stop drinking. I refused to indulge him, and since I wouldn't buy him cigarettes, he had to convince his friends to smuggle them for him. My refusal had a minimal effect on his smoking, and perhaps it was cruel, but I just couldn't be a part of it.

In August 1994 the doctors operated on George and achieved remarkably good results. George made such a good recovery after the surgery that he was discharged from the hospital and sent home. Barbara came for a visit in early 1995, and it appeared that we had finally reconciled our differences.

We celebrated George's eightieth birthday in September of that year at Aunt Mitzi's house in Gumpoldskirchen, a town near Vienna. The celebration was attended by several members of my family and many of George's friends. In November 1995 Amy also visited us.

She had packed a huge turkey in her luggage and surprised us with a Thanksgiving feast.

Another winter arrived, and the cold temperatures caused George's health to deteriorate. Slowly, he lost his strength and, with that, the will to live. During his time on this earth, George seemed to have mastered the art of self-denial, but the life-changing event that now confronted him could not be ignored. I did everything in my power to make his last months on this earth as comfortable as possible. For most of our marriage, I had played the role of a nurse, and now, as he approached the end, I also played the role of a mother. During this time, I found the strength to keep my self-composure, which gave him the strength to make this transition in life.

During these final months I took stock of my life and our time together. In doing so, I became painfully aware of the dark side of my soul, the side that is impulsive and lacks patience. I know this part of me has been difficult for my family. Perhaps others perceive me as demanding. I ask others to understand that my impulsiveness and impatience are the result of my greatest fears: not accomplishing the goals I have set for myself and disappointing those to whom I have made promises.

On May 24, 1996, George died. It was a beautiful and sunny day in late spring, one that inspired hope in the resurrection, the hope of finding lasting peace after such a troubled and difficult life. I stayed with George until he took his final breath. I stroked his head one last time and departed without saying a word.

After returning home from the hospital, I sat in an oversize wicker chair whose arms wrapped around in such a way that it reminded me of the comfort of my mother's embrace. During those hours, as I reflected upon the events of the last fifty-four years, I had the same reoccurring thought—I am now alone. A long time ago, when I was nineteen, I was supposed to remain in the maternity ward at that hospital in Karlsbad. Disobeying orders, driven by impulse and curiosity, I had hidden behind a column to view the first of the wounded soldiers who had just arrived from the eastern front. There, George and I saw each other for the first time. God places people in your life for a reason, whether it is for five minutes or fifty years.

Friends and family from the United States, South America, and Europe came to Berlin to attend the funeral. Among those present were Amy and Barbara. Our good friend Father Paul von Lobkowitz made a special trip from Denver to officiate the funeral Mass and deliver the eulogy. I arranged everything, and in the process, fate struck once again. During the service I did not want to have just organ music. On my way to the market, I saw a young man playing a Spanish love song on his classical guitar. I stopped and asked if he would perform at the funeral. This young man had studied at the conservatory in Kiev in the Ukraine before moving to Berlin. He performed at the local market to earn a little pocket money. He gladly accepted my offer.

"By the way," I asked him, "would you be so kind as to give me your name? I need to announce your name at the service."

"Madame," he answered, "I am George!"

I grinned from ear to ear. How appropriate!

The ceremony was beautiful. The young George played a moving piece, a prelude by Heitor Villa-Lobos, the famous Brazilian composer. Afterward, we held a reception, something the old George would have loved. Instead of mourning his loss, we celebrated his life, the life of a very colorful man, one who needed changes in routine like others need air to breathe.

Transition, 1996–2003

The funeral guests left, and now I was alone. Like everyone who has lost someone close, I had to overcome the difficult emotions that accompanied this life-changing event. I caught myself wanting to be left alone. I needed to sort out all the confusing events of the past, to make some peace in my heart. I also rearranged my apartment according to my taste and comfort, not erasing George so much as making it more suitable for one person. Eventually, I listened to the voice in my head, which told me, "There is still a future for me, even if limited." At Christmastime I visited friends and family in Colorado. I do not think they realize how much they helped me come to terms with my loss.

Nearly eighty years had passed since the postman came to the house in Pirkenhammer with the mail, the exact moment of my birth. I decided to really live the life I had left. In the spring of 2001, I returned to Karlsbad for the first time since the golden wedding anniversary we celebrated in 1992. Amy and her husband accompanied me, and together we enjoyed touring the city as I showed them the places that were important in my life there.

The city had taken a turn for the better, thanks in part to the large number of spa guests and investors from Russia. Before the First World War, Karlsbad had been a popular spa destination among the Russian nobility. Now the same resort was attracting those who had become prosperous after the fall of the Soviet Union. It was even featured beautifully in the 2006 romantic comedy film *Last Holiday* starring Queen Latifah and LL Cool J, and it was the filming location for a portion of the 2006 James Bond film *Casino Royale*.

As I walked the steep, narrow streets of Karlsbad, my legs no longer wanted to cooperate, yet the joy I felt when I saw the revival of this beautiful city made the journey more bearable. In Pirkenhammer I visited the house of my great-grandfather, the house where I was born. The house had received a new coat of paint, but in the middle of the facade, the initials of my great-grandparents, Johann and Aloisia Friedl, were still prominently displayed: "J.A.F. 1890." The house had survived two world wars and forty-five years of communism and was standing strong and beautiful.

Alone but Not Lonely, 2003–2011

In the time since George's death, I have become comfortable with my solitude. I started to write the story of my life, first in German and then the English translation. I am always thinking about the connections of world history and my brief time and place in that story.

I continued to travel because adventure is medicine for my soul. In 2004 I visited Orebić, Croatia, close to the island of Korčula on the Adriatic Sea, where an old friend from Colombia has a home.[1] It is

---

1   Korčula is the birthplace of Marco Polo.

a beautiful place, but it too has seen its share of war and bloodshed. Most of the damage from the Serbian-Croatian war in the mid-1990s was already repaired when I visited, but the scars were still visible if you looked close enough.

I felt the sun on my face and listened to the sea's waves lapping at the coast. It was a peaceful place for me.

In 2006, I returned to Cali, Colombia, to celebrate the fiftieth anniversary of the Residencia Stein, now under ownership of the next generation of the Frei family, who bought the hotel from us in 1966. Over the years they have had the hotel, it has done well, and it has also served as the Swiss Consulate.

It was a strange experience to visit Colombia again. I had lived in Colombia for only eleven years, but I still had the feeling that it was my home, in a small-town way, like in Pirkenhammer. I knew so many people, and after all these years, they still remembered me in a familiar way.

My Colombian friends in Berlin had arranged a welcoming party for me in Bogotá—a "skycap"—to help me with transit between the international airport terminal and the domestic terminal for my connecting flight to Cali. When a little native Colombian man first grabbed my suitcase and walked away, I thought he must be a criminal! I started to give him hell, and he said, "You are *Señora* Stein. I take you to your next plane. Come!" He tied a red ribbon on my bag so that I could see it as he walked ahead of me, and off we went.

When I arrived in Cali, I was to go to the Avianca Airlines counter. Mr. Frei, the son who now managed the hotel, had arranged a taxi for me through the airline, and I was assured several times that it was a safe taxi. It was already late at night, and Colombia was still prone to violence from the drug cartels and other criminals—in that way it was the same as when I lived there a half century before, but maybe different too. As Mr. Frei promised, the taxi got me to the hotel just fine.

A few days later, I went to the city market in Cali with Mr. Frei, and it was the same dirty, chaotic bazaar it had been when I lived there. As I wandered through the alleyways, I heard my old nickname called. *"Doña Panchita?"*

Portrait taken in 2005, Berlin, Germany.

I turned, and it was the woman selling herbs in the stand I used to frequent when I shopped for the hotel. Like me, she was an old woman now, bent with age. She had been famous in the old days for curing diseases with her herbs and witchcraft.

I stayed for two weeks in Cali, and the hotel was filled with special guests—customers who had called the hotel home for a time over the past fifty years. They had a grand party, and I am happy that I could revisit that part of my life. I was sad when I left, knowing I would not return again.

In December 2008, right after the start of the Great Recession and global financial crisis, I traveled to the United States for a long visit. As a treat, my granddaughter and former son-in-law invited me on a weeklong cruise from San Diego to Mexico, along with Amy's sisters and their families. It was a far more luxurious experience than I had endured on the *Odenwald* over fifty years earlier. But my appetite for trying local customs and experiences was undiminished—and I even ventured so far as to say hello to the friendly iguanas.

Chopin Through the Window: Last Journey to Karlsbad, 2010

In October 2009 my granddaughter Amy surprised me with a visit to Berlin. She had great news to announce: she was expecting a baby in April of the next year. At the time she was forty-two years old, and I never thought I would see a great-grandchild. Indeed, the little boy Andrew was born at the end of March, perfect in every way. I traveled to Virginia a few weeks later to visit and welcome my first great-grandson.

Now that I had a new generation in my family, I began to think about whether I should return to America. Although I still loved Berlin and my friends, I was growing more and more dependent on their kindness to help me with things such as shopping, which changed our relationship. I was getting out less and less for theater performances and lectures with them, and their visits were made more out of obligation. But at eighty-eight years, did I really want to move across the ocean again?

A year earlier, I had undergone a knee operation that included a partial replacement. Unfortunately, it didn't go well, and during the procedure they cut a nerve. Between the pain, the swelling, and the instability of a "drop foot," the act of walking on cobblestones, which were present throughout my Berlin neighborhood, was a challenge. As winter approached, I realized I simply couldn't live in Berlin much longer.

Having made up my mind, I also knew there were things I had to do before I made my last move. I wanted to go back to my first home, to see Karlsbad again and my best friend. I wanted to walk down the promenade, relishing the memories before they began to fade.

My lifelong friend and schoolmate Gerda was not well. We were the same age, but she was by this time nearly blind, toothless, and very thin. She was still living on the fourth floor of an old building, with no elevator and without adequate heating facilities. Some nineteen years after the Soviets had loosened their grip on Eastern Europe, quality housing remained difficult to get, especially for older people who had to live on small pensions.

My friend Ingrid in Berlin offered to drive with me to Karlsbad. On a gray day in early November, we traveled south toward Dresden. From there we would take the road west through the Ore Mountains to Karlsbad. We took our time because Christmas was less than two months away, and we thought we might visit some of the mountain villages, such as Seiffen, along the way. There we hoped to get some of the precious hand-carved figurines that are famous from this area. For centuries this trade has been practiced here, and it remains a viable industry for the people.

As we entered the road to the mountains, we were surprised by the first snowflakes of the season. At first it was pleasant, but as we climbed higher into the mountains, the few flakes became a blizzard, with cars stranded all over the road's shoulders and ditches. There were no hotels or other shelters to be found. The highway patrol didn't have any advice to offer—we could wait it out in our car or keep going. We decided to keep going.

About two hours later, we finally reached Oberwiesenthal, the summit of the mountain pass. The storm let up a bit on the back side of the pass, and we continued toward the Czech border, which wasn't much further on. The road conditions were still dangerous, but it was no longer a whiteout situation.

Finally, we saw the small station of the Czech Border and Customs Control. We parked the car and went inside, where we learned that we were one of only a few cars that had made it through that day without an incident. The officers assured us that the road conditions would improve quickly as we went further down the mountain, and indeed as we entered the city limits of Joachimsthal (Jáchymov), the road was clear.

After another short distance, maybe ten more miles, we arrived in Karlsbad. It was about eight o'clock in the evening, but the city seemed completely deserted. It was too late to go to see Gerda, so we headed for our hotel, the Parkhotel Richmond. We found the exit for the Panoramastrasse, a long, wide street that defined and protected the old city. The original center city features small steep lanes—so steep, in fact, that many of the sidewalks are made of stairs. Panoramastrasse ended after about three miles, and from there, via the Helenenstrasse, we entered the Imperialstrasse, a wide winding road down to the Tepel River.

Still no human was visible or audible. It started to snow again as we pulled into the entrance lane for our hotel. To the right of the entranceway was the Beethoven Monument. The famous composer is portrayed in a most unusual way here. The legend has it that his full figure stands with his fists clenching against his destiny, portraying his inner turmoil over going deaf and being unable to finish his Sixth Symphony, "The Pastorale." He did finish his masterpiece by observing the wind in the leaves of the trees, the raindrops, and all the movements in nature, imagining what they sounded like.

We turned into the short driveway to the hotel, which was marked with two Putti, fat little male children in the baroque style, holding candelabras. We crossed the bridge over the Tepel River and arrived at the grand entrance of the hotel. A young man came out from a little shelter, asked for our names, took our luggage, and asked us to follow him.

As I stood there looking into the hotel through the large, illuminated windows, I was able to see people moving. Piano music played; it was a piece by Franz Schubert. I held my breath and closed my eyes, and for a moment I submerged myself in memories. Was it not sixty-five years ago that I stood in front of the same hotel? It was early spring of the infamous year 1945. After a hard winter, the city was experiencing an unusual early spring. The war was in its final stage. The large cities in Germany had been under siege and bombed to bits of rubble. Karlsbad still remained an island in a diminishing world.

I walked with my eleven-month-old daughter in her stroller, enjoying the warm weather. Just when I was close to the entrance of the Parkhotel Richmond, a wheel of the stroller came loose. I looked around to find a bench or, better, somebody who would be able to help me. A young soldier in a German uniform stood in the driveway to the hotel. He asked if he could help me. I followed him as he looked for a tool to fasten the wheel.

Closer to the hotel, I heard someone playing a piano brilliantly. In my memory it was a mazurka by Frederic Chopin. The large windows of the salon were wide open to let in the spring air. The air moved the lace curtains like giant billows. The young soldier finished his repair work on the wheel and played with my little daughter while she sat in the stroller. Briefly, I felt detached from my worries and approaching difficulties. For that moment, I felt some peace.

As we stood together, observing and playing with Barbara, a very tall and impressive officer stepped out from the entrance of the hotel. I remember his face; he had perfect, fine features, like they had been chiseled out of marble by Michelangelo. He spoke briefly with the young soldier in Russian, greeting me with two fingers on the brim of his cap, and disappeared down the path to the garage.

I thanked the young soldier and made my way home, and my thoughts returned to the reality of daily life. I remember that I tried to find out who the unusual tenants were in the Parkhotel Richmond. A few days later, I discovered that the Russian-speaking soldier belonged to the elite Cossack unit of General Andrey Andreyevich Vlasov. General Vlasov and his regiment were defectors from the

Soviet Army. They had joined the Germans in war against the Soviets along with several thousand others on the eastern front.

It must have been ten or more years later that I read in a newspaper that at the end of the war, the Western Allies had forcibly repatriated all members of the remaining unit to the Soviets. Only a few of the officers and soldiers were able to escape their destiny by fleeing to the West with the help of some courageous British officers. Vlasov and his officers were hanged on August 1, 1946. To me this seemed a wasted opportunity to learn from these men how to deal with the Soviets and moreover, a terrible price for them to pay. But then every part of the war had been terrible.

Some six months after this memorable spring day in 1945 at the Hotel Richmond and its environs, I was expelled from my homeland along with my little daughter. Forced to leave my dying mother to the mercy of my neighbors until I was able to return, I faced an uncertain journey and an even more uncertain future.

As I stood now as an old woman in the salon of the hotel, I remembered vividly the time, the place, and the happenings. The tones of the piano, the music of Chopin and Schubert, caressed me then and now like precious pearls.

The next day, I visited Gerda, bringing her a suitcase full of winter clothes. It pained me to see her in such bad condition. Fate had given us different paths, with our own joys and struggles. She had four children and had worked her whole life only to live in old age essentially alone and in poverty. Although she had married a wonderful Czech man and her father was Czech, she had always been a second-class citizen in Czechoslovakia and later in the Czech Republic because she was German—her mother and grandparents had raised her to be German, as they were, after her father left the family when she was in preschool.

I wanted to celebrate with her—our lifelong friendship and my new life ahead in America. We had a wonderful dinner at a little Bohemian restaurant. It was the Restaurant Schwejk, named after a Bohemian soldier made famous by his daring service during the First World War. In his memory the restaurant paid homage to Emperor

Franz Josef and Tomáš Masaryk, a nice gesture to the changing land.

I finished my journey to nostalgia and memory lane by going for the last time to the Holy Mass at the Church of St. Mary Magdalene, where I was married. Then, via Marienbad, we drove on the highway back to Berlin.

The Final Move, 2011

About eleven months later, I moved back to the United States, to live with my granddaughter and her family. I am enjoying watching my great-grandson grow, teaching him songs of my childhood, and baking Old World recipes I learned from my mother. Maybe later, if destiny will give me a few more years, I will teach him more about the land of his great-grandmother, the Sudetenland, a land of brave people and kind people. I will tell him about my beloved city, Karlsbad, where kings and artists, poets and philosophers, came to visit—figures the city honors with plaques and statues still today.

Though the old historic cities of the Sudetenland have lost their names, though the cemeteries that held many generations have become parking lots, and though the language is all but gone, the natural grandeur and the houses my great-grandfather built still stand.

The family home in Pirkenhammer built by my great-grandparents Johann and Aloisia Friedl in 1899, shown in 2001.

Acknowledgements

Except as noted below, all images are from the authors' archives. The authors give grateful acknowledgement to the following for permission to use their images:

Enrique Frei and Hotel Stein Colonial (pages 376 and 377); Rumi Engineer (page 425 for the late Bruce Anderson and page 426 for the late Olga Seybert); and Robin Lee-Thorpe (page 447).

Maps on pages 1 and 245 from One Stop Map (www.onestopmap.com). Cities shown and features of interest were edited by Amy Crews Cutts. Maps on pages 179 and 379 are by Amy Crews Cutts.

Bringing my story to you was made possible by the help of many friends and family. In particular, I give my deepest appreciation to Jim and Andrew Cutts for allowing Amy and me the many hours of free time to work on this; Alexandra and Michael St. Clair for their work on translating the original German version as our starting point; to René Reiche and Sylvia Prochnow for their work to get the perfect image used on the cover, and to Gretchen Cutts, Tammy Stacy, Karen Crews Gregg, Gaby LeBlanc, and Marie Bertozzi for their detailed comments on early drafts. I am sure I have forgotten to name a few of you, but your help is no less valued.

Amy Crews Cutts is a renowned economist, author and speaker. She earned her PhD in economics at the University of Virginia, Charlottesville, VA and her BS in applied mathematics and economics at Trinity University, San Antonio, TX. She resides in Reston, Virginia, with her son, Andrew, husband, Jim, and grandmother, Franziska along with two cats, Larry and Wiley, and two horses, Bond and Jordan.

Reviews for *Chopin Through The Window*

"Stein's remembrance, which is cinematic in scope, is interspersed with 'Perspective' sections, which reflect on political and cultural conditions of the era in thoughtful, if conventional, accounts. The book also features well-composed photographs of people and places in Stein's life."

-Kirkus Reviews

From a life rich in material, Franziska I. Stein crafts an engagingly candid personal narrative with an outsized yet closely observed historical canvas in her autobiography, Chopin Through the Window.

-Blueink Reviews

Crossing nations and historical periods, the memoir *Chopin Through the Window* covers both unimaginable and everyday challenges. Franziska I. Stein's eloquent memoir [...] concerns hardships endured in the aftermath of World War II.

-Foreword Reviews

CPSIA information can be obtained
at www.ICGtesting.com
Printed in the USA
BVHW031140170322
631765BV00001B/4

9 781685 470494